BRAND
MANAGEMENT

Sara Miller McCune founded SAGE Publishing in 1965 to support the dissemination of usable knowledge and educate a global community. SAGE publishes more than 1000 journals and over 800 new books each year, spanning a wide range of subject areas. Our growing selection of library products includes archives, data, case studies and video. SAGE remains majority owned by our founder and after her lifetime will become owned by a charitable trust that secures the company's continued independence.

Los Angeles | London | New Delhi | Singapore | Washington DC | Melbourne

BRAND
MANAGEMENT

Co-creating Meaningful Brands

MICHAEL BEVERLAND

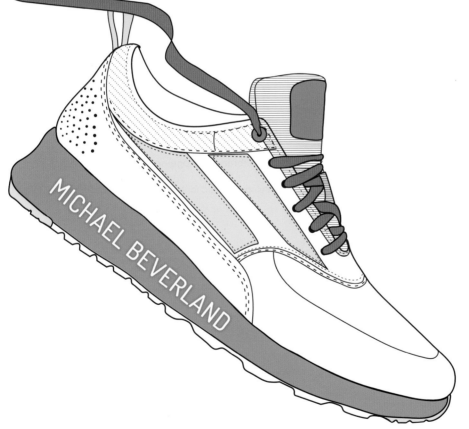

SAGE

Los Angeles | London | New Delhi
Singapore | Washington DC | Melbourne

Los Angeles | London | New Delhi
Singapore | Washington DC | Melbourne

SAGE Publications Ltd
1 Oliver's Yard
55 City Road
London EC1Y 1SP

SAGE Publications Inc.
2455 Teller Road
Thousand Oaks, California 91320

SAGE Publications India Pvt Ltd
B 1/I 1 Mohan Cooperative Industrial Area
Mathura Road
New Delhi 110 044

SAGE Publications Asia-Pacific Pte Ltd
3 Church Street
#10-04 Samsung Hub
Singapore 049483

Editor: Matthew Waters
Editorial assistant: Jasleen Kaur
Assistant editor, digital: Chloe Statham
Production editor: Imogen Roome
Marketing manager: Alison Borg
Cover design: Shaun Mercier
Typeset by: C&M Digitals (P) Ltd, Chennai, India
Printed in the UK by Bell & Bain Ltd, Glasgow

Library of Congress Control Number: 2017955497

British Library Cataloguing in Publication data

A catalogue record for this book is available from the British Library

ISBN 978-1-4739-5197-6
ISBN 978-1-4739-5198-3 (pbk)

At SAGE we take sustainability seriously. Most of our products are printed in the UK using FSC papers and boards. When we print overseas we ensure sustainable papers are used as measured by the PREPS grading system. We undertake an annual audit to monitor our sustainability.

Summary of Contents

Contents

Online Resources

Brand Management is supported by a wealth of online resources for both students and lecturers to help learning and teaching. These resources are available at: **https://study.sagepub.com/beverland**

For lecturers

- **Save time** and support your teaching each week by using the author-prepared **PowerPoint slides** for each chapter
- **Visualize** the learning experience for students by drawing on the textbook's bank of **images** saved here

For students

- **Enjoy** exclusive **videos** about a globally renowned and **real-life creative agency**, Moving Brands, to find out about their views on branding and experiences of working with some of the world's biggest brands as well as **employability tips** on how to get into this industry
- **Expand** what you learn in the textbook and from the above videos by reading author-selected **academic journals articles** that will help you to achieve high grades in your assessment
- **Explore** brand management even further using the **web links** curated for you by the author

Preface

After teaching and practicing branding for close to two decades I've always struggled to find a textbook that fits within a standard 12-week semester, is pitched at the right level, and draws on the widest range of theoretical insights and perspectives necessary to create strong brands. My usual response is to put together a reading pack; however, many students still ask me if there is one core text or book they can refer to that grounds them in the basics of brand management.

This experience is what led me to write *Brand Management: Co-creating Meaningful Brands*. My aim was to present what we know about branding to the fullest possible extent (within the context of an academic textbook), and update existing frameworks, without necessarily throwing out everything from the past. As such, this book is not aimed at the theoretical purist (there are plenty of great books in this space already, many of which I draw upon); rather, I take the view that knowledge about branding has developed in an incremental way, with different perspectives often complementing each other, most, but not all, of the time.

Our understanding of brand management comes from a wide range of different disciplines, including economics, trademark law, psychology, anthropology, cultural and media studies, design, marketing and organization studies, and sociology (to name a few). As academics, fealty to one theoretical perspective is often rewarded. However, practitioners are much more pluralistic in their choice of tools and frameworks for building brands, keeping them alive, and if necessary, returning them to health. *Brand Management: Co-creating Meaningful Brands* aims to push off from what we know about branding in 2017. As such, you will be presented with framework choices (where relevant) and a range of tools that may provide more questions than initial answers, but nonetheless are necessary for a wannabe brand practitioner.

The title reflects a specific take on building brand meaning. Co-creation refers to the idea that the line between the producer of brand meaning and the consumer has been blurred, with meaning increasingly shaped by a variety of brand "authors." Historically, consumers were largely seen as recipients of intended brand identity, giving rise to the criticism that despite claims the brand existed in the mind of the user, the user was viewed as passive in the creation of that meaning. Subsequent research identified that there are in fact many users of brands, all of whom play a role (often to varying extents) in creating the myths and cultural stories that "co-create" the meaning of the brand. In this approach, managers remain important in shaping brand meaning, but are not the sole author.

Co-creation however does not mean (nor even imply) that the consumer and brand manager literally sit down together and decide what the brand means. This is a common mistake, often drawn from the field of innovation where lead users can play a significant role in shaping new products and service systems. Co-creation simply means that the brand manager understands that the brand must speak to user needs in the widest possible sense. For the brand to be viewed as an asset by the user, it must speak to user problems within an often complex and contradictory context. As such, many of the tools within this book focus on understanding and empathizing with the world of the user, in order to co-create a brand resource that is truly meaningful to them and the networks they exist within.

Just as co-authors shape brand meaning, so too are textbooks the result of many people. To that end I'd like to thank a number of friends and colleagues who have influenced me greatly in my understanding of brand management and who have played various roles on the development of this text. I apologize in advance if I've forgotten anybody, and of course, any errors are solely mine.

A big thank you goes out to a range of colleagues, particularly Mark Ritson of Melbourne Business School (who generously shared many insights and materials with me over many years), Susan Fournier of Boston University for encouraging me to focus on the brand-as-asset perspective, Helen Edwards, Erminio Putignano, Sarah Wilner, Pietro Micheli, Julie Napoli, Tim Spratt, Anna Belogortseva, Donald Lancaster, Zoe Lee, Leslie and Maxwell Colonna-Dashwood, Richard Riddiford, and Brian Richards for providing a range of insights into branding practice over many years, and all the owners of brands that have taken the time to tell me their stories, many of which are featured in this book. Further thanks goes to various academic colleagues who have inspired me to write on branding including Stephen Brown, Avi Shankar, Giana Eckhardt, Francis Farrelly, Michael Ewing, Pınar Cankurtaran, and Colin Jevons, among many others. Thank you to Jasmin Baumann at the University of East Anglia for her thorough and insightful review of draft chapters. A big thank-you to my current Head of School, Robyn Healy, and my fashion business team (Carol, Kate, and Saniyat) for giving me the space to complete this text. Finally, thanks to my loving partner Emma for allowing me to work weekends to get this book finished.

Last, but certainly not least, I'd like to thank the team at Sage. In particular Commissioning Editor Matthew Waters for putting up with requests for extensions and, critically, providing excellent feedback and insights on the content and structure of the book. Thanks to Jasleen Kaur for editorial support and help in producing the final version, and to the various academic reviewers and other Sage team members who helped this book see the light of day.

Part I
Foundations of Co-creating Brand Meaning

1

BRANDS AND BRANDING

We use brands to project who we want to be in the world, how we want people to perceive us, and how we want to feel about ourselves. (Debbie Millman, host of Design Matters)

Learning Objectives

When you finish reading this chapter, you will be able to answer these questions:

1. What are brands? What value do brands provide to users?
2. How has our understanding of building brand value changed over time? What role does the customer play in creating brand meaning?
3. What is co-creating brand meaning? Who shapes brand meaning and what role do marketers play in managing this meaning?
4. What are the guiding principles of co-creating meaningful brands?
5. Where is branding used? What contexts are amenable to a branded strategy?

Welcome to a Branded World

Waking up, I instinctively reach for my Apple iPad, checking the time and weather (the Yahoo Weather application). Deciding I have time to go for a ride before work, I get up, put in my Daysoft contact lenses, and get dressed—Etiko shoes, Quiksilver socks, Rapha riding jersey and pants. My bike is a menagerie of brands. It was custom built by 14BikeCo but designed by a renowned Shoreditch cycling figure Super Ted (whose name also features on the logo adorning the bike) and made up of a range of branded ingredients including Reynolds Steel, Royce hubs, Shimano brakes, and Michelin tires (among many others). I put on my Camelback water carrier and Oakley sunglasses, leave my building ("Concept Blue") and head out on the road (brought to you by the good people at VicRoads).

I ride through downtown Melbourne (Australia), a tourism destination brand, and patchwork of smaller neighborhood sub-brands. I pass many branded flagship retail stores, restaurant chains, cars, branded rubbish left over from the night before, other "branded" cyclists, branded promises screaming out from billboards, and head out onto the cycle path (which features in the city's brand-driven tourism campaign). On returning home, I shower, using many branded products, before eating breakfast (surprisingly the fruit is unbranded), and head out to my "local" coffee shop (Aunty Peg's) to work while listening to music on my Pono player (the "special" Kickstarter edition if you please). I then head to work, a large university that eight years prior embarked on an aggressive "authentic" brand campaign.

By 9am, I've encountered hundreds of brands and made dozens of brand-driven choices. In fact, if you ignore the fact I was using brands, there were very few times in the three hours of my morning where I was free from brands (and this probably has more to do with the tree cover blocking out billboards on my ride). Some of my choices are practical—Oakley sunglasses adapt to different light conditions quickly and are light to wear. Some of my choices are moral—my clothing, contact lenses, and food reflect a profound belief in animal rights and are therefore sub-branded "free from," "cruelty free," and "vegan." Some choices reflect a desired identity—that of an artist rather than a business school professor. Some brands mean a great deal to me—a friend in East London made my bike and each time I ride it I recall how much I miss living in the UK. Some brand relationships are strong (I love my Pono player), while some are declining (I'm counting the days until my crowdfunded Nextbit phone arrives so I can gift my iPhone to my niece).

Marketers, my personal identity goals and life themes, and the broader sociocultural context in which I live have shaped the various meanings of these brands. Yet, the majority of textbooks fail to account for this interplay between user, identity, and social goals, the networks they're embedded in, the social forces that influence them, and the actions of marketers in co-authoring brand meaning. This book aims to do that, focusing on why brands mean what they do to users, how brands come to carry such meanings, and the ways in which aspiring marketers can influence all of this. As such, this book pushes off from all that we *now* know about brands and attempts to synthesize the vast amount of academic research and management practice that has emerged over the past three decades in particular, into a set of strategic principles.

Brands are ubiquitous. Be it work or play, we are immersed in a branded world from the day we are born to the day we die. So much of our lives involve brands that accusations of staying "on brand" have come to define a lack of sincerity on the part of political or business leaders facing a crisis. Critics write books against the ubiquity of brands featuring covers of babies covered with logos, while consumers often tattoo themselves with the very same logos for a range of surprisingly complex reasons. In many ways, known and unrecognized, they define who we are or who we long to be. This book (brought to you by the good people at Sage) identifies how brands gain meaning and how they can be co-managed for the long-term, providing value to customers, marketers, and other relevant stakeholders.

What Is a Brand?

The word "brand" is derived from the proto-German *brandr* (pronounced "brundt"), which literally means to "burn your mark into or stigmatize" and usually referred to the practice of marking ownership of captured people's (slaves) or animals (where "branding" is still in use today). Although brands say something about the user, the stigmatizing half of *brandr* is mostly forgotten. Putting aside moral concerns, it's worth thinking about the benefits resulting from such a practice:

1. Brands identify the wearer: In the case of slaves, brands mark out their status, their house identity, and therefore confer status on the branded and brander.
2. Brands signal membership: The practice of pillaging and warfare meant tribes would quickly absorb conquered peoples. Brands enabled tribal members to absorb others in spite of the range of different dialects, physiques, and markings that could cause confusion.
3. Signal information against a background of noise: In the case of animals, at round-up time, often-illiterate farmhands could quickly and immediately identify which animal belonged to which rancher—critically useful in a context defined by noise, dust, and frightened and dangerous animals.
4. Protection: This form of branding is difficult to get rid of, and at the time, most certainly attempts to do so would have resulted in infection and possibly death. Thus branded slaves are unlikely to attempt escape, while branded animals are difficult to steal and sell.

All of these ancient aspects of branding are still relevant today, although thankfully in the majority of cases concerning human animals, burning the flesh with marks usually now takes the form of deliberate tattooing. The reasons why consumers might choose to do this are the subject of Chapter 2.

Many people fail to understand that the meaning of *brandr* still has much relevance for branding today. Typically, *brandr* is dismissed as a narrow logo-centric view of branding. However, this ignores the fact that burning into and stigmatizing explain much about the emotional intensity of many consumer–brand relationships, the ways in which consumers construct their identity through brands, the ways in which particular brands mark people out from others, the notion that the "wrong user" can harm the brand's image, the ways in which employees are required to "live the brand," and finally the critical role founders play in establishing brand values. Although much has changed, the origins of the term "brand" still have relevance today.

So far we know a little of the process of branding and what some benefits were, but just what is a brand? Table 1.1 provides a range of examples from past and present, and sources, including academics and practitioners engaged in various aspects of brand management. Defining the meaning of the term "brand" remains tricky and subject to much debate. The classic definition by the American Marketing Association listed first in Table 1.1 remains the one preferred by many (but not all) academics and practitioners.

This definition emphasizes the material markers of a brand and is reflective of a historic view that brands are equivalent to legal trademarks (Conejo and Wooliscroft 2015). This definition has some useful aspects: it places a stress on competing symbolically (rather than through functional innovation or pricing) and taking a distinct position in the marketplace as a means to compete. This suggests that a brand's identity and intent can be the basis of competitive advantage.

However, although widely used, it is not without many limitations. First, although focusing on the material markers of a brand (Holt 2003), it is the meaning of these markers that truly defines the brand. Second, there is no mention of an external user in this definition. Although unintended, this definition reflects the average "person in the street" view of branding (and understandably but regrettably, many managers) as largely consisting of a cleverly designed logo aimed at extracting higher prices from gullible consumers. Third, it implies that there is but one author of the brand—the firm—a view that is not only empirically false, but in this day and age, also practically questionable.

There have been many other attempts at defining brands over the years. A few examples, drawn from a range of different perspectives, are presented in Table 1.1. In interpreting these different views it is important to keep in mind that each author has worked with the material they had available at the time and each person brings a particular professional frame to their view of brands and branding. For example, pioneering brand writer David Aaker was primarily advising senior management on competitive strategy. Not surprisingly, his definition emphasizes competitive differentiation. John Philip Jones is an advertising specialist with a focus on **fast-moving consumer goods (FMCG)**. Unsurprisingly his definition reflects the fact that consumers buying these items often make quick decisions (less than two seconds) and look for clear, eye-catching promises on the shelf. Marty Neumeier's definition reflects his background as an interaction designer, and thus he places an emphasis on the subjective experience of the user and intuitive reactions. Former Nike and Starbucks marketer Scott Bedbury unsurprisingly provides a more detailed, messy view of the brand, focusing on all the moments of truth in product and services experienced by users that create meaning for the brand, good and bad.

Table 1.1 Definitions of brands and branding

Author	Definition
American Marketing Association Mark I	A name, term, design, symbol, or any other feature that identifies one seller's good or service as distinct from those of other sellers. The legal term for brand is trademark. A brand may identify one item, a family of items, or all items of that seller. If used for the firm as a whole, the preferred term is trade name (AMA MK1).
American Marketing Association Update Mark II	A brand is a customer experience represented by a collection of images and ideas; often, it refers to a symbol such as a name, logo, slogan, and design scheme. Brand recognition and other reactions are created by the accumulation of experiences with the specific product or service, both directly relating to its use, and through the influence of advertising, design, and media commentary. https://www.ama.org/resources/pages/dictionary.aspx?dLetter=B
Oxford English Dictionary	A piece of burning, smouldering or charred wood; a stigma, a mark of disgrace; a torch, a sword; a kind of blight, leaving leaves with a burnt appearance; a special characteristic (brand of humour); an identifying mark burned on livestock or (formerly) criminals etc. with a hot iron; an iron used for this; a particular make of goods, an identifying trademark, label etc. to designate ownership
David Aaker, Vice Chairman of Prophet and Professor Emeritus, Hass Business School, University of California, Berkeley. Author of over 100 articles and 14 books on branding including classics such as *Managing Brand Equity* and *Building Strong Brands*.	A Brand is a distinguishing name and/or symbol intended to identify the goods and services of one seller and to differentiate those goods and services from those of competitors.
John Phillip Jones, Emeritus Professor of Advertising, Syracuse University, and author of numerous works on the effectiveness of advertising.	A brand is a product that provides functional benefits plus added values that some customers value enough to buy.
Jay Baer, founder of convinceandconvert.com, one of the most popular online marketing resources for business people.	Branding is the art of aligning what you want people to think about your company with what people actually do think about your company. And vice-versa.
Cheryl Burgess, co-founder and CEO of Bluefocus marketing, a web-based brand agency focused on building personal employee brands via social media.	A brand is a reason to choose.
Seth Godin, speaker and entrepreneur, creator of permission marketing, and author of 17 books.	A brand is a set of expectations, memories, stories, and relationships that, taken together, account for a consumer's decision to choose one product or service over another. If the consumer (whether it's a business, a buyer, a voter or a donor) doesn't pay a premium, make a selection, or spread the word, then no brand value exists for that consumer.
David Ogilvy (1911–1999), hailed as "Father of Advertising," founder of Ogilvy & Mather, inspiration for Don Draper character in TV show *Mad Men* and author of *Confessions of an Advertising Man*. Focus was on the BIG IDEA. Clients included Dove, Hathaway, Rolls-Royce, Schweppes, Shell, and many others.	The intangible sum of a product's attributes: its name, packaging, and price, its history, its reputation, and the way it's advertised.

(Continued)

Table 1.1 **(Continued)**

Author	Definition
Marty Neumeier, Director of Transformation for Liquid Agency, brand consultancy San Jose, CA. Author of *Brand Gap*, *Zag: The #1 Strategy of High Performance Brands*, and *The Brand Flip: Why Customers Now Run Companies and How You Can Profit from It*. Clients include Adobe, Apple, Hewlett Packard, Microsoft, and Symatec.	A brand is a person's gut feel about a product, service, or company. It's a GUT FEELING because we're all emotional, intuitive beings, despite our best efforts to be rational. It's a PERSON'S gut feeling, because in the end the brand is defined by individuals, not by companies, markets, or the so-called general public. Each person creates his or her own version of it.
Sergio Zyman, marketer behind the launch of New Coke, marketing executive and consultant, and author of *The End of Advertising as We Know It*, 1&2.	A brand is essentially a container for a customer's experience with the product or company.
Alvin "Al" Achenbaum (1925–2016), held senior positions (1951–1974) with major New York advertising agencies McCann Erickson, JWT, Grey Advertising, and Ted Bates. Clients included Procter & Gamble, GE, Nestlé, Kraft, Honda, US Department of Defense. Regular contributor to *Ad Age* and *Marketing Week*.	What distinguishes a brand from an unbranded commodity counterpart and gives it its equity is the sum total of consumers' perceptions and feelings about the product's attributes, about how it performs, about the brand name, and about the company associated with producing it.
Scott Bedbury, CEO Brandstream, former Nike Advertising Director (1987–1994, including "Just Do It" campaign) and Starbucks Chief Marketing Officer (1995–1998).	A brand is the sum of the good, bad, the ugly, and the off-strategy. It is defined by your best product as well as your worst product. It is defined by award winning advertising as well as by god-awful ads that somehow slipped through the cracks, got approved, and, not surprisingly, sank into oblivion. It is defined by the accomplishments of your best employee as well as by the mishaps of your worst hire you ever made. It is also defined by your receptionist and the music your customers are subjected to when they are put on hold. For every grand and finely worded public statement by the CEO, the brand is also defined by derisory consumer comments overheard in the hallway or in a chat room on the Internet. Brands are sponges for content, for images, for fleeting feelings. They become psychological concepts held in the minds of the public, where they may stay forever. As such you can't entirely control a brand. At best you can only guide and influence it (Bedbury 2002, p. 15).
Sir John Hegarty, founder of Bartle, Bogle, Hegarty and author of *Hegarty on Advertising* and *Hegarty on Creativity*.	The most valuable piece of real estate in the world, a corner of someone's mind.
Helen Edwards, author of *Passionbrand* and co-owner of the consultancy of the same name. Award-winning *Marketing Week* columnist.	Brand = Product and/or service + values + associations. This combination creates 'meaning' that people can connect with at the level of identity and therefore the relationship is beyond commercial. In theory the values are 'forever' and embrace the ideology, the product and/or service and associations can change over time (personal communication, February 5, 2017).
Roland van der Vorst, Professor, TU Delft, Netherlands and Managing Director FreedomLab.	A more practical definition is 'all operations executed by a brander to develop his/her brand in a positive way'. A brand is a concept that regulates the behaviour of both brander and user (personal communication, February 5, 2017).
Erminio Putignano (RMIT Adjunct Professor and co-founder of the PUSH Collective, Melbourne).	Branding is an exercise in world-making. It's about shaping a worldview anchored in values, beliefs and promises and bringing it to life through symbols, stories and experiences. It is an act of narration and a

Author	Definition
	conversation and it implies a very active contribution from all parties involved – everybody is involved in its generation and interpretation (organisations, agencies, customers and the community at large). If the worldview is convincing and relevant, then it is able to change opinions and behaviours (personal communication, February 4, 2017).
Brian Richards, founding partner, Richards Partners, leading brand and design consultancy, Auckland.	The brand is what brings together and articulates company values, both internally and externally, which is why one of the most important tasks of the manager is to ensure that everyone delivers the brand, it's no longer just a marketing function (http://richards.partners/thoughts/spiritual-intelligence).
Marie-Agnes Parmentier, consumer researcher and academic.	[A brand is] a repository of meanings fueled by a combination of marketers' intentions, consumers' interpretations, and numerous sociocultural networks' associations.
Jeff Bezos (founder and CEO of Amazon.com)	What people say about you when you aren't in the room

Definitions either sourced directly or from Brown (2016) and Cohen (2011).

Despite these differences, we can build up a clear picture of what characterizes a strong brand:

1. Identification: The purpose of a brand is to clearly identify a particular set of marketplace offers. The brand's various markers indicate authenticity and provide the user with confidence. Trappist monasteries such as Chimay, for example, use a number of cues including religious symbols, stylized gothic fonts, terms such as "double" and "triple" to indicate alcoholic strength, and overt claims of "Authentic Trappist Product" to differentiate themselves from those beers brewed by large conglomerates that attempt to trade on an imagined religious heritage (e.g., Leffe) (Beverland et al. 2008).

2. Distinction: Those managing brands have always been concerned with uniqueness. Harley Davidson went as far as to petition American courts to legally protect their motorcycle's distinctive sound. Likewise, users' brand relationships are often built around the unique benefits that the brand provides. Measures of **brand equity** (or brand value) place much emphasis on uniqueness when attempting to understand the strength of a brand relationship and its financial value.

3. Differentiation: Clearly, there is little point in simply copying a brand (unless you're in the counterfeit business). Show an image of Volvo to anyone and they will immediately say "safety." Every car arguably meets strict safety criteria but only Volvo stresses this as a USP or **unique selling point**. (In contrast, BMW equals "driver experience," while Mazda is "play and innovation.") Users may use brands to differentiate themselves from others. For example, consumers might use brand tattoos to signify their membership of different groups; a Fender tattoo for example would signify to the general public that the wearer is a musician,

although to more knowledgeable insiders Fender identifies him or her as a guitar player of early rock 'n' roll.

4. Meaning: Strong brands are rich with meaning. This meaning can include a wide array of associations, personalities, personas or archetypes, and cultural codes and myths. Some brands become so rich with meaning they become cultural icons. For example, Levi's had a rich heritage initially with working-class men, before gaining associations with the 1960s "Summer of Love," rock and roll, LBGT communities, and so on. Today, blue jeans have become a global uniform for almost everyone.

5. Value: Brands must provide value, to firms and to users. This value can include functional performance, emotional resonance, identity reinforcement, linking value, and financial return. Collectively these are forms of brand equity (defined differently by various stakeholders) and can represent in excess of 70 percent of a firm's share value.

6. Experienced: Brands represent promises to users. The true test of that promise, however, lies in use (broadly defined). For this reason practitioners often claim that "brands are built from the inside out" (the implications of which we'll return to later). In fact, for some brands, there may be nothing more than an experience and a bundle of sensations. For example, the value of the annual Glastonbury Festival lies entirely with the experience of the music, being part of a temporary community of festivalgoers, fleeting romance, camping, getting soaked and muddy, and partying all weekend.

7. Authored: Despite Neumeier's claim that only consumers define the brand, this is no more true than the managerial view that the firm is the sole author of brand meaning. Brand meaning is generated or shaped by multiple authors, especially today through social media. For example, ask consumers why they buy Apple and typically they respond with claims about "being different" or "creative." This may well define their relationship with the brand but it is unlikely they woke up one morning and decided Apple was defined that way. Instead, the brand's campaigns have highlighted these associations over time, their specialist music and film software ensures Apple products have been adopted by creative industries and feature as part of almost any band's stage set-up, and media influencers have lauded the brand's return to form as part of a wave of "design thinking" while the Apple-owned Pixar often features not so subtle links to the brand, including the signature start-up sound on robot Wall-E in the movie of the same name.

Given these seven points, recent definitions have begun to shift away from viewing a brand as little more than a logo generated by marketers aimed at differentiating products or services from one another. Drawing this together, we can define a brand as follows:

> An intangible, symbolic marketplace resource, imbued with meaning by stakeholders and the broader context in which it is embedded that enables users to project their identity goal(s) to one or more audiences.

Who Co-creates Brand Meaning?

When we say brand meaning is co-created what do we mean? Strategy scholars Prahalad and Ramaswamy (2004, p. 8) define **co-creation** as follows: "The joint creation of value by the company and the customer; allowing the customer to co-construct the service experience to suit their context." This definition has a number of implications, many of which will be identified throughout the rest of the book. Essentially, this approach to value means that value is not exchanged, but experienced-in-use. As such, the motives of users are critical to understanding meaning co-creation and managing brands. Today, co-creation lies very much at the heart of marketing, innovation, and many other business practices relevant to brand management. This begs the question: who co-creates meaning? Creator of the cultural brand model, Douglas Holt identifies four "authors" of brand meaning. Figure 1.1 identifies these four authors. Essentially, the stories told by users (including consumers), the firm (including brand managers), influencers (such as bloggers), and the brand's role in popular culture (its use in movies, etc.) shape the meaning of the brand over time.

For brand managers, the identification of these four authors changes how one approaches meaning creation. Previously, brand managers were believed to be solely responsible for creating the meaning of the brand. Now, while they certainly influence, often heavily, the shared meaning of the brand, they must also constantly adjust and align their desired meaning to that of other authors. This is demonstrated in the shifting metaphors around brand management. Classic texts, such as Aaker's *Managing Brand Equity* and Keller's *Strategic Brand Management*, display an emphasis on "creation,"

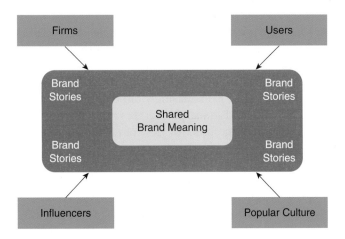

Figure 1.1   Authors shaping brand meaning

Source: Adapted from Holt (2003, p. 3)

"control," and "management" and the shifting practitioner-focused approach is framed in terms of "jams," "crowds," "conversations," and "highjacks" (as shown in *Brand Jam* by Marc Gobé and Joseph Jaffe's *Join the Conversation*).

Sometimes brand meaning can be controlled or strongly shaped, such as through sponsorship, product placement, the creation of official brand communities, and the recruitment of bloggers. In other cases, new meanings may emerge in an unpredictable fashion, which if unrecognized can change the brand's meaning for good or ill. For example, lesbian riders of Harley Davidson, self-identified as "Dykes on Bikes," co-opt the brand because of its overt masculinity. In this sense, these riders are disrupting the brand's historic image, while Harley Davidson's respectful response reinforces the core brand association of "freedom" (Martin et al. 2006).

Each author also has different, albeit not necessarily inconsistent goals. Marketers desire to build brand value by creating a desired brand identity supported with defendable associations. Customers may view the brand in ways that are different from those of marketers, and use it to achieve their desired identity, connect with others, or make sense of an ever-changing social landscape. Influencers, such as fashion bloggers, have their own identity to reinforce and are particularly aware of not damaging their relationship with their followers. For them a brand must fit their needs and be newsworthy. Those within pop culture seek a brand that both fits with their goals, and has a clear enough identity amongst an audience so as to be useful to their particular project (which could involve parodying the brand, undermining its claims, or simply reflecting a certain type of user, set of values, or context). Think of rapper Kanye West, for example, when he used to wear Polo Ralph Lauren, a seemingly curious choice of brand for a hip-hop artist, until one realizes such a choice is a form of reverse co-optation of preppy upper-class Anglo-Saxon culture. Chapter 3 discusses a framework that brings these competing goals and values of branding together.

The challenge for brand managers today is to balance the desire for a consistent brand identity (which is still crucial for brand equity) with the pressure to adapt in line with shifting customer needs and changes in the broader sociocultural context in which the brand is embedded (which also remain crucial for building brand equity). Staying "on brand" all of the time is increasingly difficult, paradoxical ("on brand" may in fact require one to go "off brand"—see Chapter 8), unnecessary, potentially dangerous, and ultimately too limiting from the point of view of enhancing brand equity.

A Short History of Brand Management

It's commonly stated that brands have been with us for centuries, while the formal management of brands is a much more recent affair. There is much truth to this. Despite archaeological evidence suggesting proto-brands or brand marks have been used to guarantee source authenticity and quality since ancient times (India, Iran, China, and Greece). Table 1.2 has details on proto-brands vs. modern brands while

Table 1.2 Brand characteristics in the ancient and modern worlds

Period	Brand Characteristics					
	Information: logistics	Information: origin	Information: quality	Image: power	Image: value	Image: personality
Early Bronze IV 2250–2000 BCE The Indus Valley	X	X	X	X		
The Middle Bronze Age 2000–1500 BCE Shang China		X	X			
The Late Bronze Age 1500–1000 BCE Cyprus		X	X	X	X	
The Iron Age Revolution 1000–500 BCE Tyre		X	X	X	X	
The Iron Age 825–336 BCE Greece		X	X	X	X	
Modern		X	X	X	X	X

Source: Moore and Reid (2008).

Figure 1.2 contains images of the earliest known proto-brands. In contrast, formalized frameworks for managing brands only began to be published in the 1990s. Despite this, many of the practices that define brand management to this day were in use for much of the twentieth century and, in some cases, well before that. Describing the evolution of branding, business historians Bastos and Levy (2012, p. 347) state:

> A general theme … is the evolution of the brand from a simple entity with limited application and whose creation, interpretation, and control are mostly enacted by one actor (i.e., its creator), to the brand as a complex entity that is multi-dimensional and multi-functional, and that receives influences from a variety of actors (e.g. the brand manager, the consumer, the media, the marketing researcher, technology).

For a long time brands were largely logos or pre-trademarks used by merchants and guilds of craftspeople to signal authenticity and quality. Ancient empires and organized religions also used the iconography of branding, including logos. For example, the Roman Empire reminded its citizens of their rights and responsibilities through the overt use of statues and architecture emblazoned with the imperial eagle on top of a tagline (SPQR—*Senātuas Populusque Rōmānus*) while the French Empire made regular use of the *fleur-de-lis*. In medieval times, craftspeople such as silversmiths were forced to mark their work with a logo to indicate that the product was indeed made by skilled craftspeople and that the buyer could trust it was made from pure silver.

Ancient Indus Zebu Bull Seal   Ancient Indus Unicorn Seal

Figure 1.2   **Earliest Known Proto-Brands**

In essence these early brands provided a degree of certainty to buyers, enabled one to trace a product back to its origins, as well as added values that came from higher status workshops or particular artisans.

However, mass branding of goods really only began in earnest during the Industrial Revolution, as supply outstripped demand and manufacturers were forced to compete for buyers' attention through mass advertising (prior to this it was not uncommon for manufacturers to sell goods unbranded to distributors and retailers). For the most part however, brand names did little more than *denote* or designate origin or relationship to a product class (i.e., brands were signs rather than **symbols**). For example, Folgers named their coffee in 1872, Kraft identified their cheese in 1903, and even Coca-Cola was originally simply a sign rather than the powerful symbol it became. Despite this, branding rarely featured in the marketing textbooks of the early twentieth century (and in some cases right up until 1988!), which were mainly concerned with sales, advertising, and managing distribution channels. The strongest brand names during this time often became generic descriptions of the category, such as Sunkist Oranges (Bastos and Levy 2012).

This approach continued until the late 1950s when academic Sid Levy wrote two influential *Harvard Business Review* articles, "The Product and the Brand" (with Burleigh Gardner, 1955) and "Symbols for Sale" (1959), suggesting brands could *connote* or imply some deeper meaning. As Levy (1959, p. 118) stated, "people buy things not only for what they do, but also for what they mean." This meant that brands could "incorporate intangibles such as identity, associations, and personality" (Bastos and

Levy 2012, p. 349). These articles in many ways captured what leading advertising agencies (such as JWT—John Walter Thompson) had been doing since the 1920s and influenced the so-called "father of advertising" David Ogilvy in his brand-building efforts after World War II.

Brands also gained more attention during this time because of the emergence of a mass consumer society whereby consumers faced a dizzying array of choices, often between products that made competing performance claims. As Gardner and Levy (1955) noted, detergents all promised to make clothes whiter, while an early famous scene in the award-winning TV series *Mad Men* (set in Madison Avenue, New York City, during the 1960s) focused on how cigarette brand Lucky Strike could differentiate cigarettes after the government banned tobacco manufacturers' health claims (which believe it or not were how brands were differentiated then). Automotive brands such as those owned by General Motors during this time were also caught in a never-ending war of feature creep, leading to an explosion of aesthetic design features such as the use of chrome and large tail wings that more often than not hampered performance and safety. At the same time, established brands started to face competition; for example, Pepsi aggressively attacked Coca-Cola's claims with its famous taste test. Since there was often little difference between these products' functional performance, the battle became symbolic.

Other practices that eventually became standard brand management tools also emerged throughout the twentieth century. When Alfred Sloan offered a car for "every purse and purpose," market segmentation was born. Drawing on new psychological theories in the 1930s research on segmentation expanded beyond demographics in the postwar period to include values, a practice that heavily influenced advertising agencies at the time. Segmentation would eventually become a key practice in branding, as it underpinned the **segmentation-targeting-positioning** model of brand identity (Keller 1993). Further advances in consumer research led to an emphasis on **brand personality** (although this was largely viewed in terms of the personality of the user and not the brand) by JWT in the 1950s. Studies on brand loyalty emerged as manufacturers became increasingly concerned at the rise of generic retailer brands. And, advertisers began studying the consumer image of particular brands in an attempt to generate more returns for their clients.

One of the first signs of the rising importance of brands (as opposed to products) was an emphasis on logo design. During the 1950s onwards, many iconic logo designs emerged including IBM, Mercedes Benz, Penguin, and Shell, as well as the use of mascots including the Michelin Man, Ronald McDonald, and the Playboy Bunny (Bastos and Levy 2012). In 1978 Wally Olins (founder of Wolff Olins—the agency responsible for repositioning BP with the now infamous "Beyond Petroleum" and producing the 2012 London Olympic Games logo) wrote *The Corporate Personality*, viewed by many within the branding world as the founding text on corporate identity, where he laid out a blueprint for organizations to holistically embody a set of values.

Organizations also started to pay more attention to the value of branding. In 1930, Procter & Gamble introduced their brand-management system, which resulted in the firm being reorganized around brands as opposed to product groupings. This saw each brand have separate managers, assistants, and budgets, and meant all marketing activities were to be driven by brand considerations (Low and Fullerton 1994). This system initially had little impact outside of Procter & Gamble, although historians noted that from the 1950s onwards the position (and eventually the power) of brand manager became more important, so much so that JWT's internal training materials bemoaned their impact on creative ideas. The systematic organization of marketing activities around brands eventually became commonplace in advanced economies.

As the power of brands started to become clearer, questions began to be raised about their financial value. Although there had long been concern about brand value, for the most part the focus had been on demonstrating to brand managers how their advertising budgets resulted in increased loyalty and/or sales. However, the deregulation of product and capital markets in the 1980s led to a wave of acquisitions and concern that the prices paid were far in excess of classic market valuations. In 1990, these questions led the Marketing Science Institute in the USA to commission a number of examinations into brand equity. The outcome of this process was a seminal article in the *Journal of Marketing* in 1993 by Kevin Keller titled "Conceptualizing, Measuring, and Managing Customer-Based Brand Equity" (which will be explored further in Chapters 2 and 3).

This article synthesized much of the research and practice into branding over the past fifty years. The **Customer-Based Brand Equity** approach (often referred to as the CBBE or "**mindshare model**") defined academic research into branding and diffused widely into practice. Even critics of this model admit it is *the* model of brand management (Holt 2004a). Subsequently research on branding has expanded dramatically to cover how organizations build, grow, and refresh brands, how they manage large portfolios of brands, how they deal with brand crises, how brands contribute to financial performance, how consumers relate to brands, the communal nature of brand consumption, experiential branding, the production of brand myths, ethical issues raised by branding, managing brands online, and global branding issues (among many others).

However, the practice of brand management and our understanding of it have changed remarkably since 1993. To see this, one only needs to look at how the dominant metaphors used to capture branding have changed (Aaker, Keller vs. Jaffe, Gobé). During the 1990s to 2000, the primary focus was on how marketers *managed* brands. The focus of most of these writers was on clearly defining the brand's identity and communicating that to consumers via advertising, design, experiential strategies, and service personnel. In these models, consumers were viewed as rather passive recipients of brand information and were assumed to view the brand exactly as marketers intended with any gaps between identity and image attributed to poor positioning and/or marketing execution.

From 2000, this began to change, with titles such as "citizen brands," "brand jam," "brand hijack," and "building brand authenticity" filling the shelves. These titles drew on a new stream of consumer research emerging in the 1990s that viewed consumers as active creators of meaning who may view and use brands in ways unintended by marketers, and often in contradiction to the intended identity or position of the brand. As the titles suggested, brands could be hijacked by tribal groups of consumers who were increasingly networked via the Internet. An empathetic approach to this hijack could often lead to brand revitalization as described in the LEGO case at the end of this chapter. In this situation, brand managers were viewed as just one session player in a jam, trying to forever align themselves with other players in order to keep the brand in time (Gobé 2007).

However, while many suggest that these various approaches are in conflict, or that brand managers now player little role in co-creating brand meaning, this book takes a different approach, which is outlined below.

Key Principles of Co-creating Meaningful Brands

1. Brand meaning is co-created: As identified in Figure 1.1, how consumers view a brand is shaped by four authors—the firm, users, influencers, and popular culture.
2. Brand marketers still matter! Although recent theory has rightly focused on the consumer/user as a meaning maker, marketers remain an author of meaning, and in the case of crises, consumers expect marketers to generate creative solutions to allow them to continue their brand relationship (Giesler 2012).
3. Context matters: Emphasizing the sociocultural context in which consumers and marketers operate is an essential part of cultural branding model. Consumers seek identity and authenticity within a wider sociocultural environment that sometimes defines and limits their choices, while marketers face the same challenge.
4. Co-creating brand meaning does mean direct interaction between consumer and marketer. This book will identify a number of methods, often drawn from the field of design, that help identify consumers' latent needs, resulting in value co-creation seemingly without any interaction.
5. Brands are primarily consumed for identity purposes. A vast amount of research identifies that in developed economies, a desired or imagined and/or authentic self (or selves), and the need to reinforce one's membership of a collective, drive consumption.
6. Brands are assets (the **brand-as-asset view**): the vast majority of a firm's share price consists of intangible assets, the most important of which are brands. For not-for-profits (including charities and hybrid organizations such as universities), reputation remains central to their viability.
7. Brands are strategic: brands help firms achieve their broad strategic goals and it is the brand that drives the marketing mix, not the other way around.

8. Branding is not an amoral practice. There are many ethical issues that arise from brand management including targeting vulnerable groups, sustainability, over-consumption, exploitation of workers, and co-optation of consumer-generated material.

The eight themes that drive this text have emerged from various streams of research in brand management, all of which are driven by different theoretical bases (considered next). Although influenced by a cultural approach to co-creation, this book takes the view that much of what has been generated by other disciplines still has much to offer brand managers if used in the right context.

Theoretical Influences on Branding Theory and Practice

There are many disciplines and communities of practice that have influenced (and continue to influence) our understanding of brands and the management of them. Below I briefly outline some of the main influences. Many of these ideas will be explored in more detail in subsequent chapters.

Economics

Economics' emphasis on rational choice, utility maximization, and exchange value has long influenced theory and practice in marketing. Brands in this approach are viewed as a way to minimize consumer confusion and search and thus aid decision-making (Heding et al. 2016). Since brands provide consumers with certainty, managers should focus on maintaining a consistent brand image and use the marketing mix (the four Ps of price, promotion, product, and place) to reinforce the brand. In this model, marketers largely communicate *to* consumers, rather than interact *with* them, and no attention is paid to sociocultural influences. Instead, brands should focus on offering clear functional performance advantages, a strategy largely regarded as unsustainable over the long term today.

More recently, different approaches to economics have had some influence on our understanding of branding. Vargo and Lusch's (2004) seminal article "The Service Dominant Logic of Marketing" drew on the writings of nineteenth-century French economic journalist Frédéric Bastiat and the early Austrian School of Economics (including Carl Menger and Ludwig von Mises) to stress the subjective nature of value and argue instead for **value-in-use** (rather than value-in-exchange). This article emphasized that marketers do not provide goods, they only make offers. And value in this context is not provided by a good but by the services it delivers to users (in this sense, all goods are services). That is, consumers do not buy a drill but buy the hole it produces. The service dominant logic (SDL) view has had some influence on our understanding of brand management, often raising theoretical challenges to classical models.

Law

As noted earlier, the AMA definition of a brand reflects a heritage of trademark law. Ross Petty (2011) provides a thorough review of how trademark law in the United States influenced marketers, and was eventually influenced by them (others have noted similar influences elsewhere). In essence, as sellers started to label their products and sell them nationally, they faced the very real problem of counterfeits. Thus, the US government expanded tort laws to provide some protection for sellers as well as for consumers. In particular, the early tort was called "passing or palming off" and was aimed at preventing fraud. Throughout the nineteenth and twentieth centuries, trademark law and legislation developed to provide further protection to sellers.

Since this protection had economic value (called "goodwill") it was not long before marketers began to realize that brands had economic value and started to lobby for further protections of brands and their associations (including logos, taglines, coloring, font). Today this practice continues with Apple unsuccessfully attempting to assert control over the use of "i."

One of course needs to be careful, as overzealous lawsuits can build resentment in local communities when large global brands try and shut down small traders using their own name. McDonald's, for example, has a long history of challenging the rights of others to use the word "McDonald" (or equivalents such as MacDonald's) in relation to the food service. For example, in 1994 the company successfully sued Elizabeth McCaughey, owner of McCoffee (which had operated in San Francisco for 17 years) (see Wikipedia, "McDonald's Legal Cases").

Psychology

Ever since practitioners began to explore how consumers viewed brands, they have drawn on psychology to understand consumer segments, brand and user personalities, and brand image. In more recent times, cognitive psychology has become the dominant influence on our understanding of brand management. Kevin Keller's customer-based brand equity model (and the many variants of this approach that followed) framed the consumer as an information processor and thus stressed the role of brand knowledge in creating brand equity. This approach treats consumers as largely rational agentic (free will) actors who are looking for clearly positioned brands with distinct advantages. Thus, this approach stresses the importance of maintaining brand consistency over time and also coherent messaging across the entire marketing program.

This type of research draws heavily on the quantitative tradition in psychology and focuses on how consumers react to particular brand related message cues, or tactics such as brand extensions or co-branded innovations (usually through the use of experimental scenarios). These models represent the dominant approach to brand management in terms of both academic research and practice, with books such as *Creating Passionbrands* by award-winning columnist and brand consultant Dr Helen Edwards (Edwards and Day 2005) as one example (see Table 1.1). This approach also underpins the two most influential brand valuation models of Interbrand (*Best Global Brands*) and Millward Brown (*Brandz*).

Not all work in this area has drawn on quantitative methods to generate important insights. Susan Fournier's seminal 1998 *Journal of Consumer Research* article drew on relationship theory to understand consumer–brand relationships. In essence, this research noted that as managers drew on personality types to position their brands, then consumers could be expected to form relationships with them. Unlike previous research, the relational approach assumes that the consumer is an active partner in creating brand meaning, and therefore seemingly mundane brands can be characterized by emotionally intense relationships. Critically, what Fournier identifies as consumer life goals and **identity projects** underpin a brand relationship and that therefore shifts in the consumer's world can lead to changes in the brand's status, sometimes leading to declining loyalty through no fault of the brand manager. Work in this area has explored a vast range of relationship-related topics, including anthropomorphism, brand love, brand attachment, and the dark side of brand relationships, and has played a role in practitioner theorizing such as former Saatchi & Saatchi CEO Kevin Roberts' (2004) *Lovemarks* that suggests the future of branding involves creating intimacy and sensuality through an emotional driven brand program.

Anthropology and Sociology

Anthropology and sociology have influenced the practice of branding (often indirectly), beginning with JWT advertising practitioners identifying ways in which to co-opt counter culture (with their metaphor of what is X-rated will soon be G-rated), Clotaire Rapielle's (in)famous use of collective subconscious archetypes (or cultural codes) to influence subconscious decision-making, and Grant McCracken's writings on consumer culture. Research in this tradition holds that consumers are active meaning makers and use material culture (including brands) to make sense of the world and achieve identity-related goals. Challenging the notion that consumers are rational, agentic individuals, this stream of research highlights the sociocultural forces that shape the actions of market actors.

During the 1980s academics began drawing more heavily on these disciplines and their qualitative methods to challenge conventional thinking about consumer decision-making and, before long, brand management. This research formed the basis of **consumer culture theory** (CCT) and gave rise to notions such as brand authenticity, brand community, consumer tribes, doppelgänger brands, brand legitimacy, brand mythologies, subcultures of consumption and, critically, Douglas Holt's (2004a) cultural brand model (which forms much of the basis of this text). While acknowledging that brands are assets for firms, these researchers emphasize that brands are also tools for consumers to achieve their identity and social identity goals, and therefore place much emphasis on how consumers use brands to achieve these outcomes.

Business Studies

This term is deliberately broad to identify the range of influences on brand-management practice flowing from finance, organization studies, marketing, operations, and strategy. Although late to the study of brands, financial concerns were responsible for the first formalization of a strategic brand-management model, and work between brand and finance researchers has crystallized into the **brand as asset** model. In this model, researchers seek to examine the value of brands on a firm's balance sheet and in relation to return on investment (ROI) and share price, as well as seeking to understand how particular brand investments drive value. Operations management has also played a role, in particular with their focus on customer journeys and moments of truth (which are critical parts of a brand audit). Intriguingly operations researchers are only just beginning to explore the role certain types of production systems play in brand image (see Chapter 8).

Marketing academics were strangely latecomers to publishing on brand management. As late as 1988, core textbooks often barely mentioned brands at all (Bastos and Levy 2012). That said, Philip Kotler in particular has played a key role in advancing marketing's appreciation of brand, so much so that in 2002 he partnered with Kevin Keller to rewrite his influential *Marketing Management* text, arguing that the marketing mix must serve the brand (this brand-driven approach is standard practice nowadays). Marketing researchers have also been instrumental in examining strategic marketing issues such as the relationship between branding and innovation, business-to-business (B2B) branding, global issues, how the marketing mix reinforces brand image, and ongoing debates regarding value co-creation and the customer experience.

Researchers in organization studies are relative newcomers to brand research (so much so that they often term it "reputation management" or "impression management"). Nonetheless, beginning in the 1990s, these scholars started to examine the organization-side of branding, identifying the need to align human resource practices and organizational cultures, systems, and processes with brand promises. Their most important insight was to identify that since brands were promises to users, the organization must be in a position to deliver those promises otherwise gaps between image and identity will emerge. In industry, this is often referred to as "brands are built from the inside out" and it is critical in ensuring brand authenticity. Much of the work of these scholars is grouped under the heading corporate branding and will be drawn on extensively in the later chapters of this book.

Media Studies

Since it involves communication, it is not surprising that branding has attracted the attention of media studies scholars. Drawing on an eclectic range of theories (and overlapping with many of the fields identified here), media studies focuses on semiotics and, in particular, signs. One critical area of influence involves the use of **cultural brand codes**. Codes often shape beliefs and help us find meaning, and are deployed by brand marketers in many ways, including in appeals to status, class, fear, envy, gender roles, and so on (Berger 2010). For example, Rowntree's Yorkie brand was advertised using subtle (humor) and not so subtle (clothing) codes to suggest it was a rugged, masculine, rural working-class brand. Over time the codes signaling masculinity had to change as manufacturing declined in the UK and notions of "male-ness" shifted. One can view these shifts on YouTube by examining the original Rowntree Yorkie advertisements from the 1970s and 1980s and comparing them with the brand's revitalizing "It's not for girls" campaign, and the current "man fuel for man stuff" online advertisements (ask yourself, "How did the brand change its approach to signaling masculinity throughout these campaigns?"). Codes are often used in other ways, especially at a category level where discount airlines and single malt whisky brands draw on cultural signs to reinforce notions of "cheap" and "authentic".

One of the most significant contributions of media studies (along with other fields) has been the recognition that brands are forms of communication and can therefore be "read" in the same way as literature and other art forms. Thus, many early studies of subcultures and consumer tribes (often co-opted by marketers to enhance their brand's coolness or authenticity) focused on understanding how insiders communicated their status through fashion, and ultimately brands. Although practitioners focused on the connotative potential of brands, for media studies scholars brands are signifiers and thus always suggestive (Berger 2010). Therefore, consumers will select certain brands (often unknowingly) because they reflect certain notions of taste, class, or status, and therefore say much about the user.

Creative Practice

Our understanding of brand management has been influenced heavily by practice. For example, when Keller developed his CBBE model in the early 1990s he noted that much of what he drew upon was common industry practice across advertising, marketing, and consumer research (the same could be said of Levy's seminal work in the 1950s). The development of branding during the twentieth century was primarily driven by practitioners seeking to understand more about consumer behavior as a means of increasing brand loyalty. Key agencies such as Ogilvy and Mather and JWT (among others) were influential in projecting a consistent brand image and in shifting from brands as signs to brands as symbols. Likewise, firms such as Procter & Gamble have played a critical role managing brands, through the development of their brand-management system in the 1930s. Furthermore, influential academics have often had one foot in the practical world—David Aaker has his own brand consultancy firm, as does Gerald Zaltman (his ZMET technique will be covered in a later chapter), Grant McCracken, Douglas Holt, and many others.

Other fields such as design have also had an important influence on brand management. Alina Wheeler's *Designing Brand Identity* (2003) remains a go-to guide for all aspiring creatives dealing with brands. The Design Management Institute (USA) has sponsored numerous conferences on branding, with a particular focus on bringing the brand promise to life through innovative products, corporate communication systems, and the physical environment such as flagship stores, corporate headquarters, and workplace architecture. More recently much work has been done examining how to create brand-driven experiences online. Public relations practitioners have also played an important role in understanding how to manage public perception, deal with crises, and engage in impression and reputation management. There are undoubtedly many more fields including fashion, arts, and technology that have all had an impact on brand management and practice.

Can Everything Be Branded?

Brands are certainly ubiquitous. A common complaint among those disillusioned with capitalism, politics, religion, social movements, or aspects of social life ("Christmas is too commercial") is that those in power too often put the brand before everything. This is partly why authenticity has such currency today although, as we'll see, authenticity is no less deliberate as an impression management strategy. In his book *Branded Nation*, James Twitchell (2004) noted that just as institutions such as religion, museums, and schools and universities had discovered branding (although many would argue that organized religions have long been brands), marketers were erecting brand museums and brand cathedrals (themed flagship stores), and building brand cults.

As noted earlier, nations have long practiced branding or proto-branding, and Steven Heller's (2008) *Iron Fists: Branding the 20th Century Totalitarian State* identifies how repressive regimes created closed brand systems to instill fear and loyalty. Today, nations, regions, cities, and even neighborhoods run branding programs targeted at travelers, business, employees, and residents. Tom Peters' (1997) *Fast Company* article, "The Brand Called You", at the height of the first dot-com era, inspired many executives to develop their own personal brands, while many commentators noted that Barrack Obama successfully drew on branding principles in the run-up to his historic US presidential election win in 2008.

Celebrities have always been at the very least proto-brands, although now most are managed as carefully as the strongest product and service brands. For example, chefs such as Michel Roux Jr, Heston Blumenthal, Attila Hildman, and Jamie Oliver (among many others) have all expanded their brand franchises to include products, books, television shows, global pop-ups, and cookware. Singers Lady Gaga and Justin Timberlake often earn more from various brand extensions such as fragrances than they do from music sales. Finally, sportspeople, artists, fashion designers, bloggers, and many others are used to promote brands, have brands of their own, and in the case of Oprah Winfrey extend the life of their personal brand beyond her core category into the lifestyle space.

Brands may have come of age in product and services marketing, and take on new meaning in the intangible world of web-based businesses, but not-for-profits have embraced branding with gusto. Among the most well known are Greenpeace, Sea Shepard, the Red Crescent and Red Cross, the World Wildlife Foundation (WWF), Habitat for Humanity, and the Salvation Army. Charities often embrace branding as a means of appearing professional, which enables them to compete more effectively for influence and corporate donations.

So what isn't branded? Commodities by definition are items with no strong point of difference and therefore branding is of little use. This often affects agricultural products and often means those transforming the commodity into a brand earn higher returns (Starbucks, for example, earns more margin than the growers of their coffee (Fottrell 2012)). Agricultural organizations face real difficulties in developing sustainable brands since farmers are disorganized, reluctant to invest in marketing programs, struggle with quality consistency, and still focus on increasing prices which undermines certainty for buyers (Beverland 2007). That said, much progress is being made in branding produce, developing ingredient brands (New Zealand's Merino NZ brand of cloth is one example), grower-friendly branding programs (such as Nordic Approach in coffee), and so on, and leveraging grower stories to enhance perceptions of brand authenticity. Finally, it is worth remembering that many commodities are in fact extremely valuable and robust brands—just think of Exxon and Marlboro.

So should everything be branded? The ethical issues in relation to this question will be covered in Chapter 11. However, it's worth bearing in mind some of the challenges faced by places, institutions, and people when branding. First, when branding a product or service, one can apply one identity across an entire organization. To do so, one conducts an audit, and removes all those unwanted elements that undermine brand image consistency. This is thankfully not possible in nation states, regions, cities, or neighborhoods. There are other difficulties too. When building a brand program for the city of Bath (UK), I identified that parking and traffic gridlock was one of the main consumer complaints; however, there was relatively little one could do to change these constraints in a Georgian city that simply wasn't built to handle four million visitors a year and large tourist buses. Likewise, New Zealand have made much out of their 100 percent Pure campaign; however, sustained environmental degradation from intensive farming and poor resource-management practices has led to one scientist saying the slogan was about 48 percent true, and many bloggers reframing the brand as 100 percent Pure Bullshit. Thus, while places can draw on some practices of branding, place marketers should bear in mind that there are justifiable limits and real uncontrollable factors.

Similarly, institutions with a strong professional ethos such as law firms, hospitals, and universities, marketers must tread carefully when implementing a brand program since lawyers, doctors, and professors have multiple logics on which they operate. Although one might be tempted to remove these in favor of a branded one, not only will this be illegal in some cases, it would also be unwanted, and ultimately undermine business effectiveness (Naidoo et al. 2011). Although personal branding sounds alluring, the rise of authentic anti-establishment politicians is just one example of a backlash against branded centrist politics (even though anti-establishment remains a powerful brand identity). Likewise, staying on brand ultimately can make individuals less interesting and less effective, particularly when circumstances change.

Chapter Summary

This chapter has explored the historical development of modern-day brand management, identified a range of approaches for defining brands and branding, explored the benefits of brands to different users, identified why branding is essential to firm success, provided an up-to-date definition of brand that reflects the current state of academic research and marketing practice, identified the various contributions different disciplines have made to our understanding of branding and co-creation, and explored a range of contexts in which branding has been applied.

Review Questions

1. Have a look around you. How many brands can you identify? Reflect on the previous day and write down all the brands you used. (Perhaps it might be easier to try to recall incidences where brands played no part in your day such as during a retreat.)
2. List five reasons why consumers may tattoo themselves with brand logos.
3. Pick five definitions of branding in Table 1.1 not discussed in the text and compare and contrast each. What, if anything, do you like about each, and why? Is there anything missing from each definition that you think is important?
4. Reflect on one favored and one hated brand. Which identity goals help account for each brand relationship?
5. In relation to each brand relationship above, identify how each of the four meaning makers in Figure 1.1 have influenced your perception of each brand.

Case Example: The Consumer Rebirth of LEGO

Founded in 1949, Danish toymaker LEGO is one of the world's enduringly iconic brands, synonymous with childhood and playtime for many children. LEGO offers a vast range of themed sets of building blocks, theme parks, computer games, television and movies, board games, magazines and books, and robotics. Although valued at US$7.1 billion today, as recently as 2004 the brand was described as "near bankruptcy" by then executive vice president of marketing Mads Nipper (see Wikipedia, "History of Lego Decline"). Failing to respond to the rise in electronic gaming, reduction in children's playtime, and a declining birth rate in Western countries, the company was on borrowed time. So what went right?

Like this book's author, most children grew out of LEGO at a certain age, moving on to more typical teenage pursuits (music, movies, fashion, parties, and romance). However, some adults continued their love affair with LEGO. Communities of adult users formed spontaneously around the brand, ordering one type of brick in huge quantities, creating building competitions (sometimes involving a blind bag of blocks that had to be shaped into something in a fixed period of time). As the Internet developed, user groups began to form, posting figures of their creations online, as well as hacks for the brand's robotic line Mindstorms.

One problem for the brand was that the initial excitement of receiving a LEGO set gave way to boredom as many children completed the model described in the instructions and then asked "What now?" Sets were passed to the next generation, thrown out, sold on, or given to other families with children. Adult users, however, went beyond the instructions, viewing the brand as raw material for their own creative visions. Artists also began to use the brand as raw material for creative works, while others developed LEGO-based jewelry, notebook covers, and other unofficial products that saw various subcultures reverse the co-optation process, using branded content for their own ends.

This did not sit well with the venerable children's brand, used to being in control of its figure as an innocent, playful and educational tool. Adult users were "off market" and their creations often decidedly "off brand." Hacking their software was also not appreciated and the company took the extraordinary step of issuing legal threats and cease-and-desist orders against fan communities and hosts of fan-dedicated websites. However, while the fortunes of the brand continued to slide, adult users continued to buy the bricks, maintain brand awareness for LEGO, and provide a range of consumer-generated content that in many ways represented the brand's long-held focus on imagination, creativity, learning, persistence, and fun.

Eventually cooler heads prevailed, and the brand team gave up on legal threats and began to embrace their adult users, generating a user-focused innovation portal whereby fans could post creations and ideas and, if adopted, gain recognition and reward. The impact was immediate and long lasting. Go into a LEGO store now and you'll find large numbers of licensed sets dedicated to film franchises such as *Lord of the Rings*, *Harry Potter*, *Star Wars*, *Cars* and other Pixar-related properties, and many others. The computer games sets in the brick-based world of LEGO featuring the iconic figurines were so popular they generated *The LEGO Movie* and further tie-ins such as *The LEGO Batman Movie*. All of these and more were generated by fan suggestions, under the LEGO Ideas program that can reward idea generators with a 1 percent royalty rate.

This led to a substantial revitalization for the venerable brand, and also saw the marketing team return the brand to its roots, updating its values, position, and tagline (see Figure 1.3). However, engaging with users is not always an easy process, as many fans wish to take the brand to places where the team would rather not go to, such as hacking figures for decidedly non-childlike uses and characters, while unlicensed commercial use is subject to legal proceedings. The brand's success also means it has become a lightning rod for important social agendas or issues, including concerns over perpetuating negative gender stereotypes and the absence of figures with disabilities.

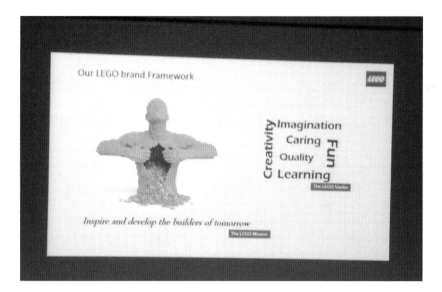

Figure 1.3   **Lego Brand Position**

(Continued)

The LEGO Friends series, for example, was subject to accusations of perpetuating traditional gender stereotypes and role behaviors. Made primarily in pink and purple, the characters in the Friends range break the design language of the brand's traditional blocky figurines, while the sets feature various suburban at-home situations such as cooking, caring for animals, equestrianism, pop stardom, and romance. The range was positively received by the target market, being one of the most successful launches for the brand ever, but earned the ire of parents and feminist critics who started a petition in 2014 calling on LEGO to embrace gender equity.

Similarly, the lack of disabled characters led to #ToyLikeMe online petitions targeting both LEGO (receiving 20,000 signatures) and competitor Playmobil. The essence of these critiques is that brands should be inclusive to all children, regardless of gender and ability, rather than perpetuating stereotypes or reinforcing barriers through exclusion. The brand recognizes that it must move with the times. This is not always easy, as the initial release of a wheelchair-bound character split advocates such as #ToyLikeMe founder Rebecca Atkinson who was delighted with the Lego range figures, stating:

> We are beyond happy right now. Lego have just rocked our brick-built world and made 150 million disabled kids, their mums, dads, pet dogs and hamsters very very happy. ... this move by Lego is massive in terms of ending cultural marginalisation, it will speak volumes to children, disabled or otherwise, the world over. (BBC, January 29, 2016)

However, Atkinson was less impressed with the brand's DUPLO range (for younger children) with the addition of an old man in a wheelchair, suggesting that having a singular character with a disability created a 'tokenistic stereotype in its isolation':

> The scant representation of disability in children's industries has long fallen into three enduring stereotypes, none of which are very positive or promote self-esteem in children with disabilities—the old (grandparents with sticks and wheelchairs), the evil (pirates with patches and hooks as manifestations of wrongdoing) and the sick or medical (the disabled body as broken and fixable with a stay in hospital). (Calderwood, August 4, 2015)

Likewise, the response to criticism regarding gender roles led the brand to launch its highly collectable limited release Science Lab (see Figure 1.4), which quickly sold

Figure 1.4   **Lego Science Lab**

out and generated much praise. Ellen Kooijman, the originator of the lab on LEGO Ideas, stated:

> As a female scientist I had noticed two things about the available Lego sets: a skewed male/female minifigure ratio and a rather stereotypical representation of the available female figures. It seemed logical that I would suggest a small set of female minifigures in interesting professions to make our Lego city communities more diverse. (Criado, August 5, 2014)

The lab featured several female characters all engaged in various scientific pursuits (astronomy, chemistry, and archaeology), controversially wearing make-up (something that generated heated criticism afterwards). However, speaking at an innovation conference in Copenhagen in 2014, LEGO's brand manager noted that the range was a big hit with parents and adults, but not so much with children, who still preferred their pink and purple Friends. Admitting the issue was a difficult one that the firm struggled with, the brand manager ultimately sided with young girls, although did not rule out further developments such as the Science Laboratory.

(Continued)

Case Questions

1. What strategies have characterized LEGO's enduring brand success?
2. How does LEGO's changing practice in relation to co-creation reflect shifts in our understanding of brand management?
3. Why did LEGO attract criticism from various activists? What would have happened to the brand's image if they had not responded?
4. Evaluate LEGO's approach to normalizing gender and disability in their product range. Is it too limited? Are they trying too hard or being too overt?
5. What challenges is the brand likely to face from online petitions in the future?

Key Terms

Brand-as-asset view
Brandr
Brand equity
Brand meaning
Brand personality
Co-creation
Consumer culture

theory (CCT)
Cultural brand codes
Cultural brand model
Customer-Based
Brand Equity (CBBE)
(Mindshare Model)
Fast-moving

consumer goods
(FMCG)
Identity projects
Segmentation-
targeting-positioning
Symbols
Value-in-use

Further Reading and Viewing

Aaker, David (2014), *Aaker on Branding: 20 Principles that Drive Success*. Morgan James Publishing, Virginia.

Conejo, Francisco and Ben Wooliscroft (2015), "Brands Defined as Semiotic Marketing Systems," *Journal of Macromarketing*, 35(3), 287–301.

Edwards, Helen and Derek Day (2005), *Creating Passionbrands: How to Build Emotional Connections with Customers*, Kogan Page, London.

Gardner, Burleigh B. and Sidney J. Levy (1955), "The Product and the Brand," *Harvard Business Review*, March–April, 33–39.

Holt, Douglas B. (2003), "Brands and Branding," *Harvard Business School Teaching Note* 9-503-045.

Levy, Sidney J. (1959), "Symbols for Sale," *Harvard Business Review*, July–August, 117–124.

Madmen "Lucky Strike Pitch." https://www.youtube.com/watch?v=yXTJhVBqWOM

2

UNDERSTANDING BRAND USERS

When brands get on the Internet, they don't really seem to get the game. They don't understand that this is about interacting with us. They're like that fat, balding guy at a party who talks too loud, drinks too much, stares at the girls, and generally thinks the world revolves around him. (McCracken 2010, p. 90)

Learning Objectives

When you finish reading this chapter, you will be able to answer these questions:

1. How have various models viewed the consumer–brand relationship over time?
2. Why are brand choices reflective of consumer identity goals?
3. What are the seven aspects of postmodernity that influence how we approach brand meaning?
4. How do consumers achieve self-authentication? What are authenticating acts and authoritative performances?
5. What is linking value and why is it important for brand managers?
6. What are the four types of "communities" that can surround brands?
7. Do all brand choices reflect identity?

Users Co-create Brand Meaning

Look at the people around you—how many brands can you see? Despite the claims of marketers, within different product and service categories, many brands largely deliver the same **functional benefits**. Yet, the people you observed probably all use many different brands, just as you yourself do. For them, and for you, these brands do mean something, and they communicate important things about you to others (and yourself). Regardless of functional convergence, you would undoubtedly argue for some time that your brand is better than others—just try suggesting your friend's favorite mass-market beer or cola is inferior to your own!

What we buy says a lot about who we are, how we see ourselves, and even who we would like to be. That is, brand choices are primarily about identity, rather than objective performance benefits. In saying that users shape brand meaning, we need to understand what they seek from the brands. This chapter draws on the significant body of research that identifies how consumers support brands that are reflective of their desired and/or authentic self. That is, in advanced (and even developing nations), where materialism is the name of the game, brand choices reflect consumers' desired identity or identities (Shankar and Fitchett 2002).

There are a few exceptions of course (see Brand Aside 2.1 and Chapter 10), but even claims that one supports brands for their functional advantages or "value-for-money" are in fact identity claims—statements that one is a savvy, informed, pragmatic consumer in control of their consumption choices (Bardhi and Eckhardt 2012; Beverland and Farrelly 2010). Likewise, as will be shown in Chapter 10, business-to-business buyers face many conflicting role expectations that closely resemble the challenges consumers face.

Since brand choice represents an extension of our **desired self** brands are often judged on their degree of genuineness, sincerity, or, as I argue here, authenticity. A number of authors have argued for some time now that authenticity is the hallmark of postmodern marketing, although how "real" claims of authenticity *are or need to be* is up for debate (Beverland 2009; Brown 2003). This chapter explores why authenticity is now the hallmark of brand co-creation, why brands play such an important role in consumers' identity, and details a range of concepts that will be used throughout this book.

The chapter begins with an overview of different ways in which users have been viewed within brand models; primarily moving from being viewed as passive receivers of brand messages to active co-creators of brand meaning. It then explores the nature of postmodern markets and identifies why consumers primarily use brands to achieve a state of **self-authentication** or acts that reveal the true self (Arnould and Price 2000). It then identifies two related but potentially competing goals: individual **authenticating acts** and collective **authoritative performances**. The rest of the chapter is dedicated to exploring the implications of these two goals for various aspects of consumption and branding. The chapter finishes by considering exceptions to brands as expressions of identity.

Changes in Our Understanding of Users and Brands

Chapter 1 identified different disciplines that have impacted on our understanding of branding over the past 100 years or so. Although our understanding of brand-meaning management has advanced substantially over the past three decades, it is important to recognize studies of branding continue to offer new insights into value co-creation through brands (i.e., there is much we still do not know).

Early approaches to branding largely focused on the denotative role of brands. For example, Lux Soap originally did not connote a set of values; rather it simply denoted that Lux was in the category of "soap." During the early part of the twentieth century, as goods became more abundant, consumers primarily desired reliability and quality, especially since consumer trade-protection laws were in their infancy. Brands in essence therefore represented trust marks (Colman's English Mustard could be trusted) or objective guarantees of authenticity (vs. a counterfeit version), much as they had in the days of medieval guilds.

Throughout this period, advertisers played a critical role in brand practice, often searching for key points of difference (or USP) in the product, its performance, and/or its backstory to use in commercials. Throughout, the most enlightened advertising agencies such as JWT and Ogilvy & Mather drew on new knowledge emerging from economics and psychology to help understand consumer choice and loyalty. Economics identified the efficiency benefits of branding, while psychology explored how and why consumers made choices.

This research identified that brands help consumers minimize the cognitive effort involved in consumption. Since consumers face literally hundreds of consumption choices every day, they are simply unable to process information regarding alternatives, performance, and value, as well as assess competing claims between brands. Brands provide simple heuristics or "rules of thumb" to enable us to make sense of a complex world (Holt 2003). For much of the twentieth century, this view underpinned much of brand-management theory and practice, leading to an emphasis on consistency, simplicity, and USPs as identified in the Lucky Strike video from Chapter 1 and Don Draper's claim the brand was "toasted."

In brand management, psychology still dominates much of the research and frames how many models, particularly the dominant customer-based brand equity (CBBE) approach, views the consumer. The CBBE model, developed by Kevin Keller (see "The Consumer Approach" below), treats the consumer as an information processor. In the simplest of terms, brands resonate more strongly if we know something about them and if that information is viewed positively (see Chapter 4 for more detail).

In CBBE, the brand manager's job is to provide small bite-sized chunks of information about the brand (often in the form of a tagline or advertising jingle), its benefits, and other associations to its target users, and to reinforce these over time. This information can be provided in a variety of ways (including directly through advertising and indirectly through packaging, sponsorship and so on) and across a range of different mediums. Although the CBBE model is consumer-focused in name, much of the effort in creating brand meaning lies with the marketer.

This view of the user began to be criticized by a number of academics in the 1980s. Responding to calls for a richer understanding of consumption, the Marketing Science Institute sponsored a group of researchers (Russell Belk, Melanie Wallendorf, and John Sherry Jr.) to travel around the United States of America on a "consumer odyssey." Published in the *Journal of Consumer Research* in 1989, "The Sacred and Profane in Consumer Behaviour: Theodicy on the Odyssey" challenged the information process-ing view of the consumer. This seminal article identified that seemingly banal objects such as plastic white picket fences erected outside of a poor consumer's trailer-park home had significant meaning, often helping consumers enforce a desired identity and communicate a sense of community with others. Things such as old toys, sporting memorabilia, or royal family ware that at first glance may seem trivial and tacky were often viewed as sacred by consumers because they had imbued them with a sense of authenticity.

BRAND ASIDE 2.1

The Extended Self

What do we use to construct our sense of self? Historically, who we were was often predetermined by our parentage, our class, our schooling, race, gender, and so on. Under postmodernity, many of these structures have broken down or have a less overt role in defining who we are (they still play a role, often in a subconscious way). Various objects including products and brands symbolically represent who we are and/or who we would like to be. That is, what we own becomes an extension of our self (desired and/or real). This spills over into all aspects of life—workers surround themselves with branded items, while tradespeople choose tools that reflect their desired status (something Black & Decker realized when attempting to extend their brand from the home into worksites—see Chapter 7), and more recently in how we build our digital self—just think about what you like on Facebook, how you carefully craft posts, what you decide to share, and how you deal with that friend who keeps posting material that conflicts with your carefully cultivated image (Belk 2013). The extended self tells us that we literally are branded!

The "sacred and profane" provided the impetus for an explosion in research focused on the lived experience of consumers, and critically viewed consumers as actively using brands to shape their identity (see Brand Aside 2.1 on "The Extended Self"). As a result, this work placed the consumer and their identity goals at the heart of branding. In contrast to psychological research, this work, informed by anthropology and sociology as well as a relational turn in marketing practice, saw the consumer as an active meaning creator and value as co-created. In contrast to psychological branding theories, cultural approaches view the consumer as an individual and social being, bounded in their choices by often subconscious socially defined structures, and motivated by the **linking value** or the ability of brands to connect one goal with another and "I" with "We."

In 2005 Eric Arnould and Craig Thompson formalized this vast body of work under the label of consumer culture theory (CCT) in the *Journal of Consumer Research*. Although not strictly a unified theory, CCT is defined by four themes:

1. Consumer identity projects: consumers use marketplace materials such as brands to construct their identity or identities. Consumers may accept the brand as it's presented to them to do so, or may have a very different relationship to the brand than that intended by marketers. The Burberry trench coat has long been seen as a symbol for success in many countries, the purchase of which signals one has "made it." Playful alternatives are shown in Figure 2.1.

Figure 2.1   Playful Identities

2. Marketplace cultures: consumers can produce culture that can offer rich pickings to marketers seeking to build brand associations (although marketers must be very careful how to leverage these relationships). Fashion designers such as the late Alexander McQueen drew on connections with the gay community in his breakthrough "Golden Shower" runway show. Consumers may commune around living and forgotten or "dead" brands. For example, fans of the Josh Whedon show *Firefly* have long campaigned for a sequel, resulting to date in the movie *Serenity* and a 2017 announced reboot), and may rework brand meaning to fit with communal norms such as *Lord of the Rings* fans' efforts to place Sir Peter Jackson's film trilogy in the J.R.R. Tolkien canon.

3. Limits to "choice" or agency: while the majority of approaches to branding assume consumers are free to choose brands (subject to resource availability), CCT researchers have identified that there are many social structures such as class, gender, and ethnicity that frame and therefore shape or limit our choices. We may be entirely oblivious to these structures, and our choices may therefore reflect societal notions of taste, status, gender, and so on. Newly rich consumers may draw on ostentatious brands to fit in line with their view of luxury as conspicuous displays of wealth, yet in doing so, they may reinforce upper-class prejudice against them for having a lack of taste (Holt 1998).

4. Marketplace ideologies: brands are part of an ideological system. For example: Coke = Freedom and America; The Body Shop = Social Ethics; Patagonia = Sustainability. This can lead consumers to preference certain types of identity projects. The fast fashion system as exemplified by Zara and H&M influences many of us to use regular changes in style and wardrobe to shape our identity, despite claims we would like to be more sustainable. Apple's call to "Think Different" ironically leverages anti-establishment figures to sell more products because it fits in with Western ideological preferences for rebellion, creativity, and independence.

Culturally informed branding work (of which this book draws upon) suggests users are active in creating meaning. What exactly does this mean in practice?

1. Consumers choose brands to reflect their desired identity or identities. These are both individually and socially defined.
2. Consumers may contest marketer brand meaning and dominant ideologies.
3. Consumers may happily play along with marketer brand meaning and market-place ideologies.
4. Even when making choices, consumers may be unaware of how that choice is shaped (and may be quite happy nonetheless).
5. Consumers can shape their own identities through consumption, although such acts may simply reinforce existing social structures, leading to dissatisfaction.

6. Consumer choices reflect a variety of motives and influences, all of which can be both shaped by marketers and shape the ways in which we can best market brands.

The CCT view sees consumers as struggling to define their true self in a context where traditional markers of identity have declined, where they face multiple, often conflicting goals, and where brands or branded contexts are ubiquitous. This view gave rise to several new approaches to understanding brand-meaning co-creation including the relational, communal, and cultural views covered below, and also highlighted that authenticity becomes the standard upon which brands are judged.

Eight Approaches to Brand-meaning Management

Research on how and why users relate to brands has exploded over the past three decades. Each of these approaches has influenced how practitioners build brands, and although each has flaws, all have something valuable to offer in different stages of the brand-building process. Different authors make assumptions about how and why users make choices, which generates different models of brand management.

For example, some models view the user as largely passive in relation to brand meaning. When we say they are "passive" we don't mean that no mental work is undertaken to understand what the brand means; rather we mean that models frame users as mere receivers of marketer-driven meanings. That means users are assumed to play no role in the meaning of the brand at all. Such approaches lead to top-down models of brand-meaning creation whereby marketers provide all the content of the brand's intended meaning (which explains LEGO's initial hostility to adult brand hacks—see Chapter 1). In contrast, where the user is framed as an active meaning creator, the focus shifts to understanding user goals and why the meaning they attribute to the brand may differ from that intended by marketers, as exemplified by Asian consumers' use of Vegemite to flavor soups (see the Vegemite case example at the end of this chapter).

Heding et al. (2016) identify seven approaches to understanding brand relationships. Summaries of the logic of each school are presented in Figure 2.2. I add one further approach that is popular among practitioners and academic researchers—the experiential approach. Together, these eight approaches are listed below:

1. *The economic approach*: Stemming from product management this approach largely views brand meaning as a spillover from investments in the marketing mix (the four Ps of promotion, place, product, and price). In this approach, consumers make rational choices (based on the optimal mix of the four Ps), have short-term, transactional relationships with brands, and play no role in generating brand meaning. This approach influenced much of the advertising industry in the first half of the twentieth century and is still dominant in some industries such as automotive and fast-moving consumer goods (FMCG).

The Economic Approach

Source: Heding et al. 2016, p.31

The Identity Approach

Source: Heding et al. 2016, p.52

The Consumer-based Approach

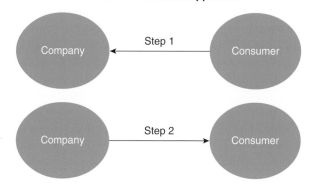

Source: Heding et al. 2016, p.105

The Personality Approach

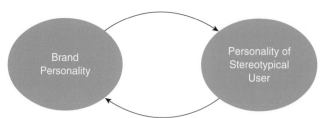

Source: Heding et al. 2016, p.133

The Relationship Approach

Source: Heding et al. 2016, p.165

The Experiential Approach

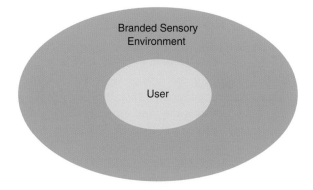

Source: Author's notes

The Community Approach

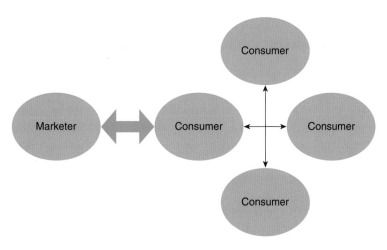

Source: Heding et al. 2016, p.199

(Continued)

Figure 2.2   (Continued)

The Cultural Approach

Figure 2.2   **Approaches to Branding and Consumers**

Source: Heding et al. 2016, p.231

2. *The identity approach*: Much like the economic approach, consumers play no role in creating brand meaning. This approach, explicated in Wolf Olins' foundational (1978) book *The Personality of the Corporation*, focuses on ensuring the firm speaks with a single, coherent identity. This approach plays a large role in the service and professional sectors today and critically highlights the importance of the customer journey and "moments of truth." Critically, firms undertake brand audits to ensure that customers' holistic experience of the firm conform to the organization's brand vision (see Chapters 5 and 6).

3. *The consumer-based approach*: This approach is synonymous with the customer-based brand equity (CBBE) model of Kevin Keller. It argues the brand exists in the mind of the consumer and is based heavily in cognitive psychology and informational processing models of choice. Although this approach emphasizes consumer perception, and thereby distinguishes between **intended brand identity** and **received brand image**, the marketer is still largely in control of shaping how the consumer views the brand. This approach remains the dominant approach in brand management today, although it has come under increasing criticism in the last decade.

4. *The personality approach*: Drawing on the psychological view of personality, this approach identifies that consumers ascribe certain personality traits or types to brands and their users. Adopted in the 1950s to identify likely users for certain brands, this approach has had a large influence on the communication of brand associations. This approach also drew on the notion of the **extended self**—or the idea that consumers see brands as extensions of their real and/or desired selves (Belk 1988, 2013). Importantly, the consumer in this view is seen as a more active meaning creator (although still dominated by the marketer). And, rather than being viewed as a rational decision maker, the personality approach highlights the importance of emotions and identity in brand choice. In theory and practice, **brand personality** is highly influential.

Figure 2.3   Consumer-brand Relationship Styles

5. *The relational approach*: Developed by Susan Fournier in her seminal (1998) article "Consumers and their Brands: Developing Relationship Theory in Consumer Research" in the *Journal of Consumer Research*, this approach varies radically from earlier work. Drawing on the emerging interest in relationship theory and marketing (or relationship marketing), this approach sees the consumer as an active meaning creator, characterizing brands according to common relationship styles (see Figure 2.3 for examples). This approach highlights that consumers can have intense relationships with seemingly mundane brands. Brand relationships are also constantly being negotiated between the user and brand as consumers seek to place the brand within a network of relationships and identity goals. Should either of these change, the relationship can also change, and there is often little marketers can do about it. An influential idea, in practice building strong consumer–brand relationships underpins models of financial brand equity.

6. *The experiential approach*: Having its roots in the pioneering work of Morris Holbrook and Elizabeth Hirschman (1982), the **experiential marketing** approach began taking off in the late 1990s when it was popularized by Harvard-based academics James Pine and Joseph Gilmore in their article and book *The Experience*

Economy. The thesis was simple: as economies developed, value moved from buying goods and services to purchasing experiences (see Figure 2.4). The approach views the user largely as a sensory being in that meaning is shaped and created through strategies that appeal to the five senses (sight, sound, smell, touch, and taste). In this approach, consumers are immersed in a branded world (often a flagship store such as SoHo's Prada store), a brand museum (such as those built by Volkswagen and Ferrari), or a themed **servicescape** or environment where the service encounter takes place. This approach remains popular especially among designers focused on products (see Brand Aside 2.2), service encounters, retail stores, and, more recently, web-based and virtual reality platforms to build more emotional and subconscious connections between brands and their users.

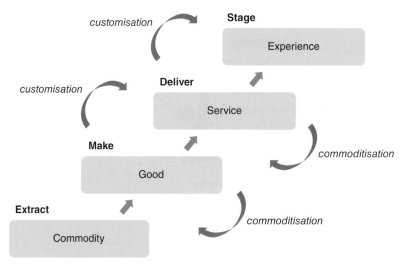

Figure 2.4   The shift towards experiences

BRAND ASIDE 2.2

The P&G Effect

Claudia Kotchka, Vice President of Design and Innovation at venerable FMCG powerhouse Procter & Gamble, gave a famous talk aimed at reinvigorating the firm's many iconic brands to make them more relevant. She labeled this the "P&G Effect" and demonstrated how the firm's efficiency logic undermined customer–brand experiences, ultimately destroying brand value. Referring to the cult brand (in America) of English peppermints Altoids (which P&G did not own), she asked,

"What makes Altoids special?" She identified a number of brand cues including the old-fashioned metal tin with embossed logo, the beautiful paper that wrapped the mints, the hand-cut mints themselves, the quirky flavors (hot cinnamon, ginger, licorice, spearmint, chocolate), and the fact that the tin was not filled to the brim. The whole package screamed authenticity. Demonstrating what would happen to the brand if P&G got its hands on it, she noted that the tin could be replaced by a plastic case (much the same as those that contain baby-wipes), the paper removed as it served no purpose, the mints mass manufactured and standardized, the logo standardized, flavors mainstreamed, and a 400 percent mark-up added. The result "Proctoids"! (See Figure 2.5.) The lesson was clear: marketers must understand how the experience of the brand enhances customer value.

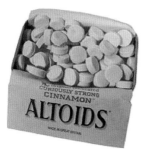
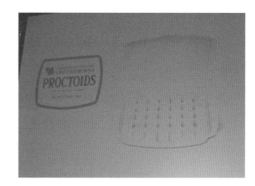

Figure 2.5   Altoids vs. Proctoids

Source: Beverland 2009

7. *The community approach*: Founded by John Schouten and James McAlexander in their study on the rebirth of Harley Davidson (1995), this approach highlights the communal aspects of brand relationships, giving rise to an interest in **brand community**, **subcultures of consumption**, **consumer tribes**, and, recently, **consumer publics**. In this model, the brand's meaning emerges through one-to-one and one-to-many relationships between consumers and the brand, but importantly, through consumers and other consumers of the brand. In this case, the brand's value may result solely from the value the community surrounding it provides to an individual consumer. This model is used to varying degrees by

marketers, especially following the shift to web-based interactivity or Web 2.0, but does require brand managers to tread carefully as they must cede some control of the brand to a community.

8. *The cultural approach*: The newest and most fragmented approach to brand building, this approach focuses upon the sociocultural context in which consumers operate and the role that brands can play in enabling them to make sense of the wider world. In this approach, emphasis is given to the brand's culture (which is driven by the four authors identified in Figure 1.1), and how brands draw on and provide cultural myths to address societal schisms. Consistent with models 5–7, the consumer is an active meaning maker, albeit one operating within (often) subconscious structures (gender, class, race, etc.) that limit choice (Bourdieu 1984). Unlike identity and consumer models, the cultural approach downplays consistency in favor of relevance, identifying the importance of changing the brand to suit the times (through "cultural innovation" see Chapter 8).

This text views brands as co-created by multiple authors (see Chapter 1, Figure 1.1), and therefore views the user as having an active role in brand-meaning development. That said, each of the eight models above provide some value in our understanding of how brands should be managed. For example:

1. The economic approach identifies the relationship between brand identity and tactics. Brand managers understand that desired brand identity must drive marketing mix activities (rather than vice versa). For example, Ryanair let their positioning around value and timeliness drive everything they do, from their choice of airports (cheaper, out of the way secondary airports), use of fees for extras, lack of airline lounges, low-quality advertising, and public relations stories about paying for the use of the toilet in air or stand-up seating.

2. The identity approach retains much currency within the corporate branding sector and has led to an interest in employee branding as well as an emphasis on ensuring alignment between intended identity, organizational culture, and user experience. When Virgin started an airline in Australia, they experienced a lot of criticism for asking potential employees to dance, sing, or act spontaneously in interviews. However, the purpose here was to ensure staff would be able to work together and solve customer problems that might emerge due to the unexpected delays that are common in the sector.

3. The consumer approach can encompass the personality, relational, experiential, and communal approaches (these are all ways in which to build brand knowledge) and is particularly useful when it comes to brand extensions (which are critical to keeping brands fresh and achieving financial performance targets) and in reinforcing the brand day-to-day (assuming no substantive change in the wider sociocultural environment). Jeep owner days, for example, mix experienced drivers with novices in order to demonstrate vehicle features and enhance driver confidence.

This community creates stronger bonds between drivers, drivers and their vehicle, and therefore ensures greater brand loyalty, positive word of mouth, and increased likelihood to repurchase a Jeep in the future.

4. The personality and relational approaches highlight how consumers frame brand relationships and can be used strategically to enhance consumer–brand bonds. Fiat, for example, identified that users enjoyed their vehicles but due to quality problems did not feel emotionally engaged with them. By running a series of light-hearted adverts for their Palio range, the brand aimed to get owners to care about their cars emotionally.

5. The experiential approach is useful in rendering the brand authentic across all aspects of the marketing mix and highlights potential new sources of differentiation. Luxury brands have gone to great lengths to embody their identity in expensive flagship stores, all of which are aimed at immersing the consumer in the brand concept.

6. The communal approach identifies how other consumers can add value to the brand relationship. Consumers for example share tips on The Impossible Project's forum focused on instant film, thereby ensuring users gain more knowledge and confidence with their old Polaroid cameras (something their rival Fuji does not do).

7. The cultural approach reminds us that brand meaning and therefore perceptions of relevance can be shaped by the wider sociocultural context in which the consumer operates. As such, it is particularly useful for understanding brand relevance, revitalization, and for new brands wishing to challenge incumbents. Dove's Campaign for Real Beauty drew on feminist ideas and parents' concerns that the influence of idealized body images in the media could harm their daughters.

Throughout this book, I will draw on each of these approaches where relevant to explore different aspects of brand meaning co-creation.

The Value of Brands to Users

Value is central to all marketing-related activities. Over time, our understanding of value has shifted. Historically, the value to the user of brands was viewed as an outcome of delivering on claims of superior performance. Since most brands started as products, advertisers often spent a lot of time searching for unique consumer benefits—as David Ogilvy stated, "great advertising cannot help a bad product, in fact the reverse is true" (Lee et al. 2017). As practices changed, and products (and services) were subsumed under brands, the value of a brand was viewed in terms of providing certainty or more accurately reducing anxiety or post-purchase dissonance. Brands were therefore trust marks that provided a lot of information very efficiently to consumers.

BRAND ASIDE 2.3

The Service Dominant Logic and Experiential Consumption

In 2004 scholars Stephen Vargo and Bob Lusch published a hugely influential paper in the *Journal of Marketing* entitled "The Service-Dominant Logic of Marketing" (S-DL). Building on the last decade of theorizing in marketing and co-creation, S-DL reconfigures our understanding of value away from economic exchange to use. In this model, value is derived through the services rendered by products, services, experiences, and brands. At first glance, this looks obvious and confusing—how can the value of a good be defined as a service? A pair of Sennheiser headphones, for example, has no intrinsic value other than their ability to provide the true benefits—sound quality and an overt signal about one's musical appreciation. Likewise, studies have demonstrated that a favored lipstick is valued for the confidence it gives the user (Fournier 1998), which is of course a service. The branding implications of this model have yet to be fully understood but S-DL focuses squarely on co-creation and user goals, and views brands as resources that can be of use to consumers and other buyers.

Brands still do this of course, but they also do so much more for users. As marketing has moved to what is called a service-dominant logic (S-DL), whereby even the value of goods is understood in terms of the services or benefits they provide to users, brands have been reframed as potential resources that users can draw on to achieve identity goals (Merz et al. 2009). Brand Aside 2.3 contains more details. Therefore, the primary value that brands offer relates to their symbolic value. Holt (2003) identifies three types of symbolic value that brands offer consumers:

1. Identity value: "the aspect of a brand's value that derives from the brand's contributions to self-expression" (Holt 2004a, p. 11). Since brands represent certain things, the act of consumption produces the emotions associated with the values of the brand and its surrounding culture. This experience is visceral, defying logic or reason (see the "truthyness" discussion below). Apple, for example, has many associations with creative communities; therefore, the adoption of this brand makes us feel more creative, as the story about the brand's stickers demonstrates (see Brand Aside 2.4).
2. Social distinction: Brands say much about who we are (the authentic self), who we desire to be (the desired self), and who we are not (the undesired self). The choice to use a brand or reject it sends a message about status (see Brand Aside 2.5). Brands are particularly important status markers in the postmodern era given the

BRAND ASIDE 2.4

Brands Shape Products and Services

Brands shape reality, often in unexpected ways. More formally, Holt (2003, p. 4) states: "Brands provide a perceptual frame through which customers understand, value, and experience the product or service." A short example illustrates this point. Apple remains one of the most valuable brands on the planet (as measured by agencies Millward Brown and Interbrand). Despite the hi-tech nature of the brand, the popularity of Macworld announcements (especially those by the late founder Steve Jobs), the iconic advertising, and the stores, the most successful marketing tool for the company is decidedly analog—stickers. Every Apple package contains some and, over the years, they have changed as the brand's logo has evolved. Fans of the brand used to indicate their love of the brand by sticking them on cars and houses. These same users often removed the stickers when they sold their car or moved homes. Older stickers are also used to indicate status within the Apple community; much in the way music fans claim to have been into certain artists before they became famous. Examples are shown in Figure 2.6. Such is the power of iconic brands like Apple that the simple application of a sticker onto a rival phone helps transform it in the mind of the user. There have even been reports of users of Nokia phones reporting that their handset was cooler and worked better after they stuck an Apple sticker onto it (Beverland 2009). Brands it would appear have magical transformative powers!

Figure 2.6   **Consumers' use of Apple Stickers**

decline of traditional social hierarchies. Related to this is the idea of the narcissism of small differences whereby consumers differentiate themselves by tiny, often unreadable differences (to outsiders) as a form of taste-based distinction. The video link in Further Reading to the "Business Card Scene" in the movie *American Psycho* demonstrates this behavior perfectly.

BRAND ASIDE 2.5

Status Anxiety

Concern with status is one of the main drivers of consumption, particularly in fast developing economies. The flipside of the extended self, status signaling involves symbolic consumption aimed at others to identify membership or lack of member-ship with a certain group. Historically, status consumption involved highly conspicuous displays of economic wealth. Such obvious displays were designed to ensure one's economic status could be ascertained quickly. However, as society became more fragmented and less hierarchical and the middle classes grew in size, it became harder and harder to display one's place. As a result, economic capital became less important than cultural capital (which will be discussed later). This gave rise to status anxiety or the feelings associated with how one is perceived by others. Giana Eckhardt and colleagues published an award-winning paper examin-ing the emergence of inconspicuous consumption (Eckhardt et al. 2015). In this model, status is defined through subtle signals and the choice of rare, older, herit-age brands and the use of ritualized language that display insider status or connoisseurship (signaling one has the time and therefore the money to invest in specialized pursuits). In China, this has led to declines in sales for ostentatious luxury logos in favor of brands that draw stronger links to art, culture, and heritage as a signal of authenticity.

3. Communal affiliation: As identified throughout this chapter, brands are often the main way we signal solidarity with others, tribal or group membership, or in rare cases provide the basis for special communities of consumption or brand com-munities. The ability to signal one's affiliation with others gives rise to a further form of value—linking value—discussed below. Austrian-based Lomography has revitalized old-school film photography through communal strategies.

To fully understand the value that brands provide, we need to understand how the wider sociocultural changes attributed to "postmodernity" have reshaped user goals and their reliance on the market to provide resources previously provided by the state, community, place, or tradition. The postmodern period emerged in the late twentieth century and ultimately changed our understanding of marketing and branding in numerous ways. In their seminal article, Firat and Venkatesh (1995) identified seven characteristics of postmodernism's influence on marketing and branding:

1. Fragmentation: The period we are currently in is defined by a sense of disconnection and instability in markets, politics, knowledge creation, and community. In marketing, a few large customer segments have given way to a seemingly endless series of micro-segments potentially including "markets of one." In his bestselling book *The Long Tail*, former *Wired* editor Chris Anderson discusses the almost infinite number of small markets for digital content providers (or "the long tail") around the globe that enables small brands to survive and prosper. He later on extends this in his work on new forms of manufacturing whereby he identifies 3D printing as a means to provide physical product to niche markets of users around the globe.

2. De-differentiation: Postmodernity is best thought of in terms of endless "shades of grey" rather than fixed categories of black and white. Traditional distinctions for example between high and low culture, local and global, news and entertainment, authentic and fake, art and commerce, and so on, have blurred. Steven Johnson's book *Everything Bad Is Good for You* identifies how genres of popular culture (including television shows and computer games but excluding movies) have become increasingly "grey" in their approaches and as a result infinitely more complex, requiring and rewarding deep consumer engagement. Compare, for example, the TV series *Battlestar Galactica*. The 1970s show reflects the black-and-white Cold War era whereby good humans fight for survival against a ruthless, collective race of hybrid machine-aliens, the Cylons. The 2003 reboot reflected a post-September 11 world whereby it was difficult to tell good from bad, with the Cylons created by humans as a servant caste. The show involved an ongoing series of shifting alliances, moral grey areas, and a reflection on what it meant to be human.

3. Hyperreality: with the ubiquity of advertising, mass media, guerrilla marketing, and social media, distinctions between what is real and what are simulacra are difficult to make (Baudrillard 1994). For example, is *The LEGO Movie* a film or an extended brand advertisement? Culturally themed pubs and retail stores, Las Vegas hotels such as the Venetian (modelled on the city of Venice), reality television, and the virtual worlds of gaming and social media are often cited as examples of the hyperreal. One outcome of this is the desire for seemingly "real" experiences or authenticity.

4. Chronology: Modernity was defined by a sense that the future would be better than the past; postmodernity takes a much more skeptical view of progress, preferring instead retro-brands, nostalgia, seeming authenticity, and mash-ups of

historic styles, albeit with modern features (such as the new MINI, VW Beetle, Fiat 500, and so on). Many sectors, such as music, fashion, film, and gaming, are now defined by endless reruns of past styles (Reynolds 2012). Consumers create new categories or segments such as steampunk (Victoriana) and revitalize legacy technology such as vinyl music and film photography (Beverland and Fernandez 2016). Retro branding also involves designers and brand managers looking to the past for inspiration in the present (Brown et al. 2003).

5. Pastiche: also referred to as "bricolage," this involves mixing or mashing up different styles in order to create something new, critique existing orders, or playfully undermine traditional dualisms such as high and low art, masculinity and femininity, luxury and mass, and so on. Since brands are treated as just another "text" to be read by audiences, value can also be created through intertextuality, or the mixing of meanings from different genres to create something new, such as the creation of brand museums (brand+museum) by automotive groups such as Volkswagen and Vespa to enhance their prestige and icon-status.

6. Anti-foundationalism: Joseph Heath and Andrew Potter's (2006) book *The Rebel Sell* identified how rebellion rather than conformity drove the creation of market categories such as punk, grunge, organics, authenticity, and (ironically) anti-consumption. In this view, rebellion is quickly co-opted by marketers and made mainstream, speeding up fashion cycles and fueling a subcultural backlash resulting in new sources of rebellion. Postmodernity focuses on undermining authorities or the status quo. Former Dior designer John Galliano drew on Parisian homelessness to reinvigorate the iconic fashion brand with his "Trash Dress," while Louis Vuitton drew on street art for their signature (and much counterfeited) Alma bag.

7. Pluralism: The previous six characteristics give rise to a live and let live, anything goes attitude. Postmodernism rejects notions of absolute truth, focusing instead on subjective experience and the social construction of reality. Brand meaning thereby comes to be defined by users and the other authors identified in Chapter 1. In this case, critical assessments of brand claims matter less than the brand's conformity to consumer beliefs about what is true or real. This is expressed in the following quote about brand myths from former Morgan Motor Company CEO Charles Morgan:

> Rather than a brand, I think it's more an attempt to interest the cult and keep the cult going. We like providing stories that people can tell in the pub and feel that makes them part of the family. So our brand is made up of a series of myths, some of which are true, and some of which are owned. The one about the wooden chassis in France, we have tried and tried to get rid of that, but it still persists. And eventually we just said, yeah sure, it's wooden. (Beverland 2009, p. 31).

These seven characteristics of postmodernity define the reality in which users and brand managers operate, and shape user goals, practices, and notions of value. This shift has enormous implications for how we manage brands as marketers.

Under postmodernity, the value of brands to users shifts from decreasing anxiety or information efficiency and trust to self-authentication and linking value. In this scenario brands become extensions of our desired self or selves, help us navigate multiple and conflicting identity-role boundaries (such as mother, worker, and friend) and connect us to "imagined communities," which are communities only in the sense that we feel that others are like us (Anderson 1983). Each of these is covered below.

Authenticity: The Morality of Postmodernity

It is perhaps ironic that postmodernity has generated a concern for authenticity, or the *pursuit* of the real, true, and genuine (Beverland and Farrelly 2010). After all distinctions between real and fake make little sense given the previous seven points. However, Giddens (1991, p. 9) identifies that authenticity is the preeminent framework for self-actualization, retro-branding expert Stephen Brown (2003) has identified that authenticity is central to postmodern marketing, while consumer researchers identify that the desire for authenticity shapes consumer expectations about brands and related experiences (Beverland and Farrelly 2010). Authenticity seemingly presents several problems to the managers of brands since commerce was viewed as artificial or motivated by base concerns prior to postmodernity, and therefore the opposite of what was deemed authentic. However, marketing experts Gilmore and Pine (2007) suggest the secret to rendering authenticity through branding lies in understanding the following paradox:

1. Everything humans create is essentially fake or inauthentic (because it would not occur naturally).
2. Everything humans create can be perceived as real or authentic by users (if it conforms to use expectations of the real).

This paradox arises out of a complex philosophical debate between what is really real and what is experienced as real. In essence, this means that although claims of authenticity can always be contested, brand managers can render authenticity through carefully constructed strategies. Research backs this assertion up, identifying how consumers will suspend disbelief or negotiate paradox in order to play along with claims of authenticity (Grayson and Martinec 2004; Rose and Wood 2005). Why might they do so?

In examining identity goals and consumption, Arnould and Price (2000) identify that globalization (the collapse of national borders and greater connectivity in trade and communication), deterritorialization (the weakening of ties between culture and place such as the use of Japanese symbols by UK-based brand Superdry), and hyperreality (difficulties in telling real from fake) have undermined traditional sources of identity. However, rather than reject authenticity, consumers have turned to the marketplace and used brands and consumption rituals as resources to achieve the true self or what they call self-authentication. However, consumers are never fully free from social obligations, and this means that achieving self-authentication in a sociocultural system requires balancing two practices:

1. Authenticating acts: These are individual actions that transcend social expectations. As identified in Figure 2.7 these involve pursuits for their own sake (such as knowledge, art, personal enlightenment, and so on), spontaneity (or the sense of flow that comes from being in the moment), uniqueness, and surprise. These are activities and pursuits that reflect who you really desire to be rather than reflect the expectations of others or conformity to social norms.
2. Authoritative performances: These are cultural displays or performances that reinforce membership of a group. As identified in Figure 2.7 these involve scripted and rehearsed actions, engagement in rituals and traditions, and stylized displays. Authoritative performances involve impression management and represent boundaries or limits to authenticating acts. That is, you may not want to follow collective "rules" but to achieve self-authentication in a social sense you must.

As described in Figure 2.7 both actions share different outcomes and we can see that these combined provide individual and social benefits. Therefore, authenticating acts involve personal "life themes" (or our long-term chosen purpose or meaning) whereas authoritative performances involve being part of a larger collective. Although the pursuit of an identity goal (or authenticating act) may be experienced as intensely personal, these goals are also shaped by social expectations or conventions, and therefore often shared by many. For example, one may desire to be creative and choose a set of brands to reflect this, but certain societies value creativity and self-expression

Figure 2.7   Authenticating Acts and Authoritative Performances

Source: Arnould and Price 2000, p.146

(and therefore set expectations about how this will be expressed), and hence many others will seek out this goal as well. Brands can represent resources for either form of self-authentication or in rare cases both.

One simple way of understanding this is through the "secretary's bag." In China, materialism defines status and success for many. For the primarily young women in secretarial roles, this means they are "forced" to purchase luxury brands such as Gucci and Louis Vuitton in order to demonstrate their success. This is an authoritative performance. Failure to do so means they are perceived as being unsuccessful and are therefore passed over for promotion, thereby making achievement of their personal goals more difficult. Therefore, self-authentication for the secretary requires the purchase of an expensive luxury handbag in order to fit in with the collective expectation regarding success and performance. This, then, provides her with the resources to engage in authenticating acts that reflect her own desires.

This would of course seem ideal for luxury houses such as Louis Vuitton and Gucci. Unlike nations where individuality is prized, writer on luxury brands Jean-Noel Kapferer (2012) notes that conformity is valued in middle-class China. For luxury brands this is an enviable situation to be in as they can continue to sell more and more, without undermining the prestige of the brand (in contrast to the carefully managed exclusivity seen elsewhere). However, Louis Vuitton and Gucci have discovered there are limits to this. Why? Their brands are now viewed as too common, literally "secretaries' bags." Already this has resulted in a new round of authoritative performances through the selection of more expensive brands such as Hermés (Willett 2015).

In an ethnographic study of Australian surfing, Beverland and Farrelly (2011) identified that the interplay between authenticating acts and authoritative performances undermined established brands and provided opportunities for smaller, local craft brands. For consumers who desired to become subcultural insiders (i.e., to achieve their desired goal of being a "true" surfer), among many others things, they needed to master the art and craft of surfing. This meant putting in many hours in the water, surfing on seemingly poor waves, falling off, getting dragged under, understanding the code between surfers when beaches were busy, and being humble in terms of achievements.

To achieve this, wannabe surfers needed to transcend expectations of looking cool with the latest surfboard endorsed by a high-profile surfer and learn to surf on longer, heavier, slower boards. Using a "second-hand board" was seen as an essential rite of passage as it meant the wannabe surfer was prepared to sacrifice image and ego for the pursuit of expertise. Established brands such as Ripcurl had engaged in inauthentic brand extensions into fashion in order to meet the needs of stockholders rather than the surf community. Many of their branded stores were staffed by non-surfers, undermining claims of authenticity and sincerity. As such, these brands declined as resources for "true surfers", ultimately losing their connection to the subculture.

In their place, smaller brands, made by local shapers (those who skillfully handcraft or "shape" a surfboard), emerged as more valuable tools because of their sole commitment to mastering the art of surfing and their dedication to making boards that were right for local conditions (similar to how winemakers emphasize the unique aspects of local conditions or *terroir* in their brand marketing). Failure to manage authenticating acts and authoritative performances has seen many global surf brands such as Quiksilver file for bankruptcy in 2015 while Ripcurl's and Billabong's brand equity (and share price) declined substantially.

Truth vs. "Truthiness" (or Keeping a Narrative Going)

What is the opposite of the real? Automatically we think of that which is "fake." However the line between real and fake is blurred. Consumers often find the seemingly real more useful and valuable than the actual real and actively create the real in the fake, such as in their engagement with highly scripted "reality television" (Rose and Wood 2005). In essence, consumers often see what they want to see when it comes to claims of authenticity.

In his book *The Authenticity Hoax*, social philosopher and journalist Andrew Potter (2011) discusses the issue of truth and truthiness in relation to claims of authenticity. Before the recent emergence of "post-truth" politics and "alternative facts," truthiness was a term used by American satirist Stephen Colbert in relation to "gut feel" claims by politicians: "*Truthiness* refers to the quality of preferring concepts or facts one wishes or believes to be true, rather than concepts or facts known to be true" (https://en.wikipedia.org/wiki/Truthiness). Consumer researchers use a similar concept called **motivated reasoning** to describe the same process whereby consumers are motivated to see only what they want to see or what confirms their personal preferences. At the same time, consumers ignore or rationalize away information that disconfirms their worldview—something many brand marketers also do, to the detriment of co-creation as it leads them to prefer "on-brand" insights generated from loyalists rather than from non-target users that may provide new directions for the brand, such as the adult LEGO users identified in Chapter 1. This leads consumers to construct a personal "echo chamber" on social media that reinforces their personal preferences rather than challenges them. This phenomenon often explains why Twitter users (who are overwhelmingly liberal in their political views) express "shock" or "surprise" at unexpected political results, such as the United Kingdom's vote to leave the European Union in 2016.

Therefore, authenticity is not so much real, as seemingly real. For example, in a study of tourist sites, Kent Grayson and Radan Martinec (2004) found that consumers preferred the iconically authentic (what we think the "real" should look be) rather than the indexically authentic (the historically real). In their case, consumers thought the house of fictional detective Sherlock Holmes more real than the actual birthplace of William Shakespeare. For visitors, Sherlock Holmes's house was more real because they could place themselves in the site and imagine that this is exactly how Holmes would have lived. As mentioned in the authenticity paradox above, authenticity is not truly real; it just feels real, something that brands can render through empathizing with customers.

Studies of product brands find similar outcomes. A study on craft beer identified how consumers understood that all claims of authenticity were marketing constructions but nonetheless they valued those brands that conformed to their expectations of what an authentic craft-beer brand should be (brewed in a small, independent brewery, by those with a true passion for the craft, respect for tradition, and not motivated by commercial gain). In this study, consumers often attributed authenticity to brands from large breweries that "looked the part" as opposed to those that genuinely had connections to place, tradition, and social programs (Beverland et al. 2008).

It is for this reason that we say authenticity is socially constructed. As a result, many have questioned whether authenticity has any value if potentially everything is authentic (to someone for some purpose). However, this view undermines the important role that brands play in helping consumers achieve self-authentication today and the work consumers engage in to transfer authenticity to particular brands.

Connecting Identity Goals: Brands and Identity Tension

Why was Nintendo's Wii console so successful? Design expert Roberto Verganti (2009) argues that reconfiguring the idea of computer games from something played alone or with others connected virtually, to something played together with real people in the same physical space, enabled Nintendo to create a game changer (no pun intended). Nintendo's insights enabled them to sell simpler games with lower quality graphics to new sets of users (as well as long-time gamers).

But this explanation only scratches the surface of the Wii's success. Postmodernity has given rise to many lifestyle changes including longer working hours, more sedentary lives, less time for loved ones, and products that blur the boundaries between real life and fantasy, often in the form of violent video games. In the middle of this are parents who are struggling with multiple roles including provider, protector, best friend to their children, and meeting societal expectations of "good parenting." The Wii solves all these problems in one go.

The Wii was released in 2006, a time of heightened concerns about terrorism, distrust in leaders, perceptions of social decline, spiraling childhood obesity rates, concern over online sexual predators, and nostalgia for simpler times. Cocooning was one result, where people stayed within the safety of the home with food delivered in and social media enabling virtual connections. The Wii's design enables players of all shapes and sizes and skill levels to play together without leaving the comfort and safety of the house. In one stroke, parents could believe they were enabling their kids to have fun, engage in exercise, and engage in wholesome play. Together, these benefits and the perceived increased time they spent with their children meant the Wii enabled them to achieve the status of "good parent" (increasingly difficult when one should at the same time worry about children playing online and not exercising, but also keep kids safe from ever present but unpredictable dangers from outside).

The Wii in this sense created "good parents." The tensions between various identity roles and goals and societal expectations, or the conflict between authenticating acts and authoritative performances, are reduced by innovative brands such as the Wii (Beverland et al. 2015). Social changes in many nations in the second half of the twentieth century resulted in more, not less, identity roles. For example, as women entered the paid workforce in large numbers they were expected to balance traditional parental roles with work-related ones. Moreover, personal empowerment and meritocracy became a dominant mantra in many Western economies, leading to further pressure to make time to be oneself while laying the blame for failing to do so on the individual. Maintaining social connections via social media websites such as Facebook and Weibo became important because these forms of virtual friendships replaced extended family ties or community relationships.

In this sense the value of a brand like the Wii lies not in its functionality or even its use (which are primarily utilitarian values), even though it delivers on both accounts. Instead brands like Wii enable us to reduce the tensions between multiple identity roles (individual vs. collective), and ensure we can achieve some fleeting sense of self-authentication. The case example at the end of this chapter on Vegemite identifies how a co-created campaign ("How do you love your Vegemite?") provided the basis for many immigrant Australians to affirm their Australian-ness for the first time. This campaign enabled new Australians to maintain immigrant traditions while also affirming their membership of a new community, while those with deeper roots in the country could reinforce the view that Australia is an open society. The ability of a mundane condiment to solve tensions between multiple cultural identities identifies the connective power of brands.

Linking Value: How Brands Help Us to Connect

As identified above, affirming social norms or connecting to communities, subcultures, and traditions are all desired by brand users. Some authors have identified brands that have "water-cooler conversation" qualities and create a sense of connective authenticity among users, resulting in an imagined community (Beverland and Farrelly 2010). Since brands can signal symbolic membership, potential users may view them as resources to connect with like-minded others. Therefore, one further value of brands in postmodernity is **linking value**, or "The brand's contribution to establishing and/or reinforcing bonds between individuals. The greater the contribution of a brand to the development and strengthening of bonds, the greater its linking value will be" (Cova and Cova 2002, p. 603). One way of thinking about this is to think about a favorite commercial place or space. Such places can be virtual (e.g., social media) or physical (a café) but for you they represent something sociologists call "a third place," which is the place after work and home that you spend significant time in. These places are typically where connections with others occur, whether they are actual connections between friends or imagined connections between like-minded people. Starbucks of course built its initial global brand empire on this simple idea, becoming a place where people could conduct meetings, connect, and hang out. Brands that enable us to imagine connections to like-minded others have strong linking value. They also provide a context in which authoritative performances can be or have to be enacted.

Research has revealed four broad types of communities involving brands that provide linking value:

1. Brand community: "A set of social relationships in which admirers of a brand experience shared rituals, traditions, and a sense of responsibility towards other members" (Canniford 2011, p. 594). In contrast to subcultures of consumption, in brand communities an individual brand is the focal point of linking value. Examples include fan-based communities (for celebrity brands such as Kat von D), sports brands, and owners clubs (e.g., Jeep). Some may be unofficial, such as various Apple-related forums, while others may be deliberate creations of the marketing team such as the Harley Davidson Owners Group (HOG), the LEGO community covered in Chapter 1, or the Linux producer community.

2. **Subcultures** of consumption: "groups of like-minded consumers that share a commitment to a certain product class or consumption activity" (Schouten and McAlexander 1995, p. 43). Examples included cyclists, wine connoisseurs, surfers, snowboarders, vinyl record enthusiasts, and so on. Here brands play more of a background, low-key, albeit important role, but the focus of the subculture is on a shared activity. Subcultures represent an important source of brand myths, authenticity, associations, and innovation, and can wield significant market power. Brands such as Absolut and Levi's for example have a mythic role in the LBGT community, largely based on their preparedness to lead on issues important to the subculture such as extending medical insurance to same-sex couples (Kates 2004).

3. Consumer tribes: These are looser, more transient groupings of consumers who gain identity benefits more from links with one another than with a focal brand or even activity. Consumers may be members of many tribes and membership does not dominate one's life in the ways subcultures and even brand communities do. Examples include clubbers, concertgoers, people with interests in platform technologies such as Wikipedia contributors, fashionistas, and those loosely associated with various sporting activities such as casual surfers (Canniford 2011). Clashes over authenticity often emerge when these tribes are created or leveraged by marketers in the form of brand myths that undermine the identity of consumers with substantial identity investments in more formal subcultures. For example, picking up on the popularity of indie music subculture (including clubs, brands of alcohol, forms of transport, and so on), marketers created a "hipster myth" that represented a highly stylized view that long-time insiders rejected (Arsel and Thompson 2011).

4. Brand publics: A relatively new communal type of consumption consisting of a cross between the looser affiliations of tribal members, the brand focus of a brand community, and social media. Rather than identifying with a brand, members of brand publics use a brand as a publicity tool for their own identity positions. Interactions among members are uncommon and typically restricted to liking a post or responding to a comment with an emoji. This concept emerged as a result of #hashtag identifiers that enable users to present various viewpoints around a shared brand (e.g., Louis Vuitton) on a global scale (Arvidsson and Caliandro 2016).

These types of communal relations are examples of contexts in which linking value is co-created around brand or where brands are present.

Is All Brand Consumption Driven by Identity?

At the end of this chapter, is it fair to ask whether all consumers or users choose *visible* brands because of their identity goals? Do organizational buyers, or industrial buyers, make large-scale and everyday purchases to affirm their true self? Researchers who study business-to-business (B2B) branding would argue against this view on the basis that organizational systems attempt to make purchasers more rational and that branding is relatively immature in this context (Beverland et al. 2007). However, a number of less rational (but perfectly legal) motives, including the desire to maintain long-term relationships, avoid personal risk, organizational status, and professional identity, do underpin many B2B purchases.

Traditionally, people have used the construct of "involvement" to examine brand motives (Rosenbaum-Elliot et al. 2015). Involvement relates to the degree of interest consumers have in the product or service category and also the degree of risk associated with getting things wrong. Therefore, a house purchase (for some) is a high-involvement category because of the risk involved and presumably because it is "one's home" and intensely personal. In contrast, baking soda may be viewed as a low-involvement purchase as it is largely a commodity and the risk of getting the choice wrong is low because of the product's inherent functionality. The latter types of brands are often called "invisible brands" or mundane brands that essentially blend into the background of one's life. Jennifer Coupland (2005) studied these brands and found that although they lacked a strong identity, they did not lack meaning. Instead, their very ordinariness meant they essentially became taken for granted within the household. These brands are typically household items and usually sold under a buyer-own-brand in supermarkets. So, do they lack symbolism?

One has to be careful in viewing certain types of product classes or brands as intrinsically lacking or having symbolic value. McCracken (1990) has noted that products tell you very little, and in the case of invisible brands their users saw them symbolically as reflective of an identity as a "good housekeeper" or "good cook." Although the brands faded into the background, the household was never without them for long, and in this sense, despite being mundane, they have important identity value, particularly since many are handed down from parent to child over multiple generations. Fournier's (1998) work on brand relationships noted that consumers might have highly emotional relationships with seemingly mundane products such as lipsticks or toothpastes. Although these brands seem mundane and we may be invisible to their presence, they do have "unrecognized loyalty" that only becomes conscious when they are changed or discontinued. The Internet after all is replete with "bring back" pages dedicated to discontinued confectionery, make-up, and other seemingly low-involvement brands.

Likewise, studies on consumption and identity typically occur in societies where basic needs are satisfied. But what about where this is not the case? What about the choices of children and young adults? Or those consumers at the margins of society? These and other contextual questions will be the subject of Chapter 11. Nonetheless, most economies are consumer societies where symbolic value is often at the heart of brand choice.

Chapter Summary

This chapter has examined the drivers of consumer brand choices in the postmodern era. Although it has not discounted the importance of functional benefits, rational appeals, or information efficiency, it has shown how these classical cues are more points of parity for all brands, and especially given the speed of convergence today. Not only are these types of appeals hard to sustain over time, they also ignore consumer-identity goals and projects, and therefore risk being seen as irrelevant by users. Instead I propose that the desire for self-authentication drives brand choices, with users looking for brands that allow for individual expression (and authenticating acts) or social connectivity (authoritative performances). From a user's standpoint, brands are judged valuable if they deliver symbolic and/or linking value. The implications for these types of value for our understanding of brand equity form the basis of the next chapter.

Review Questions

1. Think of a brand that reflects your true self. How does it do so? Is there anything that would lead you to change it for another? Do the same for your desired or imagined self (or one of your imagined selves).
2. Can you think of brands you buy that do not reflect an identity motive? Hint: check out your kitchen pantry for those seemingly "invisible brands" (salt, flour,

(Continued)

baking soda, rice, noodles). Second hint: write a food-shopping list. Which brands feature? What products are not listed as brands and why? How could these brands become identity brands?

3. Identify one example of an authoritative performance that limits the expression of your true self. Is there a brand you use that reflects a need to conform socially that does not reflect your true self?

4. Critically evaluate a brand that you make excuses for. How does it underperform relative to your expectations, which have been raised by brand authors?

5. Think of a brand that stresses "authenticity" (it may use words such as real, genuine, true, or even authentic, or suggest it via images, links to the past, subculture, or tradition). Examine its claims. Are they really true? If not, does it matter to you?

Case Example: Vegemite: The Rebirth of a Brand Icon

There are few brands that represent Australia as strongly as Vegemite. The yeast-based, thick as tar, salty spread was long a staple at Australian breakfast tables. For decades the brand, a star in Kraft's portfolio, adapted to changes in what it meant to be a "true blue Aussie," eventually becoming a local iconic brand, a regular pop culture reference, while its signature catchphrase "happy little Vegemite" entered the Australian vernacular. However, no brand's iconic status is ever guaranteed, and Vegemite began to fall out of favor with Australians, leading many within Kraft to wonder whether and how they could reinvigorate consumers' love affair with the spread.

Dr Cyril Callister developed Vegemite in 1922 as a by-product of the brewing process. The name Vegemite was chosen from a public competition in 1928 aimed at turning around poor sales (previously it had been named "Parwill"). The name stuck and the electric toaster helped the brand become a staple of Australian breakfast tables. In 1939, the brand gained an endorsement from the British Medical Association, which was leveraged by Kraft in the form of a "healthy kids are Vegemite kids" campaign.

The product was designed with the pre-refrigeration, Australian environment in mind, and therefore could stand up to the elements, and technically never expired. This, plus the brand's high salt content ensured it was included as part of soldiers' rations in World War II (to counter the effects of dehydration in the desert and jungles where many Australians saw action). Post-World War II, the brand wrapped itself in the Australian flag, becoming the patriotic choice for true Australians.

The brand team adapted to the times, shifting from associations with military heroes to athletes during peacetime, while also continuing to emphasize its usage situation (breakfast) and health-related claims, especially for growing children. The brand's iconic status is best evidenced by being included in the Men at Work song "Down Under," which became a global number one hit in 1981–2, and is viewed by many as an alternative national anthem. The brand's attributes—its salty, harsh taste, durability, and rejection by almost every nation— simply reinforced its local stature. However, its historic strengths also led to its decline.

From 2002, sales of the brand began to decline. Although the brand still had enormous market penetration in the yeast spread category, consumers were more likely to choose other condiments such as Nutella and peanut butter over Vegemite. The high salt content and historic associations with toast and lashings of butter were now seen as negatives from a health perspective. Moreover breakfast had changed, with overworked Australians often skipping the meal altogether or having something on the go. Immigration had also given rise to new food trends, while changes in the make-up of Australian families meant that the brand's historic image of an Anglo-Saxon family of mum, dad, and two kids no longer resonated with locals, let alone new immigrants. Finally, having just one market meant the brand competed internally with other brands in the Kraft stable for talent, budget, and attention, and many saw it as a cash cow in decline.

However, a new brand manager, Simon Talbot, took a different view. His belief was the brand still had strong latent equity and that many immigrants were using the brand, but felt ignored by Vegemite's old-fashioned vision of Australia. Although breakfast habits had changed, he believed that moving away from one narrow usage occasion was essential for Vegemite's long-term health. And, the brand had suffered from a lack of innovation with almost no strategic extensions in its history, and a distinct lack of customer focus among the brand team. He decided to revitalize the brand with an innovative engagement campaign called "How do you love your Vegemite?" Figure 2.8 contains details.

The campaign asked consumers to send in their favorite ways of eating Vegemite. The response was immediate and overwhelming, and the campaign itself became a talking point for celebrities and everyday Australians alike.

(Continued)

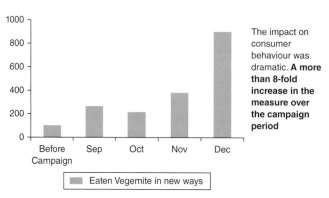

The impact on consumer behaviour was dramatic. **A more than 8-fold increase in the measure over the campaign period**

Eaten Vegemite in new ways

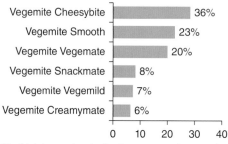

HOW YOU VOTED: Which of these names is your first choice?

Vegemite Cheesybite — 36%
Vegemite Smooth — 23%
Vegemite Vegemate — 20%
Vegemite Snackmate — 8%
Vegemite Vegemild — 7%
Vegemite Creamymate — 6%

% of total sample who had a name preference (n = 30,357)

Figure 2.8   How do you love your Vegemite?

Consumers sent 300,000 recipes, all of which generated a buzz around the brand and stimulated trial, eventually increasing sales. What the campaign demonstrated was that Australians used the brand for all types of snacking, as a stock for Asian-styled soups and stir fries, and were primarily attempting to reduce the harsh taste of the product by fattening it out with cheese and avocado, or breaking the taste down with acidic pairings such as tomatoes. The brand returned to its roots, becoming once again synonymous with Australia by reflecting changed times.

Sales took off and eventually the team extended the brand into a new combination called Cheesy Bite that combined Vegemite with Kraft stablemate Philadelphia Cream Cheese. Returning the brand to its roots, the team ran a competition under the tagline "Name Me" to name the first ever brand extension of the iconic brand. The name initially chosen by the team—iSnack 2.0—generated an immediate backlash (and generated one of the best Downfall "Hitler" parodies on YouTube), and was quickly dropped.

The preferred consumer name Cheesy Mite was trademarked by Nestlé, so the team once again involved the consumer, offering them ten legally usable choices to vote on, with Cheesy Bite the eventual winner (the extension quickly came close to outselling its parent).

Talbot's three takeaways from his experience in reinvigorating a brand that many had warned him "not to mess with" were:

1. Don't start a dance with social media and not finish it: inviting consumers to name the product and then ignoring their choices is not fair or smart.
2. We don't own our brands anymore; steer but don't control.
3. If consumers go against you, don't fight the tide.

Source: Keinan et al. 2012

Case Questions

1. Why was Vegemite so successful before 2000?
2. Why did Vegemite lose sales after 2000?
3. Which identity goals did the "How do you love your Vegemite?" campaign enable born Australians and immigrants to achieve?
4. Why was the backlash against iSnack 2.0 predictable? Was Simon right to change the name given sales were strong and only non-users disliked it?
5. Critically evaluate Simon's three takeaways with reference to examples.

Key Terms

Authenticating acts
Authoritative performances
Brand community
Brand personality
Brand publics
Consumer tribes

Desired self
Experiential marketing
Extended self
Functional benefits
Intended brand identity

Linking value
Motivated reasoning
Received brand image
Self-authentication
Subcultures of consumption

Further Reading

Arnould, Eric J. and Linda L. Price (2000), "Authenticating Acts and Authoritative Performances," in *The Why of Consumption: Contemporary Perspectives, Goals, and Desires*, ed. S. Ratneshwar, David Glen Mick, and Cynthia Huffman, Routledge, London, pp. 140–63.

Belk, Russell W. (2013), "The Extended Self in the Digital World," *Journal of Consumer Research*, 40(October), 477–500.

Beverland, Michael B. and Michael T. Ewing (2005), "Slowing the Adoption and Diffusion Process to Enhance Brand Repositioning: The Consumer Driven Repositions of Dunlop Volley," *Business Horizons*, 48(October), 385–92.

"Business Card Scene (Narcissism of Small Differences)," in *American Psycho*: https://www.youtube.com/watch?v=cISYzA36-ZY

Canniford, Robin (2011), "How to Manage Consumer Tribes," *Journal of Strategic Marketing*, 19(7), 591–606.

Fournier, Susan (1998), "Consumers and their Brands: Developing Relationship Theory in Consumer Research," *Journal of Consumer Research*, 24(March), 343–73.

3

BRAND EQUITY

All our factories and facilities could burn down tomorrow but you'd hardly touch the value of the company; all that actually lies in the goodwill of our brand franchise and the collective knowledge in the company. (Roberto Goizueta, former CEO Coca-Cola)

If this company were to split up I would give you the property, plant and equipment and I would take the brands and the trademarks and I would fare far better than you. (John Stuart, ex-Chairman of Quaker)

Learning Objectives

When you finish reading this chapter, you will be able to answer these questions:

1. What is brand equity? What does brand-as-asset mean?
2. How do brand equity and brand valuation differ?
3. Why is measuring brand equity important? What stakeholders benefit from this?
4. What is the difference between brand equity and reputation?
5. How does a brand contribute value to the firm? How might this differ from brand value to users?
6. What is employee-based brand equity?
7. How do we generate brand equity?

The Value of Brands

Among marketers, the view that the brand is more valuable than fixed assets is taken for granted, as the following, often quoted anecdotes from the CEOs of Coca-Cola and Quaker Oats highlight. Users clearly value brands, but how do we create and increase that value? How is "value" measured? These questions continue to haunt brand managers. Once legal protections for trademarks began to take effect, it didn't take long for marketers to realize names, symbols, and associations had financial value (Petty 2011). From the 1950s onwards, advertisers were also pushed by their clients to demonstrate the value of brands to ensure on-going senior management support for spiraling marketing budgets. With the deregulation of finance markets that occurred in the United States and United Kingdom in the 1980s, how to value intangible assets such as brands became a pressing issue as mergers and acquisitions resulted in share values and multiples substantially in excess of firm assets and historical norms.

BRAND ASIDE 3.1

Marlboro Friday and the Crisis of Brand Value

After losing market share to cheaper generic cigarette brands, on April 2, 1993, tobacco giant Philip Morris announced a 20 percent across-the-board price cut. This action not only decreased the value of their stock by 26 percent, but also saw all brand-driven product stocks (including Coca-Cola) fall. This event became known as "Marlboro Friday," and triggered a wave of writing about the end of brand equity and the decline of brand power. Although these predictions ultimately proved to be very wrong (Marlboro has consistently been placed in the top 10 of Interbrand's most valuable global brands index), at the time they provoked much soul searching and speculation about the failure of marketing, "the death of the brand," and the end of the "brand bubble" (Gerzema and Lebar 2008). Shocks such as this occur commonly in the history of branding, and often trigger two effects: premature claims regarding the death of branding and a greater attention among marketers, advertising agencies, researchers, and brand managers on improving strategies and measures of brand equity.

As Brand Aside 3.1 makes clear, the idea that brands are extremely valuable was once controversial. Today, however, the value of intangibles has few critics in the share market. For example, 97 percent of the US$54 billion Procter & Gamble paid for Gillette in 2005 related to the current and future value of Gillette, Duracell, Oral B, and Braun brands. When L'Oréal purchased The Bodyshop in 2006, 81 percent of the £652.2 million purchase price was attributed to the brand. This wasn't always the case. Post-World War II, less than 20 percent of the value of a company was attributed to intangibles (usually listed as "goodwill," a proxy for customer loyalty), whereas today over 75 percent of the value of any stock is derived from intangibles, which in most cases relates to **brand equity**. Leading global brand consultancy Interbrand ranked Apple as the most valuable global brand for 2015–2016, estimating the technology giant's brand value at £142 billion, while technology buzz brand Tesla was valued at a mere £3.2 billion (Interbrand 2016). Visit www.interbrand.com to view the Global 100 Brands list.

Pressure from financial markets, CEOs, and boards throughout the late 1980s to early 1990s led the Marketing Science Institute (USA) to commission a series of workshops and projects to answer the questions "How much are brands worth?", "How do brands generate value?" Arguably, the second question was easier to answer than the first, as much research had been conducted on brand choice and brand extension that provided insights into how to create customer-based **brand value**. Kevin Keller's (1993) *Journal of Marketing* article "Conceptualizing, Measuring, and Managing Customer-Based Brand Equity (CBBE)" flowed from these workshops and became the dominant way in which academics and practitioners thought about brand equity, and underpins financial estimates of brand value undertaken by the two leading agencies in this area, Interbrand and Millward Brown.

Approaches to financial valuing brands are less well developed and more controversial. The brand-as-asset view connects brand relationships to brand value, arguing that the stronger the relationship, the more valuable the brand, allowing for market risk, size, and growth potential. Leading brand consultant Helen Edwards provides some initial evidence for this relationship, arguing brands that "take a stand" build stronger relationships and therefore returns. Her views on so-called Passionbrands are covered in Brand Aside 3.2

However, others take different views and the financial impact of marketing-related activity remains a Tier One Marketing Science Institute Research Objective to this day. Long-term studies have attempted to compare the stock returns of branded vs. non-branded goods and services through boom and bust periods, generally finding that brands outperform their commodity counterparts in good times and bad (Interbrand 2016). However, how to value a particular brand is notoriously difficult, while trying to identify exactly how brands contribute to financial returns and by how much is difficult since many factors (such as turbulence, political risk, and competitive intensity) influence these variables (Aaker 2014).

BRAND ASIDE 3.2

Branding with Passion: Do Values Pay?

Marketing Week columnists Dr Helen Edwards and Derek Day published *Creating Passionbrands* in 2005. Edwards and Day run a successful agency, also called Passionbrand, and have won numerous awards for their popular articles on branding. Their hypothesis was simple: does being passionate about something pay off in terms of brand equity? Working with Millward Brown and their Brandz database of 23,000 brands worldwide, Edwards and Day identified a strong positive relationship between consumers' emotional connection to brands and brand health (a proxy for equity). Emotional connection was driven by brand belief or a commitment to something that is ultimately good for people. Values such as integrity, guts, and imagination formed the heart of a passion brand. This logic and others like it reflect the emotional brand paradigm that emerged in the late 1990s, and is built on the idea that less marketing spin and more authenticity are essential to combat widespread consumer cynicism.

What Is Brand Equity?

Definitions of brand equity vary considerably, and tend to reflect disciplinary concerns. David Aaker (1996, p. 7) provides a general definition of brand equity: "A set of assets (or liabilities) linked to a brand's name and symbol that adds (or subtracts from) the value provided by a product or service to a firm and/or that firm's customers." Aaker's definition aligns closely with a financial view of brand equity. In this view, branded-assets can be the symbolic properties of the brand as well as the size and loyalty of the brand's customer base, and other benefits. As the definition states, brands are reputational assets that can benefit or harm a firm's offering and valuation. Although we tend to only talk about increases or decreases in brand equity, sometimes a brand can have negative equity, as described in Brand Aside 3.3.

BRAND ASIDE 3.3

Negative Brand Equity

When a brand has positive equity, it simply means the brand makes a difference to its users in a positive way. However, in rare instances brands can have negative equity. This is very different from low equity or declining equity. In the case of negative brand equity, the brand itself has become so toxic that it actively drives away customers. This often happens when brands suffer scandals that are either unrecoverable or poorly managed. One classic example of this involved the UK newspaper *News of the World*. Founded in 1843, the newspaper (part of the News Corporation stable) was at one time the top-selling newspaper in the UK. However, it became embroiled in a national scandal involving journalists hacking the phones of celebrities to generate material for stories. Hacking the phones of murdered teenager Milly Dowler and the families of dead service personnel was the final straw for the general public, and sales plummeted. At the same time advertising revenue fell, with industry insiders suggesting many advertisers would never return to the *News of the World*. At this point the brand was toxic, and was closed on the July 7, 2011. Chapter 12 provides further insight into avoiding negative brand equity.

As mentioned above, definitions of brand equity often reflect particular disciplines and target audiences. Although Figure 1.1 (Chapter 1) identifies four brand authors, we know comparatively little about how influencers and pop culture value brands (Table 3.2 provides more details later in this chapter). Academics and practitioners tend to focus on four main audiences: customers, financial markets, employees, and channels. These are all important to how we manage brands over time and are described briefly below:

1. **Customer-based brand equity** (CBBE): "The differential effect of brand knowledge on consumer response to the marketing of that brand" (Keller 1993, p. 2). All those consumers camping outside of Apple stores for the latest iPhone provide an example of CBBE—users' love of the brand means they trade up to the new product, often selling their perfectly good existing phone on a secondary exchange.
2. **Financial-based brand equity**: The differential effect of the brand on the firm's balance sheet. When stock-market analysts write reports on which stocks to buy, sell, or hold, their decisions are partially based on beliefs about the strength of the brand. A Blue Chip stock, for example, is one that has delivered strong returns over many years, partly as a result of a strong relationship with its customers and an ability to outperform others.
3. **Employee-based brand equity**: The differential effect of the brand on potential and current employees. Do employees consider their personal brand to be worth more due to an association with your company, or worth less? If the firm's brand adds to their perceived personal brand, they may trade off income as a result, whereas if it's the opposite, they may require a higher salary as compensation (assuming they work for you at all).

4. **Channel equity**: the differential effect of the brand to channel partners such as distributors and retailers. Brands such as Coke are essential for retailers, while others, such as Apple, bring people into stores. A brand's equity among channel partners is important, especially when it "pulls" people into a store (which then creates demand back down the supply chain) or drives them to a website. Some brands can abuse this and find themselves subject to extreme discounting. Iconic Australian wine brand Penfolds discovered this in in the mid-1990s in New Zealand. Notorious for their arrogance, Penfolds often demanded that retailers stock large amounts of less popular wine (such as Riesling) as a condition of gaining the more popular labels. Eventually major retailers retaliated, discounting Penfolds' red wine at below cost (or as a loss leader) as a means of bringing wine lovers to their store (where their total basket purchases led to a profit). The result was diminished brand equity for Penfolds over time (Beverland and Lindgreen 2004).

As can be seen from these definitions, all refer to the *differential effect of the brand*. Keller's customer-based definition focuses on whether what consumers know about the brand affects their response to brand-driven marketing activities such as our preparedness to pay a higher price, choose one product over another, adopt new products or brand extensions, and engage with advertising, social media, theme-branded stores and so on. Keller's approach is based on three principles:

1. Brand equity arises from consumer responses to marketing for the brand.
2. **Brand knowledge**, or what consumers learn, feel, and experience over time, has an impact on brand equity (the more we know and like about the brand, the stronger the equity).
3. The **differential effect** is reflected in consumer perceptions, preferences, and behavior vis-à-vis all the marketing activities associated with the brand.

The financial approach attempts to examine the effect of brand on important indicators such as share price, return on investment, financial multiples, firm valuation, and so on. Finally, employee brand equity examines the power of the brand on current employees' satisfaction, retention, self-identity, willingness to trade off financial reward, and recommend others. Researchers also examine the power of a brand in attracting potential employees. Does a strong brand lower acquisition costs, or lead to better applications, or decrease expectations of salary? All of these are important questions and, in general, research is demonstrating significant impacts on brands across all three domains. The Sydney Apple store-opening example later in this chapter provides an example of employment branding at work.

Although brand equity and brand value are often used interchangeably, it is also important at this stage to identify the differences between the two. Financial brand equity or value is largely concerned with an estimate of the brand's worth to the firm. Customer brand equity examines the strength of the relationship between the consumer and the brand. A small, niche brand for example may have a high degree of customer brand equity, but the small size of that target market may mean its financial brand equity or value is low. Likewise, brands such as Exxon-Mobil often have very high financial brand equity, but given their near commodity status and the influence of geographic location and need (running out of gas) on choice of petrol station, the customer relationship with this brand is relatively weak (i.e., customer brand equity is low).

What Do We Know about the Financial Power of Brands?

Interest in the financial benefits of brands and brand-related activities (such as advertising) has a long history. The view that one's name or the name of a brand was valuable and therefore needed protection drove governments to develop trademark law (something that continues until this day, especially in the fight against counterfeits). Advertising agencies such as JWT spent considerable resources on understanding **brand loyalty**, the impact of brand loyalty on sales, and the power of the brand name on advertising effectiveness.

The value of brand loyalty remains subject of much debate to this day, with some suggesting there is too much emphasis on existing customers at the expense of growing sales (Singh and Uncles 2016). During times of recession, concern over the impact of low-priced generic brands on sales of branded products drove brand managers and advertising agencies to focus their messages more clearly, stress benefits, understand their target markets more clearly, and define said markets more tightly. And, as stated earlier, financial markets and therefore boards of directors place pressure on brand researchers to build frameworks for understanding how to value brands.

Nevertheless, understanding of the financial impact of brands remains in its infancy and is fraught with difficulty. Table 3.1 identifies a handful of influential studies that have examined this relationship. In general, strong brands deliver:

- Higher margins: As the Interbrand study in Table 3.1 suggests, strong brands can deliver 27–33 percent premiums over weaker brands or commodities. This may seem obvious in the context of brands such as Apple, Boeing, Microsoft, and Gucci, but it is just as true for well-positioned discounter brand such as Ryanair, who also outperform weaker brands.
- Profits: Those skeptical of brand equity often argue that brands such as Apple have relatively low market shares when compared to Samsung or laptop manufacturers such as Dell and Toshiba. This misses the point, however. Brands are not in the business of sales alone; they build their value around increases in loyalty and margins. Prior to their problems with the Galaxy, Samsung shipped more smartphones than Apple yet the Cupertino-based brand accounts for 75 percent of profits in the category. Even during the dark days of the 1990s, Apple survived

based on minuscule market shares and high profits. Similarly, prior to the global financial crisis General Motors remained the number one car manufacturer by sales, but lost money on almost every sale, whereas Toyota might have been number two, but pocketed US1,500 on each car.

- A buffer against downturns and poor performance: brands with stronger customer relationships enjoy stronger returns during good times and bad (which means they're often likely to attract low-risk, conservative investment funds). Also, brands can suffer a lot of damage and still be revitalized many years later, just as has occurred with luxury brands Burberry, Dior, and Gucci, automotive brand MINI, and, of course, Apple. Even poor reviews do not affect the box-office performance of strong franchises such as *Star Wars*.
- Better returns than weaker brands in both business-to-consumer and business-to-business markets (although this is partially moderated by the strength of commodity cycles in some industries such as mining).
- A significant amount of a firm's intangible value: this is growing all the time. Intangibles represented 50 percent of firms' balance sheets in 2007, whereas today they account for almost 80 percent.

Table 3.1 Studies on the financial impact of brands

Author	Year	Summary results
David Aaker	2014	Consumer-based brand equity increases strongly in correlation with share price increases (70%). In comparison advertising had no effect on share price (except for the indirect effect it had on brand equity). Results replicated in high technology markets.
Interbrand	2014	Global Brands Ranking demonstrated that the top 10 global brands are worth 33% on the balance sheet while those in the top 100 are worth 27%.
Gregory and McNaughton	2004	The most powerful consumer brands have a price earnings ratio of 19.5 compared to 17.9 for the least powerful, They have 4.7 Market Capitalization/Book Value of 4.7 compared to 1.6 for the least powerful. Brand equity as a percentage of market capitalization is 15.6% for most powerful brands, and 0.6% for least.
		For business-to-business brands, the most powerful brands had a price earnings ratio of 15.8 compared to 17.2 for the least, a market capitalization to book value of 2.5 compared with 0.5, and brand equity as a percentage of market capitalization of 13.3% compared with 0.6%.
Johansson, Dimofte, and Mazvancheryl	2012	Share price of top brands as measured by financial brand equity (Interbrand) fell more than the stock market as a whole in GFC, whereas those with the highest customer-based equity fell significantly less than the market. During an economic downturn, the strength of the customer–brand relationship is a better predictor of brand strength than estimates of future revenues.
Madden, Fehle, and Fournier	2006 (p. 230)	Investment of US$1,000 in strongest brand companies would quadruple to US$4,525 in six years vs. US$3,195 for overall stock market. Figures are adjusted for risk and market share and suggest brand equity has a positive effect on shareholder value.

How Do Firms Benefit from Brands?

Brands provide value to firms in many unexpected ways. Typically, we place a great deal of emphasis on how brands are valuable to customers, but this represents the tip of the iceberg, something experienced marketers realize. Why say this? Remember, in most firms, marketers very rarely have any direct impact or day-to-day contact with customers. And, marketing is expensive, often frighteningly so (although strong brands such as Apple often spend comparatively less on marketing than their weaker competitors). One recent study identified that marketing was the only function that had a positive impact on **return on investment (ROI)**, yet the influence of marketers was declining inside the very same firms that enjoyed strong marketing-driven returns (Homburg et al. 2015). Why is this? Essentially, many marketers struggle to articulate and quantify how they add value across a range of firm activities. In contrast, other functions such as finance, sales, operations, research and development, and even human resources can quantify their impact.

Thinking beyond consumers, brands can add value to many parts of the organization, all of which are often more essential in delivering brand promises than the marketing department. If we empathize with our contemporaries in finance, sales, research and development, operations, and human resources for a moment, we can identify a number of benefits of branding.

1. Finance: As stated, brands have many financial benefits. If we reframe requests for financial support in terms of return on investment rather than cost, marketers can build more influence and gain the needed resources to build strong brands.

BRAND ASIDE 3.4

Intel Inside and Ingredient Branding

Not all brands achieve a 27–33 percent price premium. Computer-chip maker Intel's famous Intel Inside campaign resulted in a 10 percent premium, so was it a failure? Not really. It's worth bearing in mind that the computer chip was just one

(Continued)

small, albeit vital, ingredient in a computer. The simple logo and supporting campaign played second fiddle to the brand campaigns run by PC manufacturers. The computer-chip industry is also subject to rapid obsolescence, commoditization, and intensive cost competition, so this campaign can be judged a success in that context. Ingredient brands are a worthwhile strategy for many manufacturers and even suppliers of raw material commodities.

Dolby Laboratories has done a great job at convincing us that their noise reduction and coding processes are necessary for a great cinematic experience (and at one time, essential for recordings and stereos). There are many other examples, including Gore-Tex, Nylon, Zeiss, Bosch, Pantone, Reynolds Steel, Woolmark, and luxury cloth brand Merino New Zealand. The owners of these ingredients usually license their use to selected users, may contribute some marketing budget, and try and generate marketing pull with end-users as a way of building loyalty with their immediate business-to-business customers.

Since brands enhance lifetime value and price premiums, they help increase returns to shareholders. As a result, they put the firm on a stronger financial footing and help financial managers negotiate better terms with lenders, attract patient investors such as Warren Buffett and extract better trading terms from suppliers. Many of the other benefits enjoyed elsewhere within the firm also have strong financial implications, especially in terms of cost efficiency.

2. The CEO: Bob Diamond at Barclays was once the darling of the share market, until a series of scandals compounded to reduce equity in the UK bank and forced him to resign. Although many CEOs stress the importance of brands, what really matters is profits and returns to shareholders. For CEOs of publicly listed companies, every quarter they are accountable for performance (leading to declines in average CEO tenure). For many of the reasons listed above, stronger brands increase returns, and help the firm expand into new markets and segments. Brands represent the single-largest intangible asset a firm has, and these make up most of the value of a share. Although brand managers may want to avoid crassly stating the obvious, building equity is essential to CEO survival.

3. Operations: In their search for operational efficiencies (often called "leads"), operations managers can do much damage to brands. Former Starbucks CMO Scott Bedbury identified how short-term savings often undermined the customer experience. In one such encounter, a proposal to use a cheaper, thinner cardboard for Starbucks' takeaway cups was dismissed by CEO Howard Schultz on the ground it undermined the tone of the brand (and would paradoxically increase costs as customers would demand an extra cup to protect their hands from the heat).

However, operations helps the brand deliver on promises, be it through service delivery, consistency of look, store fit-outs, trade shows and consumer conventions, event management, web-based services, and product quality (among many others). A strong working relationship between marketing and operations is crucial but, unfortunately, all too rare.

For operations, a strong brand can result in greater buyer power, resulting in decreased costs and efficiency savings. These benefits increase the larger the brand gets—just think of the buying power of a large global brand such as Microsoft. Likewise, suppliers (particularly those of creative services such as advertising and design) may be keener to work with strong brands on better terms, simply because it adds to their own reputation (or portfolio). RMIT University in Melbourne, for example, refreshed its brand on a relatively small budget (approximately a paltry A$1 million), largely because agencies were keen to work with a high-profile, large educational provider as a means of enhancing their portfolio and reputation.

4. Sales: Salespeople have far more direct interaction with customers than most marketers, and often have greater contact with competitive offers. Although the sales–marketing relationship has traditionally been a rocky one, brands can help salespeople in a number of ways. The financial benefits of brands obviously help commissioned salespeople earn more. Since brands pull goods through channels, salespeople representing a strong brand are likely to have greater access to retail buyers, get better shelf space for their products, enjoy insights shared with them by channel partners, access better channels, and potentially be appointed as category captains (e.g., Coca-Cola may manage the entire soft-drink category in large retailers such as Carrefour and Tesco, giving them a closer working relationship with their retailer, enabling them to produce the "own label" cola, and making decisions on behalf of their competitors). Brands high in awareness are also often higher in demand, making the sales effort easier than for unknown ones.

5. Research and development: Despite decades of research on innovation, new product failure rates, particularly in consumer markets, remain high (around 70 percent and above). Strong brands cannot save a poor product, but they can assist a good one, and help with products that do not fit known categories. For example, the iPad launch was one of several attempts by technology makers to create a market for tablets, but unlike earlier attempts by the likes of Microsoft (whose equity lay in software), Apple's brand power and loyal franchise helped ensure the product was a hit, and also helped create a brand new category. Since brand managers need to extend their brands to maintain relevance (see Chapter 7), good relationships with research and development are essential. Strong brands help innovation success by reducing risk, stimulating trial, generating public relations coverage, and gaining retailer support. They also provide firms with the income to reinvest back into future research and development activities.

6. Human resources: Much of the brand benefits enjoyed by human resources are covered below in **employee-based brand** equity. Suffice to say, a strong brand attracts good employees, helps human resources define ideal employees (who will fit with the brand's image and deliver its promise), lower acquisition costs, increase retention rates, and potentially lower salary costs. According to the founder of Southwest Airlines, Herb Kelleher (Miles and Mangold 2005), the low-cost carrier has built its entire reputation using employee branding, identifying the right people to work together to get airlines away on time, and to make the flight experience as fun as possible for tired travelers (check out the video in the Further Reading section involving a flight attendant doing the safety announcement as a rap).

These are critical, because for the most part we need all of these functions to deliver on our brand promises. We need sales to interact with customers, convince them of the merits of our offer, tailor solutions, and provide us with feedback on customer needs, wants, problems with our offer, and gaps in the marketplace. We need operations to make sure all the systems and procedures in the organization are running smoothly, manage customer journeys, deliver at important customer touch-points, and generally make certain our brand identity is delivered consistently throughout the organization. We need human resources to train staff appropriately, reward them in ways that enhance our brand promise, and ensure we get the right staff that reflect out brand. We need research and development to generate new products and services to keep the brand relevant. We need finance to give us the money to invest in brand-related marketing. Finally, let's not forget the CEO, who provides the moral support necessary to sustain brand efforts.

Reputation vs. Brand Equity

Are brand equity and brand valuation simply new names for reputation (or esteem or favorable standing relative to others; Deephouse and Carter 2005)? In many ways the answer is a qualified "yes," although there are crucial differences between the two. Historically, the value of a brand was simply called "goodwill," which represented the difference between the book value of the firm and the sales price (assuming the difference was positive). In this sense, goodwill was closer to brand valuation than customer equity, although it was rarely more than 20 percent of the final price. Reputation is also typically given to the firm by customers and other stakeholders and is therefore an outcome of firm actions over time. In contrast, customer equity, as we've seen from the discussion on the brand pyramid and will see later on in the chapter, is something managers seek to create, maintain, and grow.

Brand managers have often forgotten reputation, but this is a mistake. First, although firms may manage their customer brand equity, other stakeholders can influence the customer's image of the brand and effect its operations. For example, BP's financial brand equity (as measured by Interbrand) fell significantly after the Deepwater Horizon disaster in 2010. This reputation affected the ability of BP to drill exploratory oil wells in other locations, ultimately affecting the firm's ability to grow the brand. Poor labor practices in Nike's offshore factories still define (a decade on) the brand's image for many consumers. Likewise, poor financial reporting practices hit Krispy Kreme Donuts hard with financial markets and regulators, even though customer equity remained high. For these reasons and others, firms often complement brand strategy with reputation management.

Reputation is also important for long-established firms that have not yet invested heavily in brand equity. As we will see, brand equity involves competing symbolically in the marketplace. Many business-to-business firms, charities, government agencies, education and healthcare providers, and professions (such as lawyers) have been slow to deliberately pursue brand equity, but nonetheless have strong reputations. Even small organizations with a loyal cult following such as the Morgan Motor Company took almost 100 years to formally define their brand. In these cases, reputation is a proxy for **brand image**, and is a useful place to start when building a deliberate brand strategy, as it defines what is unique and favorable about the brand for its long-time users.

The Brand Equity Pyramid

The strength of the customer–brand relationship has historically been measured in reference to the **brand equity pyramid**. In this model, equity is equated with increased awareness of the brand and its associations. Drawing on Keller's model that equates likeable brand knowledge with brand equity this model suggests that marketers build brand equity over time, using different strategies to enhance consumers' understanding of the brand.

Keller's brand pyramid is presented in Figure 3.1. Underpinning this approach is the belief that the brand only really exists in the mind of the customer in terms of what they know about the brand, what they feel towards it, and what it was like to use. Each level of knowledge requires a different strategy, flowing from awareness and assessment of brand claims through to use, as Figure 3.2 explains. The brand pyramid thereby assumes a relationship between brand awareness and brand equity.

At the base of the pyramid lies basic awareness. This is often called brand identity and involves generating recognition of what the brand is in a very literal sense, what needs it serves, and importantly what category it belongs to. Chapter 4 first attempts to measure the value of a brand in terms of its recognition by its target users (i.e., "Do you recognize this brand [show image of brand]?") For example, a brand such as Tesla is defined by its commitment to high-performance battery technology, and primarily belongs to the category of sustainable automobiles, and a sub-category

Figure 3.1   Brand Equity Pyramid

Figure 3.2   Brand Pyramid Explained

of sports vehicle. As you can see with this description, Keller's model views the human brain much like a computer drive, whereby things are carefully filed into folders and sub-folders in a very rational way. This somewhat oversimplifies his model and certainly oversimplifies human behavior, but nonetheless brands should answer these basic questions if they are to be seen as a resource for two reasons:

brands are used as short cuts by consumers to make more efficient choices and studies do indicate that for many product and service categories, consumers choose from a small **consideration set** of around 4–5 brands in a category (Singh and Uncles 2016).

Think of this consideration set in relation to how you go supermarket shopping. Like many people you may draw up a list (if you don't, chances are you'll spend more money than planned), and on that list will be products and brands. If the brand is on the list, it is likely you will buy it (indicating a high degree of loyalty and equity), and if a product is on the list, you're open to options, albeit from a small range of known and liked brands.

Why? Although our brains are powerful things, we cannot possibly remember every brand on offer for every category we need. Like many animals at some point, it is difficult to distinguish between a number of individually different things (say "5") and a broad undifferentiated mass ("many"). For this reason, brands have an identity and try to communicate this via a consistent brand-marketing program that reinforces category-level associations. At this stage advertising is important, as is retail presence, and associations are communicated directly via images, claims, and even things such as brand names and logos, and indirectly, through the use of cultural brand codes suggestive of certain associations, such as luxury, youthfulness, glamour, value-for-money, functionality and so on.

These associations are driven by the **brand's intended identity**: "Brand identity is a unique set of associations the brand strategist aspires to create or maintain. These associations represent what the brand stands for and imply a promise to customers from the organization members" (Aaker, 1991, p.39). After building basic recognition, marketers attempt to enhance our understanding of the brand's identity through answering a second set of questions that address functional performance and emotional outcomes (see Figures 3.1 and 3.2). At this stage, marketers are still the primary driver of brand meaning, usually by stressing **points of parity** (how the brand meets accepted performance standards that all brands need just to compete) and, critically, **points of difference** (sometimes called unique selling points or USPs) relative to competitors.

From here on in, the customer takes over, and starts to form an image of the brand. As you can see in Figures 3.1 and 3.2, Keller's model does not allow for much input from the customer, as it essentially assumes users, intrigued or convinced by the brand's identity promises, are now simply judging the brand's actual performance in relation to these functional and emotional claims, and deciding ultimately if it is the very best on offer (resonance). However, while this occurs, users may make other judgments about the brand, drawing on a range of non-marketer-authored information to assess the brand.

However, customer responses to claimed characteristics are driven by trial and repurchase. As we'll see in Chapter 4, the customer-based brand equity model proposes that equity increases after positively assessed trials and therefore measurements of brand awareness move from stimulated trial to recall without a stimulus. Near the very peak of the pyramid is the brand loyal customer, who buys the brand on a regular basis out of the belief it is superior in some way. Again, in Chapter 4 we'll see that this is measured by top-of-mind awareness and this is a proxy for market share and therefore higher equity.

The peak of the pyramid is defined by the strength of the customer's bond with the brand. In essence, customers here ask, "Can anything else beat it?" This doesn't just mean that the brand outperforms others in a functional sense (i.e., is it cheaper, faster, lighter, tastier etc.?), but whether the brand is judged superior from the standpoint of self-authentication (i.e., how good is it for authenticating acts, authoritative performances or both?). There are different ways to think about this level of bonding. From a relational standpoint, the metaphor used by consumers to define their bond to the brand is important. For example, one would predict that framing the bond in terms of "a best friend" or "marriage" would be a stronger relationship than "a casual fling" (Fournier 1998). Emotional branding advocate Kevin Roberts suggests brand managers need to build "Lovemarks," where the bond between customer and brand defies reason (Roberts 2004).

Others measure the degree of attachment customers have with the brand. This focuses on whether the customer could live (in the metaphorical sense) without the brand. Studies have demonstrated a positive relationship between emotional attachment to a brand and preparedness to pay a price premium (Thomson et al. 2005). Emotional attachment is actually more effective than satisfaction and having a favorable attitude toward the brand in this regard. Such studies provide further support for an emotional branding model and are why many brand managers have reframed identity in relational terms, often through anthropomorphic designs (the human face of the MINI or Steve Jobs's redesign of apps in ways that made you want to "lick them off the screen") and innovative advertising strategies such as "Whopper Freakout" at the end of this chapter.

Attachment is also a proxy for humanizing the brand. We are more likely to bond with objects and brands that we can empathize with and that feel like us. Studies on brands driven by a higher purpose, such as those covered in Brand Aside 3.2, reinforce this. In this sense, brand equity is an outcome of self-authentication as users view the brand as an extension of the self (real and/or imagined). However, although equity is measured in this way, it is important to keep in mind that users are far more active in shaping that brand relationship than Keller's model allows. This suggests alternative strategies, including communal-based activities, authentic extensions, associations with pop culture, and cultural resonance, are essential for building and maintaining equity, all of which will be covered in later chapters.

Finally, it is important to recognize that not all brands enjoy high levels of bonding. Those that consumers view as low involvement may rate low on measures of bonding and therefore will have lower levels of customer equity (although the size of their market may mean they are valued highly from a financial standpoint).

Studies in many low-involvement categories have identified loyalty rates at around 50 percent (Singh and Uncles 2016). Consumers are rarely loyal to one brand and, in cases where they are, they are less important to future brand growth and equity than those who split their loyalty in predictable ways across several brands within the category. In fact, true loyalists are often dangerous to brands, as they get upset at even small changes, which is why many commentators associate falling equity with brand managers paying too much attention to their biggest fans, and failing to innovate (Beverland 2010).

Brand Valuation

In essence, financial brand equity is an estimate of the net present value (NPV) of the expected cash flow generated by the brand. The key word here is "estimate"! Even the sale of the brand from one firm to another is based on judgments of the brand's potential. Part of this judgment requires estimating how much difference the brand makes to a firm's revenue. So for example, what would the value of Volkswagen be if it produced unbranded vehicles? What considerations go into formulating this valuation?

1. How much revenue can be attributed to the brand in each of the markets it competes?
2. How strong is the brand? This is based on an estimate of the strength of the customer's relationship with the brand (and therefore the likelihood they will buy it again in the future).
3. What is the nature of the markets that the brand competes? A strategic assessment of the risks and opportunities faced by the brand and the category in which it competes.

Brand valuation, or financial brand equity, is an inexact science to say the least. For the most recent results of estimates of financial brand value by the two leaders in the field—Interbrand's Global Top 100 Brands and Millward Brown's *Brandz*—show that there are vast differences between each of these measures, despite the fact that their formulas (on paper) are largely the same. Although one could argue that the differences may be due to timing (Brandz is released three months after Interbrand's rating), this is unlikely.

Much of the difference comes down to how each organization estimates the strength of the customer–brand relationship. Each organization's calculation methodology (outlined on their websites) identifies how each values a brand. In essence, both firms use Bloomberg's Datamonitor database to answer points 1 and 3 above. Where they differ is in how they calculate the "multiple" or strength of the customer–brand relationship (point 2). Interbrand essentially makes a behind the scenes estimate of the relationship whereas Millward Brown conducts a very large number of interviews with brand users from around the globe. In so doing, they draw on what is essentially Keller's brand pyramid to understand where the brand's strengths lie, and provide advice to clients on where best to make improvements in their brand-building program. On this latter point, they offer a brand signature, identifying the relative strengths and weaknesses of an individual brand within a category—so a brand that is underperforming may be strong on presence, but weak on relevance, meaning users recognize it but are unsure what and who it is for. These data are then useful for honing the brand-marketing program.

Ultimately, what do these estimates of value mean? As the brand manager of Louis Vuitton, does it matter that Google and Apple are valued more highly than you? Yes and no. One could argue that since these brands are in radically different categories, such valuations do not really matter and provide little more than bragging rights for marketers. On the other hand, estimates of value may impact share-market analysts and their recommendations to buy, sell or hold a stock. Therefore, Bernard Arnault, the CEO of Louis Vuitton, may have a great deal of interest in these relative rankings and is likely to ask tough questions of the marketing team if the brand's relative value falls. But for now, the impact of these rankings on the share market is poorly understood. Also, it is worth bearing in mind that there are significant difficulties in accurately estimating the financial value of a brand including:

1. Estimates of value are subjective. Even in merger or acquisition scenarios, different analysts have varying views about the future potential of the brand. For example, the America Online (AOL)–Time Warner merger in 2000 is regarded by many as the biggest mistake in corporate history. At the time, asset and revenue rich Time Warner was in effect acquired by the promise heavy (it was the peak of the dotcom bubble of the late 1990s), asset poor AOL. However, falling revenues at AOL after the dotcom bubble burst led to the then biggest write-down in corporate history, with the value of AOL stock falling from US$226 billion to just US$20 billion. Most of this write-down reflected a reassessment of "goodwill." At the time, however, analysts were split on the value of this merger and the purchase price.
2. Many of these models rely on the ability to separate revenue attributable to the brand from other revenue. This is notoriously difficult. After all, how much of Apple's revenues is driven by the brand as opposed to new innovations or retail execution? These factors are of course all interrelated, as new innovations reinforce the brand and extend it into new categories, while the success of the new products is in part driven by loyal brand users and the power of the Apple story.
3. Brand valuation relies on a forecast, which always contains assumptions about opportunities and risk, many of which can change drastically, as in the case of the AOL–Time Warner merger above. At the time, no one foresaw the dotcom crash, and estimates of future AOL revenues and the potential to move Time Warner's titles online were within reason (Dall'Olmo Riley 2016).

Employee-based Brand Equity

Why do firms concern themselves with employee-based brand equity? Perhaps an example will help. Prior to Apple launching its flagship retail stores in Australia in 2008, the company was inundated with over 20,000 applications from potential employees. At this stage, Apple had not run any job advertisements, invested in job fairs, or spent any money on recruitment at all. The strength of the brand resulted in a record number of unsolicited applications from highly qualified employees (many of whom were fans of the brand), who were at least on paper prepared to take a pay cut to work for the brand. And, this occurred at a time of comparative economic strength for Australia (Beverland 2009).

The above example identifies why firms began expanding their branding programs beyond customers to focus on the employees who would be delivering the brand's desired identity. US-based low-cost airline Southwest was one of the most high-profile firms to emphasize employment branding, with founder and CEO Herb Kelleher going so far to state that if you took care of employees, the customer experience would follow (Miles and Mangold 2005). There are many benefits to doing so including building a strong image among potential employees as well as financial benefits. Some measures of employee brand equity include:

1. Best employees: Firms that rate high on this score (such as Deutsche Bank and Louis Vuitton) attract better applicants but also provide a halo effect for their existing employees who can all identify with being the very best and brightest. LinkedIn's "Most InDemand Employers" graph provides a recent example.
2. Lower acquisition costs: Firms with strong employment brand equity do not have to work too hard to attract high-quality applicants. As a result, the costs of acquisition, in terms of advertisements, attendance at job fares, use of recruitment consultants, and so on, are much lower.
3. Higher retention: Just like consumer brands with high levels of resonance, strong employment brands retain employees with many positive financial benefits.
4. Better performance: Brands that treat their employees fairly tend to gain a better performance from them. Although some brands such as Ralph Lauren involve notoriously long hours, especially when launching a new collection, many employees feel motivated to "do it for Ralph" (Beverland 2009).
5. Lower salaries/better value perception on salary (or employees' perceptions of salary fairness): This is an interesting measure, which means employees are trading off salary for brand associations. As a result, they have convinced themselves that their conditions are better than they are, simply because of how they view the brand, which is why strong employment brands such as Apple, Google, and McKinsey can pay less but still attract and retain the best talent.

Measuring the value of the brand to current and future employees is very similar to the brand pyramid for customers. In essence, one simply conducts the same type of analysis, but targets employees rather than customers. Therefore, knowing one's target employee market and having a clearly defined set of benefits matters in the same way as it did with customer-based brand equity. For potential employees the focus remains on measuring brand awareness, and anticipated brand associations. For current employees relative measures on brand associations including points of parity (which represent hygiene factors) and points of difference (motivators) are important in assessing the potential for turnover (a significant cost to any firm).

Perhaps the strongest question to focus on in employment branding is a version of the valuation exercise used by agencies to calculate the difference in value of the firm with the brand and without. One common question asked of current employees is the difference between the employees' personal brand and their personal brand plus the employment brand. Do employees perceive their association with the firm in a positive sense, or do they view the firm as diminishing their own reputation? If the latter, then you may find it difficult to keep your best employees and would potentially need to pay them more to remain (an effect which is likely to be only temporary).

A Framework for Building Brand Equity

When we compare most of the material in this chapter with Chapter 2, it is clear that the way in which brand value or equity is framed may differ for users or customers and brand managers. If one adds in the other two authors of brand meaning—influencers and popular culture—it is not hard to imagine further differences between how brand managers seek to build value and the value derived by these other authors. What is clear is that the brand potentially represents a resource for each author of brand meaning: marketers, users, influencers, and figures within popular culture.

Figure 3.3 provides a guiding framework for creating and managing the brand-as-a-resource. Each of the authors is identified. The main influences that shape their decisions and actions are listed underneath each author. How they assess the brand as a resource (or how they think of equity) is identified vertically at the end of each arrow. On the arrows, each author's contribution to brand equity is identified. As identified in Chapter 1, these authors all influence the shared meaning of the brand and are interconnected in various ways. I will expand on this framework through the course of each chapter (where relevant), but a summary is provided in Table 3.2.

As one can see, managing this is not so simple, and certainly not as simple as building brand awareness or creating a narrow set of associations, communicating that

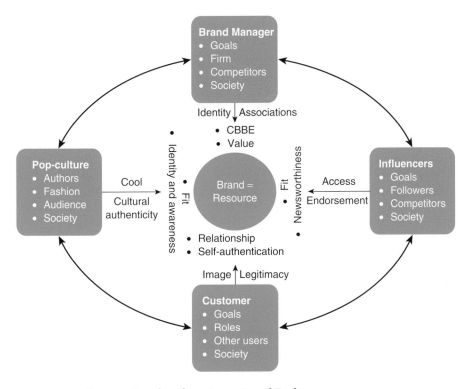

Figure 3.3   How the Four Brand Authors Frame Brand Equity

Source: Author's notes

Table 3.2   How authors of brand meaning frame brand equity

Author	Drivers of decision-making and action	Frames value or equity as	Provides brand meaning through
Brand Manager	• Goals: professional, identity, brand position, short and long term. • Firm: strategy, resources, and capabilities. • Competitors: positioning and actions. • Society: cultural worldviews, norms, and ideology.	• Customer-based brand equity. • Financial estimates of brand.	• Desired brand identity. • Brand associations (or deliberately managed markers of brand knowledge). • Cultural relevance and resonance

(Continued)

Table 3.2   (Continued)

Author	Drivers of decision-making and action	Frames value or equity as	Provides brand meaning through
Customer	• Goals: self-authentication. • Roles: various identity roles one inhabits over time (e.g., mother, friend, breadwinner). • Other users: linking value. • Society: norms that frame authoritative performances and the wider sociocultural fabric.	• Brand as relationship partner. • Authenticating acts and authoritative performances.	• Brand image: how the customer sees the brand. • Attachment: can I see myself in the brand? • Legitimacy: the brand fits with accepted beliefs about what is right and proper.
Influencers	• Goals: personal and professional aims. • Followers: an influencer's audience and their needs as customers. • Legitimacy: accepted standards of behavior within the influencer's community. • Society: cultural worldviews, norms, and ideology.	• Fit: does the brand fit with influencer's image, reputation, and audience? • Newsworthiness: is the brand worthy of comment?	• Access: the influencer controls access to their audience. • Endorsement: their stamp of approval.
Pop culture	• Authors: the identity goals and image of the particular artist or property using the brand. • Fashion: what is relevant at a particular time. • Audience: the author's target audience. • Society: cultural worldviews, norms, and ideology.	• Fit: does the brand fit with the artist's or property's desired image, purpose, and/or audience? • Identity: what is the brand's identity? How well known is the brand?	• Cool: non-commercial brand associations. • Cultural authenticity: the brand transcends the commercial world.

through the marketing mix, and maintaining consistency over time. Shifts in any part of the system in Figure 3.3 will flow through the rest of the system, resulting in the potential for further change. Even something as seemingly distant as an artist's parody of a brand may eventually flow through to the other authors and effect the target customer's framing of the brand relationship (for good or ill), as was the case with Botox's shifting image (see Chapter 4) in the media and popular culture (Giesler 2012). Brand Aside 3.5 on doppelgänger brands provides more detail.

Figure 3.4 draws this material together and identifies a model for building equity over time. As brand managers, our primary job is to bring together firm capabilities and brand associations to provide resources to customers that are meaningfully different. To do so, we must be aware of their underlying motivations and the social context and networks of influence in which they are embedded. It then follows that these considerations must flow through into the brand-marketing program and the ways in which we assess brand equity. In this model, meaning-management across all four

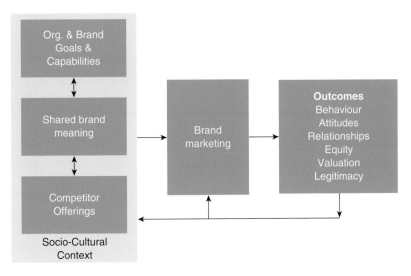

Figure 3.4   **Building Brand Equity**

Doppelgänger Brands

One way that a brand's equity can be challenged is through the doppelgänger process. Studies have identified that consumer activists and popular media can create an alternate, negative mirror image of the brand's meaning, or a doppelgänger. Starbucks, for example, suffered from culture jamming (a term used by the founders of Adbusters, an organization and magazine opposed to consumerism) or subversion of their brand identity. Although the brand presented itself as an authentic European coffee house, activists noted that the brand was responsible for sending many local neighborhood coffee shops out of business and was the very opposite of authenticity (Thompson et al. 2006). Likewise, Botox suffered a number of swings in its image (Giesler 2012). In both cases, these critiques of the brand started on the fringe, often on anti-brand websites, but crossed over to the mainstream, thereby undermining the brand's image with users. Careful management insured that equity did not decline as brand managers provided users with adjusted images and associations to ensure ongoing authenticity. Later chapters will return to this idea.

stakeholder groups becomes essential. Regardless of their many (and often substantial) differences, writers on brands all agree that meaning is essential to the brand being viewed as a resource. For example:

1. Drawing on the brand pyramid, Keller stressed the need to create favorable brand associations with target users. Once created these associations should be reinforced and refreshed over time through remaining true to the brand's identity and engaging in innovations.
2. Relationship approaches identify the need to understand how and why consumers view the brand in a particular way, why this may change, and the nature of the context that leads them to adopt a particular relationship frame. Once done, assuming no change in context and goal, the relationship frame should be reinforced and elaborated on over time.
3. Cultural brand theorists stress the importance of myths to brand meaning. Here, providing meaning that enables consumers to make sense of their place in the wider cultural world is essential. Lloyds Bank's latest campaign attempts to do this by foregrounding the brand in the ongoing narrative of Britain. The campaign attempts to return the brand to its roots and re-establish the brand as a contributor to the shared national story.
4. Writers in media studies stress the symbolic value of various texts including brands. Although they do not ascribe greater value priority to any one author's view of the brand, nonetheless an originator does create a brand text, draw on cultural codes to signal meaning, and continually communicates old and new meanings over time.
5. Others have stressed the need to enhance the brand's authenticity through the use of "truthy" stories that enable self-authentication, particularly when faced with a cultural backlash or paradoxes.

Historically brand managers have been seen as the main controller of a brand's meaning. Unsurprisingly, brand equity under this view was largely built through mass communications of a desired brand identity and image. Typically, some higher-order values (e.g., "fun," "rebellion," "ostentation') were ascribed to the brand (these were known as the brand's "position') and these drove all marketing related decisions. Brand equity was built by "staying on message" and remaining consistent with the position over time. However, under the multiple-author approach, this approach is more problematic as the brand's meaning may only ever tend toward stability. This is not to say a focus on an intended identity or building associations is a bad thing, just that there is much more to creating a shared resource than staying consistent to a narrow set of abstract values over time.

How we manage this will be the subject of the next sections. Chapter 4 will focus on measurement issues. There are accepted measures for understanding brand identity and image for example. There are also other methods, some new and some very old, for building greater empathy with the world of the customer. With the power of social media, new techniques have also emerged that enable us to track consumer–brand engagement, mentions by influencers, and the effect of pop culture on the brand.

I will also examine tools that can be used to identify brand associations and see whether these are retaining meaning or require revision.

After this, further chapters will focus on creating new brands, managing their meaning over time, refreshing tired brands, growing brands, and managing them through crises.

Chapter Summary

Brand equity is broadly equated with the value of the brand. For customers, brand equity is defined in terms of the strength of the relationship between them and the brand. Ultimately, if the brand is a resource for consumers to achieve their goals, customers will view it as more meaningful, and therefore are likely to bond more closely with it. This should then transfer through to the value of the brand (depending on the size of the market served). Financial brand equity or brand valuation is also examined. This is harder to measure, but the broad consensus is that brands do create price premiums, generate profits, and increase the share price and firm valuation. Beyond these financial indicators, brands offer many other benefits to other functions within the firm, including human resources (employment brand equity), operations, finance, sales, and research and development. Finally, a strategic model to generate and manage the brand resource is presented. This model will form the basis of the rest of the text.

Review Questions

1. What is the difference between financial brand value and customer-based brand equity? Answer this with reference to two examples from Interbrand's Global 100 Brands list.
2. Google is currently ranked highly in global estimates of financial brand value. In 2017 the firm lost advertisers on its YouTube site because their advertisements could appear side to side with material they deemed unethical. What might happen to the financial brand valuation of Google as a result? Would this crisis have the same impact on customer-based brand equity for Google?
3. Using Figure 3.3, identify how each author gains and contributes value from/to a brand of your choice.
4. Identify the differential effects of two brands of your choice with reference to Keller's three principles.
5. List three brands you would like to work for. Identify why from an employee-based brand equity perspective. Identify a brand you would not work for and think about what that brand would have to do to change your mind.

Case Example: Whopper Freakout

Burger King was founded in 1953 and expanded its menu in 1957 to include what would become its signature burger, the Whopper (the brand's slogan is "Home of the Whopper"). Despite having many loyalists the brand has always played second fiddle to McDonald's and started to lose focus during the 1980s, resulting in declining equity over the next two decades as new entrants entered the market, and existing competitors such as KFC expanded into burgers. In 2003, the firm appointed disruptive advertising agency Crispin, Porter + Bogusky (CPB) to reinvigorate the brand and attract new consumers. CPB returned the brand to its roots in many ways, redesigning the brand's mascot (the rather creepy "King") and investing heavily in social media. The 2008 "Whopper Freakout" campaign won many creative awards and generated a spike in sales.

What was special about "Whopper Freakout"? Drawing on theories of brand relationships and emotional attachment (or resonance—see the Brand Equity Pyramid) Whopper Freakout was centered on a very simple idea—what would happen if Burger King stopped making the Whopper burger? Since brand attachment is the pinnacle of brand equity and suggests one cannot do without the brand, the idea was to highlight core brand associations, authentic stories, and unguarded emotional reactions to reignite interest among lapsed and new consumers.

The advertisement was run online and presented in a documentary style, which help render it authentic. In essence, one Burger King outlet became a "Whopper-free zone" filled with hidden television cameras so as to film the results. The second part of the campaign featured giving consumers a competitor's burger including a McDonald's Big Mac and Wendy's burger by stealth, and then suggesting that the consumers were trying to pull a scam to get one of Burger King's Whoppers. The campaign is available on YouTube and well worth watching in order to reinforce the key points in this chapter.

The campaign followed up with a Facebook-based program called "Whopper sacrifice" in which consumers gained a free Whopper coupon for every ten friends they defriended on Facebook. Unsurprisingly, the social media site cancelled the Whopper Sacrifice account, but not before 200,000 friends were delisted by Whopper fans. A Direct TV campaign also ran called "Whopper Lust," requiring consumers to allow the Whopper image to remain on screen for five minutes in order to get a voucher (50,000 coupons were eventually sent out).

The first part of "Whopper Freakout" focuses on a series of vox pops (short interviews with real consumers outside of the store) on why they love Burger King and what it means to them. It becomes clear that loyalty is a function of one product,

The Whopper, and that underpinning this is a range of personal stories often centering around driving across state lines to buy Whoppers, shifting from the junior Whopper to the real thing as part of a rite of passage ("becoming a big boy") and enjoying the burger as part of a weekly routine. Clearly, these consumers are loyal to Burger King, but only through one product.

The next scene involves these same consumers placing their orders at the counter, and being told that the Whopper has been discontinued. The results are instant and powerful, showing consumers bewildered, confused, and in some cases angry and even prone to violence (an adult-rated gangsta version of the film is also available). Consumers literally cannot believe that the Whopper is gone, a situation not helped by the brave frontline staff stating that the burger was killed by head office for being "too popular." Consumers recount more personal stories about their relationship with the brand, wistfully reminiscing on what they have lost. The scene ends with vox pops with the same consumers wondering what the brand stands for—as one male consumer states, "What will they call it now? Burger Queen?"

The next scene aims to remind the audience of the brand's special attributes or associations, and in effect sees CPB taking viewers on a ride down the brand equity pyramid. As loyal consumers have their order called out, they collect their bag, sit down, open it up, and realize that they have been given the wrong burger. Confronting the service staff, they hand over a competitor burger. One older customer was given a McDonald's Big Mac, and stated forcefully "I hate McDonald's"; another told the staff member to throw away the Wendy's burger he was given; while yet another irate customer shouted, "I hate Wendy's!" Then staff, on script, implied that the customers were trying to pull a scam, identifying how McDonald's and Wendy's fried their burgers while Burger King flame-grilled theirs. At the end, they bravely asked customers if they were unsatisfied with their choice, which tipped many customers over the edge in sheer frustration.

The final scene ends the customers' torment, with staff asking them if they want to speak to the manager. Outraged customers quickly affirm this choice, and the famous King emerges from behind a screen with the Whopper they so love. Customers are told it's been a prank, with the film ending with a line about the day the Whopper went away, to remind consumers why they continue to support the brand and not take it for granted.

CPB won several creative awards for this and the follow-up campaigns, but Burger King still struggles as a brand. The agency was eventually replaced and a new campaign focused on the Whopper's ingredients launched.

(Continued)

Case Questions

1. How did the consumers in the case and video define their relationship with Burger King? Use the brand pyramid to define Burger King's customer-based brand equity.
2. Based on this case and video, would you describe Burger King's customer equity as strong? How would you rate its potential to appeal to ex-loyalists or new customers?
3. Why did the campaign fail to turn around the brand's fortunes?
4. How would you approach the Burger King turnaround?

Key Terms

Brand equity
Brand equity pyramid
Brand image
Brand knowledge
Brand loyalty
Brand value
Brand's intended

identity
Consideration set
Customer-based
brand equity
Differential effect
Employee-based
brand equity

Financial-based
brand equity
Points of difference
Points of parity
Return on investment
(ROI)

Further Reading

Deshpande, Rohit and Anat Keinan (2015), "Brands and Brand Equity," *Harvard Business School Teaching Note* 8140-HTM-ENG.

Edwards, Helen and Derek Day (2014), "Passionbrands: The Extraordinary Power of Belief," in Kartikeya Kompella (ed.), *The Definitive Book on Branding*, Sage, London, pp. 343–368.

Keller, Kevin Lane (1993), "Conceptualizing, Measuring, and Managing Customer-Based Brand Equity," *Journal of Marketing*, 57 (January), 1–22.

Miles, Sandra J. and W. Glynn Mangold (2005), "Positioning Southwest Airlines through Employee Branding," *Business Horizons*, 48(6), 535–545.

Salinas, Gabriella (2016), "Brand Valuation: Principles, Applications, and Latest Developments," in Francesca Dall'Olmo Riley, Jaywant Singh, and Charles Blankson (eds), *The Routledge Companion to Contemporary Brand Management*, Routledge, Abingdon, pp. 48–67.

YouTube, "Whopper Freakout" and "Southwest Cabin Crew Rapper." https://www.youtube.com/watch?v= IhF6Kr4ITNQ; https://www.youtube.com/watch?v=G9lZV_828OA

4

DATA, INSIGHTS, AND MEASUREMENT

Consumers have become articulate … they demand more information … changes have tended to make consumers more critical and to enhance their importance. (Kenneth Dameron 1939, p. 271)

Learning Objectives

When you finish reading this chapter, you will be able to:

1. Understand how to measure different forms of brand equity and brand associations
2. Understand the role of qualitative and quantitative approaches in brand research
3. Design a brand tracking study
4. Understand how to generate empathetic user insights
5. Understand various measures for customer–brand relationships, including engagement and authenticity
6. Apply contemporary research tools for their use in branding

Introduction

Complaints about understanding users are long-standing—the comments about consumers in the opening quote are as relevant today as they were in 1939.

Branding must start with consideration of user needs and the context in which they emerge, including the shared meaning created between the four brand co-authors identified in Chapter 1. Although brands can benefit immensely from stability in terms of identity and image, the reality is that they need to adapt, change, evolve, and, in some cases, radically rethink. However, while consumers do not always view the brand in the same light as intended by brand managers, this does not mean they always resist marketer attempts to define the brand's identity. Consumers are indeed active meaning creators, but the history of branding also demonstrates they are also co-conspirators in the development of brand meaning, as Rob Walker (2010) writes in *Buying In: The Secret Dialogue between What We Buy and Who We Are*: "The modern relationship between consumer and consumed is defined not by rejection at all, but rather by frank complicity." Nonetheless, brand managers also need to understand sources of change, potential drivers of dissonance between brand identity and consumer needs and brand image, and shifts in the wider context that may generate threats to the brand or offer new opportunities.

Building on material in Chapter 3, the first part of this chapter focuses on the methods used by brand managers to assess brand equity, measure the strengths of brand associations, understand the competitive position of the brand, and track this over time. It then focuses more deeply on arguably the most important co-authors of brand meaning—customers. This section examines recent tools for assessing the nature and strength of the consumer–brand relationship, the consumer–brand experience, engagement with brand-related material (particularly through social media), and brand authenticity. It also turns to other methods for uncovering unintended brand associations, and identifying latent (or sub-conscious) needs that may be the source of brand-meaning innovation and therefore equity. Marketing tools are often quite poor at identifying latent needs given the field's emphasis on the "customer voice" or espoused needs, so many of the methods covered come from elsewhere.

Throughout, established and contemporary measurement and data-gathering techniques are examined, as well as tools and practices associated with particular branding models, such as the emotional, experiential, and cultural branding approaches. The focus then shifts to various techniques for identifying influencer impacts on brands and for identifying the role of the brand in popular culture. The material covered here will be relevant for understanding the issues covered in later chapters, including adding brand building (Chapters 5 and 6), brand extensions and co-branding (Chapter 7), brand innovation (Chapter 8), and managing brand crises (Chapter 12).

How Do We Measure Brand Equity?

There are many different approaches to measuring brand equity. The last chapter identified how firms such as Interbrand and Millward Brown try and measure the financial value of various brands. Brand managers are also interested in understanding how customers see the brand as **financial valuation** is driven by the belief that strong brand relationships have monetary value. This chapter focuses mostly on models of customer brand equity. It will first examine the importance of **brand awareness**. This is central to the customer-based brand equity (CBBE) framework, and despite limitations is something brand managers invest in to communicate the benefits of the brand to the user, and also to measure the effectiveness of their marketing activities. Brand awareness strategies primarily focus on identifying the brand and its benefits to potential users.

Before this, however, the chapter will examine strategic approaches to measuring **brand health**. Although many of these measures are more general, they do help trigger internal conversations about how the brand could be improved, where it is struggling, and why this might be so. The most common approach is Kevin Keller's famous **Brand Score Card**. Table 4.1 provides the ten questions Keller believes are important for brand health in the first column, and the ways one can address them that are consistent with the logic of this text in the second column. Although these questions reflect Keller's CBBE model, issues of consistency, positioning, relevance, brand-driven marketing, and customer centricity are essential to any brand strategy. Remember, balance is the key—there is no hierarchy of importance in Keller's ten questions; a brand marketer must manage for all of these things, albeit with different strategies.

Table 4.1   Ten questions to ask about your brand

Question	Addressed through
The brand excels at delivering benefits truly desired by customers	Does the brand enable customers to self-authenticate? Do these benefits help consumers address identity conflicts? Does the brand provide linking value?
The brand stays relevant	Is the brand innovative? Does the brand shift to fit in with new cultural conditions? Does the brand locate itself within the evolving life world of the customer? Does the brand team monitor changes in how the other three co-authors see the brand?
Pricing reflects customer perceptions of value	Does the price reflect the relationship consumers have with the brand? Is the price perceived as "fair" in a very general sense?
The brand is properly positioned	Does the brand's identity reflect perceptions of user value (see above), provide a point of competitive difference, and can it be authentically owned by the firm?
The brand is consistent	Does the brand reinterpret its identity over time without straying from its roots?
The brand portfolio and hierarchy make sense	Does the firm strategically manage its brand architecture, brand extensions, licensees, and co-branded partnerships?
The brand makes use of and coordinates a full repertoire of marketing activities to build equity	Is the brand's shared identity the driver of marketing-related activities? Are marketers investing in the full range of tools at their disposal and at levels that are comparable with competitors and market expectations?

(Continued)

Table 4.1   (Continued)

Question	Addressed through
The brand's managers understand what the brand means to consumers	Do brand managers immerse themselves in the world of the customer and adapt their programs accordingly? Do brand managers understand the ideology underpinning consumer communities? Are brand managers communal insiders?
The brand is given proper support, and that support is sustained over the long run	Is the brand treated as an asset and invested in accordingly? Do marketers make effective arguments for the value of the brand to the firm as a whole? Does the brand achieve internal strategic objectives? Is the level of investment reflective of the desired return?
The company monitors sources of brand equity	Does the marketing team measure brand associations, both intended and emergent, via the tools listed in this chapter and elsewhere? Does the brand team measure latent customer needs, track brand hate websites, understand channels of influence (both customer and financial markets), and track how important stakeholders such as retail partners view the brand (the latter is called channel equity—see Chapter 3)?

Source: First column points taken from Keller 2000.

Another useful way of thinking about brand health is the **Brand Asset Valuator (BaV)** model developed by brand consultancy firm the Young & Rubicam Group (Gerzema and Lebar 2008, p. 44). This approach models the health of a brand as a function of two broad variables:

1. Brand strength: Strength provides the brand with its momentum and is a leading indicator of future value growth. Strength consists of two variables:

    i.   Energized differentiation: This is defined as "a brand's unique meaning, with motion and direction." Energized differentiation drives margins and cultural currency. Luxury brands such as Burberry have moved to a "see now, buy now" model whereby what you see on a runway show is already available to buy in stores (previously there was a delay of up to three months). Other brands, such as Gucci, have moved away from two seasons to multiple launches as part of a successful revitalization strategy aimed at improving energized differentiation.
    ii. Relevance: Is the brand relevant to my needs? Relevance drives consideration and trial. Uber has leveraged dissatisfaction with local taxi services in positioning their brand. Linking with music performance venues and indirectly via other events through big data (the GPS in your mobile phone) has allowed them to stimulate trial via introductory offers sent to you via text or email.

2. Brand stature: this is a measure of the brand's cumulative successes over time. This is a useful measure of the brand's historic and present value. Brand stature consists of two variables:

    i.   Esteem: How is the brand regarded (relates to perception of quality and loyalty)? For example, in employment branding, Google remains the most sought-after place to work in among the graduates at top universities

(Wells, 2017). Brands such as Chateau Margaux retain their high prices and quality perceptions year after year among fine wine buyers, influencers, and auction houses.

ii.   Knowledge: How much do I know about the brand? This relates to awareness and consumer experience. The relatively poor position of single malt whisky brand Glenfiddich was a reflection of consumers' lack of brand knowledge. When asked what they knew of the brand, consumers often mentioned "whisky," "Scottish," and "Highlands" but little more. The team used these insights to reposition the brand, building layers of knowledge via new associations and stories across different media channels.

The BaV measures brand value but also provides a useful way of thinking about the core challenge of managing brand value or equity over time: relevance vs. consistency. Figure 4.1 provides an example of how BaV data are presented. The 45-degree line is viewed as the optimal mix of strength and stature. Young & Rubicam then classify brands according to their different strength and stature combinations, identifying four possible outcomes:

1.   New or unfocused brands: low on stature and strength. Ethical shoe and clothing brand Etiko covered in Chapter 11 would probably be classified this way.
2.   Niche brands: high on strength but low on stature. Many new brands that make a lot of noise or are based around new technologies fall in here, including lager-disruptor BrewDog, non-animal-based meat substitute Beyond Meat, and fashion brand Di$count Universe (see Chapter 5).
3.   Leadership: high on strength and stature. These are "blue chip" brands and include brands that retain their equity over time, including Apple, Louis Vuitton, Coca-Cola, BMW, and IBM.
4.   Commoditization: low on strength but high on stature. These are typically tired brands largely trading on their past glory. They often have some positive associations and channel equity (as a loss leader) but have little ongoing relevance. They include The Gap, Research in Motion, and Nokia.

Remember, timing is also important. New brands may rate high on strength, but low on stature, but as they age brands must balance both, through extensions, innovations, and also consistent messaging. Brands in need of a refresh will be high in stature and low in strength. Nokia's recent attempt to re-launch a new "retro" version of their famous 3310 phone is an attempt to refresh the tired brand through innovation. Recently there has been interest in some sectors, such as luxury branding, in acquiring dead or dormant brands and re-launching them. In Chapter 8, one such example is C.W. Dixey. Others include the iconic Indian motorcycle brand or the Italian Emilio Pucci Fashion House (acquired by Louis Vuitton Moët Hennessey or LVMH in 2000). These brands are purchased because of the latent equity in their stature. Although the may have low stature and strength they are rich in associations, and

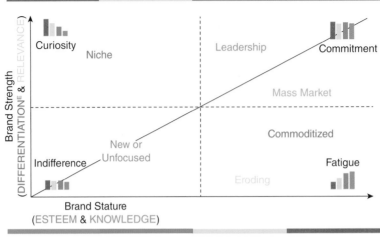

Figure 4.1   Brand Asset Valuator

Source: Adapted from Gerzema, John and Ed Lebar (2008), *The Brand Bubble: The Looming Crisis in Brand Value and How to Avoid It*, Jossey-Bass, New York, p.50.

with skillful marketing can leverage their heritage and authenticity to quickly build equity and recapture lost stature.

Much of what is covered under Keller's brand pyramid relates to building stature. While important, the brand also needs forward momentum, or relevance. As will be identified in future chapters, while both things are vital for brand health, consistency and relevance represent two competing "thought worlds" or mental frames vis-à-vis brand management, involving different assumptions about users, and requiring different strategies. They also require different types of data and measures, which will be covered below.

Measuring Brand Awareness

The previous chapter identified that brand managers attempted to create equity through a clear brand identity. To do so they use the brand pyramid and focus on building awareness of the brand, its relationship with a particular category or need, and its special features and benefits. To measure their success at raising awareness, brand managers draw on three key indicators: **recognition**, **recall**, and **top of mind** awareness (which is a function of recall). These are typically expressed as a percentage and tracked over time, relative to the brand's main competitors. The CBBE framework with specific measures is identified in Figure 4.2. Figure 4.3 identifies the order and logic of measuring recognition, recall, and top of mind awareness.

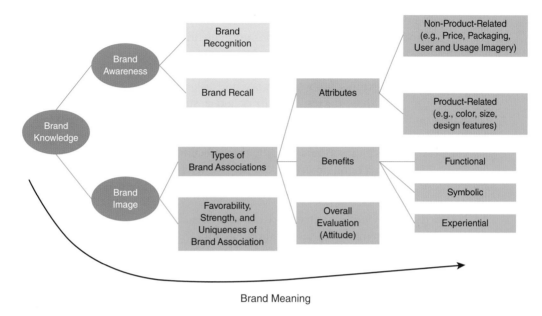

Figure 4.2   **CBBE Brand Identity and Image**

Figure 4.3   **Measuring Brand Identity**

Figure 4.2 identifies that brand equity is a function of brand awareness and brand image (consisting of brand associations that form the upper parts of the brand pyramid). To measure brand awareness screening questions are asked first to ensure the user is within the target market in order to make certain the data are valid. Figure 4.3 identifies that brand awareness is measured through aided recognition, unaided recall, and top of mind awareness. These measures are equally relevant to measuring employer brand equity, or for destinations and celebrities.

1. Aided recognition: Questions that measure recognition usually show a subject a range of brand names from a category and ask them to identify the ones they recognize. Why does having to help or aid a subject make the brand weaker? Based on the logic of CBBE and information processing, having to help a subject identify a brand means it has not registered in their memory as being part of a category of goods or services. Usually this affects new brands or smaller brands. Does this mean recognition is of no value? Not really; it does mean that your communications are being seen, but that the subject has little knowledge of the brand and virtually no experience of it.

2. Unaided recall: Questions that measure recall usually simply ask you to identify or write down as many brands within a category that you remember (without any help of course). Try it. Pick a category you buy from or intend to use—mobile phones, chocolate, beer, banks, luxury goods, or fast food—and write down as many brands as you can off the top of your head. These brands would be held to be stronger than those you left off the list but would recognize if prompted (aided recognition). Why? Returning to the Brand Pyramid (see Figures 3.1 and 3.2), it is likely you have not only heard of these brands, you may also know some of their benefits or attributes from social media posts, advertising, word of mouth, salespeople, and may have experienced them in some way, usually through trial or associations with influential figures such as celebrities. As such, you have more knowledge of them and have a stronger mental connection between them and the product or service category.

3. Top of Mind Awareness: Have a look at your list. What brand did you write first? Brand managers and their research agencies take this very seriously, as studies have identified a strong correlation between top of mind awareness and market share. Why? Think back to Marty Neumeier's definition of brands in Chapter 1, Table 1.1. He defined the brand relationship as a "gut feeling." Top of Mind Awareness in a sense measures gut feeling—you don't even need to think about the first brand to write down when you hear the category because you know it subconsciously. How? Through use and re-use. This is probably the brand you are most loyal to in a category (it may not necessarily be your favorite, however). Is this the case for you? If not, there may be reasons for this. The less favored top of mind brand may have been in the media recently (possibly for the wrong reasons), or you may have been thinking of switching brands. Also, top of mind measures are averaged over a large sample, thereby smoothing out any one-off errors.

4. The dangers of too much loyalty: Some brands have too much awareness for their own good. When you want a cola, you often ask for a Coke. Do you care if it's Pepsi? Probably not. Feeling down? Kleenex tissues are probably what you need. Do you care if they're actually Kleenex? Probably not. Fallen off your skateboard? You may need a Band Aid. But you probably don't insist on it being a "Johnson

& Johnson Band Aid" (the firm actually once tried to do this, to no effect). Stuck in a tedious away-day strategy session doing "design thinking"? You probably have become familiar with Post-it Notes (if not, you soon will be). Are you bothered if they're from 3M? Again, probably not. When a single brand becomes synonymous with an entire category, the brand has become commoditized, and once your patents expire, you can expect to receive diminishing returns. How can you avoid this? Brand innovation, including through line and category extensions and co-branding, can help avoid this problem (see Chapters 7 and 8).

These various measures are useful for measuring the effectiveness of your awareness-building efforts within a category (relative to your competitors). However, they do not give you insights into whether your brand is genuinely liked, or what are the particular strengths (if any) of your brand. That is, measuring awareness is only one part of a bigger story. To get a better handle on customer-based brand equity, you need to measure and track your brand associations (see Figure 4.2). This is a much trickier thing to do, as will be shown next.

Measuring Brand Associations

Measuring brand associations is done to assess the brand's image or, critically, how the customer views the brand. However, it is also important to keep in mind that the CBBE model assumes these associations are communicated to customers or, in other words, users are not active in meaning creation. In essence therefore, measuring brand image often means measuring the extent to which customers understand and value the associations brand managers have developed as part of the intended brand identity. This is a valuable exercise, but it must always be treated with caution—customers are experienced enough in modern marketing research techniques that they easily tell marketers what they want to hear even if it is relatively meaningless in terms of their real relationship with the brand. As such, measuring associations needs to focus on both intended meaning and customer-generated meaning.

Figure 4.2 identifies that brand associations are measured in terms of content (type of brand association), and their overall favorability, strength, and uniqueness. The latter (plus the overall rating) are relatively easy to measure on standard Likert scales (usually 5 or 7 points). Measuring the type of brand associations is somewhat trickier because it usually involves assessing brand identity (those associations that brand managers create) and brand image (how the customer sees the brand). When evaluating brand associations it is important to do the following:

1. Combine qualitative and quantitative techniques: Qualitative methods help identify the right associations and what these mean to your customers. Quantitative techniques enable you to measure these, rank them against those of your competitors, and ensure that they are widely held.

2. Focus on your target market: Where markets are segmented (not all are—see the Brand Aside 4.1) it is important to target your brand at a clearly defined group of customers (the reasons for this will be covered when brand positioning is discussed in Chapter 5) rather than the general public, or self-chosen "experts" (see Brand Aside 4.2).

BRAND ASIDE 4.1

Do Segments Exist?

As we will see, brand building is based on a segmentation–targeting–positioning model. The idea here is that segments deserve respect because they embody a unique set of needs. As a result, the brand needs to be positioned in relation to user needs, and its marketing needs to address those needs directly and/or indirectly. But this raises the question: do segments exist? Some writers on brands challenge this, at least in certain circumstances. Drawing on the work of Andrew Ehrenberg, authors such as Professor Mark Uncles argue that in some categories, such as many FMCG products sold as mass retail, segments do not really exist, and as a result brands should largely focus on standing out and appealing to less loyal buyers than in trying to increase loyalty among a particular target. In these instances, loyal buyers are small in number (often no more than 2 percent of all buyers) and therefore brand growth comes from appealing to those with split loyalties, or consumers who buy from a small set of brands in relatively predictable patterns.

This view has its converts and, as long as one understands the assumptions, it means placing greater emphasis on attracting new or light buyers, appealing to more segments, ensuring widespread availability, using communications to remind buyers why your brand is worth buying, and stressing those things that distinguish you in terms of benefits rather than focusing too heavily on points of difference at an emotional level. This view is not particularly new, advertisers have understood the real limits to loyalty for many years, as have writers such as Keller and Holt. However, these effects apply to markets that are not segmented (which is often a function of how these authors collect their data—its true segments probably don't exist at mass retail, but mass retail is not the whole market for any one category), markets are non-partitioned into different niches (which are extremely rare), and stable (true for many FMCG markets that are mature, but dynamism is the norm in many categories) (Singh and Uncles 2016).

For those working with very large brands in mature categories sold through mass distribution (these can easily cover big luxury brands as well as Coca-Cola), the "scientific" insights provided by these authors are important, although they represent only half the story in terms of building and maintaining brands (one still needs creativity to maintain the mythic profile of brands such as Coke, Nike, and Budweiser).

BRAND ASIDE 4.2

Does It Matter If Your Brand Is Cool?

There are many populist rankings of brands. The CoolBrands initiative (started in the UK but it has since expanded globally) has the highest profile. Essentially, a special group of experts generates a list of brands regarded as cool and then the general public votes upon them. Being regarded as cool by these types of reviews is not the same as brand equity. First, not surprisingly, fashions change easily, so once cool brands quickly become passé in the view of experts. Not so long ago *Encyclopaedia Britannia* (the analog ancestor of Wikipedia) was voted the coolest brand, while Aston Martin remains a regular cool brand, albeit one that has struggled continuously with profitability. Furthermore, cool brands lists seem to be full of the latest technology brands and gadgets, craft alcohol brands, and hotels in typically "hip" locations in capital cities. Second, while independent experts and the public decide whether you're cool, brand equity is a function of how your target market sees you. It matters little whether you are cool or not if your target market has little awareness of your brand, its story, and/or is not positively disposed towards it. Remember, equity is not the result of a general public vote; only those customers you want to sell to matter. That said, rankings of coolness could influence customers indirectly, via various traditional and web-based media, other users, and popular culture. CoolBrands (and others such as Superbrands) do produce beautifully illustrated books and therefore are good for public relations if strategically placed on reception office coffee tables.

3. Assess these associations relative to a set of competitors (as defined by your target market): Although it is important to understand your own associations, brand equity is based on the belief that your brand offers something unique. These are typically called points of difference or desired benefits no one else is currently providing that your brand can truly deliver. Brand Aside 4.3 provides more details and discusses the alternative to points of difference, points of parity. There are benefits for comparing your brand to others in the category, as will be shown in Chapter 5.

4. Track these associations and their strength, favorability and uniqueness relative to competitors over time: Things can change. It is important to recognize that these associations are how you build value in the marketplace. These associations reflect your brand's position (Chapter 5) or identity, or the way you intend to earn equity in the marketplace. Tracking is how you measure your expertise relative to others, judge the effectiveness of your brand marketing, and identify any problems before it is too late. The discussion below on doppelgänger brands identifies why you may also track negative conversations about your brand for similar reasons.

BRAND ASIDE 4.3

Points of Difference and Points of Parity

When building a brand, much emphasis is placed upon finding a USP or a point of difference. Tracking research focuses on identifying the strength of this point of difference in the mind of your users, when compared to other brands within the category. As will be shown in Chapter 5 on positioning, a point of difference is essential to any branding model, either mindshare or cultural. However, is this all there is to building a brand? Not at all. The flipside of a point of difference is a point of parity, and these are important. Points of parity are performance aspects that all brands within the category need to deliver on, just to survive (Keller et al. 2002).

In mobile phones, for example, battery life, durability, connection speed, and even camera quality are all points of parity now, although they initially started off as points of difference for various brands. When Apple launched the iPhone, touchscreen technology was a genuine point of difference, but competitors quickly copied this. Points of difference can quickly become points of parity, especially when they are functional performance associations, which is why brands build identity around more abstract notions. For example, Volvo embodies peace of mind or safety in its communications. It does not stress the functional aspects of safety as a point of difference as virtually all roadworthy vehicles must pass stringent safety tests; rather it stresses these at an emotional level and as something that defines every consideration the brand makes. Finally, when brands are struggling, sometimes it is the point of parity and not the point of difference that is the issue, such as Ryanair's recent emphasis on customer service, which is much more easily fixed.

Qualitative Approaches

Qualitative research collects non-numerical data, often in the form of words, images, and observations. Qualitative research takes many forms and in the context of brand-related research is used to dig deeply into consumer motivation, uncovering latent needs, consumers' lived experiences, consumer meanings, gaining insights into brand-related marketing, and identifying items to measure further with quantitative techniques (among many other uses). Qualitative research is often called "exploratory," "descriptive," or "anecdotal." Although there is a shred of truth to each of these claims, these techniques are vital to the accurate understanding of consumer–brand relationships and therefore assessing brand equity. Without qualitative insights, brand managers can never be sure that they are measuring the right thing!

BRAND ASIDE 4.4

The Focus Group Expert

Focus groups are commonly used in marketing but in some countries there are very real problems. Since it is difficult to recruit random people to be in focus groups, research agencies have developed large pools of consumers willing to take part in focus groups at short notice. However, the problem is that many of these consumers are too willing. Research has revealed that many consumers enjoy the pay, free food, and experience of being an expert and focus on pleasing the moderator in order to get invited back regularly. Unfortunately, the way to please the very human moderator seems to be to work out what they want to hear, rather than providing them with genuine insights about the brand. This renders much of the data gained from focus-group panels worthless. Agencies are aware of this problem and ensure a churn rate within groups to keep them fresh, but consumers get around this by using multiple names in order to remain in the pool (Ritson 2004).

In terms of understanding and creating brand associations, popular techniques include:

1. Focus groups: These are small groups of 8–12 consumers and a trained moderator. Focus groups are popular among marketers and even non-marketers as they provide customer feedback in ways that many can identify with. However, they are also prone to a number of problems, not the least of which is social desirability bias (for further problems see Brand Aside 4.4). Also, many great brand ideas, such as Dior's J'adore fragrance, got mixed reviews in focus groups, while they have often been criticized for killing innovations because participants can only really comment on what they know and often reject things that make them uncomfortable. When faced with the success of the Sony Walkman (a cassette-based ancestor of an mP3 player) competitors sought insight from consumers on what they desired. Many pointed out that they hated the sound of taped music and preferred records but couldn't carry them with them. The resulting innovation was the Soundburger, a portable record player that destroyed records, sounded terrible, and looked ridiculous (Beverland 2010). Surprisingly it enjoyed a hipster-led revival three decades later, sold in Urban Outfitters in 2010. Although focus groups are useful in the context of brand extension (non-verbal responses are useful for assessing brand extension "fit"—see Chapter 7), complementing tracking data, and for judging incremental innovations or advertising copy, they are not that useful for generating or assessing brand associations.
2. Depth interviews: Depth interviews have formed the basis for much of our understanding of consumer–brand relationships, consumer self-authentication, brand

authenticity, experiential consumption, and cultural branding (among many others). Susan Fournier's seminal consumer–brand relationships article was based on three depth interviews (in which she and her interviewees explored over 120 different types of brand relationships). The key benefit of this form of research lies in the name—depth. You can explore an enormous amount of detail with customers. However, the trade-off is breadth (i.e., you cannot interview many people). They also require a skilled interviewer and careful analysis. For this reason, depth interviews tend to be avoided for understanding or generating brand associations, usually in favor of projective techniques (see below).

3. Ethnography: Derived from anthropology and often called "participant observation," this form of research has become extremely popular in recent years with many brands such as Intel, IBM, Microsoft, and well-known design studio IDEO using these techniques. Basically, trained ethnographers immerse themselves in the world of the consumer in order to identify new insights, key relationships, dynamics underpinning behavior, and the nature of the consumers' lived experience, as detailed in Brand Aside 4.5. Ethnography has many other uses, which will be touched on in later chapters. Harley Davidson was literally reinvented using these techniques when two academics bought bikes and drove around America for months in an attempt to understand what connected consumers to the brand (in three words, "America," "Freedom," and "Masculinity"). This study was the first to identify subcultures of consumption.

BRAND ASIDE 4.5

I'm Not a Fish!

This is a classic saying in anthropology. Basically it identifies how difficult it is to create value for others when we are unable to see things from their perspective (the link to fish refers to failed designs aiming at enabling salmon to return to their historic spawning grounds following the damming of river pathways). Without being able to empathize, or place ourselves in someone else's shoes, it is easy to fail in branding. For example, the team behind Microsoft's Xbox failed to repeat their success with iPod competitor Zune because they had no empathy with music lovers (but lots with gamers). The generous employee discounts provided by the Big Three US automakers (Chrysler, Ford, and General Motors) meant their CEOs were immersed in a local economy (Detroit) where their auto brands dominated the roads. In contrast, national sales data demonstrated how far removed from reality their claim that "Americans love American cars" was. Had they spent time in San Francisco, New York, or Los Angeles, they would have gained vital insights that would have seen them invest in small car production (Patnaik 2009).

In contrast, toy maker Playmobil's success is based on a deep understanding of how children view the world. The iconic figures, designed by the late Hans Beck, were a product of spending time watching children play. Beck noted that children were desperate to grow up while adults were keen for them to remain innocent. However, no toymaker (in post-World War II West Germany) provided solutions that addressed both needs. Beck knew there was no point in asking young children for insights into their latent needs, but noted that children were constantly frustrated by the lack of human figures to go with their toy machines, trucks, planes, and so on, so he made the decision to fill this gap. He then noted that when children draw people, they draw them in highly stylized ways, with skinny legs, long bodies, big heads, smiling faces, eyes, and no nose. As a result, the famous Playmobil figure was born. At the time of Beck's death in 2009, over 4 billion figures had been sold worldwide. Beck had become the fish (Beverland 2009).

Ethnography's strength lies in the nature of the data gained—it is naturalistic in so much as it describes the world as it happens. This strength is also a weakness, in that results are unpredictable and often reliant on critical incidences that are also difficult to predict or interpret. Brand managers can gain much by using ethnography. Intel for example has an ethnographic unit that provides insights into the analog–digital divide, which is extremely useful when it comes to developing customer-focused breakthrough innovations. The limitations of the method, however, mean that it is often not used for assessing brand associations, particularly since the emergence of big data and netnography. Nonetheless, the method is essential for understanding how and why consumers relate to the brand and the impact of the wider sociocultural context on customers and is therefore essential for co-creating brand meaning. Ethnography is also a powerful means to help employees empathize with customers, overcoming the limitations of traditional marketing research tools and leading to enhanced innovations (Cayla et al. 2014). Below I will explore some ways firms use ethnographic techniques to maintain brand relevance and generate new brand meanings.

4. Netnography: Netnography is relatively new and was developed by communications technology expert Robert Kozinets (2009), who is a leader in understanding consumer tribes and other forms of communal consumption such as subcultures. In essence, this is the virtual version of ethnography and offers many advantages to brand managers. First, the sheer size of many online communities following the rise of social media often means one can access vast amounts of data (it is truly a form of "big data".). Second, since these data are relatively permanent, one does not need to wait for something to happen, one can check the communal history. Third, this form of research can often identify network effects, and therefore is

useful for understanding the impact of influencers and pop culture on brands. Fourth, it has many of the benefits of ethnography without the need for extensive fieldwork, making it more time/cost-effective.

5. Observational methods: Although ethnography and netnography are also observational, they usually do so from the point of view of an insider. However, there are many other forms of observation. In his bestselling book *The Science of Shopping*, retail expert Paco Underhill (2000) used in-store video cameras to uncover new insights for the customer experience. For example, he identified that consumers take time to adjust to the new environment of the store, and so any stock placed in the entrance was technically invisible. Marketing professor Mark Ritson (with Laknath Jayasinghe 2013) has used videos in the home to identify how people engage with brand advertisements, offering insights into the power or otherwise of conscious brand claims (his work, along with that of Robert Heath, 2012), and suggests subtle "low-level" messaging or indirect appeals are more effective precisely because they put us at ease and lower our defenses against marketing messages). These techniques are very useful for customer experience design and services branding.

6. Projective techniques: Projective techniques are particularly useful for identifying and assessing brand associations. Unlike focus groups and depth interviews they do not ask consumers to do the impossible (verbalize unconscious thoughts or latent needs), they are relatively easy to use and interpret, and can generate insights quickly. Although they cannot generate insights into linking value in the way ethnography and netnography can, or identify interesting "a-ha moments" (unexpected observations that illuminate the nature of a consumer-brand relationship), they are essential in understanding brand image. So how do they work?

   Basically a researcher asks a customer to project their thoughts onto a host object and then explores those responses. You're probably familiar with the simplest of these:

   "If your brand was an animal what kind of animal would it be and why?"

   "If your brand was a make of car, what kind would it be and why?"

   "If your brand was a celebrity, who would it be and why?"

The advantage of these tools is the host provides a metaphorical lens from which to explore the brand. In contrast, if you asked "Why do you like this brand?" the answers are much harder. Or "What does 'freedom' mean to you?" Brand relationships and associations like freedom are often deeply embedded in our minds so being put on the spot and asked to discuss them consciously is hard. Typically, when your lecturer asks you "Why do you like Apple?" (most students use Apple), the answer usually takes the form, "Um, I dunno, the design I guess … it's easy to use." These are obvious insights and don't tell us much beyond what the brand's advertising has already communicated. Projective techniques get around this.

One widely used form of projective techniques in branding research is ZMET or the Zaltman Metaphor Elicitation Technique. Designed by Harvard professor Gerald Zaltman (2003), this technique is used by him and his brand consultancy Olson Zaltman to generate brand associations, understand consumers' relationship with brands, and identify a personality profile for a brand, celebrity, or team. How does it work? Consumers are asked to generate images (photographs) or collages and this then forms the basis for an interview with an expert who listens carefully for metaphors, symbolic language, and personal stories that help uncover deep meanings. Constant comparison of images is also a hallmark of ZMET. For example, one study employing this technique examined the nature of brand authenticity, asking consumers to compare three self-generated images that were real and three that were fake (Beverland and Farrelly 2010). Through multiple rounds of comparison, a new process for authenticating brands was identified. An amusing but nonetheless commercial example of ZMET is used in Morgan Spurlock's (of *Super Size Me* fame) documentary about product placement, *POM Wonderful Presents the Greatest Movie Ever Sold* (2012). In this movie Spurlock is struggling to find sponsors for his film, and seeks help from Olsen Zaltman to uncover his brand personality ("mindful, playful") and then identify similar brands that would best fit with his identity (including pomegranate juice maker POM Wonderful). The clip can be viewed at TED Talks.

This type of approach was used by Fiat's brand team who wanted to understand how consumers' viewed the four core ideas underpinning the Italian car brand: easy, joyful, spirited, and innovative. These ideas were used to help refresh Fiat's image with consumers, prior to the launch of their bestseller the retro-styled Fiat 500. More details on Fiat's turnaround are provided at the end of this chapter. After a comprehensive historical study into the brand combined with consumers' insights from loyalists, the brand team believed they could rebuild the brand around these four core values. However, what did they mean to users? They asked target customers to generate images for each and then used these as the basis for an interview. In so doing, they were able to uncover measurable and actionable brand associations; for example, "easy" stood for straightforward, functional, and informal. These ideas then formed the basis of a new brand campaign aimed at changing users' relationship with their cars.

As with measuring brand awareness, the techniques identified here also apply to understanding employer brand equity (or for places and people); the only differences are the target market and content of the questions.

Quantitative Approaches

Once you have collected your qualitative data, the next step is to measure these associations quantitatively. This step is crucial as you would wish to ensure that what was identified by necessity from small samples applies more widely across your target market. How is this done? The data generated from your projective techniques (or other qualitative approaches) form the basis of your measures. So, drawing on the ethnography of the Harley Davidson community, the brand team would take the values of "American," "Freedom," and "Masculinity" and measure the extent to which the target market agreed with them on 5 or 7 point Likert Scales. They would then compare Harley Davidson with other brands within the target user's consideration set (in this case large engine road bikes) on these features. What one would like to see would be that these three associations clustered around the Harley Davidson brand (i.e., they were unique or most closely associated with this brand). Likewise, Fiat would do the same on their four values and track their performance on these over time (see Tracking below).

With this step, five conditions must be met:

1. Qualitatively generated themes must be measured using Likert scales (e.g., to what extent do you agree Fiat is "Innovative," 1 = strongly disagree, 5 = strongly agree?).
2. Robust statistical data must be collected.
3. An awareness test must be conducted. Survey respondents must have heard of the brand and be in the target market.
4. The brand must be compared with other competitor brands on these key associations.
5. Demographic data should also be collected to inform brand-driven marketing (e.g., if the majority of your customers are women under a certain age, this will impact on your messaging, product design, service strategy, and channels).

Data from these studies can be presented in many different forms, including perceptual maps, or other graphical forms. Regardless of type, they should meet the requirements listed above.

One example of these perceptual maps was used by the Victoria Tourism Board (in the southeast corner of Australia). Tourism Victoria was focused on attracting domestic in-bound tourists to their capital, Melbourne. After conducting extensive qualitative research identifying what such tourists desired from their holiday experience and how they viewed each state, they then conducted a quantitative study. The results were used to identify what associations Victoria had, what associations their competitors had, and ultimately associations such as "mysterious" that no one owned, but the market desired. Given Melbourne's positioning, the tourism marketing team also knew they could stretch the destination brand to include "mysterious" without undermining their core associations. The resulting campaign was called "It's easy to lose yourself in Melbourne" and emphasized the city's laneways and the culture of locating cool businesses behind unmarked closed doors.

Another type of geographical map was used when attracting visitors to the city of Bath, in the southwest of England. This author was involved in attempting to focus the city's branding strategy and drew upon the ArkLeisure segmentation categories (developed by Arkenford) used by Visit Britain. These segments identify what each customer seeks from their destination (the colored areas—purple and blue) and how each city rates on these features (the dark black lines within the colored areas).

For the style-hound segment, many of Bath's features do not add value, and they are probably better served by "edgier" destinations such as Bristol or Manchester. In contrast, Bath can deliver to the cosmopolitan segment, but needs to raise its game in relation to performance or communication in each. Competitor city data from Chester, Oxford, and Windsor were included but removed to aid clarity. The resulting themes focused on Bath's strengths, emphasizing "style, elegance, and pleasure," "wellbeing," and "living history," and drove a new marketing campaign that increased visitor numbers.

Brand Tracking

The final step in measuring associations is called brand tracking. In essence brand tracking is a longitudinal study of how the brand is performing against its core associations. For example, Fiat's four values of easy, joyful, spirited, and innovative would be measured against other brands within the category (low priced vehicles) as per the methods above. Tracking then involves conducting the same study annually with a customer panel to ensure the brand is increasingly being associated with these four values, maintaining ownership of these values, and/or increasing its lead over competitors. Tracking is vital for many reasons.

1. It enables you to assess whether your marketing programs are achieving their objectives.
2. It provides you with evidence of the brand's expertise.
3. If you decline on a core feature tracking represents an early warning that something is wrong (perhaps a competitor has emerged that outperforms you, or perhaps poor product quality is undermining your credibility).
4. As identified in Brand Aside 4.3, points of difference can become points of parity and therefore no longer serve to differentiate the brand. Tracking provides a signal that this is happening; performance gaps between competitors and your brand on points of difference begin to close.

Tracking Customers' Use of the Brand

The approach outlined above—projective techniques followed by quantitative measures followed by **brand tracking**—reflects how marketers assess customer-based brand equity. What does this mean? In essence, this approach seeks to measure the extent to which target customers understand and agree with the marketer-generated brand identity. There is nothing wrong with this, as marketers do represent one author of brand meaning. Measures such as the Brand Asset Valuator also identify that having a clear and consistent identity is critical for brand stature and therefore brand health.

Likewise, various forms of financial valuation also identify the importance of a clearly defined position and reinforcement of it over time.

Co-creating brand meaning, however, requires that we move beyond simply identifying, measuring, and tracking whether consumers see what we want them to see in the brand. Although consumers may rate brands such as Fiat high on their values, these outcomes are sometimes a function of the way in which questions are asked and may not therefore truly reflect how customers see the brand. Also, reliance on such techniques may blind the marketers to emerging threats through technological changes that render your business obsolete. Music retailer HMV, for example, still championed their last remaining high street presence as a core point of difference despite the emergence of streaming services such as Spotify and Netflix that undermined their business model. One may also miss out on opportunities that emerge from unexpected consumer brand use, new brand communities and tribes, and adoption by influencers and pop culture. New measures have been developed to measure brand equity that reflect a more customer-centric model of associations, while other techniques are employed to identify how the brand is viewed within consumer social networks, by influencers, and within popular culture.

Customer-focused Measures of Brand Meaning

Burberry has long played on its British heritage. Perhaps unsurprisingly the famous Burberry check was adopted by lower socioeconomic groups within the UK (often identified with the discriminatory term "chavs") as a mark of tribal identity, an anti-authoritarian statement, and as a means to demonstrate economic status (in this case that one was not poor). The brand's check cap became a favored item among this group, clashing with the marketing team's preferred image and resulting in parodies of the check and the check being banned in London nightclubs. Burberry's team had not planned this, but this adoption affected how loyal brand users in the UK viewed the brand, necessitating a temporary shift to more understated use of the check and removal of the cap from sale.

The customer-based branding approach privileges one source of brand meaning—the marketer. However, if one looks at the brand pyramid, beyond the two base layers that the marketer largely shapes (need identification and brand identity), customer-based brand equity is a function of how consumers see the brand. At the peak of the pyramid is how consumers frame their relationship with the brand. To understand this and other aspects of how and why customers view the brand as they do, we need different tools. With the emergence of co-creation approaches to brand meaning, new measures have been developed to try and understand brand image and track real time conversations about the brand and whether these conversations are positive or negative (sentiment analysis). Three of these are listed below.

Consumer Engagement

Consumer engagement is the bond between consumers and the brand and is an attempt to measure the effectiveness of co-creation efforts on the part of the marketer. This is based on interaction, shared values, experiences, and rewards (Borel and Christodoulides 2016). Engagement consists of cognitive, emotional and behavioral components:

1. Cognitive: Does the brand, brand community, marketing material, and/or other branded content engage the consumer intellectually? This form of engagement primarily assesses whether consumers will engage in mental effort to learn more about the brand and/or the value proposition at its heart. For example, Apple runs in-store "expert sessions" whereby staff give interactive lectures on various tools available on the brand's computers. Apple knows that the more consumers understand about the various capabilities of their computers and software, the more likely they will buy packages, upgrade software and hardware, and advocate for the brand. They are also less likely to consider alternatives, a critical buffer for a brand priced much higher than others in the category.

2. Emotional engagement: This refers to how the brand makes us feel. Within reason, if we are more positively disposed emotionally toward the brand we are likely to value it more highly, and therefore have a stronger relationship with it. Brand communities, corporate social responsibility, sponsorship activities, anthropomorphic design (automotive brands such as MINI use this type of design to great effect), service recovery, flash-mobs, and authentic marketing strategies (i.e., tactics that demonstrate we intuitively get the customer) may all help enhance brand trust and perceptions of brand sincerity. As a result, we are therefore unlikely to drop the brand and may forgive some failures. The flipside of this is that excessive levels of emotional engagement may have a negative impact on the brand, something that will be examined in Chapter 12.

3. Behavioral engagement: The third part of engagement focuses on behavior and, in particular, willingness to engage in user-generated interactions (Borel and Christodoulides 2016). Returning to the Jeep example above, the willingness of expert users to help out new users is an example of behavioral engagement. Other activities may involve leaving positive reviews on TripAdvisor and other ratings sites (and from the viewpoint of these sites, reviewing per se is behavioral engagement), defending the brand against online attacks or criticism, providing word of mouth recommendations, and active participation in communal events. Retro film photography brand Lomography attempts to build brand loyalty with its communal sites. Much of its focus is on behavioral engagement, encouraging consumers to upload their photos, comment on others' attempts, and provide insights into using particular films. The result of one set of user posts dedicated

to using Kodak's retired Aerochrome color infrared film resulted in Lomography being able to crowdsource a branded replacement, Lomography Purple. Similarly the LEGO case in Chapter 1 and the "How do you love your Vegemite?" campaign in Chapter 2 provide examples of behavioral engagement.

Later chapters will examine how all forms of engagement can be encouraged; however, common measures are listed below:

1. Cognitive engagement: clicking on links, viewing photos, blogs, or YouTube advertisements.
2. Emotional engagement: providing positive comments on posts, positive sentiment toward the brand, rating brands at 9–10 on net promoter scores (see Brand Aside 4.6 for details). The common measure for this is brand sentiment, which largely tracks the content of brand-related conversations. Figure 4.4 provides an example for the Burberry brand, identifying how people discuss the brand online in terms of the most popular topics (the largest words), sentiment (look at the various words), and things discussed together (those words that are closer to one another).

BRAND ASIDE 4.6

What's in a Number? Net Promoter Scores

Walk into a branch of UK high street bank Lloyds and it's likely you'll be invited to provide some feedback on your encounter. The exercise will consist of asking you to rate the encounter as "other" or "9" or "10" (out of 10). These are known as net promoter scores (NPS). Popular UK marketing columnist Mark Ritson is a big fan of net promoter scores, arguing that one simple metric is a good indicator of your brand's health. In essence the net promoter score exercise asks you "How willing would you be to recommend this brand to a friend?" on a 1–10 scale. If you rate the 9–10 you are an advocate. If you rate the brand 0–6 you are a detractor. If you rate the brand 7–8 you are largely satisfied, but not motivated enough to recommend the brand. Your NPS is simply the percentage of advocates minus the percentage of detractors (the range is −100 to +100, with above zero considered good and 50+ excellent). Why does all this matter? Fred Reichheld's (2003) research identified that this question was strongly correlated (89 percent) with firm growth. The approach is not without its critics and academics have disputed the usefulness of this measure to explain growth. Nonetheless, it is widely used within the industry and is something worth adding to your measurement repertoire (more as a tool to stimulate questions than provide answers).

Figure 4.4

3. Behavioral engagement: providing advice to other users, defending the brand against attacks, following a brand, sharing branded material on social media platforms, helping service staff recover a service failure, hashtagging the brand in conversations (#LEGO), word-of-mouth referrals, and offering ideas to help the brand innovate such as producer communities that underpin brands such as Linux.

(*Source*: Borel and Christodoulides 2016, p. 259)

To examine brand engagement, marketers often measure the customer–brand experience, since a positive experience is believed to encourage all three aspects of engagement. Research reveals that for experiences to be positive they must be consistent with the brand's position (covered in Chapter 5) and stimulate the senses, induce emotions, create a physical impression, and trigger curiosity (Brakus et al., 2009). Such measures also overlap with those of perceived brand authenticity below.

Brand Authenticity

Measures of how authentic the brand is are critical given the importance of self-authentication to users and **brand authenticity** to marketers. One measure of this involves brand–self connection. This is typically measured by asking consumers to assess whether they consider the brand to be part of who they are and how personally connected they are to the brand (Park et al. 2010). Other ways of doing this also include deploying big data techniques to identify whether consumers use the brand to project their image, either as part of a brand public or to project a desired image. One can do this using hashtag analysis and other web-based tools such as IBM Cobra (used by the team at Vegemite) to identify how consumers use the brand on social media, or through tools such as Brandwatch® (www.brandwatch.com) that helps track brand mentions and also identifies consumer–brand images such as selfies that may provide insight into how consumers are assembling the self through brands (Rokka and Canniford 2016).

There are also formal scales for assessing a brand's perceived authenticity. Studies identify that perceived brand authenticity is positively related to emotional brand engagement (including trust) and also helps drive behavioral engagement such as word-of-mouth support, preparedness to buy, and pay (Beverland 2009; Morhart et al. 2015; Napoli et al. 2014). When measuring the authenticity of a brand, one assesses the brand on the basis of:

1. Continuity: Does the brand have a history (both a sense of history and a sense of having survived), seem timeless, and above short-term trends?
2. Credibility: Is the brand honest? Does the brand deliver on its promises? Do you sense the brand will not betray you?
3. Integrity: Does the brand care about its users, does it give back to the consumers, and does the brand have a sense of moral purpose (and does it live up to that purpose)?
4. Symbolism: Does the brand add meaning to my life, does it connect to my sense of self, help me connect to important things, and reflect important social values?

(*Source*: Morhart et al. 2015, p. 213)

Customers, Influencers, Popular Culture, and Brand Meanings

Figure 3.3 identifies how customers, influencers, and popular culture provide sources of meaning for the brand, some of which may reinforce the intended identity and some that may conflict with what marketers intended. Recent research has begun to identify sources of information and tools that may help marketers to identify how these other authors see and use the brand, in order to leverage these insights for co-creation and, if necessary, preempt a backlash against the brand. These insights can be qualitative and quantitative and increasingly may take the form of images, videos, and other non-text-related material such as "likes" and "shares." Advances in technology have enabled all these sources to be aggregated into large datasets, while the Internet of Things (see Table 4.2) means that customers' preferences, behaviors, and emotions, influencer reviews and impact, and the appearance of the brand in popular culture, can be tracked and potentially influenced in real time. This is called big data and is covered below.

Another, albeit complementary approach, seeks to track how the brand is viewed socioculturally by examining how fringe ideas can influence how the brand is seen and even diffuse more widely, ultimately providing the basis for new sources of brand meaning or, if unmanaged, undermine perceptions of brand authenticity. These tools are useful for building and managing brands and avoiding and responding to brand crises, and will be explored in more detail in relevant chapters. Nevertheless, they are introduced here as they are relevant for tracking unintended but highly relevant brand associations and drivers of those associations.

Big Data: Opportunities and Pitfalls

Science fiction is often a good predictor of the future. One of the many chilling episodes in George Orwell's *1984* occurs during a mass, televised, compulsory exercise program (similar to an exercise DVD or download). The protagonist, Winston Smith, is suddenly berated on-screen for not being fully engaged in the exercises that all citizens of Air Strip One must undertake. The instructor literally stops, speaks directly to him, and then takes time out to ensure Smith understands how to exercise like a model citizen. *1984* was of course written in 1948 when this form of individual tracking was truly the stuff of fiction. However, the movie *Minority Report* was closer to the mark when Tom Cruise is offered a variety of individualized offers from digital avatars as he passes by each store in a large shopping mall. These offers are customized to his needs personally, based on his stored profile and technology that identified him accurately through an iris scan (both of which are no longer fiction today).

Users of Amazon will be familiar with the "Your Recommendations" feature. These recommendations are based on an algorithm that matches your purchases with those of others buying the same item. Let's say, like me, you enjoyed Netflix's *Stranger Things* series. If you're an obsessed electronic music fan you may decide to buy the soundtrack by Austin band Survive at Amazon. Immediately you'll be recommended a large number of similar items, including old-school electronic classics from artists including Jean-Michel Jarre and Vangelis, which may in turn trigger further recommendations to pioneering bands such as The Human League and Kraftwerk, as well as many classic eighties acts. This is much harder if you go shopping at a bricks and mortar retail store where you may at best be reliant on the willingness, knowledge, and passion of the owner or clerk.

Those with social media pages will be familiar with this type of feature too, albeit in a different form. You will find stories, pages, and advertisements for products being suggested to you, all of which may fit with your lifestyle. How do Facebook, Google, Twitter, Bandcamp, and others know what to suggest? The answer is **big data**: "Big Data takes the form of messages, updates, and images posted to social networks; readings from sensors; GPS signals from cell phones, and more" (McAfee and Brynjolfsson 2012, p. 5). Gathering data about customers used to be cumbersome, costly, prone to error, and historical. This changed with the Internet, social media platforms, and web-based businesses. Big data allow firms to collect real-time customer data regarding behavior and use this to improve message and offer targeting, identify brand publics, test hypotheses about behavior, and more accurately predict and manage demand. Big data reflect a decision to use the vast amount and variety of consumer data in order to make better, quicker decisions.

The promise of big data is often framed in terms of making data-driven (and therefore "better") decisions. For those familiar with the baseball movie *Moneyball* (starring Brad Pitt), the film focused on the decision of the manager of a financially poor team (the Oakland A's) to shift player investment practices.

Historically, baseball talent scouts (often former players) would evaluate future players based on beliefs about the right physique, compliance with established beliefs about the correct technique, and other very subjective factors that had come to be treated as unquestioned facts. This often led to an expensive system of intense competition for talent coupled with the need to write off such investments when the new player did not perform as expected (which was quite common). Such a system obviously favored larger, wealthier teams such as the New York Yankees who could afford to pay high prices to secure raw talent.

The Oakland A's instead engaged in data-driven recruitment, picking unorthodox players that had a track record of performing on key statistics such as strike-outs,

Table 4.2   Big Data: Terms and tools relevant to brand management

Term/Tool	Definition
Ambient intelligence	Electronic devices that recognize and respond to human presence, and are personalized to human needs and anticipate human behavior.
Behavioral analytics	Using data captured online to analyse the behavior of apps and game users and online shoppers.
Cookie	Small computer file that stores data about internet users' behavior when they visit a website. The information is used to track consumer activity and build profiles.
Data aggregation	The sourcing, gathering, and summarizing of data from various sources into a format that is useful for businesses.
Data mining	Analyzing data, discovering patterns, and summarizing these into accessible information with a practical application.
Internet of Things (IoT)	A connected network of "things" made by attaching a unique IP address to all kinds of items. This will allow everything to communicate remotely.
Omni-channel	A retail approach that pulls together a brand's online and bricks-and-mortar shopping experience to engage consumers across all platforms.
Personal data economy	A model that recognizes personal data is an asset and encourages a trust-based balance between businesses and consumers to regulate how those data are used.
Real-time analytics	Continuous updates on website activity that allow the site owner to monitor hits and interaction as they happen.

Source: Saw (2015, pp. 28–29).

getting to first base, hitting the ball, and so on, but were subsequently ignored by talent scouts. Such players were cheap, and when put together formed a remarkable team that almost won the Major League title. This data-driven innovation changed the industry although eventually larger wealthier teams were able to gain all the benefits as they recruited statisticians and were able to identify high-performing, relatively underpaid players.

From a brand equity perspective, big data have the potential to offer insights into the value of common consumer sentiment measures such as Facebook "Likes" or perhaps scale the various emojis now used to indicate varying degrees of passion for and against posts and Google search information (Hayashi 2014, p. 39).

Big data rely on technological tools such as Hadoop and MapReduce to examine structured and textual data (including selfies, Instagram posts, video materials, and so on). A breakdown of big data terms is provided in Table 4.2.

There are reasons to be cautious about the advantages of big data. Poorly considered use of such approaches has landed companies in hot water, leading to a consumer backlash and public relations disaster. One such case involved US retailer Target using predictive analytics to predict which customers were pregnant and then bombarding them with offers of goods (Hayashi 2014). Ethical challenges have also been raised about who owns consumer-generated data as well as concerns over privacy (Yap et al. 2011).

The other danger involves a classic marketing tension—the need to balance long-term brand equity building activities with short-term sales promotions. Why has this occurred? One of the core benefits of big data is the ability to offer targeted promotions and measure their effectiveness in real time. As a result, sales managers are now able to almost immediately identify performance measures of price promotions, in contrast to marketers who often struggle to show such returns on brand investments. The problem with promotions-based approaches, however, is that if handled poorly they can damage the brand's image, and ultimately dilute the brand's intended identity and image. Iconic news magazine *Time* destroyed its brand equity through aggressive price promotions that actually undermined the brand's credibility (Horst and Duboff 2015).

To overcome this, it's important to combine any price promotion with clear brand messages. Advertising research, for example, has identified how the dangers from price promotion can be overcome if the campaign involves core brand messages (Philip-Jones 1998). Others, however, note further words of caution, suggesting that price promotions often target loyal customers who would have purchased from you anyway, without the discount. Subway aims to overcome both problems by making sure its core messages and endorsers (such as Olympian Michael Phelps) are featured in big-data-driven price promotions and that campaigns aim to expand customers' range of preferred sandwiches as this enhances loyalty without driving down margins (Horst and Duboff 2015).

It's also important not to lose sight of individual consumers in discussions about big data, better targeting, and improved decision-making. Sponsored posts in personal

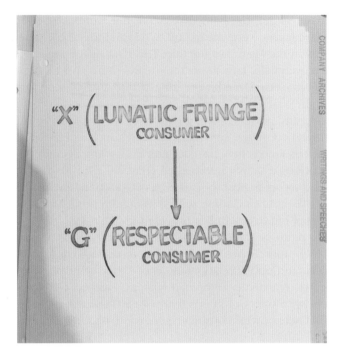

Figure 4.5   From X to G

Source: JWT Archives, Duke University, USA

Facebook feeds may be useful when marketers get things right, but they can easily backfire, resulting in wasted effort or even diminished affection for the social media brand selling rights to access. Advocates of big data often argue that the sheer size of a dataset will statically smooth out any individual errors, meaning that brand managers should worry less about getting it occasionally wrong because this will be trumped by the value of getting things right. Others are more empathetic toward customers. Domino's, for example, understands it is vital not to show specials for meat-based pizzas in the Facebook feed of vegans and vegetarians.

Monitoring the Fringe

In the 1970s advertising agency JWT creative staff attended a seminar by Lou Serrille entitled from "X to G" as part of their personal development (see Figure 4.5). The idea was simple; ideas that started on the fringe of mainstream society (at the time, feminism, black power, pornography, drug use) would eventually diffuse more widely and become accepted practice. In movie-rating parlance, what started as X-rated would eventually become acceptable for general admission. The point of this story was to encourage budding advertising creatives to "be aware" or monitor the fringe to identify potential new trends and use them before they had become mainstream.

Writers on the dangers of **doppelgänger brands** have used this same logic to manage brand backlash. Given the power and ubiquity of brands, writers on brand backlash have identified that activists may deliberately undermine central brand claims, de-authenticate market-placed myths, poke fun at brands, or provide alternate "copy" that reframes the brand's meaning in unintended ways (Arsel and Thompson 2011; Thompson et al. 2006). Organizations such as Greenpeace, culture jammers such as Adbusters and critics such as Naomi Klein (author of *No Logo*) have picked apart aspirational brand claims and found them wanting. YouTube is full of such parody ads, including the famous Hitler parodies using scenes from the award-winning 2004 film *Downfall*, as well as those made by individual consumers (check out "United Breaks Guitars" and Greenpeace's subversion of Volkswagen's *Stars Wars* campaign).

One common response to these parodies is that they do not involve target market consumers, and therefore they are not important. However, these anti-brand activities do represent a form of influence, cross over into popular culture, and through sharing and hashtagging shape the brand's image in the mind of your target users. Botox, for example, has suffered a constant backlash, all of which started at the fringe but quickly began to undermine the relationship users had with the brand (Giesler 2012). However, by actively monitoring brand hate websites, fringe criticisms and popular culture, the brand team has leveraged each of these criticisms to reframe the brand's image in a way that enabled consumers to continue to buy in to the message or place themselves in the enduring brand's narrative (self-authentication). As Giesler (2012) identified, in managing these criticisms the brand continued to increase its equity over time.

The lesson is simple, you might not like what your haters say about you, but you'd be wise to monitor them and be prepared for the X-rated to become general admission.

Chapter Summary

This chapter has focused on different ways of measuring brand equity. A variety of tools have been presented that provide insights into the strategic position of the brand, the extent to which the marketing for the brand is enhancing awareness and understanding, the brand's intended identity over time, and the generation and measuring and of brand associations. The important point to note is that all of these tools are useful, but none alone provides complete answers. Further tools and approaches were discussed that help understand how the customer perceives, uses, and relates to the brand. Quantitative measures of engagement, experience, and authenticity represent formal approaches to understanding the "what" and "why" of the brand relationship. Less structured approaches were also presented that provide more dynamic insights into what users and authors are doing with the brand and how these might provide new sources of brand innovation and potential tensions that could undermine the brand's perceived authenticity and identify new and unintended meanings for the brand.

Review Questions

1. Use Keller's Scorecard and identify a brand that scores well and one that scores poorly on each factor. Explain why for each.
2. Identify brands high on stature and strength; then identify brands high on one but not the other. Explain your choices.
3. Why is it important to use both qualitative and quantitative research on brand associations?
4. Using a projective tool or metaphor, interview someone on three brands within a category that they use and/or avoid.
5. Using the X to G metaphor in "Monitoring the Fringe," identify five issues that you believe are X-rated that will gain mainstream acceptance in the next two to three years. What does this mean for brands?

Case Example: The Rebirth of Fiat

The Fiat group (Fiat-Chrysler Automobiles) is currently enjoying a strong period of financial performance, with many of its brands including Maserati and Alfa Romeo enjoying revitalization, and in the case of Maserati, a return to its roots. Not so long ago, however, the venerable Italian automaker was in real trouble, needing to be bailed out by the Italian government. The Fiat brand of vehicles was also poorly regarded, and the equity of the brand a long way from where it is now, thanks to quality improvements and the re-launch of the award-winning, market-conquering 500. How did Fiat turn this situation around? The answer lies with using data to change users' relationships with their cars.

In the early 2000s the brand team faced a real challenge. Perceptions of poor quality and uninspiring design had led users to view their relationship with Fiat based solely on price. Table 4.3 provides details on the brand's perception. Qualitative data demonstrated that consumers saw the brand as offering value for money and so traded this off against perceptions of poor quality or tired design.

Table 4.3   Fiat image profile: Fiat vs. market average

	Italy	Germany	France	UK	Spain
Overall Image	−0.5	−1.0	−1.1	−1.4	−1.6
Price	−0.8	0.0	1.0	0.2	0.0
Running costs	1.0	0.3	0.2	0.1	−0.1
Safety	−0.7	−1.2	−1.0	−1.3	−1.2
Quality	−0.7	−1.4	−1.2	−1.5	−1.3
Innovation	−0.3	−0.8	−0.4	−0.9	−1.0

Source: author's notes.

This meant that people saw Fiat as a brand that satisfied and was good enough, but ultimately they aspired to something better,

However, the firm was also undergoing a transformation, with an emphasis on quality, design, and performance, and critically had a range of new models planned, including the re-launch of the classic 500, to follow BMW's lead with the revitalized MINI. However, the industry is beset with examples of great models, launched by poorly regarded brands that simply failed to generate sales, largely because they clashed with how users understood the brand. BMW found this with their acquisition of Rover—no matter how good the cars, it had been a long time since anyone believed Rover to be a luxury vehicle, and sales just never took off (BMW eventually sold the brand to a Chinese group). If the 500 were to conquer the world, the brand team needed to make users love the brand again, well before launch.

The team undertook research with users but also delved into the firm's history to understand what the brand could own in terms of core associations. The Fiat example earlier in the chapter provides the results: easy, joyful, spirited, and innovative. Together these were grouped under a new communications campaign entitled "Life in Primary Colors" to reflect the brand's roots and target users. The campaign was used first to support the brand's Palio range. Featuring a cyclist and increasingly irate owner of a Palio, the advertisement was fun and unexpected. At each set of traffic lights, the cyclist (wearing headphones) leans in on the Fiat to maintain balance. The owner, increasingly outraged that the cyclist is touching his precious car shouts and beeps his horn, all to no avail. At the third set of lights, the owner quickly reverses, ensuring the cyclist falls over. The advertisement conveys a simple message; Fiat is a brand worth caring about.

(Continued)

The next campaign involved the Fiat Doblo, a range of small vans and people movers. Featuring a bunch of surfers somewhere in the Caribbean and the famous Specials ska track "A Message to You, Rudy," the overall feeling is one of fun and also an emphasis on the ease of use, space, and functionality and versatility of the brand. The advertisement reminds users of the brand's strengths, but adds in a playful, fun element, once again aimed at shifting the consumer-brand relationship to a more emotional one. The advertisement features no speaking or words, other than the song, and finishes with the surfers laughing as they all sing "Rudy" in unison.

These campaigns were successful in shifting the brand relationship, and laid the groundwork for the re-launch of the 500. The 500 was launched in motor shows in bright colors, larger-than-life displays, and to great acclaim, reviving the fortunes of the company. Figure 4.6 provides an example. All of this was based on data-driven insights about how consumers saw the brand, how consumers saw the values of the brand, and how these could be communicated throughout the brand's marketing materials.

Figure 4.6   **Fiat Show Launch**

Case Questions

1. How did Fiat use data to reshape users' relationship with the brand?
2. Fiat chose four values to position the brand. Are these values authentic to the brand? Use web-based research to justify your answer.
3. The insights derived from various consumer studies were used to drive brand communications. Watch the advertisements mentioned in the case (from YouTube) and identify how these values are indicated to users.

Key Terms

Big data
Brand asset valuator (BaV)
Brand associations
Brand authenticity
Brand awareness

Brand health
Brand score card
Brand tracking
Consumer engagement
Doppelgänger brands

Financial valuation
Qualitative research
Quantitative research
Recall
Recognition
Top of mind

Further Reading

Cayla, Julien, Robin Beers, and Eric J. Arnould (2014), "Stories that Deliver Business Insights," *MIT Sloan Management Review*, 55(2), 55–62.

Horst, Peter and Robert Duboff (2015), "Don't Let Big Data Bury Your Brand," *Harvard Business Review*, November, 2–9.

Keller, Kevin Lane (2000), "The Brand Report Card," *Harvard Business Review*, Jan–Feb, 147–157.

Spurlock, Morgan (2013) "The greatest Ted talk ever sold," https://www.ted.com/talks/morgan_spurlock_the_greatest_ted_talk_ever_sold.

Zaltman, Gerald and Robie H. Coulter (1995), "Seeing the Voice of the Customer: Metaphor-Based Advertising Research," *Journal of Advertising Research*, 35(4), 35–51.

Part II
Co-creating Brand Meaning Over Time

5

THE BEGINNINGS—
NEW BRAND CO-CREATION

Building a profitable personal brand online is not a sprint, and something that happens overnight. Don't aim for perfection early on. Instead allow your brand to evolve naturally over time and focus on providing massive value and over deliver to your target audience. Then you will get more clear over your message and brand as well. Always remember that! (Navid Moazzez, Creator of Virtual Summit Mastery System https://navidmoazzez. com. Source: http://www.navidmoazzez.com/best-personal-branding-quotes/)

Learning Objectives

When you finish reading this chapter, you will be able to:

1. Understand the key decisions involved in developing a new brand
2. Understand and apply key tools and processes for developing a new brand
3. Understand the eight steps of brand building model and relate key tools to the first five steps
4. Create a brand's position using two different approaches (mindshare and cultural)
5. Apply a range of tools for uncovering underserved market needs
6. Develop brands that are new to the world or new to the firm

Introduction

To an artist or writer a blank sheet of paper (or screen) is full of possibilities and anxiety. Where should one start? How should one begin? What if we get it wrong? The same feeling confronts anyone starting a new brand—the possibilities seem endless, the anxiety is very real (especially if one's livelihood is at stake), and the concepts and ideas available seem so varied, contradictory, or dangerously obvious that it is difficult to know just where to begin.

The problem is compounded by the fact that many of the most powerful brands that feature in marketing folklore were rarely started as "brands." Instead, the founders behind brands such as Apple, BMW, Facebook, IBM, Louis Vuitton, and the World Wildlife Fund (among many others) were largely focused on following their interests, solving problems, mastering their craft, developing new technologies, or addressing unmet needs. Over time, the four brand authors often help co-create stories around the new product or service, eventually resulting in shared taken-for-granted meanings or what Holt (2003) calls "brand cultures."

These cultures represent shared brand myths and eventually can be used to define the meaning of the brand. For example, iconic English sports-car manufacturer the Morgan Motor Company only formalized its brand strategy in 2004, almost one hundred years after its founding. Its new identity, "Driven at Heart", was reflective of users' relationships with their vehicles (they rarely sell their cars), the global communities or drivers clubs that formed around the brand, the passion of the Morgan family, and their commitment to tradition in spite of sustained criticism from so-called experts (Beverland 2009). The brand's identity was already co-created through the stories told by the four authors. As a result, choosing a formal brand position was relatively easy. However, not every brand takes as long as Morgan to define its position.

Although brands continue to emerge in this fashion (Innocent and Netflix are examples), budding entrepreneurs will struggle to gain venture capital financing, investor interest, and listings in traditional and online retail if they are unable to answer key brand-related questions such as "Who is the target market?", "What need is being served?", "What does you brand stand for?", and "What is your point of difference?" For charities, service providers, tourist destinations, and even sellers of ingredient products, answering similar questions is crucial to ensuring support from other business partners, potential sponsors, and making the best use of scarce resources invested in the marketing mix. Influencers too will want answers to these questions, especially given the sheer volume of unsolicited material they receive to review, feature, and endorse (see the discussion of ZMET and Morgan Spurlock's brand personality in Chapter 4).

This chapter examines the various approaches to building a brand from scratch. Central to building a new brand is the issue of positioning. Positioning is an attempt to define the essence or identity of the brand. Although this may seem at odds with co-creating brand meaning, it is important to remember that a brand needs to be created before it can be offered to customers, and before customers can frame it in relational terms. Also, there is significant direct and indirect customer input into the positioning process, regardless of whether one uses the mindshare model or cultural approach covered in this chapter.

Before we begin, however, it is worth clarifying what is meant by a "new brand."

"New to World" vs. "New to Firm"

This chapter focuses on co-creating a new brand. Defining when a brand is new depends on understanding the difference between reputation and brand management. For example, branding is still relatively new in the business-to-business realm. However, these firms often enjoy very long-term customer relationships, often spanning over a decade (Ford and et al. 2002). In branding parlance, these firms have loyal customers, and therefore brand equity. Assuming these customers have a choice, they must see something of value in the firm to continue engaging with it. This is "reputation," and it is something largely given to the firm rather than created and actively managed, like a brand.

Brand-new firms by definition have no reputation (leaving aside the reputation of their founder(s)). However, the brand-development process is much the same for both types of firms. The first firm, with many decades of experience and customer support, can leverage these to help clarify its position (such as the Morgan Motor Company example earlier), while the brand new firm has neither the advantage of a positive reputation nor the baggage that comes with loyal supporters and a product or service culture with the four authors. Unless noted otherwise, this chapter will treat both situations as new because both organizations are adopting a new way of managing (for brand equity) for the first time.

The Eight Steps of Brand Building

This section sets out a broad eight-step process for building a brand. Think of these steps in the following way:

1. Steps 1–3: Building Internal Support for Branding
2. Steps 4–5: Building Brand Foundations
3. Steps 6–8: Brand Launch and Assessment

The logic of this process and each of the steps will be outlined, before I explore those that require more detail and attention in this chapter (steps 1-5) and the next (steps 6-7: 8 was covered in Chapter 4). What should you know about this process (apart from the fact that there are eight steps)? First, that the steps are cumulative. That is, you must

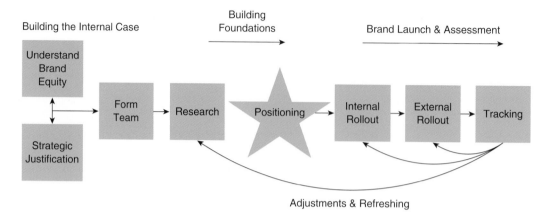

Figure 5.1   8 Steps of Brand Building

Source: Author's notes

go through each of them if you are able to build and sustain a brand. Skipping steps is not an option, nor is starting in the wrong place. Second, the highlighting of positioning is deliberate. Although each step is essential, positioning takes center stage. The first four steps provide the basis for positioning (in different ways); positioning then drives the last three steps. Third, note that external communication comes relatively late in the process. There is a reason for this—brands are always built from the inside out.

Let's break down the steps in a little more detail. The first step involves Understanding Brand Equity. What does this mean? Although it may surprise you, brands are not always useful strategic tools. In some industries, or some competitive contexts, branding cannot deliver value in terms of improved margins. Chapters 3 and 4 identified that brand equity at its simplest is simply the difference in price between a branded offer and its commodity counterpart. It is vital that you understand this otherwise you can spend a vast amount of money for no return. Likewise, focusing on whether brand equity is achievable ensures you can start focusing on just how to co-create value, and understand that the choices you make will drive all aspects of the business's operations.

For example, in 2011 the owners of Shoreditch-based (UK) custom bicycle manufacturer 14BikeCo sought my advice around branding. At the time the firm had built up a cult following for its custom-made fixed gear (or "fixies") cycles and in the sport of bike polo. The firm had a retail operation in the Truman Brewery Building in East London, their own fashion line, and a small web presence. In light of the recognition that the firm was receiving from its growing fan base, specialized cycling bloggers, and iconic firms such as Dunhill who featured the bikes in their catalogues, branding could clearly deliver value.

However, the biggest challenge would come from restraining the range of activities the owners were engaged in, the messages sent, and the product range. The owners loved making bikes and saw every request, no matter how far removed from their street credibility and origin, as a challenge. They had made road bikes, collapsible bikes, and even planned to launch a low-cost range for high-street retailers. These choices and the fashion range all took the focus away from their brand and its planned identity. Critically, the brand had less credibility in these categories and faced significant competition from other brands such as Giant, Brompton, and Rapha respectively (among many others). Although the team removed the fashion line, focusing on a brand-driven range was something at odds with their outlook, and eventually the firm was sold to a private investor who took the brand in a different direction.

Step 2 is justifying the brand program. In many ways this step (and step 3) is more critical in large firms than in small start-ups. However, thinking through the large range of benefits that a brand has is a useful exercise for start-up founders seeking investor support. What does this mean? Think back to Chapter 3, and all the ways in which brands benefit from different functions in the firm. It is vital you do this type of analysis but also ensure that you gain political support for branding from the people who matter. For a number of reasons, marketers are rarely the most influential people in an organization, and even the influence they have may be declining (Homburg et al. 2015). You will need the authority of your CEO to engage in such a large process (and maintain that momentum as you go through the period of building brand awareness and loyalty), the finance team to provide funds, the operations and human resources departments to ensure everything runs smoothly, and your sales team to make sure they stress your brand benefits.

Step 2 depends on the extent to which the firm has experience with branding. If the firm is entirely new to branding then, regardless of size and age, it is critical. For firms such as Unilever and Mars who introduce new brands all the time, the value of branding and the strategic case for them is largely taken for granted, and you can probably jump to Step 3. The same considerations apply to brand extensions which, although not technically a new brand, involve many of the same decisions covered in Figure 5.1. For first-time branders, this step is critical because you will rarely have data saying your current or desired customers want a brand. Loyal customers may list a whole range of performance features that you offer, may make mention of reputation, all of which can form part of a brand program, but will not necessarily justify the expense of one. Another reason will be that by focusing on all the benefits that your colleagues in other functions gain from branding, you will start to build or enhance working relations with those who are vital to delivering the brand (Beverland et al. 2016).

The third step is to build a team. If you've done Step 2 right, you will probably already have the senior-management team on board with your strategy. This step is often forgotten but it is vital that you reach out to others for support within an organization at an early stage. Why? Failing to do so can have dire consequences. In the 2000s a marketer at a large Australian utility decided to develop a brand campaign (under the tagline "We're excited by gas and electricity even if you're not") because she alone believed that branding was essential to the firm's ability to attract more customers. However, there were no points of differentiation in the market and almost no means of achieving them. The CEO and internal senior team remained skeptical but allowed the campaign to run for a while. When tracking data showed almost no positive results after two years, the senior team stopped the campaign.

So who should be on the team? Depending on the structure and size of your organization, you will want people with influence (including but not exclusively boardroom representation) and internal heroes. People of influence are much like the Mavens that Malcolm Gladwell discusses in his 2002 book *The Tipping Point*. Mavens know a lot of people and can connect you to new networks; in this case, they can help you cross functional boundaries internally. Internal heroes are synonymous with Gladwell's salespeople—staff who have the ability to communicate the benefits of branding in ways that make sense within functional areas (i.e., the finance person who can champion branding with other financiers). Coca-Cola, for example, developed an internal champions' program for their 2012 London Olympics sponsorship. The program was aimed at infusing the games' spirit throughout the firm and was typically staffed by people who loved sport and were highly respected in their functional areas (Farrelly et al. 2017).

In summary these first three steps are vital. Branding can involve significant upfront costs and requires ongoing financial support. Branding also forces everyone within the organization to think differently, by ensuring that what they do is driven by the brand. The first two steps ensure that the investment in time and money is likely to be recouped. Step 1 helps identify whether brand equity is possible and how much value might flow from it. Step 2 partly builds on this and helps frame branding as a return on investment issue rather than one of pure cost. The third step ensures internal buy-in and ongoing support for the brand program. It is only after these steps have been done that brand building becomes (for a while) the domain of the marketing department.

Step 4, Research, and Step 5, Positioning, are more involved and will form the focus of much of the chapter. Brands are based on customer needs, thus research is undertaken to understand the market, the customer, and their context, and to identify gaps that the nascent brand can serve. In the case of firms already in the marketplace (such as many B2B firms, 14BikeCo, and the Morgan Motor Company), research is also conducted with loyalists and the other brand authors (such as staff, influencers, and using some of the tools covered in Chapter 4 to understand how the firm is viewed in web-based conversations, for example) to identify any unique and enduring associations the potential brand has. Positioning, or Step 5, flows from this research. Positioning is simply the brand's identity or essence, or more formally:

> Brand positioning refers to the specific, intended meaning for a brand in consumers' [customers'] minds. More precisely, a brand's positioning articulates the goal that a consumer will achieve by using the brand and explains why it is superior to other means of accomplishing this goal. (Tybout and Sternthal 2005, p. 110)

Positioning defines the brand over time (and therefore should rarely change—see Holt's cultural branding model below for a counter view) and, as Figure 5.1 identifies, drives all marketing activities. Historically, positioning flows from an analysis of market segments and decisions regarding targeting (or the **segmentation–targeting–positioning** approach). However, there are competing views about how to understand target users and the nature of a brand's position. These will be explored in more detail in the discussion of mindshare and cultural branding later. However, in essence positioning involves providing users with compelling answers to the following three questions:

1. Who are you?
2. What do you do?
3. Why does it matter?

(*Source*: Neumeier 2005, p. 31)

Next we launch the brand, although in fact we do two launches (or more depending on the number of stakeholders). To budding marketers, Step 6 seems strangely out of place, but the order is essential. Since the brand represents a promise to the user, you must first ensure that everyone within the organization understands the brand and that a thorough brand audit has been conducted to ensure that users' experiences match the rhetoric. Essentially, to make the brand authentic to the user the organization behind it has to be rendered authentic. This is why we often say "brands are built from the inside out." It is also one of many reasons why organizations invest in employment branding. Chapter 6 will spend some time in identifying how this is done.

It is only after the organization is ready to deliver the brand position that one starts communicating externally. As identified in Chapters 3–4, awareness, knowledge, endorsement, and associations are all essential components of brand equity. At this stage, the brand strategies are engineered into the marketing mix including design, service, formal communications (advertising), public relations and corporate communications, channel management, innovation, and pricing and promotions. The term "engineering" implies that every marketing mix element will contain aspects of the brand's position and be aimed at enhancing or protecting brand equity (Holt 2003).

The eighth and final step, Tracking, has been covered in Chapter 4. In summary tracking is essential because it represents feedback from our users and helps guide future activities, and may require adjustments to the brand program or even further research to understand why points of difference are not being achieved or sustained. This may require refreshing the brand or even changing tack in a more radical way, along the lines of Holt's cultural brand model. Critically, it is also vital internally to demonstrate that the brand program is working as intended. Failing to do this step can have serious consequences. Returning to the utility example earlier, poor tracking results reinforced management views that consumers focused on price and that branding was an expense that could not be justified. Failing to engage in tracking can have disastrous consequences. Attempts by cooperatives to develop upmarket branded versions of their commodity products have come unstuck when commodity prices rose and members could not be convinced that branding was generating returns over and above the normal changes in demand and supply (Beverland 2007).

Positioning: Two Approaches

Although each of the eight steps is essential, the technical aspects of brand-related research, positioning, and internal launch warrant more attention. The external aspects of branding will feature more heavily throughout the rest of the text, while Tracking has been covered previously in Chapter 4. Steps 4–6 in effect create the brand and help render it authentic. Authenticity is achieved in research by identifying underlying user goals and needs. Authenticity is then achieved in positioning by ensuring the brand's identity is grounded in user goals and needs, ideology, competitor gaps, and firm capabilities. Finally, internal rollout or launch ensures the firm has done their utmost to ensure the user experience of it is authentic because it meets expectations shaped by the brand's marketing program.

Positioning is considered to be the most important decision made in relation to building a brand, although controversy surrounds how best to do so. There are two approaches to positioning in the literature. The mindshare model remains the most popular approach to positioning theory and practice, while the cultural approach is more recent, but based in recent advances in consumer research.

1. **Mindshare positioning**: this approach is derived from Ries and Trout's (1981) classic *Positioning: The Battle for Your Mind* and is used in the CBBE framework. As the term "mindshare" suggests, the brand is positioned in the mind of the customer, takes the form of quite abstract values, and is expressed externally via a USP or unique selling point, reinforced with taglines, slogans, personalities, tone of voice, experiences, and so on.

2. **Cultural positioning**: this approach is derived from Douglas Holt's (2004a) cultural branding framework that challenges the assumptions and strategies of the mindshare approach. Here the brand is positioned in relation to wider schisms or fractures in society (or in our terms the gap between an authenticating act and an authoritative performance) and is often expressed in terms of myths that enable consumers to make sense of their place in the world.

Although often seen as oppositional, we believe both approaches have value, if understood carefully. The mindshare approach is useful in ensuring consistency over time. As Holt has stated (in an interview in Heding et al. 2016, p. 263), mindshare-driven strategies are perfectly appropriate in an environment characterized by stability or incremental change. By way of contrast, the cultural approach is useful in ensuring relevance in terms of turbulence, and emphasizes tools and methods that focus on identifying and responding to wider cultural shifts that can render mindshare positions irrelevant, requiring radical change in the brand's stated position (Beverland et al. 2015).

Given this, I will examine both models in an extended presentation of how to define one's position. Both involve research (Step 4), though the focus is different. The mindshare model concentrates on individual users and their choices, while the cultural model focuses on consumers and the sociocultural context in which they struggle to balance authenticating acts and authoritative performances. Regardless of the model chosen, the sequence of steps in Figure 5.1 is broadly the same, as are the steps flowing from positioning in terms of internal and external rollout and tracking. In discussing both approaches to positioning, I will also weave back and forward between Research (Step 4) and Positioning (Step 5) as this reflects real world practice.

Positioning: Mindshare (Step 5)

> Positioning is identifying the real estate in a consumer's mind that the brand will and can own. (Wheeler 2003, p. 37)

The above quote, taken from a manager in global biomedical giant Cephalon (now Teva Pharmaceuticals), is typical of the mindshare approach to brand positioning. The term "positioning" is credited to marketing practitioners Al Ries and Jack Trout who wrote *Positioning: The Battle for Your Mind*. Released in 1981, this book is regarded as an industry standard and reflects how many practitioners and academics define a brand's position. Ries and Trout argued that a brand's position is equivalent to its foundation, upon which all its equity is subsequently built. In essence, the brand's position involves generating two to three abstract ideas or a mantra that balances customer needs, competitor gaps, and firm capability (Figure 5.2). Industry insiders such as Helen Edwards often use sporting metaphors like "the sweet spot" to describe the words that balance the three Cs of customer, competitor, and capability. How does this work?

Step 1: Engage in segmentation.

Step 2: Pick a target segment.

Step 3: Conduct research to identify the customer need or goal that the brand will serve. This is called the **frame of reference**.

Step 4: Use the frame of reference to define your competition and then analyze competitors to identify strengths and weaknesses. This process helps identify **points of difference**.

Step 5: Analyze your capabilities relative to the frame of reference being served. Typically this analysis provides the credibility for your brand and is often called the **reason to believe**.

Figure 5.2   Mind-Share Positioning

Source: author's notes

> Step 6: Identify two to three words or a short positioning statement that simultane-ously addresses the frame of reference, competitor gaps, and capabilities.

> Step 7: Engineer this position into all aspects of your marketing mix and operations.

Why do we seek a balance between customer needs, competitor gaps, and firm capa-bilities? The answer lies in understanding the three outcomes a brand must achieve:

1. Customer needs analysis ensures **brand relevance**.
2. Competitive gap analysis ensures **brand differentiation**.
3. Capabilities analysis ensures deliverability and authenticity.

Brands must achieve all three of these things simultaneously. Brands that lack rele-vance quickly fail. Brands that have relevance but no point of difference also fail, or must be better resourced, cheaper, and more accessible than competitors. Brands that have relevance but cannot deliver on their promise are seen as insincere or inauthen-tic. The three Cs exercise therefore seeks to build a brand position that balances all three of these considerations.

This process looks deceptively simple and logical, but in practice it can be very difficult to do for a number of reasons. The important issue to remember is that this exercise assumes a certain context—before segmentation, targeting, or positioning can occur, the firm has to first be market or customer oriented. The decisions about the frame of reference need to be based on research, and the process requires firms to make tough choices and avoid their brand being all things to all people. Then, organ-izations need to *consistently* stick to it over time, while paradoxically, reinterpreting it to ensure the execution of the position remains relevant (Keller 1999).

So what's involved? Start with **market segmentation** (see Step 4: Research). Segmentation divides the market into groups of (potential) customers with distinct characteristics, behaviors, or needs. These segments should clearly be different from one another (heterogeneous between), but there should also be a lot of similarity within each segment (homogeneous within) (Silk 2006, p. 86). There are two main ways to segment markets:

1. Benefits sought: the customer goal or need that the brand can serve.
2. Observable characteristics: often demographics, geographic locations, cohort effects (Generation Z, Y, etc.), lifestyle, and usage occasions (Silk 2006).

It's important to keep in mind that observable characteristics map onto the benefit being sought. It's common to see marketers talking about "female consumers," "generation [XYZ]," or "Millennials" (cohort effects), "sea-change" (lifestyle segments)," "ethical consumers" (value segmentation), "retirees" (age), "working class" (socioeconomic), and other such easily observable segments, but these often fail the test of homogeneity within because there can be huge variation within groups of retirees, cisgenders or transgenders, age cohorts, and so on. Typically reliance on this form of segmentation alone results in very bland positioning statements which, as will be shown, are increasingly dangerous in markets characterized by high choice and partitioning between large value-driven and niche prestige brands.

The following points identify how marketers should approach the tricky challenge of segmentation—a process that requires experience and a degree of creativity (Silk 2006):

1. Understand the benefits sought. Qualitative research is a necessity here in order to understand the context that customers seek to enact their identity goals.
2. Segment the market and use a design tool such as personas (see Brand Aside 5.1) to develop customer profiles of each segment (especially valuable for non-marketing staff such as creatives and product designers).
3. Search for observable characteristics that help distinguish each segment (heterogeneity) and clarify membership of each (homogeneity) as these can assist with tactical marketing decisions such as the content of advertising, the range of products designed, and so on.

BRAND ASIDE 5.1

User Personas

Once the target has been selected, a customer profile needs to be developed. This may draw on the relevant observable characteristics identified in market segmentation. However, these types of profiles (lists of characteristics) often suffer from being too abstract and unreal for many of the people who will be needed to launch the brand. One useful tool that overcomes this problem is user personas. A persona is an imagined character that represents the target segment or segments. For example:

> The Longchamp woman likes fashion, but she's not a fashion addict or victim. She is a real woman living a real life. She is active, dynamic, and takes her

(Continued)

life into her own hands. She's several women at the same time; she can be a businesswoman, a mother, a party girl, multifaceted and multitasking. She needs to feel self-confident. She pays attention to what she buys and likes to find a good balance between quality and fashion. The Longchamp bag is a part of her life. She can wear it a lot as it becomes nicer with age, and she always comes back to it. She is emotionally attached to it; women feel like they are part of the family. (Avery et al. 2016, p. 5)

In essence the persona is given a name and then a world is created around them that enriches our understanding of, and empathy with, the target, their goals, and the sociocultural context that helps define it. A persona should include:

1. Behavior patterns
2. Goals
3. Skills
4. Attitudes
5. The environment
6. A few fictional personal details to make the persona "real"

A hypothetical example of persona is provided in Figure 5.6.

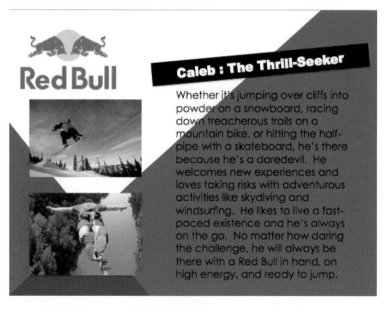

Figure 5.6   Hypothetical Persona for Redbull

The next step involves **Targeting** (which can be considered the second part of Step 4: Research). This involves evaluating each segment in terms of its attractiveness and appropriateness for the potential brand. How does one evaluate the appropriateness of the segment if the brand position has not yet been defined? This is where creativity comes in. If we return to the segments identified for the city of Bath in the last chapter, how did we know that the city could not appeal to "style hounds"? The simple answer is that the team lived in the city, knew its heritage, the key components of its offer, the fixable problems (tired advertising), the more difficult issues (such as parking and traffic), and the advantages enjoyed by other cities in each segment's frame of reference. For a new to the world brand, the judgment is similar (although you may have less to go on), although much comes down to the level of resources one has.

Generally, targeting decisions are made with reference to the following:

1. Size of segment: how many consumers? Generalist, value-based brands often target the mass market whereas nice specialists target a smaller, typically higher value segment.
2. Profitability: usage, price sensitivity. Apple has built its success on targeting highly profitable segments, at the expense of market share. In contrast, Samsung targets more price-sensitive segments, albeit much larger ones than Apple.
3. Ability to win: ability to conceive, produce, market, finance, execute, and sustain one's position (Silk 2006, pp. 88–89). Craft-beer brands such as BrewDog beat out brands made by larger conglomerates because being a pioneer genuinely committed to making great beer is the standard for authenticity in this segment (Beverland et al. 2008).
4. Underserved: the classic "blue ocean" market, or uncontested markets (Kim and Mauborgne 2015). Aaker (2012) argues that category extensions by Apple enable them to avoid product life cycles associated with single categories and shut out competitors by creating whole new categories of products in which they can attract valuable early adopters. Kraft's Dairylea Dunkers targeted the "third thing" in packed school lunches and found that no other competitors were targeting a frame of reference involving parental considerations of nutrition and children's considerations of fun.

Once the customer's world has been brought to life, the next step in developing the brand's position is competitor analysis. Competitor analysis draws on one of the most influential articles in marketing and business strategy ever written: "Marketing Myopia" (1960) by Theodore ("Ted") Levitt. This article argues that firms often define their competitors too narrowly, by focusing primarily on their immediate industry competitors offering similar functioning products or services. The result is myopic vision, whereby entrenched firms fail to see the threat posed by potential competitors in tangential industries.

UK high-street music retailer HMV, for example, was still trumpeting its physical retail presence as a core advantage at the time of its bankruptcy, even though customers had switched their music and entertainment purchases to online sources, including legal and illegal downloading, online retailers, and streaming services. Customers did not lose their appetite for music and/or movies; they just no longer saw any reason to go to a physical store to purchase them. Had HMV focused on defining itself according to a customer frame of reference defined as "entertainment," it may have realized the danger provided by new players such as Apple and Spotify, and potentially invested in its own online platform early on. Many previously dominant brands such as Kodak (supplanted by digital photography), Toys R Us (beaten by Amazon.com), and Blockbuster (disrupted by downloading and streaming) have suffered due to marketing myopia.

Now that the frame of reference has been used to identify competitors, the next step is to evaluate competitor offerings. Let's examine how this is done with reference to a competitive map. Figure 5.3 is a hypothetical example taken from the luxury sports car category. Qualitative research was conducted to identify that range of associations that loyalists and target users desired from brands in this category. These associations were then turned into five-point Likert scales and each brand in the category assessed against them (e.g., "To what extent do you agree that Audi is …"). A statistical tool called factor analysis then builds the competitor map (these maps can be represented in a variety of ways but all involve the same underlying process).

At this point one can identify potential gaps in the market, existing brand strengths and weaknesses, and even new associations that the brand can own without undermining its authenticity. The final step is to examine the firm's capabilities. The focus on capabilities is rooted in the **resource-based view of the firm**. In this view, firms are bundles of resources and capabilities (Teece et al. 1997). The difference is important—resources are static and often tangible (such as money, factories, and equipment), whereas capabilities are intangible and reflect our ability to leverage our resources

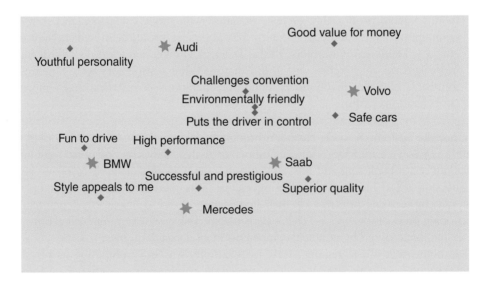

Figure 5.3   Positioning Map for Luxury Sports Car

Source: author's notes

effectively and/or in unique ways. Capabilities are necessary for ensuring we can execute and deliver our positioning to customers.

How do we do this? Return to the frame of reference. Only capabilities valuable to customers matter. These can include a range of things including the symbolism inherent in the organization's founding story, motivation of founders, founders' backgrounds, story of the product or production process, innovation ability, service quality and delivery, heritage, user-profiles and associations, or for new to the firm brands, organizational reputation with loyal customers. How do you do this?

1. Even for a new to the world brand, there will be some backstory. This backstory could spring from founder beliefs, heritage, motivation, background, the region they are located in, or many other factors. For new to the firm brands, the heritage may be richer and well worth documenting.
2. For new to the firm brands, interviews, or focus groups of loyalists, can provide unique insights into your unique capabilities. Another means of doing this is through simple web-based tools such as hashtag (#) analysis, Google analytics, or even typing your firm's name into Google and seeing what the most common inquiries are. Insights from industry insiders (influencers), salespeople and new and potential employees can also help.
3. Review your existing stock of resources including your potential partners (retailers, other brands, websites) if you are truly new to the world. In this case, you may only have potential capabilities, but you will at least gain some insight into what you can promise and deliver sustainably.

At this stage you will now have the material you need to develop your brand's positioning statement. You may find that you have to revise your decisions as you go, especially since you may also find that your target need is overserved, or you lack the capabilities to do so, or existing customers identify strengths you had not thought of that could be leveraged more effectively. At this stage it is good to involve your brand team and a moderator to ensure you stay on track and don't fall into the trap of a comfortable consensus rather than identify a controversial but more effective position. Positioning statements are then usually structured along the following lines:

Our brand is positioned toward _____ (target segment) and offers a solution that is superior in terms of _____ (competitors) because of the following _____ (capabilities).

The following quote from former Abercrombie & Fitch CEO Mike Jeffries provides an example. The identification of a target segment is clear—the cool kids at school. The difference to competitors is implicit in the last statement about being exclusive as this drives the brand to refuse to make clothes in size ten and above (among many other actions they undertake). The capabilities are hinted at, but relate the brand's long heritage of providing clothing for the well-to-do, predominantly Anglo-American upper-middle-class and upper-class consumer.

In every school there are the cool and popular kids, and then there are the not-so-cool kids. We go after the cool kids [target segment]. We go after the attractive all-American kid with a great attitude and a lot of friends [capabilities]. A lot of people don't belong [in our clothes], and they can't belong. Are we exclusionary? Absolutely [competitors]. (Mike Jeffries, Abercrombie & Fitch, quoted by Cohen 2016)

How narrow should your positioning be? This is a critical question because the decisions you make now will define your brand's identity for the future. Although you may change the marketing mix of the brand to ensure relevance, the brand position under the mindshare model does not change (rather it is simply reinterpreted for the times). Brand expert Mark Ritson argues that most brand positioning is the equivalent of vanilla ice cream (apologies to lovers of vanilla)—a flavor no one really dislikes, but no one gets very excited or angry about it either. In contrast, the best brands are like Ben & Jerry's crazy flavors—many detractors (who may talk about them), but enough lovers that keep returning to buy again and again. Ritson argues that too often brands are defined by ideas that have no workable opposite. These include words like:

1. Different: being different is essential for all brands.
2. Innovative: staying relevant is essential for all brands.
3. Quality: all brands must perform to expectations.
4. Integrity: all brands must walk the walk.
5. Ethical: some stakeholders may view a brand as unethical, but being overtly so is not sustainable in the long term.
6. Reliable: a brand that does not consistently deliver on promises is certain to disappear.
7. Honest: brands must follow through on their promises.
8. Trust: trust is at the heart of all brand relationships.

The problem with these choices is that they are really preconditions of any strong brand. One cannot develop strong brand relationships without a point of difference, without keeping the brand fresh through innovation, by being unethical and unreliable and so on. However, these words are often comforting and easy to gain consensus on. This suggests that developing the right position involves two processes:

1. Does the brand meet a defined need, or fill a gap in the marketplace? Can the firm deliver it? This is known as the "three Cs" test. Each idea you choose to define your position must pass every test.
2. Does the idea have a workable opposite? The words above do not. But think about how Volvo uses the idea of "safety" to position its brand. All cars must meet basic safety tests, but Volvo is the only brand that talks about safety in its marketing campaigns as a clear point of distinction. In the context of automobiles, does safety have a workable opposite? Figure 5.2 identifies plenty, including "sportiness," "driving experience," "prestige," "youthfulness," and so on. Likewise, Virgin is positioned as anti-establishment, a value not all brands desire.

In the mindshare model your position should be defined narrowly and strictly controlled and communicated. Ryanair for example owns the value or "cheap" end of the market and engineers this into all of its operations, including the choice of airport, the seemingly poor quality advertising, strict bag policies, understaffing, cheesy on-time arrival jingle, rumors about charging for toilet use and standing up seats, and garish colors. The message is clear—we will do everything to keep prices down. The brand is paradoxically one of the most hated in the industry, but also one of the most profitable. Vanilla it certainly is not!

What are the downsides of such an approach? Douglas Holt is the most vocal critic of the mindshare model, as he argues that the approach, despite widespread use, has little empirical support (other than in assessing brand extensions), involves values so abstract as to be meaningless to marketers, creative staff, and consumers, and locks one into a focus on consistency at all costs. Instead he provides an alternative to this mindshare model, the cultural branding model.

The Cultural Model of Brand Positioning (an Alternative Step 5)

The above model assumes that the wider sociocultural environment in which the consumer and brand are located is relatively unchanging. However, should this prevailing cultural or national worldview or *zeitgeist* change, it can have profound effects on the authenticity of brands, often rendering their long cherished positions irrelevant. Figure 5.4 represents the cultural positioning model of Douglas Holt. Immediately it is clear that this approach is very different from the mindshare model above. The cultural branding model argues that brands exist in "myth markets," which emerge due to

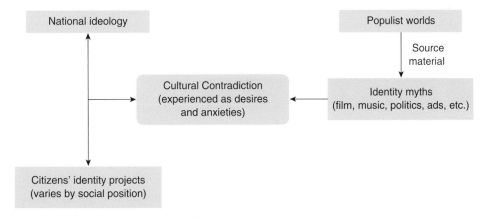

Figure 5.4   Cultural Brand Positioning

Source: Holt 2004a, p.58

contradictions in national ideology. Consumers experience these contradictions and look for brands that help them self-authenticate against a background of a shifting sociocultural landscape. In effect, this model argues brands must tell stories that enable consumers to align authenticating acts with authoritative performances (see Chapter 2).

How does this work? Let's say an important cultural norm is that hard work will be rewarded. This is what Holt means by a national ideology (Figure 5.3) or worldview. Consumers will often frame their identities in terms of being self-made or self-reliant and chose brands that reflect this identity. Brands focused on rewarding effort are likely to win out while consumers view the national ideology as true. However, in many developed nations, workers are experiencing flat or even falling real wages, and populist political movements argue that connected elites rather than hard-working people get ahead. And continued employment often has little to do with hard work, as firms may automate or send jobs overseas to save on costs.

As a result a gap emerges between the national ideology (which frames an authoritative performance) and an individual's experience of it (which frames authenticating acts). This produces anxiety, and leads consumers to question existing truths, including the identity-value of existing brands. One result of this is the emergence of doppelgänger images that undermine the authenticity of brand claims, thus undermining the consumer–brand relationship. When this occurs (or your data suggest such a shift is emerging), Holt argues one must radically switch position as a simple refresh will not deal with the root cause of a brand's declining relevance.

To do so, Holt argues brand managers must look for alternative associations from "populist worlds" or subcultures to build new brand myths that speak to the emerging reality consumers find themselves in (see Brand Aside 5.2). For example, rather than beliefs in hard work generating success, brands may draw on the creative sector and frame their benefits in terms of the "gig economy" whereby being able to multi-task, adapt, and connect (through social media) is essential for success. Through careful historic analysis, Holt argues that it is constant change, not reinforcement of position, that defines the success of iconic brands such as Nike, Harley Davidson, Mountain Dew, and Budweiser.

BRAND ASIDE 5.2

Crowd Cultures and Brand Opportunity

The cultural positioning models propose that sources brand insights from crowd cultures or populist worlds. These subcultures typically form to meet certain identity needs of their members. Over time, a shared ethos emerges that governs what is acceptable or legitimate in terms of behavior. Marketers must be very careful in how they approach this consumer-owned space. Historically, marketers would simply cool-hunt or appropriate cultural material and use it without "permission" or offering anything in return. Recent research has called into question whether this model is likely to generate authenticity for the brand. Holt (2002) argued that brands must move from being "cultural parasites" to "cultural innovators" and adopt the standpoint of a "citizen artist" whereby the brand team provides material that strengthens the subculture. Likewise a review of marketing to consumer collectives identifies the need to provide resources that strengthen linking value (Schau et al. 2009). Consumers will push back against marketer-generated myths that co-opt or "steal" subcultural material (Arsel and Thompson 2011), consider brands authentic if they play by communal rules (Kates 2004), and prefer brands that act as cultural insiders (Beverland and Ewing 2005).

The Vegemite example featured in Chapter 2 provides an example of this. The brand was built on the basis of owning breakfast time, the meal most associated with a "good start to the day." However, sociocultural shifts such as increased working hours and an increased emphasis on health changed meal patterns and what Australians ate. Often breakfast was on the run, and featured a coffee, snack bar, or smoothie. Slowly Vegemite became the product that defined Australia's past, rather than the present. The "How do you love your Vegemite?" campaign was a strategy to revitalize the brand by encouraging users to tell their stories about it. The revitalization of the brand's equity had nothing to do with recapturing breakfast, but with reconnecting users to a new Australian identity myth as urban, cosmopolitan, and multicultural. The brand team leveraged populist associations with user groups and celebrities, and shifted the brand's functional role to snacking (Keinan et al. 2012).

Brands that follow this approach do position themselves relative to a customer goal or need, but this frame of reference is very different from that of the mindshare model. The cultural model does look to competitive gaps, but in terms of ideology rather than function or emotion. The cultural view implies a different view of capabilities as well, focused on brands' ability to identify cultural shifts, generate populist authenticity, and create new myths that may destabilize the brand's previous position or accepted market norms (Beverland et al. 2015).

In light of these differences, how does one build a new brand using a cultural approach? Holt built his theory examining iconic brands or brands that had stood the test of time. His work did not examine how these brands were founded. However, since shifting the brand's myth essentially means beginning anew, we can use the cultural model for new brands. How?

1. Iconic brands such as Converse, Harley Davidson, Hilton Hotels, and Leica began with a product or service (Holt 2003). Surrounding these products were populist worlds such as basketball, musicians, creatives, biker gangs such as Hell's Angels and

other rebels, the wealthy, and professional photographers such as Alfred Eisenstaedt. Nike was and continues to be embedded in the world of elite sport. This world has its own ethos, while each individual sporting code such as skateboarding or basketball represents populist sub-worlds that the brand can draw authenticity from and contribute back to in terms of innovations and cultural events.

2. **Cultural contradictions** arise from schisms between national ideology (authoritative performances) and citizen identity projects (authenticating acts). There are ways of identifying these schisms and positioning a new brand with the relevant myths to address it. For example, historically children usually enjoyed more economic prosperity than their parents. In many developed economies this is breaking down, with young adults feeling shut out of the housing market, having less job security, carrying large student debts, and less income and wealth. How does this affect luxury brands that have been built around aspiration and economic success? A Burberry trench coat was historically a signifier that one had "made it" but what happens to this position when "making it" is not experienced as possible or realistic? Will such a contradiction lead people to buy less, or own less and access more services via sharing economy brands such as Zipcar and Airbnb? Can discount brands such as Aldi, or heritage brands such as Zippo and Woolrich, position themselves as smart choices for their price/quality ratios or durability and longevity?

3. Schisms usually appear in popular culture (film, literature, music), art, political debates, activist sites, and other areas seemingly peripheral to the brand. Since the September 11, 2001 attacks on the Twin Towers in New York and the fallout over involvement in the Iraq War, there has been a distinct shift in popular culture, especially in television shows. Increasingly the historic anti-hero, such as Saul Goodman (*Better Call Saul*), Lorne Malvo (*Fargo*), Tyrion Lannister (*Game of Thrones*), Walter White (*Breaking Bad*), or Frank Underwood (*House of Cards*) has become the focus of our affections. These shows challenge our perceptions of good and bad, as they focus on characters forced to break the law because of a broken system, or expertly manipulating a corrupt system for their own gains. Dystopian fiction, computer games, and movies are also all the rage, finding audiences perhaps convinced that the capitalist system is rigged against them. Holt would argue that there is currently plenty of material to suggest brands need to develop new cultural myths to appeal meaningful to a narrative of decline and systemic breakdown.

4. Cultural intermediaries, including those in design, advertising, fashion, and other professions that intersect art and commerce, are often best equipped to pick up on these schisms or shifts. These fields help shape how individuals see themselves in relation to the whole (or individual identity vs. national identity). Christian Dior has built on this ability, shifting tastes to address the contradictions of the times. After World War II, for example, his business was built on returning to the glamor of the 1920s, as he understood the need to move on from wartime

austerity and functionality. In Chapter 8 we identify how designers enhance brand equity by destabilizing accepted brand or market truths, in order to make the brand more ambidextrous (where it balances its past with seemingly contradictory external demands).

5. Methods such as ethnography, netnography, trend analysis, and big data identify shifts in the wider *zeitgeist* or worldview, or identify the identity tensions experienced by your potential user. Brands such as Di$count Universe and Etiko (Chapter 11) were built on these types of insights. Etiko is an ethical clothing brand that was based on tracking insights on the so-called attitude-behavior gap. This occurs when consumers' behavior differs drastically from their stated intent. Etiko realized that while consumers wanted to be ethical in their clothing choices, they had no idea where to start and how to proceed, and they also did not want to sacrifice fashionability and performance to do so. These insights drove product development, marketing campaigns, and partnerships with designers and social movements.

So how should one begin? To understand the aim we need to understand cultural innovation. Holt and Cameron's cultural innovation theoretical model identifies this logic. In Figure 5.4, brands innovate culturally by positioning themselves against the orthodoxy that is breaking down for our target users. In essence, they get the jump on established brands by being more relevant to the identity needs of those users experiencing the cultural contradiction. In this sense differentiation is defined in terms of the extent to which we speak to the current and emerging ideological world rather than the past. To build our position we must therefore do the following:

1. Identify the cultural schism or contradiction.
2. Identify how different segments experience this contradiction. For example, the notion of self-reliance is still important for white-collar and blue-collar workers, but the anxiety arising from cultural contradictions can be experienced very differently and in different intensities, each potentially representing different opportunities for a new brand.
3. Targeting involves two steps: first target the frame of reference in terms of the anxiety or tension experienced by your user (e.g., a breakdown in job security vs. beliefs about rewards for individual effort) and then target the **populist world** or web-based crowd-culture (e.g., artists, musicians, creative industries, trades, and crafts, all of whom enjoy little economic reward but have high cultural status and focus on doing things for the love of it) you want to source material from to address the cultural contradiction (Holt 2016).
4. Articulate your position in a cultural brief for the brand and your agency partners in advertising, product development, web strategy, and so on.

As you can see capabilities analysis is not included here. The cultural model does assume one can jump from one position to the next, without considering whether one is credible or capable of doing so. Partly this is because cultural models downplay the power of the brand relationship in situations of significant cultural contradictions or schisms. However, capabilities are given consideration in the development of the cultural brief (Step 2 below) as firms are encouraged to reposition themselves as authentic insiders in the populist world they seek to inhabit. Budweiser, for example, parodied itself when seeking to reposition itself around slacker myths, something that was viewed as essential to making the new myth authentic (since beer is no longer for hard-working men, it must be for cynical, slacker types who have figured out the system is rigged against them) (Holt 2004a).

This model also takes for granted that the firm has some dynamic capabilities such as learning, the transformation of existing resources, innovation, ambidexterity, integrating, and executing (the nature of which will be explained in later chapters). The cultural brief (or cultural positioning statement) must address the following three areas:

1. Myth treatment: What will be the brand's mythic story? Identify the plot, characters, and setting of the story that will address the cultural contradiction. BrewDog, for example, drew on the logic of punk rock to challenge entrenched corporate brands' claims to making quality beer. Their initial web campaigns focused on the founders using bottles of Stella Artois as bowling pins (with predictable results), refusing to play by the rules set out by the Advertising Standards Authority (ASA) (with a hashtag #kissmyASA on their official Twitter feed when the brand's advertisement was ruled offensive), and challenging conventions about beer styles and alcohol levels. The story was obvious: the two founders were the equivalent of punk pioneers seeking to destroy conventions that had resulted in stale conformity and dominance by corporate brands who took their audience for granted.

2. Populist authenticity: Which **web-based crowd culture** or populist world will the brand source its material from? What are the important rituals and language that define the populist world? What is the ethos that defines the populist world? The BrewDog example above identifies that the populist world chosen is the punk movement, thus conventions must be challenged, the tone of voice must be aggressive, in your face, nonconformist, and rude (the brand is positioned as "a post Punk apocalyptic mother fucker of a craft brewery"). The brand's employees have a range of nonconformist titles such as Master Gunner and Mr World. The brand's consumer share ownership scheme, "Equity for Punks," also reflects the communal nature of the punk movement.

3. Charismatic aesthetic: What is the unique style that reflects the populist world above that will help make the mythic story compelling? Following the example of BrewDog above, the brand's product names reflect the punk ethos (including "Born to Die," "Dog E," and "Dead Pony Club"), while the imagery draws heavily on street art with its graffiti-styled font and colors.

(*Source*: Adapted from Holt 2004a, pp. 64–65)

Once this is done the firm then moves on to Steps 6–8 in Figure 5.1: internal launch, external launch, and tracking. However, there are some important differences. Populist authenticity is a different approach to internal rollout from that in the mindshare model. While the brand is built inside out in the mindshare model, in the cultural model the firm draws from the populist world to render it authentic. This is why many brands adopting this model insist staff engage directly in the activities and communities that they draw from. Nike, for example, require staff to engage in their various sports communities, just as Ripcurl require staff to surf, and the Morgan Motor Company encourages staff to participate in amateur vintage car competitors. These are strategies not only to enhance the brand's image within its communities but also, critically, to ensure it speaks as an authentic insider and picks up on the nuances of the populist world it chooses to leverage. Communication and tracking also shift somewhat. Communication or external launch will be covered in Chapter 6, but tracking involves monitoring the brand's position within the populist worlds it draws on and contributes to, tracking the anxieties of our target market, and being mindful of any doppelgänger images that may emerge on the periphery, typically using big data, ethnographic, and netnographic techniques.

Reconciling Both Models

The cultural model was developed as a critique of the dominant mindshare model of branding. However, it is better to think about the two models as complementary. Holt (Heding et al. 2016) has suggested that mindshare is useful in periods of relative stability, while the cultural model is necessary in times of radical change. One way of framing these models is to borrow from new product development with its focus on radical and incremental innovation. Radical innovation is disruptive and often reshapes existing markets (e.g., sharing models such as Uber). Incremental innovation involves minor changes that are often cosmetic or focused on functional improvements and new markets or price points (the launch of a next generation iPhone). In branding, consistency and relevance are both critical to building brand equity over time. The mindshare model places a premium on consistency and staying on message, and is therefore incremental in focus. The cultural model places a premium on relevance and challenging orthodoxy, and is therefore more radical in nature.

Recent research has identified that brand ambidexterity, or balancing the needs of both approaches, is essential for maintaining brand value over time (Beverland et al. 2015). What this means is that building and sustaining brand equity requires balancing radical innovation with incremental, or relevance with consistency. Figure 5.5 identifies the relationship, with the mindshare model appropriate in periods

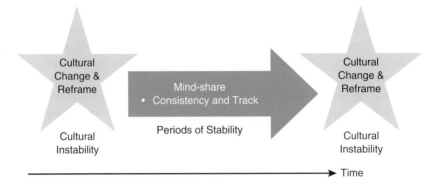

Figure 5.5   Punctuated Equilibrium Model of Brand Building

Source: author's notes

of sociocultural stability and the cultural model essential during periods of national schism and contradiction.

Brand Names, Logos, and Elements

Now that you have your brand defined, the next step is to develop a name and/or logo, and then consider other **brand elements** such as slogans, characters, packaging, jingles, and so on. As naming involves legal considerations in terms of trademark protection globally, it is not unusual to employ an agency (see Brand Aside 5.3) such as Interbrand to moderate naming discussions. Logos and other elements of the brand identity system are best left to professional design agencies who have the skills and resources to provide what you need. The critical issue is that brand position should drive naming, logo, and identity systems, and therefore having a brand positioning statement and the underpinning research is necessary to get the best result here.

What is the process for brand naming?

1. Brainstorm a list of names. Preferably use an agency that specializes in this because it's harder than you think.
2. Evaluate each in relation to the brand position.
3. Check that you have legal rights globally to various options and that they do not translate negatively in different languages.
4. Test the name with target users, usually through focus groups.
5. Register the final choice.
6. Use a similar process for the other brand elements as well.

BRAND ASIDE 5.3

Brand Agencies

Although they cost money, employing a brand agency can represent a very good investment in the future. If the agency has a comprehensive set of skills, then they can provide insight into the positioning process, help moderate team meetings, conduct research, develop names, logos, taglines, personalities, and identity systems, and help with the internal and external launch. Brand agencies typically provide the following services: brand identity and strategy, design (product, website, corporate communications, logos, mascots, publications, packaging, point of purchase displays, retail fit out), research, communications, internal branding, and brand launch activities (Neumeier 2005). Since these agencies employ people from many different backgrounds, they can also provide unique outsider insights on your brand more easily than you could within your firm or team.

What defines a good name, logo, slogan, brand character, jingle, packaging, or brand element? First, they should be meaningful in so far as they communicate something about the brand to its users. The words used can be literally meaningless, but still convey meaning in the sense mentioned above. Second, they should be memorable in that they are distinct, easy to remember, pronounce and (especially for web searches) spell (consider why the band Chvrches changed their spelling slightly to use a "v" instead of the normal "u'). Third, they should be future-oriented in that they allow the brand to grow, extend, and change. Fourth, they should all be protectable, in the legal sense. Fifth, they should be positive and devoid of negative connotations. Finally, they should be visual in that they will lend themselves to use in different media (Wheeler, 2003, p. 41).

There is a range of different options. Some common ones include:

1. Founder: These names are easy to protect but may not communicate much about the brand, especially when the founder dies. Ford, Louis Vuitton, and Chanel are examples.
2. Descriptive: These clearly communicate intent but may not be future-oriented and can be too descriptive to protect. Examples include Fuji Film, American Airlines, and Weight Watchers.
3. Fabricated: These are easy to protect and can be very distinctive, but do not obviously communicate intent. Starbucks, Dr Pepper, and Apple are examples.
4. Metaphor: Things, places, people, animals, processes are widely understood and can easily communicate an idea, but may be difficult to protect. Innocent, Nike, and Virgin are examples.

5. Acronym: Think IBM, GE, CNN, and so on. These can be difficult to remember and protect and are usually used by firms who have shortened their official names.
6. Combinations of the above: These often combine advantages but do not go overboard. Examples include Google Android, Microsoft Vista and XP, littleBits/Korg.

(*Source*: Wheeler, 2003, p. 41)

Articulating the Position

However you define the brand's position, you still have to bring it to life for users. The brand's position is often articulated in ways that do not translate easily into advertisements, slogans, packaging design, tone of voice, and so on. As a result, the brand team with help from creatives and specialist agencies now have to translate the position for various audiences. Table 5.1 identifies the difference between a brand's position as defined internally and the external translation of that position.

So what are the options for bringing the position to life? Popular options include:

1. **Brand personality or archetypes**: Research reveals that consumers do imbue brands with personalities. As a result, firms attempt to do the same. Brand personalities are underpinned by five traits: sincerity (Animals Asia, Dove, Stella McCartney), excitement (BMW, Virgin), competence (Deutsche Bank, Boston Consulting Group), sophistication (Louis Vuitton, Krug Champagne), and ruggedness (Jeep, Marlboro) (Aaker 1997). Archetypes are a Jungian take on personality and can include roles such as trickster (Virgin), matriarch (IBM), warrior (Under Armour), sage (Go Compare), angel (Innocent), enchantress (Aesop), and so on.

Table 5.1   Brand position vs. external articulation

Brand Position	Articulation of that Position
Apple: "You will never be part of the machine."	"Think different"
Nike: "If you have got a body, you're an athlete."	"Just do it"
Amazon: "Make it easy to sell people lots of stuff."	No tagline, but innovations such as i-click and Amazon Prime are designed to reinforce this position implicitly.
Lego: "To inspire and develop the builders of tomorrow."	"Play on"
GE: "GE creates things that make our world work. Amazing, forward-reaching, inventive things. Smart things. Powerful things. Things of consequence. Things that change the world."	"Imagination at work"

2. **Tone of voice**: This is often the outward expression of the brand personality and is sometimes called brand style. Tone of voice is engineered into all the marketing aspects of the brand including language, messaging, music, colors, sensory aspects such as smell, taste, and touch, the experience, spokespeople, and so on. BrewDog, discussed earlier, demonstrates an "in your face" anti-establishment tone of voice, while Innocent's tone of voice reflects fun, purity, and homeliness.
3. **Taglines or slogans**: See Brand Aside 5.4.
4. **Corporate identity systems**: Organizations often ensure every customer touch-point is covered by the brand. Corporate identity systems are a visual system that communicates the brand identity and can cover everything from signage, websites, uniforms, vehicles, business cards, pens and stationery, retail stores, corporate head office, letterhead, and so on. Think of UPS's consistent identity across its uniforms, delivery vehicles, website, and corporate communications. Likewise, although it appears amateurish, Ryanair's consistent use of blue and yellow across is a deliberate strategy to reinforce its identity and position.

BRAND ASIDE 5.4

Tagline, Basics

Design expert Alina Wheeler (2003, p. 43) suggests taglines should be:

1. Short
2. Different
3. Unique
4. Able to capture the brand position
5. Easy to say and remember
6. Free from negative connotations
7. Easily displayed
8. Protected
9. Able to evoke emotions

Types of taglines include: imperative (Nike and "Just do it"); descriptive (Who Gives a Crap's "Premium Loo Roll"); superlative (BMW and "The ultimate driving machine" or DeBeers and "A diamond is a girl's best friend"); provocative ("Avis, We Try Harder"); or specific (M&M's "Melt in your mouth, not in your hands"). Similar rules apply to other brand elements such as names, slogans, jingles and so on.

Chapter Summary

This chapter has explored the process of building and positioning a brand. Decisions made at the founding of the brand have a long-term effect and thus creating a new brand needs to be done with care, although one also needs to be flexible enough to adapt the emerging brand position to shifts in the marketplace (as covered in Chapter 6). The tools and processes discussed within this chapter relate to new brands, whether they are truly new to the world or new to the firm. An eight-step process was presented, which included discussion of two different approaches to brand positioning: the mindshare and cultural approach. The chapters that follow will expand on and extend the material presented here, focusing on steps 6-7, and strategies for reinforcing, growing, and refreshing the brand.

Review Questions

1. What are the challenges facing new brands from (1) unknown firms and (2) established firms?
2. Looking at Figure 5.1, what would be the downsides of leaving out individual steps (i.e., skipping over one or leaving one out)? Do this for each step.
3. Develop a brand persona for the style-hound consumer identified in Chapter 4. What would new destinations, products, and service brands need to offer to this user?
4. The recent rise of political populism (Brexit in the UK; President Trump in the USA; Marine Le Pen in France, etc.) can be argued to reflect a cultural schism for some consumers. Drawing on the cultural brand model, what type of brand opportunities does this shift offer?
5. Identify two brands in your own country that draw on populist worlds for their cultural relevance? How do they embody this in two of their brand elements?

Case Example: Di$count Universe

Di$count Universe is a small luxury fashion label founded in Melbourne by Cami James and Nadia Napreychikov (see Figure 5.7). The two met while studying for their fashion degree and quickly realized they had much in common. Their student dissertations contained the essence of what would become Di$count Universe—a belief that anything goes in postmodernity, that authenticity is suspect, and that online communities could help nurture a brand and shake up what they saw as an elitist industry. Choosing to name their luxury fashion label "Di$count Universe" is one example of their beliefs about authenticity, given that the name is hardly consistent with traditional category codes. Rejecting the idea that clothes are only made for one season, the brand is staunchly anti-seasonal in always carrying stocks of their past designs, as Nadia states: "Clothes aren't just made seasonally to go out of fashion the next season. If something has resonance with people over and over again we will keep releasing it."

The brand began at the time when few online-only labels existed (platforms such as ETSY and eBay were not used by serious designers as their main channel) and blogging was something you'd rather not admit to. Examples of Di$count Universe clothes are presented in Figures 5.7 and 5.8.

The pair used their blog originally as part of their research focused on introducing the online world as a legitimate place to display their garments (up until then only shows and galleries were considered legitimate "spaces" in the academic world of fashion). With the shift to Web 2.0, the idea of the blog as a community space took off, and Cami and Nadia's clothes quickly generated a large fan base, many of whom wrote posts or comments of considerable length (demonstrating engagement) about each product and release. Nadia describes the brand as being grassroots and pushed by the people.

Figure 5.7   **Di$count Universe Founders and Clothes**

(Continued)

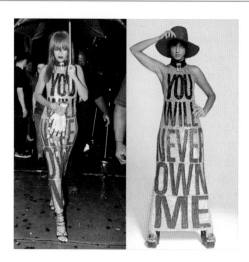

Figure 5.8   Di$count Universe Clothes

The pair's big break came when Miley Cyrus was photographed in one of their tops. At the time, Cyrus was transitioning from her Hannah Montana character to a more mature performer, and Nadia and Cami were initially reluctant to use the endorsement, as Cyrus didn't fit their perceived identity. Cyrus's photograph featuring Di$count Universe was printed on her tour t-shirts, and the awareness and licensing fee literally saved the struggling business and took the nascent brand to the global stage.

Further adoptions by stars such as Rihanna, Katy Perry (on her Prismatic world tour), and most recently Kylie Jenner have driven sales higher and built awareness of the brand to such an extent that the pair relocated to New York in 2017 in order to take advantage of a larger market, a natural target user base, and the closer links to entertainment icons such as Lady Gaga (who asked for a dress two days before the Oscars, an opportunity that couldn't be taken advantage of because of geographical distance).

Although the brand has been built around a community, no formal positioning has yet been done. The community approach is a direct assault on the perceived elitism of the luxury fashion industry in which a just a few privileged insiders get to attend shows and launches. In contrast, Di$count Universe shows give priority to the brand's online fan base, and are set up like rock shows or giant parties where cheering and hedonistic expressions are encouraged, and content is available to any fan who wishes to blog, post, or tweet about the collection. As Cami states: "It's about having that relationship with the people who got us to where we are more so than someone who might have come up through [a magazine] nurturing them."

Nadia and Cami have built up a decade's worth of collections (over 1,000 garments), which they presented as a retrospective in Australia before leaving for New York. Remaining independent (the pair have refused investor money) Nadia and Cami have saved virtually every penny earned to fund further expansion of the brand's operations in New York, including new workspace and showrooms and specialized marketing and public relations staff. With the help of interns, both still design the collections and sales remain primarily online. Di$count Universe's Instagram page has over 200,000 followers from over 80 countries and is the main form of communication. Describing their look, Cami James stated: "It's obviously excessive in style ... it's anti-industry, that's part of the DNA of the brand. There's a lot of messages and certain innuendo and humour in the brand."

Source: author's interview notes and Singer (November 26, 2016)

Case Questions

1. Who is the user of the brand? Develop a consumer persona for Di$count Universe.
2. The brand has a ten-year history but no formal position. Using the mindshare approach, identify three words or a short positioning statement that address the three Cs and are not vanilla.
3. The brand is built on an anti-establishment position. How would you position the brand culturally?
4. Regardless of how you have positioned the brand, describe its personality and tone of voice.

Key Terms

Brand articulation
Brand differentiation
Brand elements
Brand personality and archetypes
Brand relevance
Cultural brand positioning

Cultural schism or contradiction
Frame of reference
Marketing myopia
Mindshare positioning
Populist worlds
Positioning

Resource-based view of the firm
Segmentation–targeting–positioning
Tone of voice
Web-based crowd culture

Further Reading

Holt, Douglas (2004), "What Becomes an Icon Most?" *Harvard Business Review*, 81(3), 43–49.

Holt, Douglas (2016), "Branding in the Age of Social Media," *Harvard Business Review*, 94(3), 40–50.

Holt, Douglas B. and Craig J. Thompson (2004), "Man-of-Action Heroes: The Pursuit of Heroic Masculinity in Everyday Consumption," *Journal of Consumer Research*, 31 (2), 425–440.

Levitt, Theodore (1960), "Marketing Myopia," *Harvard Business Review*, July–August, 45–56.

Tybout, Alice and Brian Sternthal (2005), "Brand Positioning," in Alice M. Tybout and Tim Calkins (eds.), *Kellogg on Branding*, John Wiley & Sons, Hoboken, NJ, pp. 11–26.

6

BUILDING AND MAINTAINING A BRAND'S POSITION

A brand is a living entity—and it's enriched or undermined cumulatively over time, the product of a thousand small gestures. (Michael Eisner, former CEO Walt Disney Company, 1984–2005)

Learning Objectives

When you finish reading this chapter, you will be able to:

1. Understand the basis for maintaining brand equity over time using the mindshare and cultural approaches
2. Understand different approaches to infusing the brand throughout the firm
3. Understand the importance of an internal brand audit
4. Understand how to leverage communal and/or consumer content in ways that enhance the brand's legitimacy and authenticity
5. Understand the role of different communication tools for building and maintaining brand equity
6. Understand the nature of the brand experience

Introduction

In the previous chapter, two approaches to building a new brand were identified: the mind-share and cultural positioning models. Since tracking has been covered in Chapters 4–5, this chapter expands on Steps 6–7 in Figure 5.1: internal and external launch. Beyond that, it also examines the challenges involved in maintaining the brand's equity over time. Maintaining a brand's equity is often called **brand reinforcement**, which is contrasted with brand repositioning, the latter of which focuses on how to grow a brand's equity after a period of decline, which will be the subject of Chapter 8.

The Challenge of Stability and Change

The mindshare approach commits one to stability. Under this approach, brand equity is a function of consistency, and ensuring that brand considerations are engineered into every aspect of the firm's activities. In contrast, the cultural approach downplays consistency in favor of relevance and adaptation. Brand considerations are still engineered into every aspect of the firm's operations, but in radically different ways.

This tension between stability and change lies at the heart of much modern brand writing. Those adopting the mindshare approach typically frame their ideas in terms of "strategic brand management" or "building strong brands" where marketers are primarily responsible for creating brand meaning while the user passively receives brand messages as intended by marketers. As mentioned in Chapter 1, recent writings have taken a different tone. Using metaphors such as "the crowd," "hijack," "accidental," "citizen," and "jam," these writers have begun identifying how brand meaning is a function of multiple voices, can change frequently, and much like musicians jamming together, management involves providing a place for the jam, keeping in time with and feeding off other brand authors to cohere around a single tune. This obviously implies that managers are savvy enough to understand how to correctly adapt to other members of the jam session.

This tension lies at the heart of this chapter and will frame our discussion of building and maintaining brand meaning and equity. Following Figure 5.5, and the discussion of the brand asset valuator model in Chapter 4, brand equity involves balancing stability and change over time. Stability is primarily managed through consistency, or truly reinforcing the desired image among stakeholders. In the context of co-creation, this can refer to authentically living the brand's ethos, which paradoxically may involve adapting it over time. For example, Harley Davidson attempts to own "freedom" as an idea, and therefore makes sure it welcomes all comers to the brand and provides resources for them to express their tribal or subcultural identity (this example will be expanded on later). Financial requirements also meant the brand positioned itself as a "lifestyle brand" in order to extend its franchise beyond motorcycles. Over time, the brand has changed as a result of trying to appeal to all these users (Martin et al. 2006).

Change is managed through **relevance**, defined as "is the brand relevant to my needs?" (Rosenbaum-Eliot et al. 2015). In the mindshare approach relevance largely relates to adaptations to the marketing mix (Keller 1999). Here, the position remains set in stone but the means of communicating are constantly updated for the times, such as through new products (iPhone 3G, to 4, to 4s all the way through to the iPhone 7, for example), new product placement strategies (in films, television shows, games, YouTube advertisements, sponsorships, pop-up events, etc.), new retail store fit-outs, new celebrity endorsers, evolving marketing campaigns, new price points through line extensions, and so on.

Articulating a stable position through adapting the mix is perfectly fine when the sociocultural environment is characterized by ideological stability. However, we use "relevance" more broadly to relate to consumer (and stakeholder) relevance. As a result, we also identify how maintaining brand equity can involve changing position, through leveraging consumer-generated content, allowing for "brand hijacking," managing doppelgänger images, and generating new myths to address emerging cultural schisms (Beverland and Ewing 2005; Giesler 2012; Holt 2004a).

It's popular to question the value of stability in an age of co-creation and consumer sovereignty, but this is dangerous. Researchers from different perspectives (see Chapter 2) have all identified the dangers of handing over authorship of the brand to customers and influencers. Co-creation does not imply the lack of consistency as users gain value from being able to trust the brand as a resource for their authentication goals (Beverland and Farrelly 2010). Research on doppelgänger brand images, for example, identifies that consumers of the brand suffering the backlash desperately want marketers to solve the problem and enable them to continue using the brand (Giesler 2012).

That said, brands cannot remain stubbornly defiant in the face of change. The success of the "How do you love your Vegemite?" campaign, for example, resulted in the brand team launching a new brand extension, and asking consumers to submit recommendations for a new name. However, running counter to the spirit of the campaign, at the last minute, the brand team decided to choose "iSnack 2.0" as the winning name. Unsurprisingly there was an immediate social-media backlash, and the team rightly changed their approach within 48 hours by submitting the ten most popular that consumers submitted to popular vote. Ultimately this ensured even greater success (leading to the creation of conspiracy theory myths that the team had planned it all along) and reaffirmed the people did indeed own the brand. Why did they change? Their own analysis of various backlashes to changes to iconic brands identified things only got worse when you went against the tide of consumer sentiment (Keinan et al. 2012).

Brands can also be hijacked in unforeseen but positive ways. **Brand hijacking** refers to the process whereby a market actor uses the brand in unintended or unplanned ways (Wipperfürth 2005). Brands such as Tommy Hilfiger and Australia's Crumpler (cycling bags) and Smiggle (stationery for children) turned initial failure into success when they adapted to unforeseen events (Beverland and Reynolds 2010). Hilfiger wanted to target white American males with his brand but failed. However, when 1990s rappers Puffy and Coolio started to wear his gear, African American teens adopted the brand, which in turn ensured that white teens would follow (as they looked to African American males for insight into what was cool). The brand quickly embedded itself in the rap community and turned around its flagging fortunes (Beverland 2004).

Adidas's shift from sportswear to street wear was similarly inspired (Beverland 2009). Crumpler and Smiggle both wanted to target photographers and business stationery needs respectively, but failed. Instead cycle couriers and school kids lapped up the products (bags and fun stationery) and both brands' quick adaptation eventually positioned them beyond their originally desired usage and functional positioning (and they eventually succeeded with their original target markets through the same diffusion process as Hilfiger) (Beverland and Reynolds 2010). That is, by being flexible, these brands achieved an identity far beyond what was intended and came to occupy important positions within specific sub-cultures that enabled them to benefit from populist worlds—Hilfiger and 1990s rap music, Crumpler and street cycling (and eventually hipsterism), and Smiggle with the 2000s' creative class.

One way to think about this interplay is through Henry Mintzberg's (1987) comparison of planned, emergent, and realized strategy. This is diagrammed simply in Figure 6.1. Mintzberg identified that the best strategy was the outcome of planning, while also being prepared to engage in trial and error and adapting to unforeseen events (what he called "realized strategy"). In branding terms, the planned position (mindshare) cannot be maintained in a vacuum, and may need to be revised, or even revised substantially. Parts of it may have to be dropped ("unrealized strategy"). Unforeseen opportunities may emerge over time that force change or offer opportunities for brand innovation. These can include cultural schisms, but may also involve brand hijacking, doppelgänger images, user innovation, influencers, and pop culture, as LEGO found to their advantage in Chapter 1. Managing a top-down brand position (mindshare) with bottom-up change (cultural branding but also day-to-day shifts in brand meaning generated by the other brand authors) is the equivalent of realized strategy or realized brand position.

How one does this, how one organizes for this, and the strategies, tactics, tools, and capabilities necessary to realize valuable co-created brand meaning over time are the focus of the rest of this chapter. To begin, it examines Step 6 in Building a Brand (see Figure 5.1 in Chapter 5)—internal launch—before examining externally focused strategies and tools to help identify emergent ideas that represent triggers for change and/or innovation.

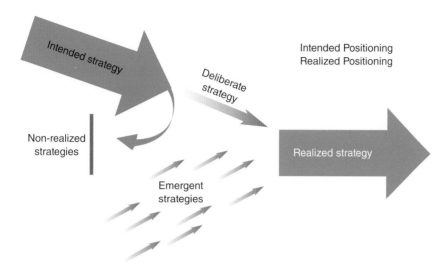

Figure 6.1   Maintaining the Brand

Source: Mintzberg

Internal Brand Launch: Organizing Authentically

Why do organizations talk about the importance of "living the brand" (Ind 2014)? Just what does this entail? There are several important activities required of brand managers. One can examine the **customer journey** (see Figure 6.2) and all the **customer touch points** to identify crucial areas where the brand's promise can be reinforced or undermined. One should survey all **brand stakeholders** (the authors in Figure 1.1) and identify gaps between intended identity, received image, and the firm's culture (Hatch and Schultz 2008). Building on Chapter 4, the brand team (and other staff) should immerse themselves in the target culture, populist world, or web-based crowd culture they seek to leverage associations with.

Why do we do this? Based on a lengthy ethnographic research program of the North American LBGT community, Kates (2004) identified the value and eventually the necessity of what he called "**brand legitimacy**." Brand legitimacy takes three forms:

1. **Pragmatic legitimacy**: This refers to the brand's ability to deliver on its functional promises and provides benefits that speak to users' self-interest. For example, that Levi's made good jeans that were hard wearing and stylish was never disputed.
2. **Moral legitimacy**: This refers to whether the brand has the moral right to operate within the subculture it seeks resources from. For example, beer brand Coors was found to be contributing to the politically conservative Heritage Foundation, an organization campaigning against equal rights for LBGT people. At the same time,

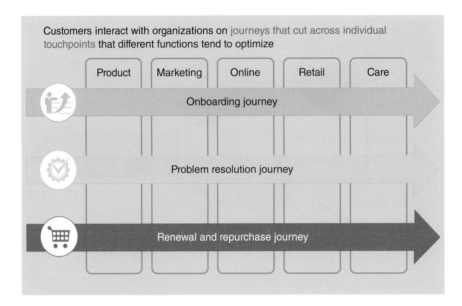

Figure 6.2   The Customer Journey

they were cynically trying to benefit from this community because of the value of the "pink dollar." The brand was quickly dropped from LBGT clubs and bars, eventually having negative equity in the community. In contrast, Levi's decision to take the lead on extending health care to LBGT employees' partners enhanced its moral standing (Kates 2004). In essence, the brand is viewed as sincere in intent and colloquially "walking the walk," both important drivers of legitimacy (and authenticity).

3. **Cultural legitimacy**: This is when the brand has become a taken-for-granted part of the subcultural landscape. In this instance, that the brand had the right to operate within the community is unquestioned. This type of legitimacy characterizes iconic brands and lies at the heart of authenticity. Although the LBGT community rejected Coors, Absolut Vodka's and Levi's constant early adoption of LBGT political issues and financial support resulted in them being viewed as an insider or "one of us." This meant these brands enjoyed high awareness and loyalty, strong levels of attachment, and sentiment. These brands had subcultural authenticity and therefore had every right to leverage community associations for their own gain (Kates 2004).

How do we render ourselves authentic relative to a community of users in the way that Absolut and Levi's did? First we conduct a brand consistency audit to identify customer "moments of truth" and gaps between intended identity, user perceived image, and firm culture (Hatch and Schultz 2008). The brand consistency audit involves mapping every aspect of the firm's operation in order to identity weaknesses and inconsistencies. A **customer journey analysis** is conducted to identify the target user's experience and identify inconsistencies between promises and delivery.

When conducting a **brand consistency audit** rate the following against the brand position:

1. Products and services: Are the products or services on offer consistent with the brand's position? When Steve Jobs was rejuvenating Apple, he used the brand's "Think Different" slogan to reduce a planned product release list down from over 800 to just a few, including the iPod, iPhone, iPad, laptops, iTunes store, and retail offer. Anything that was focused on incremental improvements over competitors, "me too" innovation, and processing power was dropped. The rest is history.

2. Services: Even product-oriented firms offer services, including in-store sales, after sales support, web communications, and so on. Lloyds Banking Group (UK) invested a substantial amount of resources and training into their call centers in order to ensure that "right first time" scores improved in line with their brand's claim of high-quality, expert service. Virgin Blue (Australia) focused on hiring airline cabin crew who could "think outside the box" because of their industry disruptor positioning.

3. Practices: Naomi Klein's bestselling anti-brand book *No Logo* held brands accountable for their impact on the environment, treatment of employees in overseas factories, and their impact on local communities. Nike's labor practices in its factories failed to live up to their aspirational position expressed in "Just do it!" Greenpeace countered Dove's Real Beauty campaign with one identifying the impact of palm oil use on the environment and families within Indonesia, resulting in Unilever changing suppliers of sustainable palm oil. Starbucks' doppelgänger brand image emerged when activists complained they shut down the very local coffee shops their brand was modelled on (Thompson et al. 2006).

4. Customers: In 2011 Abercrombie & Fitch made the headlines with an offer to pay actor Michael Sorrentino (from MTV's *Jersey Shore*) to stop wearing their clothes. The public relations strategy was designed to send a message to Abercrombie & Fitch's target customers who were concerned the tone of the show undermined the value of the brand as an identity resource. Other customers also influence the image of the brand, and although difficult to manage, the bravest brand teams do consider how to remove customers at odds with their position. Burberry retail staff were instructed to politely turn away older male customers (at odds with their refreshed brand image) from their stores as part of their turnaround under Rose Maria Bravo.

5. Production: How a firm produces its products or services can be a significant source of brand equity. Although operations managers have pursued lean production strategies for many years, studies of automotive brands suggest those with less lean strategies are more valued by users (in effect what is lean for production is often mean for customers) (Beverland et al. 2015). Brands such as luxury brands often emphasize their craft traditions (real or imagined) in their communications (Beverland et al. 2010), while Disneyland's experience is the result of careful training and scripting to ensure all of the firm's "hosts" communicate with customers in ways that reinforce the Disney image.

6. Removals: Apart from customers, what aspects of the firm's operations need to be removed to make the brand position authentic? For example, BP's 1990s repositioning to "Beyond Petroleum" (from British Petroleum) has long been the subject of green-washing claims given the firm's continued reliance on non-renewable energy sources. This strategy would have required the firm to have a clear plan to phase out its reliance on petroleum, and therefore was probably a stretch too far for the brand's owners.

7. Customer journey: The experiential brand approach has identified the need to align customers' sensory experience with the brand's position (this is covered in more detail below). During their heyday, Abercrombie & Fitch carefully crafted their stores to ensure the music was loud, the lighting low, the staff scantily clad and muscle-bound, and the scent strong and simple. The logic was clear, if you didn't like these aspects of the store, you were probably too old for the brand. In the early 2000s influential automotive ratings agency JD Power shifted their rankings away from vehicle returns to complaints within the first three months of ownership. The logic was simple—investments in total quality management had reduced true failings so that there was little difference between brands, whereas analysis of customer complaints not requiring a replacement revealed poor attention to user-interface design. One's ability to program the satnav, open the petrol cap, and adjust the seats was how most customers initially engaged with their new vehicle, and many of the most expensive marques failed handsomely in these rankings (Beverland 2005a).

The results of a brand consistency audit identify where things are going right, wrong, or need to be given special attention and investment. They often do not tell one why, however. To understand why gaps can emerge between the brand position and users' experience of it, we need to examine the nature of the gaps between three areas:

1. Intended brand identity or what they firm would like users to believe.
2. Received brand image or how users experience the brand claims.
3. Firm culture or the values and assumptions that determine whether staff engage in the behaviors supportive of the intended brand identity.

Chapters 1 and 2 identified the contribution made to branding of organizational theorists and also briefly covered the "firm personality" approach. Both highlight the importance of understanding the organizational side of branding in order to ensure that the firm, customer, and brand are in alignment. Hatch and Shultz (2008) have expanded upon this in their organizational identity framework, identifying three gaps that can emerge and undermine the delivery of a brand's position. These are identified in Figure 6.3 and expanded upon below.

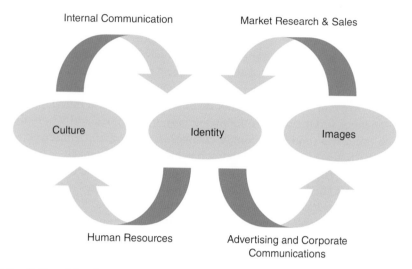

Achieving Brand Alignment

Figure 6.3   **Culture-Identity-Image Gaps**

Source: Hatch and Schultz 2008, p.78

Figure 6.2 identifies why we launch the brand internally first. Gaps between the three areas listed above represent problems for the brand. For example:

1. Identity–Image Gaps: This is the classic difference between the brand's intended identity and how users view the brand. This gap does not refer to user-generated content that can be positive for the brand's realized position, but to genuine failures that create a negative experience for the customer, or eventually influence the customer via negative publicity arising from doppelgänger attacks, influencer backlash, reports on scandals and unethical behavior, and so on.
2. Identity–Culture Gap: This is the difference between how your employees see the brand and the intended brand identity. This is partly why interest in employment branding has emerged over the last decade, but it is also why internal branding and marketing are conducted to ensure employees understand the brand, and are treated in ways consistent with the brand's identity.
3. Image–Culture Gaps: This is the difference between how your customer views the brand and how your employees see it. This is perhaps the more difficult gap to close because it can reflect a lack of customer focus on behalf of the firm, poor communication of intended brand identity to employees, a lack of training, poor performance-management systems, a lack of staff investment, or real antagonism between customers and employees.

Figure 6.3 clearly implies that these gaps can be avoided through clear communication between marketing, sales, and human resources, and a strong **internal marketing** or branding program. Image-based gaps are also based on stakeholder surveys of brand perceptions and through the use of tools that provide direct insights into identity–image–culture gaps in terms of the customer journey. For example, mystery shopping involves appointing someone to "play the customer" (they can be an external appointment but are often people within the firm) much like an ethnographer. Banks, for example, often use employees from other divisions to apply for a mortgage at a branch to identify whether service staff are following brand guidelines and where the experience can be improved (and also identify changes in training and employee support).

Returning to Kates's (2004) focus on achieving brand legitimacy, a brand consistency audit and the gaps identified above help ensure pragmatic and to some extent moral legitimacy for the brand. They also line up strongly with the emphasis by adherents of mindshare positioning that the brand position must be "lived" and engineered into all aspects of the firm's operations. The cultural positioning approach also emphasizes "living the brand" and legitimacy but achieves it in different ways, focusing on ensuring the firm achieves cultural or cognitive legitimacy or becomes an authentic member of the community it seeks to associate with.

The cultural approach to internal launch involves authenticating the firm so that customers and other users view the brand as a cultural insider. In this approach, the firm draws on insights gained from the populist world it wishes to link to and leverage in its cultural myths. Historically many marketers have done this through a process called "**co-optation**" whereby they adopt culture from marginalized groups, strip them of their authenticity, and use them to enhance the cool factor of their brands with the mainstream (see X to G, Chapter 4). This often creates a backlash among the original creators of culture who feel exploited, which may eventually destroy the claimed authenticity of the brand. Holt (2002) has argued this approach is no longer viable in a connected world where a backlash can go viral and create a crisis of authenticity overnight.

For example, many brands have sought to benefit from "hipsterism" ("white cool") or what was once ostensibly created by struggling inner city Anglo-Saxon wannabe artists and creatives (Arsel and Thompson 2011)). Predating the "gig economy" these consumers typically built their own music venues in order to provide a place where their own bands could play (as they were shut out of the mainstream). The 2016 documentary *Death by Audio* featured one such club, built by music fans in a derelict building, and eventually becoming viewed as the most innovative music venue in Brooklyn. Eventually the building was sold to Vice Media, who closed the club down at short notice. The irony, however, was that Vice Media had built its empire on championing the do-it-yourself culture at the heart of inner-city hipsterism, a point not lost on the documentary's audience. The documentary had challenged the myths underpinning Vice's claim to authenticity, presenting it as a cultural parasite (Holt 2006).

Co-optation, whether through direct appropriation of cultural content, or the purchase of "rights" to associate with cultural events and communities such as sport, music, and art, has largely ignored the other meaning creators in the co-creation process. Although brands may have the legal right to use unprotected content and leverage associations purchased through sponsorship or endorsement deals, fans or community insiders enjoy psychological ownership (or felt-attachment) to their content, and are not always happy for it to be exploited commercially. Football clubs such as Cardiff City have experienced a backlash when fans feel outsiders are mishandling "their club."

As a result, firms have attempted to move from marketing to populist worlds to marketing through them, through a process of cultural immersion. The idea here is simple in theory but challenging in practice—firms need to embrace the ethos at the heart of the populist world and engineer it into everything they do, just as Absolut did with the LBGT community and Harley Davidson with their Harley Owners Group. In this sense, they render the firm authentic from the point of view of the customer they target and the populist world they draw on, and, importantly, contribute back to. So how is this done

1. First start with the cultural brief process identified in Chapter 5.
2. Focus on learning the rules of the game or the ethos that frames what is right, proper, and acceptable within the populist world. This takes time, and involves immersing employees in the marketplace through policies that require engagement with community and its focal activity. For example, L.L. Bean requires all of its employees to engage in at least one of the outdoor activities of its many subcultures, including fishing, hiking, and hunting. Nike requires its staff to participate in sport, and use the insights gained from engaging with customers to frame branding activities. The end result of this is staff that ultimately believe they are marketing to themselves because they are so embedded in their communities (Farrelly et al. 2017).
3. Market through cultural codes: These codes are cues that signal one is a cultural insider. For example, New Zealand Vodka brand 42-Below realized that to overcome its lack of country-of-origin authenticity (it had no link to traditional vodka-producing nations) it needed to position itself differently. Seeking to build a buzz about the brand through being served at the hottest clubs rather than through extensive advertising, the brand team aligned closely with LBGT clubs (standard setters in alcohol choice and frequented by customers with a high disposable income), producing a series of controversial social media videos (search on YouTube for 42Below) playfully featuring high-profile gay iconography, musicians, clothing, stereotypical activities, the brand team loudly claim "they love the mighty pink dollar." Outsiders viewed these adverts as outrageous stereotyping, but insiders viewed them as legitimate camp humor (the brand received no complaints regarding discrimination). Knowledge of these insider cues came from a decision to invest much of their marketing budget in entertainment—that is, staff were paid to go clubbing! The brand was eventually sold to Bacardi for $US140 million.

4. Innovate culturally: Cultural co-optation lacks reciprocity—the brand benefits from the associations taken from the populist world, but the community gains little in return and, in some cases, members can feel their identity being diminished through mainstreaming. The large global surf brands such as Ripcurl and Billabong have found this out to their detriment. Extending into fashion lines brands have undermined their authenticity with core surfers who react negatively to non-surfers wearing "their brands." Brands that seek to benefit from their relationship to a populist culture render themselves authentic when they give something back via cultural innovation. Returning to surfing, the brand Roxy gained instant credibility by supporting female professional surfers. The brand ensured prize money for competitions was equivalent to that for men, ensured competitions were professionally run, and offered top of the line sponsorship deals to female surf stars. Historically, female surfers were viewed in negative terms by men, often seen as "beach bunnies" and objectified sexually (Beverland and Farrelly 2011). Other forms of cultural innovation are covered later in the chapter on community-oriented branding.

5. Be prepared to let go of brand control: This is difficult for many firms, but in seeking to associate with a populist world it is only logical to allow members input into brand meaning co-creation. Harley Davidson attracts many different subcultures, many of which are openly antagonistic. For example, the brand has attracted misogynistic men (who think women should "ride bitch" as passenger, but never be in control) and lesbian riders seeking to undermine the ultimate symbol of masculinity by riding the bikes and forming their own club (Dykes on Bikes). The brand welcomes all comers and focuses on supporting each group in different ways, happily sponsoring music concerts for each that reflect their deep knowledge of each subculture. All of this ultimately renders their position of "freedom" as authentic.

Internal launch at the simplest level ensures that the brand's intended identity is seen as genuine or authentic. This involves not only aligning the internal operations of the firm to ensure a brand's functional promises are delivered on consistently, but also increasingly requires the firm to render itself authentic at many levels including its ethical behavior, political outlook, employee engagement, and cultural role. This requires a detailed brand audit involving surveying stakeholder perceptions, studying consumer contexts, understanding consumer goals and identity projects, and aligning employees' interests and passions with brand values in ways that genuinely ensure they live the ethos of the brand. Although much of this results from trial and error, brand managers should try and step lightly in consumer space before engaging in innovations, seeking to leverage associations they may or may not have the right to use, and communicating brand promises more broadly through marketing communications.

Communicating Externally

Communicating the brand's position to the target audience is actually the second-to-last step in brand building (see Step 7, Figure 5.1, Chapter 5). Regardless of what type of positioning model one uses, it is only once the organization is ready to deliver on the brand's promise that it begins to communicate externally with its intended customers. The first step in designing a communication strategy is to ensure that the brand position drives marketing-related actions across the expanded marketing mix (remember that price, promotion, placement, product, processes, people, physical environment, and purpose all communicate). As the quote by Michael Eisner at the beginning of this chapter states, the brand's position must be engineered into all subsequent strategic and tactical activities aimed at building awareness, stimulating trial, and encouraging loyalty over time. Since this is not a specialist text on marketing communications, we will limitation our discussion to four broad approaches to brand communications:

1. Integrated Marketing Communications (IMC): This approach covers the other three strategies detailed below, but also includes discussion of traditional tools such as advertising (in all its forms), sponsorship and celebrity endorsement, product placement, and personal selling. The basic logic of IMC is that all the tools used should cohere around a single campaign strategy, although each tool may be used at different stages of buyer readiness (i.e., awareness, interest, desire, action).
2. Experiential Marketing Strategies: The experiential branding approach (see Chapter 2) focuses on appealing to the five senses (hearing, sight, taste, smell, and touch), often through flagship stores, carefully crafted servicescapes, temporary events such as pop-up stores, product and service design, and website design.
3. Community Focused Marketing: The communal branding approach (see Chapter 2) is detailed below in terms of subcultures of consumption, brand communities, consumer tribes, and brand publics. The Lomography case at the end of the chapter provides an example of this approach.
4. Social Media: Although social media play differing roles in the strategies above, there are also some specific things to bear in mind when seeking to build your brand through this medium.

Integrated Marketing Communications

Chapters 3 and 4 discussed the importance of building brand awareness (recognition and recall) through communicating important associations to customers. When a brand is positioned relative to a customer's goal (whether it is defined through mindshare or cultural positioning), we need to make customers aware of our brand and its promise, and do so in a compelling way. The primary way to do this is marketing communications.

Marketing communications involves a range of tools including advertising across different media channels, sponsorship and celebrity endorsement, event marketing, personal selling, product placement, point of sale, and public relations. I will not go into each in detail here, but the important point is that these different tools should be used in an integrated fashion and for different outcomes.

Integrated marketing communications (IMC) involves just that, integrating every tool and message so that they communicate (1) a consistent message and (2) work in harmony across the **consumer-decision journey**. The consumer-decision journey consists of four stages:

1. Consider: the user becomes aware of the brand through communications and personal sources (word-of-mouth or social media sharing for example).
2. Evaluate: users search for information about the brand from a wide array of formal and informal sources.
3. Buy: the consumer buys the brand (this can involve a long considered process, impulse purchase, or *in situ* choices based on feelings that the brand fits intuitively with my goals or sense of self).
4. Experience, advocate, and bond: the user experiences the brand, judges its value, engages in positive or negative advocacy, and starts to frame their relationship with it.

(*Source*: Darley 2016, p. 202)

BRAND ASIDE 6.1

Strategic Ambiguity and Multiple Messages

Although consistency and clarity are viewed as essential for brand building, for many organizations managing multiple stakeholder expectations requires strategic ambiguity. Law-enforcement organizations such as London's Metropolitan Police (which do invest in corporate image), for example, have to manage between being seen as part of the community while also having to appear impartial and, by necessity, apart from their communities (Brown et al. 2008). The pursuit of authenticity has also led many organizations to communicate multiple messages, often in deliberately ambiguous ways, simultaneously referencing the past and the future, tradition, and modernity, being non-commercial and user focused (Dickinson-Delaporte et al. 2010). This is because authenticity is not merely fealty to tradition but involves an evolving story through time. Likewise, different stakeholder objectives may render the pursuit of message clarity pointless. If a brand has one (or more) of these core tensions at its heart, it must carefully craft its messaging accordingly.

A common mistake in regard to IMC involves the belief that every form of communication should say the same thing. This is often expressed in terms such as "One Voice, One Look." While consistency is important, especially in terms of design cues such as color, font, store fit out, and brochures, clearly the medium chosen and the message must differ for different stages of the customer journey. Brand Aside 6.1 provides further details on managing multiple messages across different stakeholder audiences. In reality, IMC means the messages should be integrated into the customer journey, so that the campaign is aimed at ensuring users take the full journey, and that each form of communication achieves particular goals (defined by the four stages of the journey) and helps transition the user to the next phase. So which tools are best at each stage?

1. Advertising: Advertising is best used in the "consideration" stage of the customer journey, and is valuable in reinforcing brand image in general. Non-print advertising remains a powerful mechanism for communicating brand myths, and identifying ideal users, usage situations, and other core associations about the brand. Print-based forms can then reinforce these messages, often through the use of taglines or by focusing on particular parts of the overall brand message. Brand Aside 6.2 provides a counterpoint to classical attention grabbing advertising strategies.

BRAND ASIDE 6.2

Does Gaining Our Attention Build Brands?

In the 2015 UK election, advertising for the two major political parties (Labour and Conservatives) seemed to be deliberately vague and bland. Long lead-ins with soft music and snippets of leaders' speeches and voter concerns seemingly played at random dominated the television advertisements, with the leaders and their core messages appearing briefly, and at the end. Similarly, Leica launched their new innovative X-1 camera with a 45-minute YouTube film identifying how a camera was shaped from a block of polished aluminum, with no overt appeals to brand claims. These advertisements go out of their way not to grab our attention, which is the exact opposite of what good ads should do. High attention, for example, helps generate awareness, which of course builds brands. Or does it?

Robert Heath (2012) proposes an alternative approach called low-attention emotional processing, which argues paradoxically that the less attention we pay to advertisements, the more powerful they become (assuming they're crafted carefully). Low-attention ads work directly on the emotions, which are key to building

(Continued)

strong brand relationships rather than high-attention rational appeals (Fournier 1998). Seemingly, low-key advertisements put us at ease precisely because they don't seem like advertisements. As a result, we lower our defenses or "marketing bullshit detector" and as a result are more likely to be influenced at a subconscious, emotional level. For example, the advertising campaigns referred to earlier made each party's leader seem in touch, real, and concerned. No clear positions were enunciated, but this was the point; the advertisements were about reinforcing the political brand. In contrast, minor parties who made strong appeals often communicated solely with their base rather than appeal to the swinging voters they needed. Heath's arguments are rejected by many, but align with work on neuro-marketing, Big Data, "nudging", theories of the subconscious, and much work in consumer culture theory.

2. Sales promotion: Sales promotion provides an incentive to buy, primarily through reducing risk of purchase, and is therefore useful for the "buy" stage. This often takes the form of a price or volume discount. Sales promotions can be a fact of life for most FMCG brands (and may help gain retail listings), especially in large retail chains; however, they should be used carefully. Sales promotions can simply encourage loyal users to buy brands they would have purchased anyway, but at a lower price. Sales promotions have also been linked to declining brand image, although should the promotion occur as part of a strong brand campaign this effect is mitigated (Jones 1998).

3. Direct marketing: Typically, this form of communications occurs via email or posts into social media feeds. Drawing on big data or customer relationship management (CRM) systems, messages can be targeted at individual customers with relatively ease. This form of communication is useful in the "buy" stage and may also help with "bonding" (particularly stimulating re-buy).

4. Event marketing and sponsorship: these forms of communication are useful in the "consider" and "experience, advocate, and bond" stages. Typically, these forms of communication have been judged according to whether they fit the brand. However, recent research has suggested sponsorship with low fit can be even more valuable because it is viewed as more authentically motivated. For example, Walmart's provision of help and materials to re-start the New Orleans Mardi Gras after were viewed positively because they were low key and seemingly had little to do with the brand or any commercial motive (Weinberger and Wallendorf 2012). Events can also be essential to building legitimacy, creating the place for experiences to occur, and for reinforcing communal brand bonds (see below). Further detail on the logic of endorsement strategies is provided in Brand Aside 6.3.

BRAND ASIDE 6.3

Celebrity Endorsements and Brand Meaning

How do brands benefit from celebrity endorsement? Essentially, it involves meaning transfer. Figure 6.5 provides details. Anthropologist Grant McCracken's (1989) meaning transfer model identifies that celebrities transfer meaning to the brand, while the brand also transfers meaning to the celebrity. Since the celebrity occupies the cultural world, endorsement enables the brand to transcend the world of commerce. Although widespread exposure to sponsorship deals and endorsement strategies makes this less meaningful, A-list celebrities are viewed as more discerning in this regard. If the match is done carefully, both parties can benefit (the opposite is also true). Celebrity endorsement is also a useful way to reach a wider audience, reinforce the brand's position with your current audience, adding in associations, renew the brand potentially by reaching the next generation of users, and enhance perceptions of the brand. One must be careful, however; celebrities are human, and any missteps can backfire on the brand as well—Nike, for example, has had to carefully manage its relationship with endorsed athletes such as Tiger Woods and Maria Sharapova who suffered scandals.

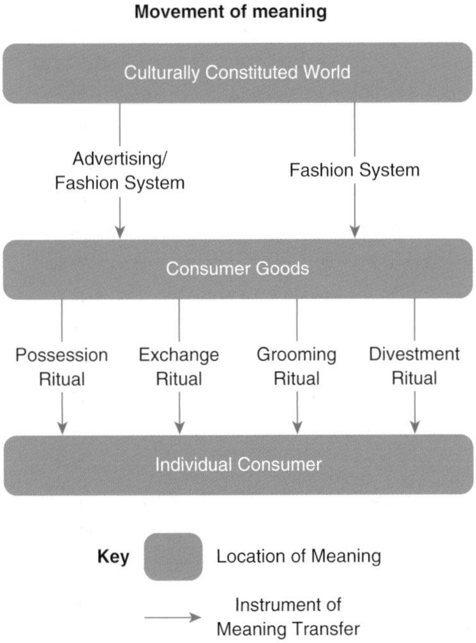

Movement of meaning

```
                    ┌──────────────────────────────┐
                    │   Culturally Constituted World │
                    └──────────────────────────────┘
                         │                    │
                   Advertising/          Fashion System
                  Fashion System
                         ↓                    ↓
                    ┌──────────────────────────────┐
                    │        Consumer Goods          │
                    └──────────────────────────────┘
                    │          │          │          │
               Possession  Exchange   Grooming   Divestment
                 Ritual     Ritual     Ritual     Ritual
                    ↓          ↓          ↓          ↓
                    ┌──────────────────────────────┐
                    │      Individual Consumer       │
                    └──────────────────────────────┘
```

Key ▭ Location of Meaning

→ Instrument of Meaning Transfer

Figure 6.5   Cultural Meaning Transfer Model

Source: McCracken, Grant (1986), 'Culture and Consumption: A Theoretical Account of the Structure and Movement of the Cultural Meaning of Consumer Goods', *Journal of Consumer Research*, 13(1): 71–84.

5. Personal selling: This involves face-to-face selling and is typically used more in business-to-business branding efforts than in business-to-consumer contexts due to the cost. This form of communication is useful in the "evaluate" and "buy" stages, as personal interactions can help build trust in the brand, provide more tailored solutions to needs, and provide the opportunity to build empathy with the customer. Research reveals that strong bonds between salespeople and customers can provide positive spillover effects for the brand both in B2B and B2C contexts (Beverland 2001), and such bonds may often be framed in terms of "commercial friendships" (Price and Arnould 1999). The downside is that loyalty is often primarily to the salesperson not the brand, resulting in diminished brand equity with the loss of a salesperson (MacIntosh and Lockshin 1997).

6. Mobile marketing: Communication through mobile devices or application technology is on the rise (in-app advertising in particular is growing rapidly). Big data enable content to be customized, although marketers need to take care in ensuring accuracy and that it does not become intrusive in what is customer space. This type of advertising is most useful for the "buy," "experience, advocate, and bond" stages.

7. Online advertising: Over 50 percent of marketing communications budgets in developed economies is allocated to social media. This involves advertising through established platforms such as the "big four" of Facebook, Twitter, LinkedIn, and YouTube, as well as blogs and company-sponsored sites. The advantages are many—marketers face less restraints in terms of time and content restrictions, and potentially can reach a very large, global audience. And such content can be easily shared, helping to generate a buzz about the brand. These forms of communications can be useful across all stages of the customer journey.

8. Public Relations: Public relations relates not only to the brand but also the organization behind the brand. Public relations is often more about generating a reputation with the broader public, or key stakeholders such as shareholders, than in communicating specific brand associations. Public relations is also essential in dealing with brand crises (Chapter 12) and in building and maintaining moral and cultural legitimacy (depending on the ethos of each populist world). Public relations can help with all stages of communications but is particularly useful in the "consider" and "evaluate" stages.

There are many more considerations to make regarding media, including the different media options (radio, vs. television vs. online) and the mix of these options. These are beyond the scope of this book, and the choice of channel and mix depends on the budget available, the technological context at hand, and the habits of your target audience. Critically, all should be integrated in terms of message, and in terms of moving customers through the buyer journey stages. The effectiveness of each tool is also measured differently, depending upon what stage one is in—"consideration" might be measured with recognition and recall, while sentiment and authenticity might be more appropriate in the "experience, advocate, and bond" stage.

Crafting the Brand Experience

Marketers have long understood the value of the experience. Emile Zola's 1883 novel *Au Bonheur des Dames* was inspired by the Paris department store Le Bon Marché (now owned by the LVMH group). Zola described the store in detail, identifying how its design was carefully crafted to seduce customers that the experience of visiting was more important than the goods purchased. Although value as experience was popularized in Pine and Gilmore's 1998 *Harvard Business Review* article "Welcome to the Experience Economy," how users experience your brand (relative to their needs) has always lain at the heart of brand value. Holbrook has been instrumental in helping us understand the nature of experiences. His typology of experiences is presented in Table 6.1 below.

Holbrook's value typology models consumer experience in terms of it being experienced in relation to the self or others, the extent to which the consumer is active in the experience or not, and the degree to which value is framed as a gain or avoidance of loss (extrinsic) or is valued for its own sake (intrinsic). No value is better than the other; rather Holbrook identified the basis on which different brands could appeal to customers. This idea lies at the heart of different models of brand positioning and in framing the customer need. Ultimately, the way in which value is expressed and experienced should reflect the brand. For established brands, this is often why it is difficult to reposition (see Chapter 8), as awareness and understanding of the brand frame expectations about the experience, and these act as barriers to change.

These types of value are useful for helping us understand how we might frame brand communications. Nike, for example, focuses primarily on Efficiency—one gets as much out of exercise as one puts in. Johnnie Walker in contrast focuses on Status—the whisky is a sign of success and creates an impression that the drinker is a high flyer. The typology can also be used in store design. Prada creates stores that are a blend of retail, technology, and museum gallery. Here the focus of the store is on Aesthetic appreciation, with many garments placed on pedestals off limits to customers to be enjoyed for their own sake. LEGO engineers Play into its communications, product designs, flagship stores, theme parks, games, and movies.

Table 6.1 Holbrook's typology of value in the consumption experience

		Extrinsic	Intrinsic
Self-oriented	**Active**	Efficiency (Input/Output; Convenience)	Play (Fun)
	Reactive	Excellence (Quality)	Aesthetics (Beauty)
Other-oriented	**Active**	Status (Success; Impression Management)	Ethics (Justice; Virtue; Morality)
	Reactive	Esteem (Reputation; Materialism; Possessions)	Spirituality (Faith; Ecstasy; Sacredness)

Source: Holbrook (1999, p. 5).

A similar way to think about creating an experience is Pine and Gilmore's experience economy model. Pine and Gilmore proposed that economies developed through cycles, and that experiences simply represented a new stage of evolution in the search for differentiation in an age of commoditization. Pine and Gilmore's value in the experience economy model (1998) presents their approach to creating experiences (much of which is consistent with Holbrook's ideas above). This models experience in terms of how active or passive the customer is in co-creating the experience and the extent to which they absorb the experience or are largely immersed in it.

This framework has impacted on how retailers have carefully crafted servicescapes in their flagship stores. Apple, for example, emphasizes education in its retail stores, providing a small lecture theatre for customers to attend information sessions on using different programs and tools. Lomography does the same with its sponsored "Lomo Walks," ensuring novice Lomographers learn about the joys of film photography and learn new tricks through active participation (reinforced through a sharing communal website). This makes sense in terms of both brands—Apple is positioned as a tool to enable creative expression, while Lomography stresses a "no rules" do-it-yourself approach to film photography that stresses the value of happy accidents and experimentation. In contrast, cinema chains focus on entertaining experiences, doing all they can to make customers comfortable so they can sit back and enjoy the movie, and hopefully large amounts of heavily marked-up food items.

Other brands take a different approach, albeit in line with their position. Many gaming brands such as *World of Warcraft* (and real world equivalents such as Games Workshop) encourage active participation in other times, places, and realities. Through extensive engagement in these activities, consumers experience a sense of flow whereby they lose track of time and feel immersed in an alternate hyper-reality. Aesthetic (or "esthetic" in Pine and Gilmore's figure) experiences follow from Holbrook's typology. Pioneering German electronic group Kraftwerk creates these experiences in its highly sought-after 3D concerts. These concerts usually take place in iconic locations such as New York's MoMA museum, the Sydney Opera House, or London's Tate Modern Turbine Hall. Here, the audience is immersed in a world of light, sound, and laser visuals (which can be viewed through specially branded 3D glasses). The experience is largely passive, with no interaction between band and the crowd, and reflects the band's robotic "man machine" imagery.

As with all aspects of brand communications, the brand's position is engineered into the experience (Brakus et al. 2009).

Communal Branding Strategies

Chapters 1 and 2 identified how communities grow up around brands, or groups of consumers use brands for linking value. We have identified these as brand communities, subcultures of consumption, consumer tribes, and brand publics. Although the origins of these communities have often had little active involvement from the brands' marketing teams, marketers need to have a clear strategy for creating, influencing, or engaging with different communities, all of which can influence the image of the brand. This strategy is particularly important if one is following a cultural brand positioning approach, but is also important in the case of mindshare branding. Brand Aside 6.4 provides further insight into populist authenticity and communal brand strategies.

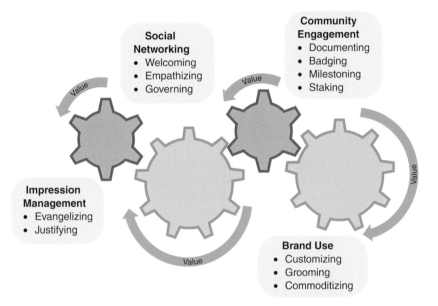

Figure 6.4   The Process of Collective Value Creation in Brand Communities

Source: Schau et al. 2009, p.36

BRAND ASIDE 6.4

Getting Communities Right

Susan Fournier and Lara Lee (2009) have identified the basis of successful brand community strategies. They challenge a number of myths about communities that align with how value is created by users. First, brand community requires the organization to change instead of just representing another marketing strategy. In essence, the organization must embody the ethos of the community in order

(Continued)

to render itself authentic. Second, brand community is primarily there for the benefit of users. Organizations can benefit immensely from these communities, but many communities were set up without brand support or involvement and thus may resent increased encroachment into their space. Third, as identified in Figure 6.4, brands benefit from strong communities, rather than vice versa. The focus of community strategies should be on enhancing the community first. Fourth, organizations should embrace communal tension (between old and new, real and fake, insider and outsider) because these conflicts ensure communities endure. Trying to create a community of unquestioning followers is a waste of effort. Fifth, online networks are simply one form of communication tool, rather than central to a community strategy. Finally, communities are strongest when marketers give up control.

To understand how to build the brand through communal activities, it is useful to explore how value is created collectively. Figure 6.4 identifies that a combination of four processes (underpinned by particular practices) helps create strong and enduring brand communities:

1. Social networking: These practices provide linking value between members. They aim to create, strengthen, and sustain bonds between members. How? Members welcome newcomers, empathize with them (by remembering what it was like to be a newcomer and cutting them some slack), and govern them (making sure members adhere to the communal ethos).
2. Impression management: These practices are externally focused and aim to present a positive view of the community, the brand, and its members to outsiders (largely in an attempt to sustain and grow the community, and, by implication, the brand). How? By talking about the many benefits of the brand and its community, members act as evangelists. Related to this, members typically justify an ongoing commitment to the brand community.
3. Community engagement: These practices focus on increasing members' engagement with the community (i.e., making them more loyal and attached). How? Figure 6.4 identifies four practices (staking, milestoning, badging, and documenting). In essence, these practices focus on building the community rather than using the brand. As such, the main focus is on respecting sub-groups within the community, maintaining distinctions between members, and in valuing diversity. Staking for example involves setting out one's degree of engagement. Milestoning involves participating in key events including one's first exposure to the brand and transitions from novice to experienced practitioner. Badging involves a representation of the milestone in a visual form. Documenting involves creating and sharing a personal narrative of community involvement (a timeline so to speak).

4. Brand use: These are practices that enhance members' use of the brand. One benefit of brand communities is that they encourage deeper participation in the activities at the heart of the brand, and in so doing create more and deeper associations, generating stronger perceptions of value and beliefs that it is unique, resulting in greater attachment and equity. How? Grooming involves sharing best practice tips, including how to pass difficult levels of online games, how to get the best of out certain types of photographic film, how to drive off road, and so on. When community members innovate in their use of the brand, they are customizing their relationship with it. In sharing their innovations, they help with grooming. Finally, commoditizing is about maintaining access to the brand, often by highlighting where one can buy it cheaply, guaranteeing tickets to desirable events, and so on.

(*Source*: Schau et al. 2009, pp. 34–35)

The practices above were derived from studies of how consumers within brand communities co-created value. Table 6.2 identifies examples of how different brands play a role in enabling this value co-creation to occur, and offers advice on different strategies for each practice.

Table 6.2   Communal branding practices and examples

Practice	Example	Branding Approach
Social networking: bringing new members into the fold and enabling them to learn the ropes		
Welcoming	Local chapters of Morgan Motor Clubs contact new owners and welcome them and their car into the fold.	Provide forums for new members to be formally welcomed to the community; provide members with welcome packs; identify and acknowledge quasi-official "welcomers"; acknowledge new members and profile them in forums.
Empathizing	Virgin managers are required to work airline check-in counters regularly in order to understand one of the more stressful parts of traveling.	Ensure staff engage directly in the community and reflect on what it was like to be a new entrant in an unknown space.
Governing	Lomography provides 10 rules to set the tone for commenting on posters' photos.	Learn the basis of legitimacy judgments and communicate and act appropriately.
Impression management: identity building with outsiders		
Evangelizing	Filmmaker Peter Jackson held daily debriefing sessions for fans during the making of *Lord of the Rings* in order to bring them into his decision process and the necessity of diverging from the text. This communicated his love and respect for the material and overcame the shock of an inexperienced director being placed in charge of a sacred text.	Provide deeper insight into the brand through the provision of behind the scenes materials, personal engagement with key brand figures and community events in general.
Justifying	Copic provides instructional videos to identify how different types of marker pens unique to the brand enhance one's drawings, leading to more professional effects.	Celebrate the subcultural identity of members.

(Continued)

Table 6.2   (Continued)

Practice	Example	Branding Approach
Community engagement: maintaining community harmony		
Staking	Harley Davidson provides targeted concerts to each and every subculture, allowing them to celebrate their differences.	Understand the subcultures or groups within the community; acknowledge each and support each with sub-sites and targeted support/events.
Milestoning	Facebook's memories app provides a personal and public reminder of important events from your past.	Use CRM systems to acknowledge important milestones; develop apps and web-based systems that enable milestones to be entered and captured.
Badging	Pioneering New Zealand-based bungee-jumping brand AJ Hackett provides t-shirts to actual jumpers (they are not available to non-jumpers). A film of each jumper's encounter is also provided and loaded up onto social media.	Provide physical and virtual signs of key milestones; small rewards for engaging in such activities.
Documenting	14Bike Co developed a "My Story" webpage to allow owners of their custom-made cycles to describe their design processes.	Provide a platform and format for narratives to be created and shared. Provide a place for "my story" narratives in official brand archives.
Brand use: enhancing engagement with brand		
Grooming	Lomography hosts photography walks whereby novices and experienced film shooters mingle and share tips with different types of cameras.	Provide spaces and places for knowledge sharing between experts and novices.
Customizing	LEGO allows fans to post ideas for new lines and innovations on their website. This has reinvented the brand and led to a range of movie tie-ins.	Provide spaces for users to share customized creations within the community; offer creative commons acknowledgment of such works; seek permission to use some works in brand communications or activities.
Commoditizing	BrewDog runs a cellar-share scheme that ensures fans get advance access to specialist releases, beer as a dividend, and favorable pricing.	Give the community preferential treatment and access to brand-related material including new launches, extensions, and so on.

In Figure 6.4 the cogs identify that these processes work together to shape the community. The tighter the cogs, the more the community provides benefits for members. The more practices in operation in relation to each process, the stronger the community, meaning it is more likely to endure over time and continue to provide value to its users. Marketers add value in this process if they provide an abundant array of practices that enable consumers to engage in linking and identity value, and of course tighten the relationships between each of the cogs. Communal-based communications involve investing in a broad array of practices identified in Table 6.2, and monitoring their use to ensure they are effective and relevant.

These practices help generate the moral and cultural legitimacy identified as being essential to associating with populist worlds. In providing these practices and ceding a degree of control over the brand to community members, the organization indicates its sincerity and therefore is believed to be genuine in intent, which is a core component of moral legitimacy and authenticity (Beverland et al. 2008). The ability to provide the right practices and adapt them to the needs of the community means the brand becomes taken for granted and seen as essential to the communal context (subculture, brand community, and tribe), resulting in cultural legitimacy.

Social Media

Although social media communications are covered or implied in the discussion of IMC and experiential and communal brand strategies, it is also important to consider a few pointers when using other social media strategies. Marketers invest in social media for many reasons, but in the context of brand building, web-based content has been developed in the hope of generating a "buzz" about the brand, which will hopefully lead to increased sharing among viewers and viral success. However as Holt (2016) has noted, success in this realm for brands is often rare. It is worth remembering that the most successful web-based content is rarely branded—low-key, amateur-generated content often ranks the highest in YouTube viewership and Instagram subscribers, while celebrities are far more likely to attract engaged fans to their social media pages that brands. Holt (2016) argues that brand marketers forget that social media are the space for cultural innovation to occur. Studies of brand publics have identified that although big data may demonstrate that brands are widely talked about online, users are more focused on projecting their own image than in engaging with each other or with branded content per se (Arvidsson and Caliandro 2015).

So, what are some things to be aware of when using social media to build brands?

1. The mindshare approach is problematic online as it is predicated on marketers owning the message and being the sole author of brand meaning. Although on-position ads that are humorous, surprising, or challenging may form the basis of viral campaign success, these are few and far between (Dobele et al. 2007).
2. The cultural position model may have more relevance online. If one is primarily building a brand in this space, then web-based crowd cultures replace populist worlds as sources of myth making and outlets for brand innovation and authentic engagement (Holt 2016).
3. Each online forum has a different ethos that frames how branded content is received. Although sending bloggers free products or services in the hope they will endorse your brand is common, these may breach the unwritten norms or rules that define the blogger community (and of which even the blogger may be unaware since they are also in a co-creation context). Knowing the rules of the game prior

to engaging with bloggers will ensure the blogging platform remains valuable to its users and therefore potentially valuable to your brand (Kozinets et al. 2010).

4.   Subscribers to blogging sites with a strong communal basis (i.e., where the focus is on the blogger offering a service to a like-minded community) react best when any word-of-mouth campaign is fully disclosed by the owner of the site. Brand managers should therefore avoid guerrilla-style campaigns in this area (Kozinets et al. 2010).

5.   Subscribers to sites with a more individualistic ethos (i.e., where the site is largely a focus for celebrity bloggers identity) may react positively if the product and campaign fit the personality of the blogger. Those that do not are likely to be contested by followers and this may result in damage to the blogger's reputation (Kozinets et al. 2010).

6.   The effective seeding of word of mouth strategies through social media sites requires a full understanding of the positioning of the site and its owner, fits with community norms and objectives, and/or is consistent with the celebrity persona of the site's host (Kozinets et al. 2010).

Chapter Summary

Brand building involves preparing the organization to deliver the brand's promise (or live the brand) and communicating externally with target audiences and stakeholders that can influence the image of the brand in the mind of core users. Although brand audits are essential for identifying whether the firm can deliver on brand promises, rendering the organization authentic by embodying the ethos of a target populist world is essential for achieving moral and cultural legitimacy and therefore authenticity. Through engagement with these populist worlds, organizations identify the basis of authentic brand communications, including messages used in IMC campaigns, communicated implicitly through experiential strategies, engagement with brand communities or subcultures, and online.

Review Questions

1.   Why do we undertake a brand audit? Describe how the mindshare and cultural models differ in their approaches to internal launch.

2.   Identify a brand that is inconsistent. Identify all the messages the brand sends across its different communications tools.

3.   Examine how the brand Volvo reinforces its position of "safety" over time.

4.   Identify a brand community and analyze how the brand helps or hinders consumer value creation using the strategies listed in this chapter.

5.   Why might brands struggle to build strong social media communities?

Case Example: Lomography

The Lomography Society was formed in 1992 in Vienna, Austria, by a group of art students who fell in love with a Communist-era Soviet-made film camera, the LC-A (see Figure 6.6). This camera was one of many made in the USSR to cater to the needs of the local mass market. Other models included the Diana and Holga (see Figure 6.7), both cheap, plastic cameras. Although the LC-A featured a very good lens and was well respected, models such as the Diana and Holga were notorious for light leaks, which have the effect of exposing the film. Although most serious photographers try and avoid light leaks at all costs as they view photos suffering from over exposure as "flawed" the Lomography Society took a different view, looking upon light leaks and other flaws (the ease of double exposure for example) as offering potential for individual artistic expression (see Figure 6.8).

In 1995 the Lomography Society became the sole distributor for Lomo cameras outside of Russia and have subsequently updated the various models, launching the LC-A+, wide-angled versions of the Holga, and co-branded versions of the Diana

Figure 6.6   Lomo LC-A Camera

Source: author's collection

(Continued)

Figure 6.7   Holga and Diana Co-branded Cameras

Figure 6.8   Lomography Photo with Light Leaks using Turquoise

with well-known pop artists such as Tara MacPherson (see Figure 6.7), among many others. As digital cameras began to replace film, the Lomographic Society morphed into a full-blown brand community, under the tagline of "The Future is Analog." The organization now operates a number of flagship Lomography Stores around the globe, has launched many of its own models of cameras, and collaborated with Russian lens makers to produce nineteenth-century Daguerreotype brass lenses to fit standard digital and film DSLR cameras by Canon, Leica, and Nikon. Furthermore, the brand has been responsible for revitalizing film photography.

The brand is based around its community. The Lomography community is based on ten rules:

1. Take your camera everywhere you go.
2. Use it anytime, day or night.
3. Lomography is not interference in your life, but part of it.
4. Try the shot from the hip (literally).
5. Approach the objects of your Lomographic desire as close as possible.
6. Don't think.
7. Be fast.
8. You don't have to know beforehand what you have captured on film, or,
9. Afterwards either.
10. Don't worry about any rules.

The community is built across a number of platforms. In each store, Lomographers are able to pin their favorite prints to the wall to create a collective, consumer-owned "Lomo Wall" (see Figure 6.9). Each store hosts a range of user events, often called Lomo Walks, which involve going out together to shoot in different light conditions, different parts of cities, or with different film and camera types. Consumers can sign up to the brand's communal website, create their own page, and share photos, tips, and discuss different cameras, techniques, films, and the stories behind shots they are fond of. They even contain discussion of "rules" when shooting, contradicting rule number 10.

Community support has been mobilized around new product innovation. For example, a number of advanced Lomographers began posting photographs taken with Kodak's long extinct Aerochrome film. Aerochrome was developed for military aerial surveillance and is one of the few color infrared films. The films create purple and red effects (see Figure 6.10) and was usually discovered by fans with US military contacts who were more than keen to get rid of the thousands of meters of Aerochrome that had been carefully frozen in bunkers and warehouses.

(Continued)

Figure 6.9   **Lomo Wall**

Source: Lomography

Figure 6.10   **Aerochrome Shot that Inspired Lomo Purple Campaign**

Since Aerochrome must be hand spooled into classic 35mm cassettes, it is often upwards of 50 euros a roll, and notoriously unreliable. Fans called upon Lomography to find a cheaper alternative.

The resulting Kickstarter campaign was oversubscribed and saw the launch of the brand's genuinely new film *Purple* which was a film with infrared effects. This was followed by other films such as *Turquoise* (mimicking Kodak's expired transparency film), 110 films, super-8 movie films, and re-made old lenses including 19th brass lenses, Petzval, Jupiter, Minitar, and Russar effect lenses, and the recently launched Lomo'Instant Automat camera, all via Kickstarter, and all oversubscribed. The brand has also partnered with Urban Outfitters to pick up on the hipster trend toward analog technology (including film cameras and vinyl records), and has become a genuine force in the photographic world, running competitions, keeping brands such as Kodak alive through their co-branding arrangements, and investing heavily in high tech "Lomo Labs" to provide development services to film photographers unable or unwilling to develop their own films.

Case Questions

1. How does Lomography help strengthen their brand community? Refer to Table 6.1 for community value creating practices.
2. How do the 10 Rules of Lomography reinforce the firm's brand position?
3. How does Lomography co-create brand value with its users?
4. Identify how Lomography gains the three forms of brand legitimacy (pragmatic, moral, and cultural).

Key Terms

Brand consistency audit
Brand hijacking
Brand legitimacy
Brand reinforcement
Brand relevance
Brand stakeholders

Communal branding strategies
Consumer decision journey
Co-optation
Cultural legitimacy
Customer journey

analysis
Integrated marketing communications (IMC)
Internal marketing
Moral legitimacy
Pragmatic legitimacy

Further Reading

Beverland, Michael B. (2016), *Building Brand Authenticity: 7 Habits of Iconic Brands*, Palgrave Macmillan, London.

Fournier, Susan and Lara Lee (2009), "Getting Brand Communities Right," *Harvard Business Review*, 87 (April), 105–111.

Hatch, Mary Jo and Majken Schultz (2001), "Are the Strategic Stars Aligned for Your Corporate Brand?," *Harvard Business Review*, 79 (Feb.), 128–134.

Kates, Steven M. (2004), "The Dynamics of Brand Legitimacy: An Interpretive Study in the Gay Men's Community," *Journal of Consumer Research*, 31 (Sept.), 455–464.

Rosenbaum, Mark, S. Mauricio Losada Otalora, and Germán Contreras Ramírez (2017), "How to create a realistic customer journey map," *Business Horizons*, 60 (1), 143–150.

7

EXTENDING THE BRAND, PARTNERING, AND MANAGING BRAND PORTFOLIOS

When asked why Virgin Brides failed, Virgin Chief Richard Branson responded: "We soon realised there weren't any."

Although the perfume is called fruity, what woman would want to pull out a perfume bottle looking exactly like a lighter and start spraying herself in public? It brings up thoughts of smelling like smoke and lighter fluid! [Comment on Zippo's extension into fragrances]

(Shané Schutte 2016, commenting on six failed brand extensions)

Learning Objectives

When you finish reading this chapter, you will be able to:

1. Understand the role of **brand extensions** in reinforcing and refreshing brand image and achieving growth objectives
2. Differentiate between "brand image fit" and "brand extension authenticity"
3. Differentiate between **line and category extensions** and understand the risks and benefits of both
4. Understand the factors behind brand extensions success
5. Understand and evaluate the opportunity represented by **co-branding**
6. Understand the importance of brand architecture and how to manage portfolios of brands
7. Examine strategies used to change brand architecture options and their potential downsides

Introduction

Can you name a brand that has not extended? If we loosely classify an extension as any transfer of the brand from its original product or service category, it's actually very difficult. As soon as a brand offers the ubiquitous t-shirt, coffee cup, or key ring, we realize that most brands have at some point extended. Many would argue these are not true extensions and may in fact represent marketing material or licensing arrangements, but in the eyes of the customer they are in fact extensions and can impact upon the brand's image. Nonetheless, extensions are also a fact of life for brand managers. Extensions help achieve strategic growth objectives (handed to us from above), can clarify the brand's meaning, can help neutralize competitors, and are essential to maintaining the brand's vitality or relevance. In fact, a lack of extensions is often one sign that a tired brand has been poorly managed.

Although the assumptions underpinning the mindshare approach are at their strongest in regard to brand extension success, when we factor in co-creation, brand communities, celebrities and other influencers, and the emergent opportunities posed by brand hijacks, doppelgängers, and popular culture, the opportunities for brand extensions increase exponentially. However, there is a lot of superstition and folklore surrounding brand extensions—the old maritime map features of "here be dragons" when describing what lay beyond the edge of the known world are a good parallel. Brand extensions are held to dilute the parent brand, cannibalize existing sales, reduce brand equity in favor of short-term sales, and confuse the user. This chapter addresses these views and focuses on how to grow brand meaning through extensions, and co-branding.

One outcome of brand extension is growth in the brand portfolio. Coupled with the development of multiple brands, mergers and acquisition, and culling, senior brand managers need to understand how they should structure their brand portfolio effectively. This is referred to as **brand architecture** and is viewed by many brand strategists as one of the most important foundational concerns for brand managers (Aaker 2009; Ritson 2012). This chapter will examine this area in detail.

Overall, this chapter is focused on maintaining the growth of the brand without diluting its authenticity. Since many of the decisions made or avoided here can result in brand-meaning decline, this chapter precedes the chapters on brand innovation (Chapter 8) and managing brand crises (Chapter 12).

What Is a Brand Extension?

Brand extensions are "the use of an established brand to launch new products or services" (Völckner and Sattler 2006, p. 18). Extending the brand is one of the most commonly used strategies by marketers to grow the brand, increase sales, attract new users, and clarify and enhance brand meaning. Why do marketers extend brands?

1. Brand extensions are assumed to be a less risky form of innovation because users already know the brand, retailer acceptance may be higher, and in the case of line extensions (see Figure 7.1), the costs may be lower.

2. Brand extensions are ways to increase the return on investment in the brand. Brand extensions can grow sales, use up production capacity, appeal to new segments, and help the brand enter new markets. For example, Coca-Cola extended from Coke to Diet Coke after female consumers identified that although they desired to drink soft drinks, they felt guilty for doing so. Years later, male consumers identified a similar desire and tension, but did not want to drink Diet Coke (it was seen as too feminine), so Coke Zero was launched to increase sales in this market. This strategy has seen Coke dominate the cola category across the globe.

3. Brand extensions are an essential form of brand innovation. Maintaining the brand's relevance involves extending it, while also maintaining the brand authenticity. Recall the Vegemite case covered in Chapter 2—one reason why the brand's equity started to decline was because it had failed to engage in strategic brand extensions (as opposed to ad hoc, random extensions with poor **brand-image fit**).

4. Brand extensions are essential if the brand is to avoid becoming commodified. Chapter 3 identified that the pinnacle of the brand pyramid resulted in the dangerous position of commodity status, whereby the brand name becomes synonymous with the product or service category. Two classic examples, 3M's Post-it Notes and Johnson & Johnson's Band Aids, had no extensions (until it was too late) and over time lost margins and sales to generic competitors.

5. Brand extensions are a useful way of clarifying the brand's meaning. Recent research on **brand-extension authenticity** has identified how extensions that remain true to the brand's core meaning help further clarify that meaning. For example, French luxury wine brands such as Chateau Margaux have, in the last two decades, extended their brands into lower price points. The move helps with cash flow but ultimately is about reinforcing their dedication to quality as such moves emphasize further how selective they are in terms of quality when it comes to the wines bearing the parent-brand logo (Beverland 2005b). This benefit will be discussed further below.

6. Brand extensions may be essential to business model success. For example, haute couture (made-to-measure) brands such as Chanel and Dior usually lose substantial sums (upwards of US$20 million per year). As such, extensions into fragrances, accessories, and ready-to-wear fashion help generate the cash flow necessary to recoup losses on haute couture. Likewise, Ralph Lauren developed the brand extension "Purple" as a means of enhancing his brand's prestige through associations with haute couture. This strategic use of brand extensions will be discussed further in brand architecture.

7. Brand extensions can be necessary preemptive or reactive competitive moves. Aaker (2012) contends that Apple's extension into category after category ensures that it remains ahead of competitors. Just as competitors enter into categories pioneered by Apple, the brand moves a step ahead again through further category extensions (see Figure 7.1). All of this also reinforces the brand's "Think Different" position and their image as a creative powerhouse. Likewise, brands may find they need to extend their brand into lower price points or offer fighter brands as a means of protecting themselves against lower cost competitors. Brand Aside 7.1 on **fighter brands** provides further information on this strategy.

BRAND ASIDE 7.1

"Fighter Brands": Protecting Vulnerable Points

In the discussion of positioning, it was identified that many brands were caught in partitioned markets—between low-cost, value brands at the bottom, and high-end brands at the top. This scenario is an evolving one and once established in the value end of the market, such brands may attempt to expand up the value chain, much as Android has done. Since position dilution is the wrong response to being outflanked on value, developing a fighter brand or a brand that protects your weak point is one possible response. Australian Airline Qantas did just this with its low-cost Jetstar brand. Due to airline deregulation, Qantas's dominant position in the local market was challenged by strongly capitalized brands such as Virgin Blue and Tiger Air.

Unable to lower the cost of its operations due to union power and employment legislation, Qantas set up a fighter brand to protect its flank. Jetstar drew on the typical codes used by low-cost airlines (youthful customers, enjoying beach holidays) and went head to head with Virgin Blue on key tourist routes. Qantas was refocused on important business travel routes and international long-haul travel. The strategy succeeded in seeing off the domestic threat. Successful fighter brands are rare, however, and their success is predicated on addressing the following questions:

1. Will it cannibalize your premium offering?
2. Can it defeat the competition?
3. Will it be profitable?
4. Will it be relevant to customers?
5. Will it shift your focus away from the main game?

Source: Ritson 2010

8. Brand extensions improve efficiencies in marketing and other related expenditure. Coca-Cola, for example, can spread distribution, research, and development, marketing expenditure, sales expenses, human resources, public relations, sponsorship investment and others in relation to the parent brand over all of its extensions.

9. In the age of co-creation, unforeseen consumer-driven innovation, including use or hacking, may represent opportunities to extend the brand. Chapter 1 identified how LEGO has formalized this process through entry into new categories (electronic games, movies) and line extensions (see Figure 7.1) involving the strategic use of licensing with entertainment franchises such as *Star Wars*, *Lord of the Rings*, and *Harry Potter* (among many others).

Brand extensions typically take one of two forms: a line extension or a category extension. Examples and definitions of each are provided in Figure 7.1.

Line extensions are the most common form of brand extension and involve extending the brand within an existing product or service category. This can involve the addition of new product variants, such as has occurred over time with Coca-Cola, moving from the original recipe Coke, to Diet Coke, Cherry Coke (and then Diet Cherry Coke), Coke Zero, Vanilla Coke, Coke Life, and so on. The second form is less common, and involves extending the brand franchise into new categories, such as Apple's move into different technological categories (many of which it created), or Virgin's move from music to airlines to banking to cola, and so on.

Each strategy has strengths and weaknesses, although many marketing commentators confuse the two when warning of the dire risks to the **parent-brand equity** of a failed extension. Although line extensions are less risky in terms of acceptance and cost, they potentially can involve greater risk to parent-brand equity when they fail. In contrast, category extensions are more likely to fail, and in the absence of shared costs through licensing, endorsement, or co-branding, can be more expensive. However, they are less risky in terms of parent-brand equity. Why? Extension success involves perceptions of brand-image fit. Fit is defined as: "The perceived similarity

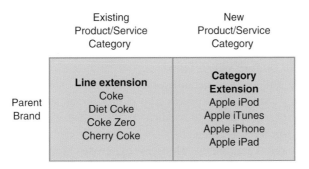

Figure 7.1   Brand extensions

Source: author's notes

(e.g., product category, usage situation) and relevance of parent-brand associations (i.e. attributes or benefits) for the extension category, which should positively influence consumer attitudes toward the brand extension" (Spiggle et al. 2012, p. 967). As this definition identifies, fit has two forms: similarity and relevance. For line extensions, similarity is the most important consideration. This is why line extensions are low risk in terms of potential acceptance and high risk if they fail. Line extensions speak to the brand's expertise. Imagine, for example, if Diet Coke was a terrible product. We expect Coke, with over 100 years of production expertise, to be able to produce a good cola. Likewise, extensions into lower price points, such as BMW's move to the Series 1 and 2 (and originally 3), need to deliver as we expect them to be able to produce a good automobile. This is the ultimate danger of brand extensions for parent-brand equity—your expertise and capabilities (i.e., your positioning) are on the line every time you engage in this strategy.

In contrast, category extensions primarily involve considerations of relevance. That is, does the parent brand bring something meaningful to the product category? When Nike first made a foray into the skateboard market, its corporate image was at odds with the anti-establishment ethos of the marketplace. As a result, its range of gear emblazoned with its Swoosh logo (plus the lack of commitment to the product line) resulted in failure. Likewise, Virgin, the brand held up by many as the exemplar par excellence of category extension, fails more often than it succeeds. So, why does this not hurt the parent-brand image? In simple terms, do we expect a music label (Virgin) to successfully run an airline? Not really. Category extensions involve issues of relevance—Virgin uses its playful, anti-establishment, disruptive ethos to act as a challenger in mature categories. When category extensions fail, they may come at a substantial cost (although careful licensing can mediate this), but not to parent-brand image. As Brand Aside 7.2 on "Silly Brand Extensions" identifies, this confusion is why even experienced marketing commentators get it wrong when judging the danger of extensions.

In summary, perceptions of fit relate to:

1. Product attributes and benefits: French brand Bic is associated with small, cheap, and reliable everyday products such as pens, lighters, stationery, key rings, and USB sticks; however, these attributes are not benefits when it comes to perfumes and underwear, both of which failed.
2. Substitutability and complementarity of parent and extension: Colgate's various extensions from brushes and pastes into related areas such as dental floss, electronic toothbrushes, and mouthwashes makes sense as all of these reflect the brand's emphasis on oral care.
3. Brand assets and capabilities: Honda's expertise in high performance small engines works well for motorbikes, vehicles, outboard motors, motor mowers, and snowmobiles.

BRAND ASIDE 7.2

Silly Brand Extensions

Every year professional marketing publications give raspberry awards to worst brand extensions. Past luminaries have included Harley Davidson's eau de toilette (who wants to smell like a motorbike?), Burger King's "Have it Your Way" boxer shorts featuring a creepy picture of brand mascot The King, Zippo Lighter's perfume, Bic ladies' underwear and perfume, and Chicken Soup for the Dog Lover's Soul, among many others.

It's easy to laugh at these and wonder, "What were the marketing teams thinking?" However, if you look at each of these category extensions, there is little cost involved in developing and launching each as each one involves licensing, and there is no danger to the parent brand's equity when they fail. Why might marketers engage in this type of activity? In some cases, they are trying to create a buzz around the brand and figure that all news is good news. In other cases these often appear late in the financial year and involve marketers allocating spare budget to ensure they receive at least the same allocation the following year. And, in some cases, the low cost of development and lack of risk can pay off with brand loyalists.

Brand Extension Authenticity (BEA)

The ideas of fit above reflect a mindshare approach to brand extension. Even ardent critics such as Holt identify that mindshare assumptions are correct in relation to brand extension and concerns of fit. However, recent research challenges this. A cultural approach to brand extension proposes that brand-extension authenticity (BEA) complements traditional ideas of fit (similarity and relevance) in explaining extension success. So what is BEA? "A consumer's sense that a brand extension is a legitimate, culturally consistent extension of the parent brand" (Spiggle et al. 2012, p. 969). BEA defines fit in cultural and relational terms (in contrast to similarity or relevance), focusing on the extent to which the extension is both true to the brand's essence and the ability of the consumer to connect the extension to the brand's enduring story. There are four components of BEA:

1. Maintaining brand standards and style: Caterpillar's extension toys and fashion maintain the parent brand's rugged toughness. Luxury winemakers such as Chateau Margaux engage in line extensions to reinforce their stringent selection standards for their elite parent brand (Beverland 2005b).

2. Honoring brand heritage: Retro-branding strategies such as those of Volkswagen and Fiat in rebooting the Beetle and the 500 are tied back to each firm's heritage. Likewise, Korg's various extensions into small analog synthesizers are a means of honoring the heritage of electronic music.

3. Preserving brand essence: Stella McCartney's partnership with H&M is an attempt to bring her sustainability focus to a larger audience and change people's expectation of fast fashion. Leica's shift into a mirror-less camera was a shift away from its use of rangefinders that many fans argued were more accurate and "authentic" (as they require skill and patience). As a result, the launch of the X-1 focused heavily on continuing the brand's quality standards, heritage of innovation, and dedication to craft.

4. Avoiding brand exploitation: Brand authenticity arises when the brand somehow transcends perceptions of commercial intent. Australian winemaker Penfolds' decision to develop White Grange (extending its iconic Red Wine Grange) under the Yattarna label was seen as too commercial and failed to reflect the original intent of Grange winemaker Max Schubert's desire to produce a wine that truly expressed the unique nature of Australian growing (Beverland 2009). Likewise, Leica's recent shift into instant photography was viewed by users as lacking in seriousness and many viewed the resulting range as simply expensive versions of Fuji cameras.

Should extensions meet these criteria and consumer self-brand connections are strong, then the extension will increase its chances of being purchased, attitudes toward it will be favorable, and willingness to recommend it will increase.

BEA is critical for consumers with a strong self-connection to the brand and less relevant for functionally oriented brands (such as many FMCGs). Brand extensions that fail to cohere with the brand's essence may dilute the identity value of the parent brand, thereby reducing its equity. BlackBerry is a case in point. While Apple had a strong consumer focus, BlackBerry was the must-have brand of handset for serious movers and shakers in the business world. With high-profile users including US President Barack Obama and Russian President Vladimir Putin, BlackBerry's associations included absolute power, security, and seriousness. Consumer-focused extensions such as its Pearl handset and, more disastrously, its tablet the *Play*Book (italics added) undermined this identity value. Coupled with a serious security lapse in 2011, the brand lost its way and has never been able to regain momentum.

The field of extreme sports including surfing, snowboarding and skateboarding is another good example of BEA. The major surf brands such as Ripcurl, Billabong, and O'Neil have struggled to maintain their authenticity and equity over time. Much of this has to do with inauthentic brand extensions into fashion lines. This has meant consumers can appear to be surfers even when they do not surf, which undermines the identity value of these brands for real surfers. As a result, original consumers of brands have migrated to smaller, craft brands focused on the act of surfing, while the larger brands have lost the basis of their authenticity. The major brands did not help themselves when they coupled their extension strategy with retail expansion whereby flagship stores were staffed by employees who had never surfed (Beverland et al. 2010).

The difficulties in balancing BEA with strategic necessity are covered in Brand Aside 7.3.

BRAND ASIDE 7.3

Sometimes Extension Is a Strategic Necessity

For many marketing commentators, Porsche's attempt to launch a sports utility vehicle (SUV) was a classic example of brand extension gone mad and would guarantee a loss of equity. Certainly, on the surface, it is difficult to see how the Cayenne fits with Porsche's iconic design, its tradition of focusing on classic two-seater sports cars, and its historic customer base. There seemed to be little fit in terms of similarity and relevance, and commentators and loyalists were quick to criticize the move. The extension blurred the lines between line and category extension and as such could place the parent brand at risk if the Cayenne (developed at substantial cost) failed to impress. So why did a brand known for its caution extend into this category? The Cayenne was launched to address a key strategic challenge facing the brand—Porsche desperately needed a financial injection to maintain its performance edge and the SUV market was the only major growth market at the time. The backlash forced the brand to use careful photography angles in their advertisements and an emphasis on the Cayenne being a legitimate addition to the Porsche family (which focused on drivability) aimed to convince skeptical loyalists of the extension's authenticity (with mixed success). The thinking behind this form of renewal is covered in Chapter 8.

Why Not Develop a New Brand? Plusses and Minuses of Brand Extensions

Why launch a brand extension instead of developing a new brand? The answer to this question relates to how far one can stretch the parent brand. Toyota could not stretch their brand to the luxury automobile market, so launched Lexus. Likewise, Black & Decker could not stretch their brand (associated with female homemakers and lightweight, plastic toy-like design) into the professional trade market, so developed DeWalt instead. Likewise, as Brand Aside 7.2 details, Australian flag carrier Qantas could not stretch its luxury positioning into the low-cost airline market so developed Jetstar as a means of protecting the parent brand against low-cost rivals such as Virgin Blue and Tiger Air.

What are the benefits of extending the brand?

1. Efficiency: Because extensions share identity with the parent brand one can spread the costs of marketing, distribution, research and development, packaging, printing, and communications across both. With a new brand, you need a separate marketing program, which is expensive and can place you at a disadvantage when competing against corporate brands or **branded houses** (see brand architecture below).

2. Growth in Sales and Coverage: Apple's various **category extensions** have reinforced its image as a technological leader (see clarifying brand meaning below) and also increased the number of sales it can make to loyalists, while also increasing its customer base overall. Likewise, Unilever's decision to extend Axe (or Lynx, depending on where you live) to women has significantly impacted on sales without diluting parent brand equity.

3. Clarify brand image and frame of reference: When Unilever launched Axe (Lynx) Attract, they changed the image of the brand, away from a young men's frat party brand (where man + Axe = women^2) to one that focused on providing a solution to the sexual insecurities for both genders. As such, the brand owned the "attract" space, something valuable when dealing with teens nervous about sexuality. Apple has done the same, moving away from computing into technological mediated creativity. This strategy is particularly useful in reviving single product brands that are in danger of becoming commoditized or irrelevant. Further examples are provided in Figure 7.2.

4. Refreshing the brand: Extensions are a form of innovation and as such help keep brands fresh. Crayola for example was long focused on drawing crayons for kids. With the emergence of electronic gaming and more exciting toy brands, it was in danger of becoming irrelevant, while low-cost competitors could easily make crayons. As such, Crayola extended away from crayons into crafts more generally, and as such expanded the meaning base of the brand from crayons to colorful crafts for kids.

Expanding Brand Meaning Through Extensions

BRAND	Original Product	Extension Product	New Brand Meaning
Weight Watchers	Fitness Centers	Low Calorie Foods	Weight Loss AND Maintenance
Sunkist	Oranges	Vitamins, Juices	Good Health
Crayola	Crayons	Markers, Paints, Pen, Clay, etc	Colorful Crafts For Kids

Figure 7.2   **Examples of Brand Extension Meaning Clarification**

5. Build customer relationships: As the LEGO case in Chapter 1 identifies, customer-generated innovations can represent opportunities for brand revitalization or innovation. Extensions that draw on these innovations enhance the legitimacy of the brand within its communities, increase linking and identity value, and enhance perceptions of authenticity.

Brand extensions can also have downsides however. So, apart from the opportunity cost associated with not launching a new brand, what are the potential downsides of brand extensions?

1. Customer confusion and reduction of category identification: Poorly planned extensions, particularly through licensing, can confuse customers about the brand's position. Prior to Burberry's revitalization under Rose Maria Bravo, the brand, through uncontrolled licensing, had extended into literally thousands of product lines, all of which diluted the brand's luxury image and worked against any coherent brand identity. Many luxury houses, such as Gucci, suffered this fate in the 1980s and 1990s before culling licensees and lines and refocusing on luxury.
2. Retailer resistance: Retailers have limited shelf space and may demand that an extension replace one of your existing products.
3. Cannibalization: The *Independent* newspaper in the UK released an extension called *i* to counter falling sales and refresh after a crisis involving concerns over editorial independence. The newspaper was aimed at train travelers and priced at just 20 pence. Sold under the banner "only the news that matters," *i* quickly cannibalized sales of the flagship *Independent* (although the extension did create more advertising revenue for the brand). Cannibalization is one of the big concerns with brand extensions, particularly lower-cost line extensions. General Motors found this to their peril, especially when its salespeople would encourage customers to choose the lower-cost brand (Chevrolet or GM) because it was essentially the same vehicle as a more expensive Oldsmobile, just with a different grille and badge. Brand Aside 7.4 provides more details.
4. Parent brand dilution: Poor line extensions and excessive licensing can of course dilute the parent brand image over time. Even Unilever's decision to extend Axe (Lynx) initially raised concerns that it could undermine the brand's image with its original teenage male audience. Certainly initial web sentiment analysis suggested this did occur. Likewise, many of Starbucks' extensions, such as automated coffee machines and instant coffee for the home, have undermined the brand's claim to offer fine coffee in traditional European-styled cafés.
5. Declining authenticity: Extensions can of course undermine claims of authenticity (see BEA above). Even responding to customer-driven innovations must be undertaken with care as brands can quickly lose identity coherence and also the act of responding can be seen as too commercial, something that created intense debate when George Lucas sought to revive the *Star Wars* franchise with *Episodes I–III* (extensions of this sort should involve respecting the community narrative). Brand Aside 7.5 provides a further example.

BRAND ASIDE 7.4

Dangers of Brand Dilution: General Motors

General Motors (GM) was one of the originators of a house of brands architecture. In contrast to Ford, which focused on offering consumers one model of cars, solely in black, GM focused on capturing consumers at different life stages with different brands. The logic was simple: first-time car owners started with a Chevrolet and retired in a Cadillac. Between that, they were offered Pontiac (to celebrate their first job and leaving home), and sensible family and middle-aged (and middle-class) options in Oldsmobile and Buick. The firm understood the role of each brand, positioned each clearly, and as a result avoided cannibalization.

This strategy worked for many years and helped ensure GM was the biggest car brand in the world. However, due to a desire for cost efficiencies, the firm engaged in modular production whereby each brand shared a basic platform (the chassis, tires, engine) while retaining unique styling. However, over time, the differences between each brand diminished, resulting in little more than logo and engine grille-based variation. As a result, consumers traded down: after all why buy a Pontiac when the Chevrolet is essentially the same vehicle but at a lower sticker price—salespeople told customers as much. As a result each brand's equity declined, several were ended altogether, and the firm's brand architecture stopped working.

BRAND ASIDE 7.5

How Brand Growth Can Trigger Doppelgänger Brand Images

Brand extensions can eventually undermine a brand's authenticity and lead to doppelgänger images, and the dilution of parent brand image. One brand experiencing this is Harley Davidson. The iconic American motorcycle manufacturer almost went bankrupt in the 1980s, but a management buy-out ensured the brand returned to its roots and enjoyed an incredible comeback. What were the brand's roots? The firm had never positioned the brand formally and sought help from academics John Schouten and James McAlexander (1995) who conducted an ethnographic study of Harley loyalists. These academics identified that the brand's image was defined by three ideas: American, Freedom, and Masculinity.

These were very much born of the time and place, but the brand team used these insights in their campaigns to great success. Relisting on the stock exchange as a lifestyle company, the team was keen to emphasize that Harley Davidson was not just a manufacturer of motorcycles, but could also earn substantial income streams from extensions into clothing, accessories, perfumes, and so on. However, over time, as the brand became more successful, its image changed. A follow-up study suggested that the brand was largely defined in terms of freedom, although even this was waning (Martin et al. 2006).

Further extensions and market expansion resulted in more parodies, the most high profile of which was in 2009 on the Comedy Central animated satire show *South Park*. In an episode called "The F Word", creators Trey Parker and Matt Stone featured wannabe rebels (typical Harley Owners Group members) riding through towns annoying lots of people. Eventually the four boys at the heart of the show (Stan, Kyle, Kenny, and Cartman) petitioned the English Dictionary Officiates to have the homophobic slur "fag" redefined to mean: 1) an extremely annoying, inconsiderate person most commonly associated with Harley riders; and 2) a loud and obnoxious person who owns or frequently rides a Harley. The Officiates agree to a change of definition, which is widely welcomed by the townspeople of South Park, including gay community members Big Gay Al and Mr Slave. The show was one of the highest rating for the long-running series and given its controversial content featured widely on subsequent news and talk shows. Is this a case of a brand being hijacked because of over-extending?

In summary, brand extensions are a critical means to enhance brand equity and achieve the firm's strategic goals. They are something most brand marketers will need to engage in at some point in time. Moreover, extensions are a critical means of keeping the brand fresh. However, there are downsides and consistently poor extensions and overuse of licensing usually signal that a brand is in trouble or that the brand team has a poor understanding of the customer–brand relationship and the brand's meaning (see Keller's Scorecard in Chapter 3).

The Five Steps of Brand Extension

1. Ascertain what users know and like about the parent brand.
2. Identify possible extension options (line and category).
3. Evaluate proposed extension with: associations of the extension (authenticity), perceptions of fit (similarity, relevance, and authenticity), and against internal factors such as ability to compete and level of marketing support. Focus groups can be particularly useful here.
4. Develop supporting marketing programs and brand elements.
5. Launch the extension.
6. Track the extension and its impact on the parent brand.

Further strategic considerations regarding brand extension success are covered in Brand Aside 7.6.

BRAND ASIDE 7.6

Brand Extension Check List

The following are some important strategic considerations when developing brand extensions:

1. Is the market growing? Many luxury brands have extended downwards in terms of price because of the increase in middle-class consumers who aspire to access the world of luxury.
2. Are the brand assets transferable? Toyota's decision to develop a separate luxury brand (Lexus) was based on consumer insights identifying the inability of Toyota's classical strengths (efficiency, value for money, reliability) to transfer into the luxury market. Although consumers had no doubt that Toyota could produce a high-end vehicle, they did not see the brand as useful in symbolizing their success or wealth. A brand can only stretch so far.
3. Will the extension have a positive impact on parent brand equity? Nike's decision to extend into different categories of sports, including less intense forms of exercise such as yoga, all reinforce its positioning around an active lifestyle. Likewise, its Nike Goddess brand extension aimed at active women enhanced its equity in the overall sportswear market.
4. How entrenched are competitors? When Kodak attempted to extend its strengths in color printing (developed from decades of experience of film processing), it found that it faced powerful competitors with loyal users. Although the value equation of Kodak's offer was high, competitors could easily counter with their own high-quality prints and longer-life print cartridges.
5. Does the product have a clear differential advantage? In the early 1990s Pepsi and then Coca-Cola launched clear cola variations. Although they tried to play on notions of purity (hence "clear") these were simply not advantages in the soft drink market, and both were quickly discontinued in the United States.
6. Will retailers accept it? For bricks and mortar retailers, shelf space is a finite resource, so the decision to accept a brand extension may involve dropping another product line or brand. Likewise, high price points (along with poor parent brand-image fit) killed Levi's attempted Classic range of off-the-rack formal business wear in the early 1980s.

Co-branding and Brand Alliances

Although sponsorship, celebrity endorsement, and co-optation have all involved forms of partnership between different brands, co-branding or brand alliances are a relatively more recent way to grow the brand. Co-branding is defined as "a marketing partnership between two or more brands" (Singh et al. 2016, p. 121). Unlike extensions, co-branding or branding alliances involve growing each partner brand through accessing the other's market and associations.

UK fashion designer Stella McCartney has used this strategy to her advantage, turning a struggling brand committed to sustainability into a profitable enterprise. McCartney's partnership with Adidas brought a strong fashion sense to the sports brand icon and helped it create stronger relationships with female consumers. For McCartney, the partnership exposed her to a much larger audience, and added associations with sportswear, street style, and activeness to her high-fashion brand. Her partnership with H&M helped the Swedish fast-fashion brand improve its sustainability credentials and increase prices, while exposing McCartney to a younger audience, creating a significant buzz when the collection sold out in 30 minutes, and added younger, more casual associations to her brand (Keinan and Crener 2015).

McCartney's partnerships have helped grow exposure of her brand to new audiences, add brand associations, generate buzz, and enhance parent-brand equity. This last outcome seems strange in light of her own brand's commitment to environmental sustainability and luxury, which seems inconsistent with the lower-cost fast-fashion position of Adidas and H&M. So how does co-branding work?

When partners are selected carefully, customers attribute the positive aspects of each brand onto the co-branded product or service. Customers take the comfort, durability, functionality, and street cool from Adidas and the sustainability, high fashion, and femininity from McCartney when presented with the co-branded range. Co-branding is a way of combining seeming opposites to enhance the performance and image of the brand, without diluting the parent brands.

Research supports this. A co-branding scenario representing a hypothetical partnership between chocolate maker Godiva and diet brand SlimFast was given to consumers in a seminal 1996 study (Park et al. 1996). At first glance, a co-brand between diet-minded SlimFast and rich luxurious chocolate brand Godiva looks too good to be true. Somehow, one can literally have their cake and eat it too! Is it really possible to combine two brands positioned so differently and even contradicting one another? Well, yes. The authors found that consumers did believe that the co-brand was the best of both worlds—that the hypothetical cake mix would be tasty, rich, and luxurious, and low in calories. What the authors concluded was:

1. Consumers take the positive associations from each brand and attribute these positive features to the co-brand.

2. Consumers then think more positively about both individual brands. That is, the co-brand enhances the equity of each parent, by making Godiva seem healthy, and SlimFast seem tasty and indulgent.
3. Both brands benefit from accessing each other's customer base and sharing resources.
4. Brands with strong awareness and image that are paradoxically complementary work better than substitutes. In a follow-up experiment, consumers were presented with a hypothetical cake-mix brand between Godiva and Häagen-Dazs. This seems a perfect match, but consumers could not see what the benefit of the co-brand was. By themselves, each brand seemed to deliver the same benefit, so together it was a case of too much of a good thing.
5. Poor co-branding, such as the hypothetical case between Häagen-Dazs and Godiva, had no downsides in terms of parent-brand equity.

In relation to the five points above, it would seem that co-branding offers brand managers a lot of upside, without much attendant risk. Co-branding practice does support the hypothetical scenarios above. LVMH developed a co-brand between Champagne icon Veuve Cliquot and its newly acquired fashion brand Emilio Pucci. The co-brand involved launching Cliquot's elite champagne, La Grandes Dames, in a Pucci-colored box, replete with a story about both houses, albeit with more emphasis on Pucci. Why? As a brand Pucci needed revitalization and lacked awareness amongst consumers, although had recall with fashion insiders. Cliquot on the other hand had authenticity in spades, but was seen as old and staid. Pucci therefore built awareness with the vast number of champagne consumers, while Cliquot got featured in fashion magazines such as *Vogue*, was exposed to a different audience, and freshened up its image.

Are there no dangers to co-branding? The downside depends on how far you stretch co-branding to include any form of partnership. If you equate co-branding with sponsorship and celebrity endorsement (and in an age of personal branding this seems fair), then dangers arise when one partner gets tainted through scandal for example. Nike suffered when South African Paralympian Oscar Pistorius was accused of murdering his girlfriend (Nike's "I am the bullet in the chamber" campaign using the disgraced athlete was a little too close to the truth). These are typical downsides to sponsorship arrangements and the effects are well known (Quester 1996), and largely involve putting distance between the sponsor and the celebrity. Nonetheless, it is possible that a crisis experienced by one brand could taint the co-brand and possibly spillover and effect the innocent partner. Ford experienced just such a problem when the Firestone tires on its cars had quality problems.

In regard to brand partners, it would appear that brands with strong awareness and identity with some stakeholder group can benefit from some form of alliance. Also, co-branding with a strong local brand may help with market entry for unknown brands seeking out overseas markets. This is particularly the case in industrial or B2B markets, where partnerships of some form can reduce perceptions of risk and enhance credibility (Singh et al. 2016).

Brand Architecture: Managing Brand Portfolios

One result of growing brands is an increase in the complexity of the brand's activities and coverage. This is further complicated in the context of adding new brands instead of, or as well as, extensions. Managing the structure of a **brand portfolio** is known as brand architecture. An example of brand architecture showing the giant companies and the umbrella brands they own can be found online. This identifies how a small number of global companies own a vast number of brands that we assume are independent and part of the vast choice we enjoy as consumers (the image has originally did the rounds on social media as an anti-brand meme). Brand architecture is defined as follows: "An organizing structure of the brand portfolio that specifies brand roles and the nature of relationships between brands" (Aaker and Joachimsthaler 2000, p. 8). Brand architecture involves the application of portfolio management techniques to brand management. Critical to the definition above is that chief marketing officers or other senior managers within an organization must understand the strategic role that each brand or group of brands plays, and ensure that each brand is positioned carefully so as not to encourage cannibalization. Obviously junior brand and product managers need the same understanding as many of their day-to-day activities and campaign decisions will impact on (and be impacted upon) other brands within the firm and the firm's overall brand architecture strategy. To explore this further, let's examine LVMH's brand portfolio, which can also be found with a quick Google search.

LVMH is split up into a number of different divisions, within which exists a range of brands. What is the role of each division? The Wine & Spirit's division is relatively low margin (the high prices are offset by the high cost of production and storage) but generates ongoing cash flow across a number of demographic and target groups. In contrast, Fashion & Leather Goods is high margin, but unlikely to be purchased as regularly as alcohol. So luxury fashion provides the group with margin, but also high-brand awareness, and core associations such as glamor, status, prestige, and lifestyle factors. This then provides a halo effect for each fashion brand's extensions into cheaper accessories, but also for fragrances (that also help with both margin and cash flow). Watches & Jewelry provides a similar glamor and prestige effect for the group. Selective retailing means LVMH can control the channels that sell their goods and recoup more margin as a result, not to mention leverage their research and development expertise to launch new brands and own labels as they do through their cosmetics supermarket chain Sephora. Those parts left out of this discussion are investments made to benefit the group and take advantage of unique opportunities within the market.

That deals with the strategic role of each brand group but what about the differences between the brands? These are also carefully positioned to ensure strong points of difference as well as a shared sense of luxury and heritage (luxury buyers are rarely 100 percent loyal). If one looks at Wine & Spirits, for example, the various champagne houses all have different positions. Krug, for example, is the rebellious, artisanal champagne house, significantly more expensive than any of the other brands, and seen as a convention breaker within the industry. Veuve Cliquot's identity is built around Madame Cliquot and her love of champagne and life in general. Moët and Chandon is more of an entry-level brand, while Dom Perignon (a line extension of Moët) is one of the iconic, elite brands of the region, priced extremely high and built around the myth of the inventor of champagne making (Beverland 2005b).

Brand architecture strategy concerns the ways in which firms organize their brands. Brand architecture strategy is defined as:

> The hierarchical specification describing (1) whether one or two levels of brands are used, (2) whether, how, and how strongly individual brands within the company's portfolio are grouped and relate to each other, and (3) the visibility and role of the corporate master brand. (Hsu et al. 2016, p. 1)

What does this refer to? The key decisions for firms in relation to managing their brand portfolio's relate to the number of individual brands, how to group these brands and whether or not to identify to users a connection between them, and, finally, whether, and how, to use the corporate master brand. Returning to LVMH for example, LVMH is the name of the group, is listed on the stock market under that moniker, is used in corporate partnerships and hiring, but has no individual visual identity or relationship with customers. LVMH is known as a **house of brands**. This strategy involves retaining all the individual brand identities, supporting them separately, and subordinating the master or corporate brand to them (assuming it appears at all).

In contrast, Sony, Samsung, Nike, and Huawei are branded houses. In this situation, there is only one brand, the corporate or master brand, and, at best, any individual identity is subordinated to the master brand (such as Nike Goddess or Sony PlayStation). Many large services firms (PriceWaterhouseCoopers), technology groups (Samsung), business-to-business brands (Caterpillar), charities (Greenpeace), and government agencies (The Royal Mail) use this strategy. Typically, few packaged goods or FMCG companies (Heinz would be one counter-example) use this type of strategy. Others take a hybrid approach, including automotive firms such as Toyota (with Lexus and Prius), hotel groups such as Sheraton with its various endorsed properties, and sports brands such as Adidas with its co-branding strategy. So which one is best? There is no right or wrong answer to this as both have strengths and weaknesses, and understanding these are critical.

The Brand Relationship Spectrum

David Aaker and Erich Joachimsthaler developed the **brand relationship spectrum** in 2000. Figure 7.3 provides further details. This attempted to formalize different organizing principles to manage brand portfolios. Envisaging these options as a continuum, the brand relationship spectrum has at one end the house of brands (many brands, no umbrella) and at the other the branded house (one corporate brand umbrella or master brand). Each was viewed as an ideal, and it is important to remember that there are times when one should step away from these ideals, as this is best for the brand, its users, and the firm overall.

This framework has become the industry standard for managing brand portfolios, and recently research has identified that there are different stock-market returns for each strategy. These are:

1. Sub-branding, or "brands connected to a master or parent brand that modify or augment that master brand" (Aaker and Joachimsthaler 2000, p. 14), has the strongest returns (by a substantial margin). However, they also have the strongest risk profile and need to be approached carefully.
2. There is virtually no significant difference between the performance of branded houses or house of brands. The purist strategy depends on context.
3. Hybrid architectures or those that combine house of brands and branded houses offer mediocre results, despite their popularity amongst practitioners.
4. Endorsed brand or individual brands linked officially to the master brand represents a low-risk strategy, but correspondingly delivers the lowest returns of all architecture types. This runs counter to the industry belief that it is a best of both worlds approach.

(*Source*: Hsu et al. 2016)

Let's consider the two ends of the relationship spectrum in turn.

The House of Brands

The house of brands approach respects the individual identities of each brand and does little to draw connections between them. Made famous by General Motors and FMCG stalwarts Procter & Gamble, Kraft, Nestlé, Unilever, and Mars among many others, this strategy is very popular in consumer goods marketing.

What are the benefits of a house of brands strategy?

1. Contradictory positioning across brands: Two of Unilever's star brands were Dove and Axe (Lynx). Both are positioned in radically different and oppositional ways. Dove builds its identity by rejecting the beauty myths and encouraging women to feel good about who they are. They take a strong anti-fashion line, and through

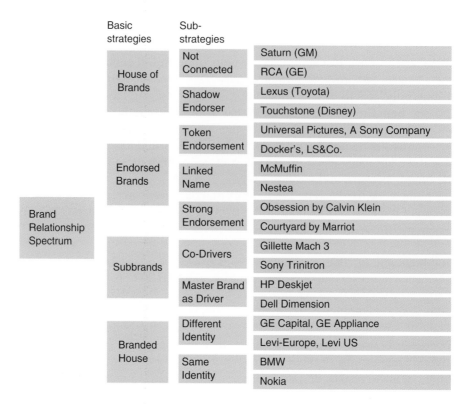

Figure 7.3   Brand Relationship Spectrum

Source: D. A. Aaker & E. Joachimsthaler, *The Brand Relationship Spectrum: The Key to the Brand Architecture Challenge,* 2000a. p. 9.

their Real Beauty campaign, reject stereotypical notions of the ideal women. In contrast, Axe (Lynx) targeted at teenaged males treats women as sex objects who are drawn uncontrollably to the nearest male using the fragrance. The advertisements regularly get rejected on gender discrimination grounds, and their portrayal of the ideal female draws on a very narrow set of stereotypes. Both, however, work for their target audiences, and it is like the parents buy both for their children without realizing they are both sold by the same firm.

2.   Allows one to operate across multiple categories: What does Mars sell? Your answer is most likely to be "chocolate bars." And it is true that the Mars Corporation built its business on confectionery. But it also sells pet food under its Pedigree brand. When buying a chocolate bar do you want to know that the company making it also makes dog food? Probably not. The opposite is also true. Chocolate is extremely toxic for dogs. The strategy allows firms like Procter & Gamble to enter categories as diverse as household cleaners, food, sanitary products, and healthcare

3. Category ownership: The house of brands strategy was founded by Procter & Gamble when they realized that it was cheaper to buy a competitor brand than build a new one, or shift loyal consumers away from their preferred option. At the local Cooperative Store on my former university campus, there are five brands of deodorant, all produced by Unilever. This allows firms to offer the illusion of choice, while dominating entire categories of goods. This is beneficial to retailers who only have to manage one relationship but also want to provide choice for their consumers.

4. Lack of contamination: When one brand suffers a scandal, the rest of the group is unaffected. Not so for branded houses.

House of brand strategies are appealing on many levels, especially when choice is valued by customers, in fragmented markets with split loyalties, and in contexts where diversity is important (such as fashion), or decisions based on impulse (confectionery). However, the two downsides of house of brands are:

1. The inability to cross-promote: General Motors' brand architecture was designed to migrate you from one brand to the next as your life stage changed. Although you would remain loyal to the group, you would do so by moving up an aspirational brand ladder, from humble Chevrolet all the way through to luxurious status signifier Cadillac. But to make this work, the brands needed to be clearly separate. Likewise, despite the high trust that Procter & Gamble inspires, they have struggled to leverage this master-brand connection in order to encourage consumers of laundry detergent (Ariel) to also seek out Procter & Gamble brands in hair care (Clairol), women's sanitary products (Tampax), and baby care (Pampers). This is the biggest limitation of this strategy.

2. Stretched resources: General Motors competes against a number of different brands, including Ford, Honda, Toyota, BMW, and so on. Notice the difference? These brands are all branded houses (or hybrids). While General Motors has to invest scarce resources in multiple brands, Ford and Toyota can concentrate the same total marketing spend on just one brand. This is why many large house of brands have begun to reduce the size of their portfolios in order to concentrate on their star brands and purchase brands in new categories or acquire new brands with strong potential.

A Branded House

A branded house involves just one brand that encompasses all of the firm's offerings. Sometimes known as **master branding** or **corporate branding**, this approach is popular with consumer and industrial service firms, business-to-business organizations, charities, professional services, and government agencies. It overcomes some of the limitations of the house of brands, including the inability to cross-promote and spreading resources too thinly across many brands. There are other advantages:

1. It is efficient: One brands means savings across a huge number of areas, including marketing, training, retailing, and also printing, label design, and so on. Coke has taken this to extremes in recent times with a redesign to ensure all their products have the same design language and are easily identifiable as part of the Coke family.
2. One can leverage the master brand's credibility across different segments of users. American Express for example has managed to expand its franchise by offering different levels of status to users (from Green through Gold, Platinum, and Black) and also leverage the brand down into the standard credit-card carry-over-balance market. Technological companies such as Apple and Samsung do the same, leveraging off their respective innovation images to add credibility to their range of different products. In the latter case, if users have a positive experience with the brand in one context, they are more likely to adopt new products for other occasions or usages.

However, the branded house also has some problems. The biggest one relates to risk. If anything effects the master brand, then the whole group of products can suffer as a result. Toyota suffered this problem when drivers experienced issues with brakes in some of its models, just as Volkswagen has recently suffered due to its fraudulent emissions claims for some of its cars. The firm initially did not handle the problems well, but after a false start recalled the problematic models. However, despite it only affecting a few models, sales of all Toyota vehicles fell, with many industry insiders suggesting this problem was responsible for the sales revival of rivals Ford and General Motors. Interestingly sales of Lexus (also owned by Toyota but with no brand connection) did not suffer while the company began marketing its sub-brand Prius more aggressively as the sustainable choice, downplaying the master brand at the same time.

Dangers of Combining Both

As mentioned earlier, both ends of the continuum represent ideal types. Many of the examples identified in this chapter involve firms that primarily lean to one end or the other but for critical strategic reasons have adopted exceptions to their preferred approach. Toyota, for example, could not stretch its brand to luxury, so chose to develop a separate brand (Lexus) instead. Suffering a crisis, Toyota sought to leverage its sub-brand's environmental credentials in order to contain the damage suffered by the master brand (see Chapter 12 for more detail). Apple has also taken a mixed approach, using Apple across all its products but with strong sub-brands using the "i" prefix, and acquiring Beats by Dre to reinforce its music industry credentials.

However, the large FMCG groups (Unilever and Procter & Gamble) have recently tried more hybrid forms in order to gain the best of both worlds, largely hoping the master-brand connection will enable cross-selling, while retaining the benefits of a house of brands. Procter & Gamble have largely done this through marketing communications and in-store promotions (involving discounts for buying several of their brands). Unilever have gone further, using master-brand endorsement and corporate advertising to identify the relationships between its products, under its so-called "One U" program.

Unlike Procter & Gamble, many of Unilever's brands have a much more emotional, aspirational, and even risky positioning strategy. Drawing links between Dove and Axe (Lynx) has resulted in a backlash as campaigners have pointed out the lack of sincerity of the real beauty campaign driving the Dove brand, when at the same time Unilever is portraying women using negative stereotypes in Axe (Lynx) advertisements. A mash-up video called "A message from Unilever" featuring mash-ups of the brand's original messages with images from various Axe (Lynx) advertisements, and concluding with the line "talk to your daughter before Unilever does" (a play on Dove's "Talk to your daughter before the fashion industry does"), has had almost twice as many views as Dove's official onslaught video and generated a brand backlash.

Acquiring New Brands: Using Architecture to Bring Brands into the Fold

How do you treat new brands you have acquired? For a house of brands, this is not really an issue. Their main consideration is where to group them and how to differentiate the brand relative to other brands within the group. Merging two organizations is a trickier issue and involves larger strategic considerations well beyond the marketing department. But how do you treat acquired brands under a branded house? Two considerations emerge: how do you gain the benefits of bringing the acquired brand into the fold while also respecting existing customers' relationship with the brand? Unless the brand is very weak, simply rebranding the newly acquired brand immediately can result in a customer backlash and sends the wrong message about your intent vis-à-vis their relationships (which they may be entirely happy with).

This is where endorsements and sub-brands and finer uses of the logo such as those options listed under sub-strategies (see LVMH brand architecture) come in. One example of this is American banking group TD Banknorth. This bank expanded beyond its original base in America's northern states (Vermont, Oregon, Maine) by acquiring small local banks. Banknorth realized they could offer customers of local banks many advantages of a big bank, but that those same customers valued the personal touch of a small local bank. With each acquisition, Banknorth wanted to signal to the target brand's customers that everything they loved about their bank would remain the same, while they would also be able to access all the benefits in terms of services that a large bank could bring. How?

Through endorsement. On acquiring the new bank brand, they immediately renamed the bank "MetroWest (acquired in 2001), a member of the Banknorth Group." Over time, they slowly moved MetroWest's look toward the Banknorth identity and invested most of their communications budget into building awareness and likeability of the Banknorth brand. When Banknorth awareness reached 50 percent, they removed the original (MetroWest) brand name. French-based Aviva followed a similar strategy when they decided to phase out their Norwich Union brand. They announced it would be phased out over a two-year period in 2008, although eventually were able to remove the brand altogether a year ahead of time. To assure worried customers and members of the local community, the Norwich Union identity was at first rebranded in Aviva colors and fonts with the addition of an Aviva Group endorsement. Aviva also continued important local traditions such as sponsorship of the local football team to signal that local traditions would continue.

Harvesting Brands

This final section seems a strange addition to a book about branding, but is there a time when one should sell or harvest brands? Or even discontinue them altogether? Portfolio management techniques are useful not only for managing complex groupings of brands, but also for making investment decisions regarding each brand's future. It is useful to think of brands in classic portfolio terms, including "cash cows" (Nike's Air Jordan), "stars" (Dove for Unilever), potential "stars" (Beyond Meat for Tyson Foods), and "dogs" (SAAB for General Motors). However, one should be careful not to forget the relationship between different brands—so although haute couture loses money for LVMH, they would be foolish to remove these brands as they provide the halo effect for all their other brands (Ralph Lauren's Purple label was developed in the knowledge it would lose money but enhance the group).

However, portfolio management also suggests that the majority of sales, margin, and growth is likely to be generated by just a small range of brands (often expressed as the 80:20 rule). As a result, large house of brands groups such as Procter & Gamble and Unilever have begun reducing the size of their portfolios, selling off third- and fourth-ranked brands in categories, which has freed up funds to invest in new categories and brands and put behind proven winners. Cadbury also made a similar move, reducing its individual brands in favor of the master brand. As a result, Caramel became Cadbury Dairy Milk Caramel and Fry's Turkish Delight became an ingredient in Cadbury Dairy Milk Turkish delight and the Fry's name was sold, with positive financial results and enhanced brand equity.

Chapter Summary

This chapter has moved from building brands to focusing on how to use brands to achieve corporate growth objectives. The main way that firms do this is via brand extension, which involves line extensions and categories extensions. Both strategies have different risk profiles and different requirements for success. A cultural approach called brand extension authenticity was also identified, and four criteria discussed. Importantly all must raise the equity of the parent brand. Co-branding and brand alliances were also examined, identifying further ways in which marketers can leverage the equity in their brands. Finally, brand architecture, or how to organize large portfolios of brands and/or offers, was examined. Two types of approaches were identified (house of brands and branded houses), their strengths and limits discussed, before examining the benefits of reducing the size of brand portfolios.

Review Questions

1. Evaluate the benefits and risks for each type of brand extension. How would you moderate the risks associated with each?
2. Examine some examples of co-branding that (1) you think work, and (2) you think are mismatched. Explain your answer.
3. Starbucks planned on launching a brand extension of instant coffee that they described as "as good as what you get in store." What type of extension is this? Evaluate its likelihood of success.
4. Co-branding appears to be without risk. Do you agree with this? Explain your answer.
5. How might brands overcome the limitations of the two extremes of brand architecture strategy (a house of brands and brand house)?

Case Example: Pantone

Look around you. Wherever you are, there is color. If you look at your clothes, the colors in this book, and the colors that surround you (excepting nature) there's a good chance each has a reference and a unique name.

The Pantone Color Matching System® was launched in in September 1963 but the brand's origin goes back to 1956 when Lawrence Herbert joined the

(Continued)

firm, which at the time was a small printing operation run by M&J Levine Advertising in New York. At the time, printers and their clients struggled with color. There was no common agreement or system to classify color and as a result costs were high, clients were often unhappy that the colors did not match their original sketches, and printers struggled with the lack of standardization of ink supplies because every supplier had a different way of classifying colors such as turquoise. In innovation terms, the market had yet to agree on a dominant design when it came to classifying hue (Suárez and Utterback 1995). Herbert described the situation as follows:

> Every design had about half a dozen books in his [sic] drawer. Every ink company used different sets of pigments ... Obviously, there was a lot of confusion. That's when I had the idea: "Why couldn't everyone just use the same color book?" (Kim 2016, p. 98)

Herbert set about developing a common language for color, and eventually the Pantone Color Matching System® was born. In 2016, the Systems Reference Library cost around US$1,500, and came in physical and digital forms. This was revolutionary at the time as now printing could be outsourced to specialist suppliers or even sent overseas because each party shared the same color language. An example of this is provided in Figure 7.4. Following its launch, the system quickly became the industry standard, used by printers, designers, educators, magazine editors, and

Figure 7.4   Pantone Colour Matching System

even appearing in software packages such as Photoshop. Furthermore, consumers became familiar with the color system, as it was often used in interior design. The brand's ease of use is what set it apart from others; for example:

> There's another commonly used system called DIC Color Guide. It is a color standard, similar to Pantone's. It could potentially fit the market in Korea, where printers don't use Pantone ink. But DIC didn't think about the next step. After releasing their product, the people at Pantone reflected on how to make it convenient for consumers to compare and assess colors, and then focused entirely on the colors themselves. (Designer Youngsik Oh, Total Impact, interviewed in Kim 2016, p. 24)

Every year Pantone feature a Color of the Year (2017 is Greenery 15-0343). Some designers rail against what they see as Pantone's stranglehold on the industry choices when it comes to the "in" color, but the system has no competitor and features over 1,800 colors. However, with a high price, the need for annual updates, and a focus on the business-to-business market, Pantone had nowhere to grow, and faced the real risk of becoming commoditized. It solved this challenge in the early 2000s, when picking up on a cultural *zeitgeist* favoring individual creativity and expression (exemplified in Richard's Florida's book *The Creative Class*), the brand extended its famous color system into a range of household products, fashion items, consumables, ice cream (all in Pantone shades), and even the Pantone Hotel (opened in 2011). Figure 7.5 provides examples.

Figure 7.5   Pantone Extensions

(Continued)

First leveraging the elegance and simplicity of the color system in a range of fashion and household items, the brand enabled consumers to identify as designers or wannabe creatives by associating with an industry standard with widespread awareness. Furthermore, since high-profile brands had become associated with particular Pantone colors, including Starbucks (3425), Hermes (16-1448), Barbie (820), Christian Louboutin (18-1663), and of course Tiffany (1837), consumers could reinforce their brand love in subtle ways that could be read by other members of the brand public or community. Finally, licensing opportunities were used as part of co-branding strategy with rapper Jay-Z getting his own color, Jay-Z blue, which was used on his 2001 album *The Blueprint* and referenced in the name of his daughter Blue Ivy.

The brand was eventually sold for US$180 million in 2007 and continues with its Color Matching System®, Color of the Year, and further extensions.

Case Questions

1. What type of extension has Pantone primarily used? Evaluate the risks associated with this strategy? How might these risks be reduced?
2. What other extensions could the brand team undertake? Consider this with reference to fit and BEA.
3. What did the brand originally stand for? What is the brand's new meaning after the extensions?
4. Can you think of other dominant design standards that could be extended in this way?

Key Terms

Brand architecture
Brand extension
Brand extension authenticity (BEA)
Brand-image fit
Branded house

Brand relationship spectrum
Category extension
Co-branding
Fighter brands
House of brands

Line extension
Master brand
Parent-brand image/ equity
Portfolio-brand strategy

Further Reading

Aaker, David A. (2012), "Win the Brand Relevance Battle and the Build Competitor Barriers," *California Management Review*, 54(2), 43–57.

Aaker, David A. and Erich Joachimsthaler (2000), "The Brand Relationship Spectrum: The Key to the Brand Architecture Challenge," *California Management Review*, 42(4), 8–23.

Park, C. Whan, Sung Youl Jun, and Allan D. Shocker. (1996), "Composite Branding Alliances: An Investigation of Extension and Feedback Effects," *Journal of Marketing Research*, 33(4), 453–466.

Ritson, Mark (2010), "Should You Launch a Fighter Brand?" *Harvard Business Review*, 87(10), 86–94.

Spiggle, Susan, Hang T. Nguyen, and Mary Caravella (2012), "More than Fit: Brand Extension Authenticity," *Journal of Marketing Research*, 49(6), 967–983.

8

BRAND INNOVATION: REVITALIZING AND REFRESHING BRANDS

Apple's continued success lies in its ability to take risks and to endanger its life with each new product. (Steve Jobs 1998, quoted in Kapferer 2014a, p. 154)

We must always change, renew, rejuvenate ourselves; otherwise, we harden. (Johann Wolfgang von Goethe 1749–1832).

Learning Objectives

When you finish reading this chapter, you will be able to:

1. Understand the basis for declining brand equity and how to respond
2. Understand the difference between innovation, revitalization, re-launch, and refreshing
3. Examine different strategies for revitalizing and refreshing brands
4. Apply approaches from the mindshare and cultural positioning models
5. Use design thinking to build brand ambidexterity
6. Examine how to approach user-generated innovations

Introduction

The previous chapter examined two forms of brand innovation, brand extension and co-branding. However, brand-related innovation involves more than these two strategies. First, brands need to innovate just in order to maintain advantages or points of difference in order to reinforce their position, which may not involve extension or co-branding. Second, brands need to innovate culturally, to ensure they retain relevance in the face of ideological change (see Chapter 5). Although we'd prefer to avoid it, brands can also get tired and require **revitalization** (often called "**repositioning**"). Finally, consumer-generated content and use, and/or the use of the brand by influencers and in popular culture, can be a source of innovation in meaning and in terms of the product, services, and stories that underpin the brand. These forms of innovation form the basis of this chapter.

Brand Equity: Relevance vs. Consistency

Previous chapters have highlighted the important role than relevance and consistency play in brand equity. The mindshare approach places a great deal of emphasis on consistency, focusing on ensuring that users clearly understand the brand's promise, core associations, and image. Adherents of mindshare do not ignore relevance; rather, they argue it is built into the positioning process (in defining the frame of reference—see Chapter 5), and that it is a function of the marketing mix. In regard to the latter, relevance is addressed through changes to the supporting brand-marketing program, including product, service, pricing, promotion, and so on, while the position of the brand never changes or shifts. In this sense, relevance and consistency involve understanding the difference between brand tactics and brand strategy.

The cultural positioning model in contrast emphasizes relevance over consistency. By examining the approaches of iconic brands over time, adherents of this approach note how regularly brands change their position to take advantage of cultural schisms, and address new ideological challenges. Adherents to this approach do not ignore consistency. Like the mindshare approach, the cultural brand position requires a consistent expression of the brand position through the marketing program. And consistency with position requires rendering the organization authentic in the eyes of the populist worlds or crowd cultures one is drawing inspiration from. In this sense, authenticity may involve change and adaptation as well as consistency. In his study of the North American gay subculture, Kates (2004) identified that investing the firm in the subculture's political program drove brand legitimacy and authenticity. This involved regular adaptation, but arguably was also a furthering of the cultural position of brands such as Absolut and Levi's.

Both models share a concern with relevance and consistency, and of course both models are useful in combination for building brand equity over time. It's also important to remember why both relevance and consistency are necessary. Studies on brand equity have identified that brands that are inconsistent have less equity than those that take a strong stand (both in terms of culture and mindshare) (Edwards and Day 2005; Keller 1999). Inconsistency is also a common theme in brands that have suffered declining fortunes. Studies of luxury brands, for example, identify how extensive licensing eventually diluted the up-market image of brands such as Gucci (Forden 2000) and Burberry (Moon 2004). Maintaining fealty to one's roots has also been identified as an essential component of brand authenticity, which subsequently drives consumer attachment and pro-brand behaviors such as paying a premium and positive word of mouth (Beverland 2009; Napoli et al. 2014).

However, remaining true in the face of change is also a reason why brands decline, as we saw in the cases of LEGO and Vegemite in Chapters 1 and 2. The cultural model has identified how previously strong brands lost wider relevance despite high levels of marketing investment in remaining consistent. Recent studies have also identified how consistency per se represents a barrier to brand innovation that can ensure relevance and new sources of brand meaning and equity (Beverland et al. 2015; Holt and Cameron 2010). However, constantly changing the brand's position (especially during times of ideological stability), straying off into different segments and categories, and trying to be all things to all people ultimately undermine the stability necessary for achieving legitimacy and authenticity (Gerzema and Lebar 2008).

So, brand managers need to strive for consistency and relevance, both strategically and tactically, but need to understand when to emphasize one over the other, and also understand that each requires a very different mind-set and approach.

Why Brand Managers Struggle with Change

Although it is easy to say a strong brand requires stability and change, the overwhelming message that brand managers receive is "be consistent" (Beverland et al. 2015). Over time, this leads to a set of taken-for-granted assumptions that ensure consistency is privileged over change. We call this an "interpretive frame" (Dougherty 1992), which represents the lens through which we frame problems, identify and interpret data, and define solutions. This frame ensures we focus on information essential for ensuring consistency, while screening out ideas, requests, occurrences, and information that are inconsistent with our desire to remain "on brand" (Holt and Cameron 2010). In one sense, this is useful and often unavoidable as it ensures we do focus on consistency, which is actually important. On the other hand, it leads to a form of brand-management myopia whereby information that may warn us of impending danger, or identify sources of innovation that could enhance brand equity, is ignored or tuned out. Despite knowing relevance is important, it is often very difficult to achieve if your whole world is defined by an emphasis on consistency.

So, can brand managers innovate and remain consistent? This issue will be examined in more detail in this chapter, drawing on research in design thinking to identify the basis of **brand ambidexterity** (Beverland et al. 2015). This balance is not easy, and many writers note that the "**iron cage of brand bureaucracy**" means that relevance may be best left to creative disciplines such as design, advertising, and anthropology, "chief culture officers," and lead- and end-users (Holt and Cameron 2010; McCracken 2009). However, this so-called iron cage of brand bureaucracy is a function of an over-emphasis on one model of branding, so it is worth identifying the signals that should trigger discussions about relevance and transform the brand in ways consistent with its heritage but ensure relevance for the times.

Repositioning, Refreshing, Revitalization, Re-launch?

I have included the words "**revitalizing**" and "**refreshing**" in the title of this chapter for good reason—they more accurately describe what is involved in turning around tired brands and/or restoring relevance. Although this chapter goes into other forms of innovation, the main focus will be on revitalizing and refreshing brands that have lost equity. However, practitioners often use many terms to refer to revitalizing and refreshing brands, the most common of which is "**repositioning**." However, this term can be misleading. If you think back to the discussion of positioning, repositioning would literally mean changing the brand's meaning entirely. From a mindshare view-point, this is obviously quite dangerous because it would mean directly challenging the user's idea of the brand. Those adhering to this approach usually argue that should a brand need repositioning, it is probably not worth saving, and may be best harvested or retired (Trout and Rivkin 2009). They also point out that there are very few examples of actual repositioning in the truest sense of the word.

From a cultural point of view, repositioning happens throughout the life of the brand (Holt 2004a), although the difficulties involved in changing how users see a brand they have experienced in one way are often downplayed. The cultural approach has been built on cases of brands that went through periods of strength and growth (driven by relevance and rendered authenticity) and then decline, which was only solved through the generation of new cultural myths. However, these new myths often appear to involve much less change to the brand's historic roots than adherents of this approach would argue. Partly this is because the cultural model assumes that users will readily and easily reframe how they view the brand, dropping old knowledge and buying into new myths. As well, the cultural model downplays capabilities in its approach, and therefore underestimates the degree to which brands can simply change position and engage in the required organizational change needed for organizational authenticity.

What both models share is an interest in innovation. Mindshare argues innovation is essential for brand equity growth and relevance, identifying the importance of extension and other "on-brand" innovation activities. Cultural positioning argues for cultural innovation, identifying that relevance is achieved through identifying and exploiting emerging cultural schisms. In so doing, brands will be viewed as a legitimate relationship partner and cultural first mover able to outflank and undercut larger entrenched brands. In this chapter, I use the following terms to refer to specific aspects of brand innovation:

1. **Brand innovation**: This broadly captures proactive approaches to growing the brand (including brand extension and co-branding—see Chapter 7), identifying opportunities, revitalization and refreshing, and avoiding decline.
2. **Brand revitalization**: This refers to brands that have declined but are still in the marketplace. This replaces the term "repositioning" and refers to turning around brands that have suffered declines in their equity but nonetheless still have an actual market presence. Vegemite and LEGO are examples of brand revitalization we have examined already.
3. **Brand re-launch**: This refers to brands that have lain dormant for some time. In effect, these brands were removed from the market but may still have some latent equity through low levels of recognition. The C.W. Dixey & Son case at the end of this chapter is an example. This strategy is increasingly popular in certain sectors as it easier to re-launch a brand with a backstory than create one anew. The recent crowdfunded rebirth of Ferrania Film is another.
4. **Brand refreshing**: This generally refers to tactical shifts in the brand program to ensure relevance. Such changes can involve those covered in reinforcement and extension (see Chapters 6 and 7) and/or regular changes made to logo design, font, colors, and other more cosmetic actions brand managers undertake regularly. Coca-Cola's regular redesign to their identity system represents an example of refreshing.

Why Does Brand Equity Decline?

Customer-based brand equity (CBBE) (see Chapter 3) is usually defined in terms of the *aggregated* strength of the customers' relationship with the brand (Keller 2003). Although cultural positioning advocates do not address the issue of equity in-depth, they do focus on decline, identifying that as the meaning of the brand dissipates (vis-à-vis addressing the cultural schism), customers respond less favorably to the brand's marketing and reduce their use of it (Holt 2004). Both approaches therefore take a broadly similar view of brand equity but ascribe very different processes to build, and therefore rebuild or recover equity. So, what are the common reasons for users to reduce the strength of their brand relationship?

1. Points of differentiation become points of parity: What once differentiated the brand is simply now the category standard. Since differentiation lies at the heart of brand equity, a lack of it causes users to look at other alternatives, substitute generic products for the brand, move to low-cost options, switch in response to promotions, or try buyers' own brands (such as those offered by Aldi, Carrefour, Sainsbury, Tesco, and others).
2. The brand underperforms on points of parity: Points of parity are really hygiene factors—they won't motivate a user to prefer your brand but the lack of them will

ensure your brand is not preferred (Keller et al. 2002). Focus groups with target users can quickly get to the source of this problem, although feedback is just as likely to come from retailers, salespeople, influencers, and social media posts. Fortunately this type of decline is relatively easy to fix and primarily tactical.

3. **Disruptive technologies** or business models: The highest valued organizations at the beginning of the twentieth century were not the highest valued firms 50 or 100 years later. Why? Typically the inability to change one's business model in the face of foreseeable change. Eastman Kodak built their brand equity on providing innovative film-photography solutions—they sold the film and camera, and provided the processing. Although they invented the digital camera in the 1970s, share-market analysts berated them for investing in such a low-margin business model, and the rest is history. Technological disruption usually emerges from unexpected sources despite entrenched leaders having the resources to counter it (Christensen 1997). Netflix CEO Reed Hastings identified how the brand's early postal model could have easily been copied by then market leader Blockbuster and ensured the early demise of what is now an industry leader (Seo and Kim 2016).

4. The user's life-goals change: Prior to Fournier's (1998) celebrated work on consumer–brand relationships, brand-equity decline was mostly seen as something brand managers could avoid. Fournier, however, identified that brand equity could decline for reasons largely outside of a marketer's control. For example, several years ago I switched to a vegan lifestyle. This had an immediate impact on my existing brand relationships—previous relationships (of brands such as Schott New York using non-human animal products) framed in love-type terms (New Zealand Merino producer Icebreaker) were dropped. Correspondingly, new brand relationships were formed, with previously unknown brands such as Tofurkey, Etiko, and Moo Shoes New York. Could Icebreaker's brand manager do anything to address this? Beyond transforming their entire business model, no. Such changes speak to authenticating acts—the act of dropping brands or downgrading a relationship frame (from "best friend" to "casual fling") reflects shifts in one's defined true self.

5. The user's life-world changes: Fournier also identified that life transitions such shifts in roles (single woman to partner, to mother, to empty nester) could affect the goals we set and the brands we value. Any number of transitions, including those between child and teenager, at home and moving out, in work and retirement, can impact on the context in which we engage in authoritative performances. Others have noted that changes in collectives such as the family unit can affect the brands we relate to and the way in which we frame those relationships (Epp and Price 2010). For example, new arrangements arising from merging the families of divorced couples can result in new life worlds—the addition of a new family on top of the relationships one may desire or be forced to continue with the old family collective (Epp et al. 2014). Brands that can help you navigate both collectives (such as Skype for example) will be especially valued, while brands reflective of the old collective may be downgraded or dropped.

6. Ideological shifts that render the brand culturally irrelevant: The cultural position-ing model is predicated on addressing cultural schisms. Brands such as Mountain Dew built their equity on their ability to tap into cultural discontent and offer new solutions. However, should societal changes render the brand's underpinning ide-ology irrelevant, the brand will decline, and managers will need to create a new cultural brief (see Chapter 5).

7. The death/removal/retirement of the brand's founder: This may seem a strange inclusion, but brand founders intuitively get the brand and are often associated closely with it in the eyes of users. Steve Jobs' death, for example, raised many questions about the future of Apple, while any subsequent perceived misstep made reference to what Jobs would have done. One challenge for managers post-founder is that they become too respectful of their legacy. This happened at Christian Dior following the death of the founder and namesake. Managing the founder–brand link is tricky as Brand Aside 8.1 explains.

BRAND ASIDE 8.1

The Tale of Two Crowns: Managing Brand Founder Image

Founders are often essential to the brand's ethos and external identity. However, they are also human, subject to errors and mistakes, and ultimately, may need to be replaced, wish to retire, or die. How does one therefore manage the tension between a human founder and the abstraction of the brand that will hopefully endure for a longer period of time?

The theory of the two crowns is an old idea that is used to manage the institu-tion of the Royal Crown in the United Kingdom. Basically, the king or queen is the real but temporal and earthly crown, whereas the "Crown" is an enduring, abstract, institution. The former will perish, but the latter will always continue. Fournier (2016) draws on this idea to identify how professional owners seek to manage founder-driven brands (such as Martha Stewart, Christian Dior, Richard Branson's Virgin, and so on). In essence, management teams and financiers seek to distance the brand from the owner over time in order to ensure the brand can endure with-out them. This approach is tricky, however, as scandals such as those suffered by Martha Stewart (who went to jail) can undermine the brand.

8. Mismanagement: When Quaker Oats purchased Snapple, for example, they treated the brand in the same way as Gatorade, but the two brands had very different images with customers and eventually Quaker had to divest Snapple to new owners (who happily returned it to its original roots and reversed the decline) (Deighton 2003).

As we've seen, poor licensing decisions and over-extensions are another form of mismanagement. Cost cutting can also harm a brand, as managers begin to reduce the value of the customer experience, as happened at Harley Davidson in the 1970s when they removed chrome from their cycles to save money (Beverland 2009).

9. Crisis: This is covered in detail in Chapter 12, but beyond those fatal to the brand's future (where negative equity arises), a range of authenticity crises can negatively impact brand equity. In contrast, well-managed crises can represent important moments of clarity for the brand and eventually become part of the brand's folklore. Coca-Cola's infamous New Coke, Vegemite's iSnack 2.0, or Johnson & Johnson's Tylenol scare in their own ways all helped reinforce important brand associations.

10. De-legitimization: Chapter 7 identified how legitimacy was essential for ensuring brand authenticity and therefore equity. Legitimacy goes beyond pragmatic claims of performance or rights to trade, but involves considerations of the brand's moral standing and cultural embeddedness. The tobacco industry has faced increased regulation over time because it has lost legitimacy in core markets, with dramatic impacts on brand equity. These sources of decline are difficult if not impossible to manage since they involve considerations on whether the brand has the right to exist at all.

The above ten points contain things brand managers have varying degrees of control over. Brand managers can be expected to manage points 1, 2, scenario plan and mitigate for point 7, and clearly avoid points 8 and 9. They should have input and influence over points 3, 7, and 9. Points 4 and 5 are harder to manage and may require more radical solutions, involving careful use of brand extension and architecture and/or may involve investment/divestment considerations. Point 6 is difficult for brand managers to respond to and they will often need outside help from cultural creatives to enact a new cultural positioning. Point 9 is covered in Chapter 12. Point 10 is probably outside the influence of brand managers although picking up on changing social values and identifying the risks to their brand are something that should be part of any review process.

The rest of the chapter will examine (1) how to avoid some of these sources of decline through mindshare and cultural innovation, (2) rebuild brand equity in the cases of decline, and (3) use design thinking tools to ensure brands remain relevant and true to their roots.

Brand Innovation: Three Perspectives

This book has split brand innovation into three perspectives. The first is mindshare-based innovation whereby the brand's position is engineered into all innovation activities. This approach is valuable for reinforcing the brand. However, while it can often result in a focus on incremental innovation there is no reason why radical innovation (often through category extension) cannot occur. The second approach is cultural innovation with an emphasis on spotting cultural schisms or moving the brand from one cultural position to the next. In this approach, brands must also contribute to the populist worlds or web-based crowd cultures they draw from and therefore both radical and incremental innovations can result. Although this approach is much more user-centered than the mindshare approach, there is no reason why this needs to be the case (and vice versa). Finally, the **brand ambidexterity** approach will be examined, which draws on design thinking or the practices and thinking methods used by designers to address tricky problems (such as relevance vs. consistency for example).

Mindshare Innovation

Mindshare branding involves building equity through developing a series of distinct and strong brand associations in the mind of the user (Keller 2003). Innovation therefore involves activities that reinforce and/or enhance these associations (Beverland et al. 2010). As Jean Noel Kapferer states: "The twin engines of brand building are innovation and communication. Consistency is the key to managing these dual engines. Innovations build brands if and only if they create a consistent picture of what the brand is about" (2014a, p. 150). This innovation of course can involve new products and services, new messaging, new user-associations (through endorsement and sponsorship), usage associations, and other activities that aim to keep the brand "fresh" without straying too far from its roots. For example, Apple used a number of strategies to reinforce its commitment to user-centered innovation, including:

1. Radical "new to the world" product innovations such as the iPod, iPhone, and iPad (category extensions)
2. Incremental product innovations such as within category line extensions (the iPod Nano, iPod Shuffle, MacBook Air, iPad Air, and various software updates)
3. Service and experience innovations: Apple retail stores featuring Genius Bar helpdesks, educational experiential events, and the ability to interact with technology; the stores reflected the brand's iconography, look, and feel
4. Campaigns with musicians including Irish superstars U2 and their special edition red iPod, and of course the failed free download of U2's 2014 album *Songs of Innocence* given to everyone with an iTunes account
5. The adaptation of their famous Mac vs. PC Guy campaign to take account of Apple's and Microsoft's various updates and their differences in user experience
6. The Macworld events that generated worldwide free coverage of the firm's new releases and plans
7. Strategic "leaks" of new designs, all strenuously denied by the firm but nonetheless reported widely throughout the globe, all with the air of authority that came with news content rather than paid publicity

8. Constant software releases and updates in areas historically owned by the firm including photography, movie making, and electronic music; reinforced through a strategic program with various educational partners (particularly design schools), which ensured the brand became taken for granted or culturally legitimate in creative communities, all of which reinforced the brand's associations and ensured its cool status (itself reinforced through product placement in specific television shows and films)

All of these innovations reinforced the brand's "Think Different" message, enabled Apple to stay ahead of competitors and therefore earn higher margins (category extension was particularly important here), and keep the brand fresh and relevant through a careful mix of radical and incremental product innovations, and advertising campaigns that generated a buzz (Aaker 2012). The retail store expansion also ensured greater control over brand presentation (consistency), enabled the building of closer relationships with customers, encouraged trial for new users, and helped protect margins.

In the case of Mac vs. PC Guy, the campaign achieved wider cultural resonance and helped ensure user identities for both sets of consumers. It is not unusual for cafés and bars in hipster areas of various cities to be framed in terms of "filled with bearded, tattooed Mac users", all of which helps reinforce the brand's creative identity. The other thing this campaign does is reinforce a sense of them and us, which is essential for brand community (Muñiz and O'Guinn 2001). After all, most forget that Apple is a Microsoft client in terms of software and that the two firms' respective focus (on hardware and software) complements more than competes. However, in symbolic terms, PC Guy is a perfect foil for the hip, cool Apple guy, while both represented a nice foil for upstart Linux who tried a doppelgänger approach by presenting both as comfortable elderly men (vs. the female Linux user), focused on incremental innovation and controlling the market (Beverland 2009).

Historically, innovation scholars have paid little attention to branding-related issues. With a focus on research and development, innovation specialists often treat the brand as something that happens at the end of the process (Beverland et al. 2015). This approach holds that the "real innovation work" involves generating new concepts and workable prototypes, after which it can be handed to marketing to make it user friendly (who then as often as not hand it to design to get the styling right). Brand leaders, however, do the opposite, ensuring that all innovation is "on brand", and then leverage their creative processes as part of their brand's authenticity.

Figure 8.1 identifies a mindshare approach to innovation. This figure identifies different branded approaches to innovation that are determined by the degree to which the brand seeks to drive the market or be driven by the market, and the extent to which it is defined by radical versus incremental innovation. Different brands should according to their position engage in different types of innovation strategies:

Figure 8.1   Mindshare-driven innovation

Source: Adapted from Beverland et al. 2010, p.33

1. Creative brands: These are brands within creative sectors that attempt to create or shape trends. This includes design-driven brands like Alessi, Apple, Diesel, Di$count Universe, Dyson, Google, IBM, Phillips, Sea Shepherd, Stella McCartney, Umpqua Bank, and Tesla. These brands are expected to do things differently, take risks, and attempt to create new market categories, often through category extensions. Although not everything may work (i.e., Apple TV), they do not necessarily suffer for failures in the eyes of their users.
2. Share leaders: Creative brands may dominate profits even though they do not lead in terms of share. Share leaders such L'Oréal, Mars, Cadbury, Samsung, H&M, and Toyota engage in radical innovation (e.g., the Prius), but do so with reference to espoused user needs. Typically, they are not first to market with new concepts, but when they do enter, they often shape the category and determine performance benchmarks. Here innovation is more typically driven by the **Stage-Gate™ process** (see Figure 8.2 and Brand Aside 8.2) and a planned acquisition strategy.

BRAND ASIDE 8.2

Stage-Gate™ Innovation Process

Figure 8.2 represents the famous Stage-Gate™ Innovation process. This process is the dominant model in innovation studies, particularly those focused on new product development (although the logic applies equally to service innovation as well). The gates at the end of each stage are not just metaphorical; they consist of series of tests (usually involving a mix of marketability, feasibility, and strategic and

(Continued)

brand considerations). Should the idea fail at a gate, it is removed. The idea is the gates should weed out poor ideas and ensure that only a few strong ideas make it through the next stage. Each stage represents furthering investment, and therefore reducing ideas ensures decreased risk and a greater concentration of resources.

The beginning is usually called the "fuzzy front end" and this is where there is a free-flowing ideation session (designers are often involved here). The end is launch and hopefully sustained adoption and diffusion. Prior to that is prototyping, which can be an expensive stage, although with technological advances and crowdfunding operations, developing workable prototypes has become a lot cheaper and led to new models focused on "failing fast" (whereby multiple rough workable prototypes can be developed and removed quickly, although the learning in each is invested in later designs). The model is useful, although as design academic Roberto Verganti (2009) identifies it is not the only model, primarily results in incremental innovation, and does not explain the success of many lauded breakthrough designs that have rebooted brands.

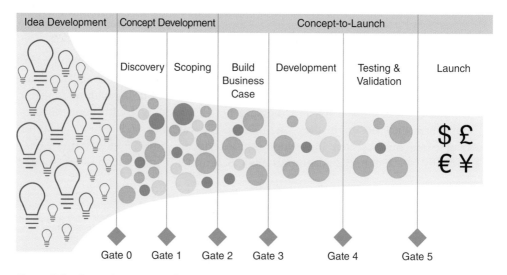

Figure 8.2   Stage Gate Innovation Process

Source: www.winsightsmarketing.com/services/new-product-development/

3.   Heritage brands: Many brands in the market look backwards and inwards rather than forwards and outwards. Typically, these brands leverage their lengthy (real or imagined) heritage, focusing on incremental improvements through greater mastery of their craft. Jack Daniel's is one such brand (as are many alcohol brands), Champagne Krug, C.W. Dixey, The Morgan Motor Company, Red Wings Boots, Claridge's, and

Savile Row brands such as Gieves & Hawkes. Culturally these brands draw their power from their associations with the world of craft and making, and often deploy language and cultural codes associated with "slow production" (see Brand Aside 8.3). New innovations are always framed in terms of "this has been a long time coming."

BRAND ASIDE 8.3

Fast vs. Slow Innovation

With the emergence of the Slow Food movement (vs. fast food), speed-based metaphors have become cultural codes to define certain types of innovation approaches, design models, and business models (there are now movements dedicated to slow living, slow fashion, slow design, and even slow branding). The emphasis on brand authenticity has also emerged as part of this, with authentic being more associated with the slow world than the fast. So what do they refer to? Definitions are difficult to come by, but the two terms are interrelated—one cannot have slow without fast.

The fast model is typically associated with mass consumerism, ever-quickening production cycles, globalization, cheap disposable products made by machines or cheap labor, sameness of style, and a lack of concern for society and the environment. Brands such as H&M are often seen as examples of this, with cheap clothes, made in developing world factories, designed to be worn just a few times before being thrown away. Slow, in contrast, is everything that fast is not. Heritage and craft brands typically play up this identity, stressing their localness, timelessness, durability, handmade nature, and concern with local communities and the environment (Beverland 2011).

However, large brands can also play up their slow credentials with much success—brand authenticity is often a combination of careful delineations between the front (what we say we are) and back stage (what we do). Many brands that draw on slow cultural codes such as Jack Daniel's, Red Wing Boots, Dom Perignon, the Savoy Hotel, and Camper are a mix of slow messaging and fast business systems. The benefit of this is that it enables one to be relevant in terms of product and service standards while also exuding an old-world charm (Beverland 2005b). Although users often know that this is all stage-managed they are willing to suspend disbelief as long as you manage the illusion carefully.

4. Follower brands: Many brands define themselves in terms of a leader, often stressing points of difference and matching points of parity. Avis's "We Try Harder" fits this model. They define themselves in relation to the market leader (Hertz), match them in terms of offers, and try and do better on performance. This process defines fast-fashion brands such as Zara. Zara, H&M, and Primark all copy the ideas of luxury design houses and ensure they are quicker to market with ready-to-wear,

sharply priced options. Likewise, retailers' buyers own brands fall into this category. Here innovation is always incremental and always defined in reference to competitor offers and proven concepts. Typically, these firms also place a great deal of emphasis on process-based innovations to ensure continuous improvement, cost efficiency, and speed to market.

It is important to remember that brands can mix and match their innovation strategies somewhat, as their respective positions are often flexible enough to stretch across radical and incremental innovations. However, the categories in Figure 8.1 identify the innovation strategy that should be the dominant approach for each type of brand. For example, consider how incremental innovations such as iPhone upgrades from Apple are greeted with disappointment, especially when no new radical products are announced. The company needs to engage in this type of innovation to ensure relevance, reinforce points of parity and difference, and to recoup its initial large investment in radical innovation; however, influencers and users expect the company to regularly excite with new technological wonders.

Likewise, heritage brands such as The Morgan Motor Company do engage in radical innovation, often leading the way in hydrogen-based prototypes, aluminum forming (their Aero models are literally blown into shape much like glass), and sleek design; however, failing to integrate these stories into the brand's design language (open-top sports cars with a significant amount of handmade content) can be dangerous, such as the move to a fiberglass closed top model (the +4+) in the 1960s. Just 24 were made before it was abandoned as a failure although currently the model is the most valued because of its rarity (Beverland 2011).

Far from being an afterthought, brand marketers must ensure that their position is engineered into R&D, innovation, design, and production or service delivery, to ensure that innovation reinforces the brand over time.

Cultural Innovation

For the cultural positioning model, relevance rather than consistency is central. Inherent in the cultural positioning model is the idea that brands must change when they cease resonating culturally. As we saw in Chapter 5, the cultural positioning model is a disruptive one in relation to the brand's recent past. When the gap between national ideology and the users' daily experience grows too great, the brand is at risk of losing equity, its myths no longer creating the desired differential effects in terms of user behavior and financial performance.

Budweiser for example is considered an archetypical iconic brand in the cultural positioning model. Although the brand has loosely owned the idea of masculinity over its life, given that gender roles and expectations are framed culturally, the brand has endured because it has radically shifted from a middle class to be enjoyed at home premium beer, to a reward for hard work and effort, to being cynically self-denigrating (Holt 2004a). Why?

Masculinity changed. As the 1950s gave way to the 1960s counter-culture, the idea of the predominantly white American male being a breadwinner lost cultural resonance. America's economic, political, cultural, and military decline meant men were unable to buy into classical cultural roles, and therefore began to desert the brand. The brand's revitalization came through aligning with a new populist world—that of working-class craftsmen dedicated to the love of work for its own sake. The "This Bud's for you" campaign resonated with men again and gave them a new myth to buy into—the man as action hero (Holt and Thompson 2004). This too eventually gave way with ongoing outsourcing, automation, and the decline of local manufacturing rendering belief in the idea that hard work would be rewarded or "making" defined anyone, to be replaced with the self-depreciating, mocking slacker ethic reflected in shows about nothing such as *Seinfeld* (and the character Kramer) and movies such as *The Big Lebowski* (exemplified by Jeff Bridges' iconic "The Dude" character). Here, workers were seen as dupes for "The Man" (1960s slang for the system), and the only thing that really mattered was male bonding over sports and masculine rituals (Holt 2004a).

As this example shows, relevance is a moving target. It's important to remember that each campaign defining the brand's cultural position ran successfully for long periods of stability and on-brand (mindshare) incremental adjustments. Innovation in this model has already been discussed in Chapter 5 and the method behind the cultural brief. In essence, when sales suggest the brand is losing relevance (even if tracking suggests otherwise) it is time for a new myth. This requires understanding the nature of the cultural schism experienced by your target users, identifying a new populist world or web-based crowd culture to draw from, rendering your company and offer authentic in terms of these mythic sources and your heritage, and in some cases changing position radically. After all, Budweiser's shift from man as action hero to slacker is openly contradictory, which is why the brand's lizard advertising campaign openly mocked the firm's marketing approach (Holt 2004a).

However, as Brand Aside 8.4 demonstrates, brand managers struggle to make these changes, which is why they often need the unique input of creative personnel, or design thinking. Differences in how each discipline approaches brand innovation challenges are presented in Table 8.1.

BRAND ASIDE 8.4

The Brand Bureaucracy

Holt and Cameron (2010) challenge the idea that brand managers are able to innovate culturally and manage relevance. They argue that brand managers operate within a mental "iron cage," which they call "the brand bureaucracy." The brand bureaucracy emerges out of the idea that branding can be distilled down

(Continued)

to a few rules, the effects of which can be measured. This is a further critique of the mindshare model. This model has attempted to make branding a science (or "sciency"—science like) and is seen as too abstract, reductionist, standardized procedures, a preference for control, quantification, and an emphasis on rational and rigid rules. Anything that sits outside of these rules or that cannot be measured is ignored or rejected. However, it is precisely this type of information and the disciplines that prefer to work with it that drive relevance and the basis for cultural brand innovation.

Table 8.1   Brand managers' vs. designers' approach to innovation

Brand Issue	Marketers, brand managers	Designers
Brand concept	Reference brand positioning	Up for discussion; assumptions can be challenged
Brand articulation	Write brand mantra, promise	Bring promise to life
Brand communications	Communicate brand consistency in marketing communications and programs	See brand consistency as a three-dimensional construct, including product form, sensory components.
Role of brands in consumer's life	Focus on satisfaction; loyalty, Individual product function and performance ("new and improved")	Brands are part of a customer's or end-user's life and products; holistic, systems perspective
Brand's role vis-à-vis other corporate assets	Brands tend to be managed in separate portfolios; they compete for resources and to create value	Brands have emotional meanings and convey them, e.g., trust, innovativeness
Role of product innovation	Necessary to maintain growth; brand and line extensions	Opportunity to challenge assumptions; activate brand experience, experiment
Meaning of consistency	Predictability, reliability	Authenticity of meaning
Communication of brand values	Pictures, messages, events	Experiences, objects, senses, symbols

Brand Ambidexterity and Design Thinking

Maintaining consistency and relevance is an enduring "wicked" brand problem. **Wicked problems** are typically those where no obviously simple answer can be found and are defined as: "A wicked problem is a problem that is difficult or impossible to solve because of incomplete, contradictory, and changing requirements that are often difficult to recognize" (Churchman 1967, p. B-141). The defining characteristics of wicked problems are:

1. The problem is not understood until after the formulation of a solution.
2. Wicked problems have no stopping rule.

3. Solutions to wicked problems are not right or wrong.
4. Every wicked problem is essentially novel and unique.
5. Every solution to a wicked problem is a "one-shot operation."
6. Wicked problems have no given alternative solutions.

(*Source*: Conklin 2003)

One discipline that deals with these types of problems is design. Tim Brown of Californian design firm IDEO (responsible for many break through products including the first laptop) popularized the phrase "**design thinking**" in an influential 2008 *Harvard Business Review* article of the same name. The idea is that if managers can think more like designers, they too can solve wicked problems or see things in a new light. So what is design thinking?

> Design thinking is a collaborative, iterative, experimental and human-centered process that adopts a holistic approach and applies abductive reasoning to problem solving. It draws on design methods and tools, and it is both an individual cognitive feature and an organizational one. (Micheli et al. 2017, p. 20)

Design thinking consists of the following practices:

1. **Abductive reasoning**: induction seeks to generalize from instances to theory, whereas deduction involves making predictions from theory. Induction is most consistent with a creative logic focused on relevance. Deduction is much more about consistency (deducing from brand position to tactics). Abduction combines the two and asks, "What could be?"
2. **Iterative thinking and experimentation**: a preference for trial and error, and learning from feedback. Rather than perfect the offer first time around, design thinkers engage in quick prototyping and adjust quickly.
3. **Holistic perspective**: a focus on the wider system in which a user's problem or opportunity exists. Similar to the assumptions underpinning relational and cultural models of branding.
4. **Human centeredness**: a focus on the user, but one that acknowledges cognition, emotions, and behavior, and seeks to understand the context in which such users seek self-authentication.

(*Source*: Beverland et al. 2015, p. 593)

Together these practices are used by design thinkers (who are not necessarily designers) to generate brand ambidexterity: "Brand ambidexterity is defined as a marketing capability whereby a brand is strategically managed to create value through the pursuit of both consistency and relevance" (Beverland et al. 2015, p. 592). Table 8.2 identifies the practices deployed by design-thinkers in the three stages of building brand ambidexterity. Beverland et al. (2015) identified that design thinkers addressed common consistency–relevance tensions through a three-stage process of:

1. Destabilizing the common assumptions underpinning so-called brand-truths
2. Defining and developing new solutions
3. Transforming the brand in such a way as to remain true to its roots (which may have been reinterpreted or broadened) while also being relevant to stakeholders

Outcomes of this process included greater brand equity and a stronger meaning platform with which to reinforce and refresh over time. As a result, the brand ambidexterity approach helps balance the competing but necessary logics underpinning the mindshare and cultural positioning models. Figure 8.3 identifies the different options under an ambidexterity approach.

Table 8.2   Brand-related design practices and design thinking

	Abductive reasoning	Holistic perspective	Human-centredness	Iterative thinking and experimentation
Destablization: (1) naïve questioning (2) problem interrogation (3) contextual immersion.	Why can't we be relevant?	Where did these categories come from?	User empathy	What happens if we play with the assumptions underpinning mental categories?
Define and develop: (1) capabilities matching (2) problem scoping (3) solution development.	What could help us achieve relevance?	Mapping the wider context of the problem.	Respecting stakeholder needs.	Innovating in ways sensitive to (but not 100% respectful of) the brand story.
Transformation: (1) mapping innovation to brand (2) restabilizing.	How does the innovation link the brand's past and future?	Ensuring the brand delivers value in use to stakeholders	Innovation enables the brand to become the relationship partner	Innovation expands the brand manager's mental horizon about future possibilities.

Source: Beverland et al. 2015, p. 598

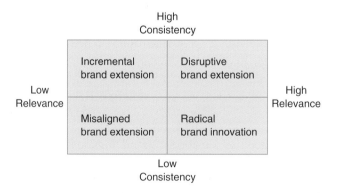

Figure 8.3   Brand Ambidexterity

Source: Beverland et al. 2015b, p.592

Co-creation: What Role for the User?

When co-creation and innovation are discussed, the role of the user often comes up. Many innovation scholars propose that co-creation involves direct input from **lead-users**. Typically, these innovations are large business-to-business (B2B), new-to-the-world innovations and involve technical specialists, and key or lead-users have always played a significant role in the innovation process (Hultink et al. 1997). Lead-users in this sense have deep levels of expertise and unique skills that are vital to the success of the project (for example, clients seeking new ships, aircraft, defense platforms, power plants, and rail tunnels all have to have significant expertise to develop the brief and make informed decisions among alternatives). Likewise, studies of producer communities such as Linux developers reveal that not all ideas are treated equally, and therefore one needs a large amount of coding expertise to engage in the requisite authoritative performance (contributing code to the open source software) (Cromie and Ewing 2009).

However, outside of these specialized areas, does co-creation have to involve direct engagement with or input from users? Not really. In fact, it is usually more incremental innovations that value direct input—asking users to rate the various treatments of proposed advertisements, or what they like and dislike about their current services or products, are useful strategies when it comes to gaining insights for small incremental improvements that keep brands fresh and maintain points of parity. However, they're not much use when engaging in radical product innovations, developing the myths for new cultural positioning campaigns, or identifying how to challenge existing service expectations in order to reframe expectations of certain categories (key to new service innovations) (Verganti 2009).

In fields such as design, and more recently marketing and brand management, co-creation is equated with user centeredness (Merz et al. 2009; Verganti 2009). A user-focused approach does not mean merely asking target users for their wish list; rather it is a much more empathetic approach, whereby the innovator places themselves in the shoes of the user and tries to work out what would provide value from their perspective. In some cases, this is simple. When IDEO co-founder (the late) Bill Moggridge was designing new workstations, he imagined how he would like the workstation to be designed, an approach he called "interaction design." These insights could inform prototypes that could then be tweaked and adjusted with input from other users. In this case, the users themselves may not have been able to come up with the innovation, but they could see its value because it spoke to their latent needs (as opposed to espoused needs) and everyday frustrations of working with technology that had not been designed with the user in mind.

Figure 8.4 identifies the difference in approach to co-creation. Roberto Verganti (2009) differentiates between a user-centered version of design whereby users define what improvements they would like in their existing offers and a design-driven approach. User-centered approaches are appropriate for incremental improvement

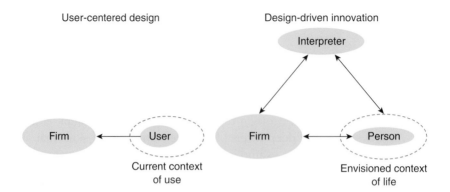

User-centered design   Design-driven innovation

Figure 8.4   Design Driven Innovation

Source: Verganti 2009, p.118

and do not differ from the stage-gate™ model of innovation (Figure 8.2). However, breakthrough, radical innovations require a different approach to co-creation, one that Verganti calls "design-driven innovation" whereby the designer acts as a sociocultural-technical interpreter to generate insights that are missing in terms of the target person's life world. This is much more akin to the cultural brand positioning approach, whereby creators seek to generate user-focused insights that address latent rather than espoused needs (Beverland et al. 2015).

This is more difficult when one is more distant from the user, or when one is trying to develop campaign ideas for cultural relevance and revitalization. Here the brand team, usually in conjunction with professional creatives, have to generate an outcome that reeks of insider-authenticity (from the point of view of the populist world) while also connecting to the target audience and somehow reflecting or overturning the brand's previous cultural position (Beverland 2009).

Refreshing and Revitalizing Tired Brands

Refreshing the brand largely involves keeping the brand's position relevant and is largely achieved through tactical updates to the brand's marketing program. Firms that invest in and act upon tracking research, engage in regular brand and creative reviews, and have a strong level of market or customer orientation are typically able to ensure the brand remains fresh in the mind of the user. The greatest challenge in ensuring freshness relates to balancing on-brand reinforcement (the brand's heritage) while taking advantage of emergent opportunities that have the potential to keep the brand fresh while also adding associations.

This challenge is particularly relevant given that such opportunities can come from unexpected sources, and may be generated by customers, users, fans, influencers, or actors in pop culture (e.g., Vegemite gained unexpected momentum when it was mentioned in Men at Work's global number one smash single "Down Under" in 1981). For example, while Tommy Hilfiger benefited from being "adopted'" by American rap stars, his was not the only preppy white American brand to experience this situation. Ralph Lauren also experienced this uptake but unlike Hilfiger decided to ignore it, feeling it was off-brand and the influencers would move on to the next "hot" item quickly enough (Beverland 2004). Who's to say who was right—Hilfiger was a brand in desperate need of relevance whereas Lauren was a powerful brand arguably at the top of its game.

Pepsi in contrast has been quite adept at reinforcing its brand image among younger users (its traditional "Next Generation" base) over time through quickly responding to emergent adoption. In 2006, as part of the FIFA World Cup (held in Germany), Pepsi ran a humorous advertisement featuring a soccer match between the world's top footballers and a team of Bavarians decked out in traditional lederhosen. The bemused footballers quickly realized the Bavarians were more than a match for anything they could throw at them. The advertisement was set to the quirky 1980s hit "Da Da Da" by German band Trio. In China, a group of teens called The Back Dorm Boys (so named after their lip-synched YouTube hit cover of the Backstreet Boys' ballad "I Want It That Way") quickly loaded up their cover of "Da Da Da." Pepsi signed the duo to feature in a range of advertisements and helped boost the brand's profile in China during the FIFA World Cup and beyond.

A successful reaction to emergent events like this involves (1) having a clearly defined brand position, (2) having a shared understanding amongst the brand team of this positioning, (3) knowing the brand's audience and the networks of influence they exist in, and (4) being open to new opportunities and possibilities. Although 1–3 represent basic skill sets for any brand manager, too many marketers move between jobs meaning that such shared understanding of the brand's heritage and position and empathy for the brand's audience is often rarer than one thinks. Being open to new opportunities, while being mindful of points 1–3, is unusual, especially when consistency tends to frame brand-management practice. This requires a different set of skills, such as those covered in the design thinking and brand ambidexterity section above.

Revitalizing tired brands is trickier. Typically, these brands have suffered periods of decline for some time. Much depends on how far the respective brand has fallen. Arguably, those brands with lower equity have more potential in terms of new associations, but they also have less brand strength (see Chapter 4). In contrast, brands with stronger equity have more strength to build on, but potentially less scope to be made over anew. Revitalization involves addressing the causes of decline. Revitalization will undoubtedly involve revisiting the brand's marketing mix, and the brand's consumer and cultural relevance, as well as require insights from design thinkers who can balance relevance and consistency. In some cases, revitalization may require organizational change, such as the movement to a more market-oriented culture (Gebhardt et al. 2006). On top of the aspects of innovation covered so far (which are also relevant to revitalizing brands), revitalization involves the following steps:

1. Conduct a brand audit: Identify through the eyes of users the good, bad, and ugly of the brand. Which aspects (or mix) of the brand's identity, image, user associations, ideology, practices, and marketing mix have played a role in the brand's decline? Does the brand align with users' life worlds? Does it appear to be authentic in terms of helping users achieve their goals? Is the firm behind the brand authentic? Does the brand speak to the times—that is, is its core messaging in tune with the ideology that frames a user's authoritative performance and their lived reality?

2. Examine competitors also targeting your user base: What do they do differently to you? What are the points of parity and points of difference? Where are the gaps? What can your brand do to address those gaps and be relevant to users?

3. In addressing points 1–2, conduct research with current users but more importantly lapsed users, industry experts, influencers, and previous employees: Look at conversation trends in netnographic or big data studies to identify how often the brand is discussed, the sentiment toward the brand, and the associations. It is likely that the sentiment will not be wholly negative; more often among lapsed users there is a desire to see the brand do well again, to return to its former relationship status.

4. Ascertain the brand's strengths and weaknesses: The focus on your revitalization program is to play to the strengths, but critically address the weaknesses. It's not strictly true that you only get one shot at revitalization, but every time you fail you reinforce negative perceptions about the brand with users and influencers and, of course, waste increasingly scarce resources.

5. Depending on the approach you adopt, you either need to revisit the brand's historic position or devise a new cultural brief: Regardless, one important and often overlooked step is to conduct a historical analysis of the brand. If mindshare is the frame of choice, this historical analysis identifies long-held brand truths that can be refreshed for the times. If cultural branding is the frame, you need to locate the brand's historical successes and failures in relation to the ideology of the day, identifying how the brand enabled users to perform authoritatively and why the brand ceased providing this user benefit.

6. Develop the brand's internal programs—see Chapter 6.

7. Develop the brand's external programs and tracking—see Chapter 6.

8. Remember that revitalization is rarely revolutionary: This may seem contradictory in light of the cultural approach's emphasis on change and overturning previous myths, but the success of a brand's cultural myths requires political authority or authenticity born of a long-term engagement with particular ideas and audiences.

Let's examine how this worked in practice. After purchasing Maserati from Fiat in 1999, the Ferrari Group (now ironically owned by Fiat) set about returning the iconic grand touring car marque to its former glory. Maserati has a long heritage including iconic designs, racing success, and rivalry with Ferrari.

However, after World War II, the brand was swapped among various owners all of whom seemed to lack any empathy for the marque. Maserati was removed from racing, and in the 1980s moved out of the sports-car category altogether, launching its ill-fated Biturbo coupé, which by design standards was rather conventional and resembled many mass-market vehicles of the day. The range was also beset by engine and rust problems. The brand's fortunes slowly slid and while many models were launched in a bid to capture the glory days, quality problems and a lack of performance credibility dogged the brand. Exciting new models were often cancelled due to the expense, and eventually the brand was sold.

In 2002, new versions of the Coupé and Spyder were the first releases aimed at revitalizing the brand. Prior to this, the brand team had invested a substantial amount of work into understanding the brand's strengths and negatives. The revitalization was to be driven by two positioning values: "sporting spirit" and "pure style." Where did these come from? These values were based on historical research and research with market actors including motor enthusiasts, journalists, and bloggers, current and former owners, distributors, and staff conducted by marketing consultants at Sapient. These values were seen as paths between the past and the future of the brand. Maserati's strength lay in four areas: exclusivity, Italian heritage, authenticity and craftsmanship, and sportiness. Its weaknesses included concerns over the credibility of the vehicles and their reliability and support network.

Studies of the consumer relationship to the brand were also conducted. As the brand team were keen to position Maserati away from Ferrari (also in their stable), they identified that whereas owners of the latter were emboldened by their car, the relationship between a Maserati and driver was symbiotic and complementary. In terms of personas and personality, the owner of a Maserati was self-assured, confident in themselves, and did not need a prop for their ego. For them, the Maserati was about the joy of driving and being at one with the road and vehicle. Like all brands, owning it was an identity statement, but one that communicated taste, refinement, and self-confidence.

Brand revitalization involved rebuilding a strong dealer network, engaging with members of the press, returning to racing, and a communications campaign stressing cultural elegance and brand heritage, and road handling. Owners were also given access to maserati.com, a brand community website and forum to share information, gain advice, explore the brand's story, and gain access to special services and promotions. The results were impressive. Maserati has become one of the strongest upper luxury sports car brands in the United States, increased sales while also increasing prices, and won praise for their vehicles from the motoring press. The brand has expanded its range but maintained its focus on the upper end of the luxury car market (selling no more than 70,000 cars per year globally).

Re-launching Dormant Brands

The C.W. Dixey & Son case at the end of this chapter is a case of **re-launch**. Re-launch involves reviving brands that have been dead or dormant for some time. These brands typically have a backstory, representing potential esteem but no strength of forward momentum (see Chapter 4, Figure 4.1). Why re-launch a brand? For Simon Palmer of C.W. Dixey & Son the reasons are quite personal, albeit with clear professional goals and commercial insights. For firms specializing in acquiring the rights to old brands, such as River West, the reasons are simple—old brands retain some awareness, are cheap to acquire, and therefore potentially a low-risk way to create value (and potentially be re-sold to larger groups).

River West has purchased a number of dormant US brands including coffee brand Brim (which disappeared in 1995), Salon Selectives (hair care), and many other FMCG brands that have disappeared usually after being acquired by larger groups (Walker 2008). Although these brands have no reality, they are often remembered fondly by previous users and therefore have potential. Whether brands such as Indian Motorcycles, Polaroid Instant Cameras, Pac-man, and Brim coffee can re-emerge from the dust is questionable. However, their owners are banking on the "MINI factor" that saw the iconic British brand re-launched successfully by BMW and go on to be arguably bigger than it ever was. *Star Trek*, *Star Wars*, and other film franchises have also recently been re-launched. What should one remember when re-launching such brands? Know your target market, remember the fans, modernize and differentiate, and connect back to heritage.

Chapter Summary

This chapter has focused on brand-related innovation, with a particular focus on rebuilding brand equity in cases where it has declined. As such, it complements the previous chapter with its focus on innovation through extension, co-branding, and portfolio management aimed at keeping brands fresh that helps grow brand equity and, if done carefully, avoid decline. A number of reasons for brand-equity decline were covered, including those that are within the control and/or influence of brand managers, those outside of their control, and those largely determined by shifts in the consumer's self-authentication goals and the context in which they are enacted.

Options for brand innovation were covered with reference to the mindshare approach (in which the brand position drives innovation), the cultural approach (in which the brand's position is the focus of innovation and therefore subject to change when required), and the design thinking approach that seeks to balance these two approaches over time (brand ambidexterity). The chapter identified why brand managers often struggle with questions of relevance and change. It then moved on to ways in which brands can be refreshed, revitalized, and re-launched (see the C.W. Dixey & Son case study below). The commonly used term "repositioning" was rejected as it rarely achieves success and runs counter to how consumers relate to brands.

Part III begins with the next chapter, which explores global branding.

Review Questions

1. Identify some brands that have genuinely repositioned? Why are they so rare?
2. What is a brand that you think needs a refresh? Why? Do the same for a brand you believe needs revitalizing. Compare the differences.
3. Using Figure 8.1, identify brand examples for each quadrant not listed in this book. Identify examples of brand innovations that feature in two or more quadrants and identify the strategic connections between them.
4. Identify two wicked problems in branding. How might design thinking help with one of them?
5. Identify three examples of brands that you view as ambidextrous. Explain your choices.

Case Example: Re-launching C.W. Dixey & Son

C.W. Dixey was founded in 1777 and focused on making optical instruments and eyewear for the wealthy, including nobility. The brand was eventually on-sold and became C.W. Dixey & Son in the nineteenth century. Counted among its patrons (the brand has never called its clients "customers") are "Mad King" George III, Emperor Qianlong of China, Napoleon Bonaparte, Queen Victoria, James Bond author Ian Fleming, and most famously Sir Winston Churchill (among many others). C.W. Dixey's most famous design were the round frames favored by Churchill. The brand has been awarded 15 Royal Warrants (which are given to brands that serve the English Royal Household) for its dedication to quality and luxury.

The brand was viewed as market leader among wealthy patrons up until World War II. After that, the firm slowly declined, stopping production of eyewear in the 1960s, while an employee theft dealt the brand an almost fatal blow in the late 1970s. After that, the brand was sold and declined in awareness, eventually being the name of three up-market opticians in London. In 2006 Simon Palmer inherited the brand from his father (who had been responsible for placing the business on a sound financial footing) and decided to re-launch it in the luxury eyewear market.

This was not easy, however, as much of the brand's heritage had been lost over the years, with the firm's headquarters destroyed during a bombing raid in World

(Continued)

War II, and its Coat of Arms (given to the brand by the Duke of Norfolk in 1978) rotting in Simon's garden shed. Eventually Simon built up a rich historical portfolio through his own research, purchases on eBay, and contacts with former employees.

As part of rebuilding the company's historic story, Simon believed that his brand provided retailers and consumers with an authenticity than few luxury eyewear brands could match.

> In the world we live in there's so much false branding, false marketing, false provenance, that having something that has a true, really unusual story is more relevant than ever for people who will always want something special and rare. There will always be people that will move away from designer logos to something with depth and authenticity.

This comment refers to the grey area of country of origin labeling in luxury goods production. Although many of the world's largest luxury brands trade on their European origin, they are often made in China, under license from the big three manufacturers: Luxottica, Safilo, and Marcolin. Luxottica owned or had exclusive licenses for numerous eyewear brands, including Ray-Ban, Persol, Oakley, Vogue, Oliver Peoples, Polo Ralph Lauren, Prada, Paul Smith, Chanel, Burberry, D&G, Donna Karan Eyewear, Miu, Stella McCartney, and Versace. Luxottica had a near monopoly on the eyewear channel and owned retail chains such as Lenscrafters, PerleVision, and Sunglass Hut. Safilo produces branded eyewear, including Alexander McQueen, Dior, Emporio Armani, Giorgio Armani, Gucci, and Hugo Boss, while Marcolin owned licenses to Harley Davidson, Mont Blanc, Tom Ford, and Tods.

European law enables brands to label their products as "made in France" or "made in Italy" (and so on) as long as some production is done in the European Union. As many industry insiders report, this often means little more than final assembly or even sewing in the "made in France" label. For the licensee and license holder eyewear is hugely profitable because final production costs for a pair of luxury branded glasses (without corrective lenses) made in China can be as low as 10 euros (including packaging). On top of this, shifts in fashion mean the market for eyewear is now part of the fast-fashion sector, as Simon states:

> In the past there was the threat from laser surgery or contact lenses, but now people love to wear eyewear; it makes people look serious, it makes women look incredibly attractive—or it makes a statement if you're a cool designer or hipster; it's incredibly popular around the world now.

Table 8.3   The market for eyeglasses (non-sunglasses)

Tier	US$ Price*	Channel	Example Brands	Attribute	Made in
Low (large cost-focused players)	$30–$140	Chain optical retailers & pharmaceutical chains	Specsavers, Boots, Optical Express, Dollond & Aitchinson	Ready-to-wear; cheap; functional	China
Medium (large luxury and mass-luxury brands, many players)	$140–$400	Upmarket optical retailers and specialist brand stores	Dior, Ray Ban, Lenscrafters	Brand name; ostentation; fashion; mass luxury	China (finished in Europe)
Luxury (fewer players, small)	$400+	Specialist retail	Cartier, Cutler & Gross, Lindberg, Mykita	Heritage; customization; craft; design aesthetic; old world luxury	Europe

Source: Keinan and Beverland 2016, p. 7

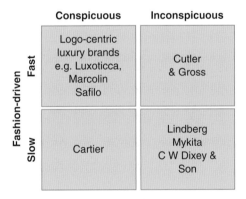

Figure 8.5   Positioning for Luxury Eyewear

Source: Authors' notes

The control that large license holders such as Luxottica exerts over marketing channels has also meant there is little differentiation between retailers. For many up-market retailers with discerning clientele, a unique brand provides them with a point of difference and is therefore likely to enjoy substantial channel equity.

(Continued)

The market for eyewear can be broken down into three broad segments, contained in Table 8.4 below.

Simon re-launched his brand into the luxury eyewear segment, and focused on appealing to the inconspicuous, slow luxury market contained within Figure 8.5. Simon based this idea in historic brand truth and also beliefs about the emergence of inconspicuous luxury whereby consumers signaled their status through cultural taste, downplaying logos in the process (and preferring classically crafted products) rather than overt displays of economic wealth through logo-centric brands.

Simon had gained permission to leverage the historic association with Sir Winston Churchill (he could not afford to do likewise with the James Bond 007 franchise) through the brand's first new collection in 50 years, entitled the Chartwell Collection (after Churchill's country house). His glasses would be priced high (£450 and above), sold via his own website and through select optician-run retail outlets, target men and women, sold without corrective lenses, and, for now, ignore sunglasses (as these represented a different type of purchase and market segment). Interest in Churchill remained high, and the brand retained a small amount of awareness among consumers who had Dixey glasses as children and experienced retailers and opticians, but otherwise enjoyed little recognition or recall.

The Chartwell range was designed and produced in the Jura region in France. Although Simon desired to make his products in the UK, there was no manufacturing base in eyewear any longer and the highest quality frames were hand-produced in France, Italy, and Japan. His products would be made from the most expensive acetate, and with an all up cost of around 30 euros (including a leather case, branded glasses cloth, and hand-printed card containing the brand's story). Simon aimed to re-launch the brand globally, as "Englishness" was popular amongst the wealthy. Once re-established future ranges, drawing on the connection to Napoleon and Emperor Qianlong, would be rolled out along with further expansion of the Chartwell collection.

Case Questions

1. Assess Simon's chances of successfully re-launching his long-dormant brand? What challenges will he need to overcome?
2. Using both a mindshare and cultural approach, identify how Simon can position his brand with his target audience in a compelling way.
3. How could Simon innovate in his brand marketing in order to generate brand awareness and traffic to his website and partner stores?
4. Is being produced in France a problem for an inherently English brand?

Key Terms

Abductive thinking
Brand ambidexterity
Brand innovation
Brand refreshing
Brand re-launch
Brand revitalization

Design thinking
Disruptive technology
Incremental
innovation
Iron cage of brand
bureaucracy

Iterative thinking and
experimentation
Lead-user
Repositioning
Stage-gate model™
Wicked problems

Further Reading

Beverland, Michael B., Julie Napoli, and Francis J. Farrelly (2010), "Can All Brands Innovate in the Same Way? A Typology of Brand Position and Innovation Effort," *Journal of Product Innovation Management*, 27(1), 33–48.

Beverland, Michael B., Sarah J.S. Wilner, and Pietro Micheli (2015), "Reconciling the Tension between Consistency and Relevance: Design Thinking as a Mechanism for Brand Ambidexterity," *Journal of the Academy of Marketing Science*, 43(5), 589–609.

Brown, Tim, "Design Thinking" https://www.ted.com/talks/tim_brown_urges_designers_to_think_big.

Verganti, Roberto (2011), "Designing Breakthrough Products," *Harvard Business Review*, 89(10), 114–120.

Walker, Rob (2008), "Can a Dead Brand Live Again?", *New York Times Magazine*, May 18, 49–53.

Part III
Brand Management Challenges

9

GLOBAL BRANDING

Rather than hope to communicate with and convince consumers using consistent messages and images, many advertisers may opt to micro market their brands, select speciality media, and radically alter their brand positioning to attain a strategic *in*consistency that still resonates with consumers from different backgrounds and allegiances with the richness, complexity, and diversity of local cultural meanings. A brand morphing approach to positioning poses logistical and strategic challenges, however. (Kates and Goh 2003, p. 66)

Learning Objectives

When you finish reading this chapter, you will be able to:

1. Differentiate between the "global branding" and the "brand as culture" perspectives.
2. Explore decisions around adaptation-standardization in global brand management.
3. Explore local–global tensions in relation to brand meaning co-creation.
4. Understand country-of-origin effects.
5. Examine contemporary and enduring challenges in relation to global branding

Introduction

In the lead-up to November 25, many people living outside of the United States were no doubt bombarded with messages about Black Friday. Some may even live in countries (such as the UK and Australia) where this previously unknown shopping event is fast becoming normalized. A common response was "What the hell is Black Friday?!" Usually followed by "I'm not in America!" But the latest complaint is beside the point—globalization and digital technology have rendered borders porous and seen commercial rituals and holidays go global (see Brand Aside 9.1). Brands too, exposed to a global customer base, are forced to play along with this, lest they miss out on sales in key markets. Charities have also fallen in line, with Giving Tuesday (which follows Black Friday) now becoming a normal fundraising drive that transcends its original national context.

BRAND ASIDE 9.1

McDonaldization vs. eBayization

"McDonaldization" is a term developed by economist George Ritzer in 1983 to refer to the process of standardization and uniformity that would sweep the globe. Ritzer saw this process as inevitable due to globalization and neoliberalism (economic deregulation). Although Ritzer's idea primarily referred to the spread of an organizational form (primarily a traditional mass manufacturing system complemented by uniformity of look and scripted service encounters) the idea has become highly influential in debates regarding global branding, particularly in the emphasis on efficiency and predictability (one global brand) and control (protecting the desired brand identity across the globe). This idea is not without its critics and recently some have questioned whether a command and control system makes sense in a postmodern economy characterized by fragmentation and co-creation.

Consumer culture scholars have offered eBayization as an update on the McDonaldization thesis (Ahuvia and Izberk-Bilgin 2011). Whereas McDonaldization did not allow for consumer identity work, eBayization reflects the fact that consumption is about identity building. eBayization draws on the emergence of peer-to-peer networks to suggest that high variety and unpredictability are desired outcomes for consumers. Unlike an industrial process focused on efficiency of outcomes (limited variety), eBay allows for high variety (See Brand Aside 9.3, The Long Tail) and relatively smooth transactions through its internet site. Variety allows for consumer self-authentication. Rather than control, eBay allows for peer-to-peer influence and self-monitoring, stepping in only as an arbiter of disputes. This is not to say it is inefficient or lacking in measurement; Big Data techniques, for example, are a way of mining disaggregated data to identify general trends, patterns, publics, subcultures, doppelgänger threats and so on. Such a system pushes the work of consumption and even production onto the consumer. Although the latter enables co-creation it also results in benefits to marketers that are subject to intense ethical debates (see Chapter 11).

Global branding has typically referred to the process of taking a brand beyond its original country of origin in order to expand its franchise. We call this the managerial approach to global branding. In this approach, the main consideration relates to the trade-off between global consistency and local relevance, or to what extent does one adapt the brand from a standardized global approach to fit local cultures? Although adaptation may seem intuitively obvious or even be reflected in local market data, the efficiency gains from standardization are considerable, and with the Internet exposing consumers around the globe to particular lifestyles, adaptation is often not as desirable or as necessary as one would think.

Studies in consumer culture take a different view of global branding, however. Whereas the managerial approach defines global and local from the standpoint of the brand's geographic operation (rather than exposure), the cultural global branding approach focuses on consumers' experience of notions of "global," "national," and "local." This approach not surprisingly identifies a much more complex and dynamic picture of globalization and branding, identifying how consumers may use brands to self-authenticate, how brands may give rise to culture, how marketers may create shared cultural myths that tie different people together in an **imagined community**, and how brands can be involved in any local backlash against globalization.

In this chapter, we explore both these approaches, identifying a range of managerial and consumer-related considerations in relation to global branding.

What Is Globalization?

Along with difficulties in tracing connections back to particular places or deterritorialization (see Chapter 2) and difficulties in distinguishing real from imagined (or hyperreality), **globalization** is an important antecedent in consumers' use of brands as a means of self-authentication (Arnould and Price 2000). What this means in the context of branding, is that consumers make use of brands and engage in other consumption-related rituals to re-connect to real and, more often than not, imagined notions of place, community, and nationhood. This may involve consumers drawing on retro brands to connect with an imagined "golden age" of past traditions, seeking out old favorites overseas (or taking brands with them), seeking places to celebrate national days with like-minded others (again often overseas), and adopting local traditions on a global scale, such as the St Patrick's Day celebrations on March 17 in nations with a large Irish diaspora, and Christmas around the globe.

Globalization is defined as the process of international integration arising from the interchange of worldviews, products, ideas, and other aspects of culture (Albrow and King 1990). The International Monetary Fund (IMF) (2000) identified four aspects of globalization:

1. Trade and transactions
2. Capital and investment movements
3. Migration and movement of people
4. The dissemination of knowledge

With the onset of globalization and trade deregulation, brand owners began to look at expanding their markets offshore. Chapter 3 examined various forms of brand equity including financial brand valuation. It is important to remember that the most influential rankings of brand equity are in fact measures of **global brand value**. For example, Interbrand's valuation metrics dictate that no less than one-third of a brand's sales must come from foreign markets for it to be considered in its Global 100 Brands. However, marketing across cultures presents unique challenges for brand managers, not just in terms of local relevance, but also because they and their brands are carriers of culture (ethnic, ideological, and lifestyle).

One interrelated challenge relates to whether the brand's position and execution (particularly messaging but also pricing and other marketing elements) can drive equity in other markets characterized by different cultural values, legal frameworks, and marketing systems. This challenge lies at the heart of global branding research and practice, and is best characterized as the **adaptation–standardization problem**. As Schroeder et al. (2016, p. 153) state:

> The term global brand encompasses multiple dimensions, which include marketing standardization, consumer perception and international management. Furthermore, a key tenet of branding strategy posits that global branding decisions should cohere with other marketing elements, such as the brand's core essence, the brand personality and positioning and the brand's execution. The process of global branding refers to a complex process of reinforcing and aligning multiple elements on a global scale.

The process described reflects what I will call the managerial approach to global branding. This approach defines a brand's global-ness and local-ness in terms of how many markets the brand owners formally operate in. It ignores how consumers think about global or local, but nonetheless offers useful insights in terms of the strategic expansion of brands from its historic national base. As the quote above makes clear, the managerial approach focuses attention on one core challenge: standardization vs. adaptation. The general plusses and minuses of global brands are identified in Table 9.1.

Table 9.1   Benefits and drawbacks of global brands

Benefits	Drawbacks
Increased equity	Equity requires relevance and a lack of adaptation may decrease effectiveness
Easier penetration of emerging markets	Difficulties of building a cultural position
Economies of scale in marketing communications	A lack of local management flexibility to adapt to local conditions
Cost efficiencies in terms of product and services	Negative country of origin image in some categories
Favorable reviews by stock analysts	May create a backlash if brands are seen as representative of political ideals

Adapt or Standardize?

In his famous *Harvard Business Review* article "Globalization of Markets" (1983), Theodore, or "Ted," Levitt made the case for undiluted brand **standardization** (or **McDonaldization**) or one brand position and supportive marketing program across the globe. He did recognize it was difficult to achieve at any one point in time, but nonetheless held this aim to be an ideal worth striving for because of cost efficiencies. The HSBC case at the end of this chapter concerns the central challenge facing global brand managers: how does one maintain a consistent global brand identity while remaining relevant to locals? What is standardization in this context?

> Standardization involves developing a distinctive brand identity and reproducing this identity across differing cultural, historical and structural terrains, is a cost-effective means to target and fulfil those consumer demands generally shared by affluent and youth markets across the world. (Schroeder et al. 2016, pp. 153–154)

Although some may challenge the benefits of a singular brand identity (given the importance of relevance to brand equity), it is also important to remember there are a number of benefits to standardization, especially when one considers issues of scale, cost, and of course exposure through social media sites. For example:

1. Having one brand identity across the globe is efficient. As the HSBC case demonstrates, high equity can be achieved with relatively little investment (albeit still significant in absolute terms). Furthermore, there are significant financial benefits to standardization including maximizing profits, reducing marketing costs, and costs in research and development, manufacturing, and staff training.

2. Many brand users (not just consumers) source brands from around the globe and therefore may value the certainty that comes from a singular identity. For example, it is not uncommon for global brands such as Infosys to purchase services from other large global professional services firms such as PriceWaterhouseCoopers or IBM. Research on authenticity, for example, suggests users in these situations may value the feelings of control generated by the predictability of a global brand above other forms of self-authentication such as connection and morality (Beverland and Farrelly 2010).

3. Social media and porous borders mean that users are just as likely to embrace global lifestyles while also seeking to maintain some imagined local connections. This is particularly true for younger consumers who have never known the pre-Internet era, let alone the pre-globalization period. Andrew Potter (2011), for example, identifies how hipsterism has become a global lifestyle, resulting in worldwide demand for brands such as Urban Outfitters, Lomography, and so on.

4. In many sectors such as fashion (Chanel and H&M), technology (Apple, IBM, Samsung), fast food (McDonald's), finance (Citibank), and entertainment (Sony and Disney), global brands often set the standard for others to emulate. The sheer scale of these brands' operations gives them incredible reach and influence.

5. As economies develop, emerging middle-class consumers often value global or international brands because they are perceived to be of better quality and more exotic. Global brands represent important signifiers for the newly wealthy to display their status. Gucci's seemingly culturally sensitive market entry strategy in China in the early 2000s required adjusting after consumers rejected local imagery and messaging in favor of what they imagined to be the more real and desirable Italian or European approach, which in reality reflected a very stylized, iconic rendering of Italian heritage (Beverland 2009).

6. Population diasporas (or mass immigration of peoples around the globe) often provide a beachhead or staging point for foreign brands to enter new markets without adaptation. As many of these communities represent populist worlds or are attractive to cosmopolitan locals, seeming purity of brand image (remaining true to origin) may be more effective than adaptation. Korean popular culture is spreading around the globe partly as a result of this influence while Filipino brand Jollibee has driven its global expansion through expatriate communities abroad (who act as early adopters).

7. Related to the above point, the movement of people around the globe has resulted in cross-cultural cross-pollination in many sectors, with consumers being more exposed to global cuisines, art, fashion, and pop culture than ever before. In many cases, what is global or local is very hard to discern. Hybrid food styles such as Tex-Mex have become authentic cuisines in their own right, while trends such as Pacific cuisine represent a mash-up of styles. Australasian baristas have moved around the globe, establishing coffee chains and roasteries, and shaping consumer expectations, (the New Zealand invented "flat white" has travelled well beyond its home environment).

8. As covered in the C.W. Dixey & Son case study in Chapter 8, shifts in **global supply chains** have undermined the truth-value of many claims of origin. European luxury goods for example are often made in China and finished in Europe (European Union labeling laws allow this practice). Likewise, the shift of manufacturing to low-cost labor countries or countries with supportive ecosystems (made up of R&D, suppliers, and raw material suppliers, other services) has seen a split between making, designing, and marketing. At the same time, large global brands' marketing and branding strategies reinforce perceptions about country-of-origin and iconic authenticity (Beverland et al. 2015). Consumers are used to this global–local greyness (especially as many experience it in their workplace).

9. For consumers in developed economies, the opposite may be true; local brands or foreign brands or associations from developing economies may be deemed more authentic because they are harder to attain, reflect cultural rather than economic capital, and also reflect people's desired identity goals in terms of connection and morality (Beverland and Farrelly 2010). Netflix's global coverage has seen them invest in shows from around the world because their customers are seen as discerning viewers. This includes popular shows from France (*The Returned* and *Marseille*), Colombia (*Narcos*), Germany (*Deutschland 83*), Norway (*Occupied*), and so on.

10. Cultural industries such as fashion and entertainment are forever co-opting cultural traditions, rituals, and symbols from around the world, making it difficult to discern the real "foreign" from the "global melting pot." Celebrities (including bloggers and other influencers) such as Miley Cyrus have a global or multiregional audience (as in the case of Korean pop culture throughout South East Asia), and therefore are able to lend a new brand such as Di$count Universe (see Chapter 5) instant credibility or expand their own brand franchise across the globe without adaptation.

11. Influencers such as Richard Florida have had an enormous impact on creating "global cities" through their work on the "creative class" (see Brand Aside 9.2). These ideas, and the development of branding by cities, regions, and countries' marketing councils as a means of attracting business investment, creative knowledge workers as well as high-end tourists, have created a sense of cultural convergence between places. Neighborhoods often noted for their hipness, for example (including Mitte in Berlin, Shoreditch in London, Fitzroy in Melbourne, Williamsburg in New York, and Newtown in Sydney), all largely resemble one another in terms of aesthetics, types of business, residents, brands, and retail formats. Along with the emergence of social media, this global provides opportunities for the smallest of brands, as detailed in Brand Aside 9.3

BRAND ASIDE 9.2

The Creative Class

Richard Florida's (2002) book *The Rise of the Creative Class* has had an enormous effect on regional policymaking, ensuring many cities converge towards a unified positioning in order to attract knowledge workers that produce value through creativity. Florida's thesis was that the cities most likely to flourish in the future (as the shift away from manufacturing and service work toward knowledge work continues) would embody the three Ts: talent, tolerance, and technology. The idea is simple—creative professionals like to be around other creative people in order to spur further innovation, move to tolerant places because challenging the status quo is accepted, and need to access web-based technology to connect globally. This has led many cities such as Auckland, Minsk, Stockholm, and more recently the team charged with rebranding Detroit to engage in relatively similar strategies, including investments in high-speed internet, free Wi-Fi, support for the gay community, innovation districts and hubs, and so on. Brands locating in these places can benefit from cultural innovations, technological breakthroughs, and of course the populist world that these creative cultures represent.

BRAND ASIDE 9.3

The Long Tail

The Long Tail is the title of a book by former *Wired* editor Chris Anderson. Anderson uses this title as a metaphor for global digital markets. For producers of physical goods, making a sustainable living by being highly specialized or appealing to only a few customers is difficult because of the costs associated with shipping globally, performing to audiences, or adapting to local legal frameworks. However, in digital marketplaces, this changes. Anderson argues that since there is no cost to delivering digital-based products and services one can easily tap into an infinite number of specialized niches on a global scale. The long tail refers to this infinite number of niches that are available to the vast majority of producers (while just a few typically service the largest niches as they have the power to do so). This gives new meaning to the "born global" debate as even the smallest brand can build equity with a small, often intensely loyal following and do so sustainably.

These ideas have much value for cultural branding as these small niche markets represent populist worlds that can be tapped for greater meaning and authenticity. For those using a mindshare approach, the same applies, although typically one would coopt such markets to enhance a brand's authenticity, often by mainstreaming the imagery and ideals of the small communities that grow up around these micro brands or cultural producers. Combined with crowdfunding models such as Kickstarter and Indiegogo, these communities can also generate challenger technologies and brands to large incumbents. For example, folk-rock singer Neil Young crowdfunded his hi fidelity Pono music player as an alternative to low fidelity mp3 players, generating substantial buzz and eventual investor interest. Many so-called slow fashion brands such RPM West with their Quarter Century Jacket have also used this approach to respond to consumer exhaustion with fast-fashion approaches. Legacy technologies such as camera film (Ferrania and Cinestill), vinyl music, old-school computer gaming, and board games (such as Kodama and Dreamwell by Action Phase Games) have been revitalized by initially targeting the long tail (often embedded in subcultures of consumption) through crowdfunding models (Beverland and Fernandez 2016).

12. Brand equity measures through Interbrand, Brand Asset Valuator, and Brandz are a reflection of global coverage and assumptions about brand consistency.
13. Firms often overcome country-of-origin disadvantages through co-branding with local or global players such Huawei's upmarket push with its P10 phone involves a partnership with legendary German camera manufacturer Leica, a co-branded relationship conspicuously advertised throughout the globe (see Figure 9.1). Furthermore, commonly used international expansion strategies involving strategic

Figure 9.1   Huawei-Leica Co-brand

alliances (50 percent of which result in a merger) or merger or acquisition are often followed by brand integration, such as Citibank's expansions around the globe whereby they eventually integrate local banks into the global brand franchise.

14. All too often, cultural differences or local market conditions require adjustments in the brand-marketing program but not in the intended identity or (mindshare or cultural) position (which may offer the same appeal to target markets across countries). Clever use of local spokespeople, a local distribution partner, or local agencies can help ease the transition of a wannabe global brand in particular markets. Critically, service providers such as design agencies, advertisers, financial and brand consultants, and market research firms have also expanded their brand franchise globally, resulting in purchasing efficiency gains for their large clients when they chose agencies with global coverage.

Adaptation and Brand Morphing

So what are the reasons to consider the local adaptation of brand elements and even brand identity and position? Authors focusing on adaptation argue that differences in culture, stage of economic development, and structural issues in the marketing system may necessitate adaptation. At first appearance, this may look reasonable, but such studies also come with assumptions that can be challenged, especially when considered in light of the points listed above. For example, reasons for adaptation are often framed in relation to uniform measures of culture such as Geert Hofstede's famous framework (see Brand Aside 9.4) that do not hold up empirically or stand up to critical scrutiny under postmodern market conditions where, even within nations, multiple interpretations are possible by difference audiences: "Contemporary culture is no longer a monolithic, shared way of life among a majority of people (if it ever was). A more advanced view of culture is that it is a complex melange of symbols, diverse practices, and hybrids" (Kates and Goh 2003, p. 65).

BRAND ASIDE 9.4

Geert Hofstede's Cultural Dimensions

Researchers have long sought ways of measuring cultural differences. Such attempts are fraught with difficulty as well as assumptions that can be challenged in today's postmodern markets. The most famous measure is Geert Hofstede's cultural dimensions. Developed using a worldwide survey of IBM employees (a population that shared "IBM-ness" but differed in terms of location and, potentially, culture) in the late 1960s through to the early 1970s, the framework is widely used by researchers, especially when seeking to understand how to communicate across cultures. Hofstede identified six dimensions of culture:

1. Power distance: This index measures perceptions regarding equality. In high power index countries (e.g., Latin, Asian, and Arab countries), equality is low and authority is unlikely to be questioned. In low power index countries, the opposite is the case (e.g., Northern Europe, the United Kingdom, USA, Israel).
2. Individualism vs. collectivism: Individualism vs. collectivism relates to the strength of ties and social obligations. Individualistic societies are characterized by few social obligations and loose ties, even between family members (e.g., Western Europe, the USA, Australia, and New Zealand). In collectivist countries, "we" takes precedence over "I" and obligations to others are often extensive (e.g., Asia, Africa, Latin American, Pacific Rim).
3. Uncertainty avoidance: This index measures a culture's tolerance of ambiguity or the unknown. Those high on the index tend to prefer one truth or authority (law, beliefs, religion, codes) (e.g., Latin America, Germany, Japan) in contrast to those rated low who are more tolerant of multiple options and accepting of different views (e.g., Sweden, Denmark, China).
4. Masculinity vs. femininity: This index measures societal preferences for what would be viewed as fairly stereotypical gender roles. Feminine societies (e.g., Nordic countries, Chile) would place a high degree of emphasis on caring and cooperation, while masculine societies emphasize achievement and materialism (e.g., Anglo-Saxon countries, Germanic-speaking countries, Japan).
5. Long-term vs. short-term orientation: This index refers to time orientation in terms of preferring to look forward rather than backwards. Those cultures with a low degree of time horizon have a preference for tradition (e.g., Anglo-Saxon countries, Islamic nations, Africa, and Latin America), while those with a high degree of time horizon have a strong preference for change (e.g., China, Japan).
6. Indulgence vs. restraint: This index measures the extent to which people are free to gratify their desires and act on their emotions. Those high on this index

(e.g., Latin America, the UK, Nordic countries) tolerate more indulgence while those low are more restrained (e.g., East Asian nations, Eastern Europe).

Source: Wikipedia, "Hofstede's Cultural Dimensions Theory"

This model has been widely used (especially the first four dimensions—much less is known about the latter two), but is not without its critics. Much of the critique comes down to methods and measures, including whether there are other dimensions to measure national cultures, whether the original IBM sample was truly representative of the diversity of culture, sampling discrepancies, and so on. However, postmodern writers critique this model from a different view, arguing that stable unified cultural characteristics are in short supply and may have never really existed. In line with this text, these authors argue that cultures are rich and varied and cannot be measured against false binaries such those listed in 1–6 above.

However, it is also the case that such differences may exist, and may require changes to aspects of the brand program (or **glocalization**), or even the brand's position. Reviews also suggest that communication standardization is risky because of social, cultural, and market differences, and, as such, the brand or aspects of it must be "morphed" across different markets. There are a number of reasons why adaptation beyond simple linguistic translation might be appropriate:

1. Many of the effects noted above are often conditional on certain moderating variables. For example, although consumers in so-called less developed or developing economies may believe global brands are of higher quality or offer greater prestige, these beliefs are subject to socio-historical conditions. For example, for the past two decades middle-class Chinese consumers have driven demand for Western luxury brands such as Louis Vuitton, Gucci, and Chanel. These brands play on strong traditions of bespoke and craft production, yet in centuries past China was viewed as the standard for luxury.

   However, Chinese artisans were restricted in terms of who they could sell to, usually only being able to produce goods for the Royal Household and certain nobles. The Chinese Communist Party downplays pre-revolutionary history for political reasons. As such, the general Chinese consumer has little knowledge or experience of the long tradition of local craft production (ironically, many luxury brands use China as a manufacturing base precisely because of the availability of skilled artisans). By way of contrast, Indian consumers regularly use local artisans to produce high-quality goods (especially clothing) and have little interest in purchasing saris made by luxury brand Hermès (Kapferer 2014b). Both markets would therefore require very different approaches in terms of brand messaging and positioning.

2. Brands at different stages of development may require different strategies to eventually become truly global, standardized brands. Johansson and Carlson (2014) for example differentiate between **international novice brands** and **global brands**. An international novice brand, for example, will need to adapt to local market conditions in order to be successful, while a truly global brand often has the power to shape markets to its own ends, disrupting existing market conditions, service scripts, and setting new standards of performance and operation. Novices are more likely to require local partner assistance when entering new markets, and only through learning over time can they eventually take on more of a marketing driving role. Although useful, this way of thinking also needs to bear in mind the reasons for standardization listed above. There is no reason why even new brands such as Di$count Universe or Netflix cannot shape markets to their advantage or why global brands such as McDonald's and Coke should not adapt in particular situations when the need calls for it.

3. Different institutional requirements, legal restrictions, and cultural norms related to the role of religion, traditional taboos, gender roles, and cultural meanings among many other local issues require changes in the brand program. For example, Google's founding commitment to freedom of speech and freedom of information (their positioning is articulated as "Don't be evil") was impossible to live up to in China where information is regulated by the state. Adaptation in this case, through the use of a sub-brand or even the purchase of a local operation would have ensured they were more successful in this large market and avoided much of the criticism they suffered as a result of their public mental gymnastics around whether the brand mantra was authentic or aspirational.

4. Country of origin images may be negative within the category or generally negative or unknown, requiring a shift in strategy. Brand Aside 9.5 provides more insight. Many US brands can carry negative connotations in some categories or in general as a result of that country's military policy around the world. Likewise, Danish brands suffered in the wake of a backlash in Muslim countries over the publication of cartoon images of the Prophet Muhammad.

BRAND ASIDE 9.5

Country of Origin Effects

What do you think of when you see the brand Havaianas? These simple rubber flip-flops have gone global by leveraging their Brazilian roots. A brand's country of origin can represent a useful set of associations. Where something is made (or perceptions thereof) can provide brands with certain advantages. This is often referred to as the "country of origin" effect. Typically, this is measured by assessing the link between a place and certain classes of products. For example, Russia is associated strongly with vodka, so much so that many producers, regardless of origin, build their brands around stylized Russian imagery. However, Russia is not known as a producer of quality cars or electronics, and in fact for those classes of goods "made in Russia" may be a negative association (just as "made in the USA" for some classes of food and cigars is a negative for users). This has led to a large amount of research on understanding such effects, identifying ways in which to use country of origin, or overcome unknown or negative perceptions of origin. But how real is this effect?

Country of origin effects involve priming consumers with images of particular nations or the names of the country and then probing associations between countries and certain categories of products. These effects therefore tend to be easy to generate but harder to replicate in real-world purchase situations. This is partially why "made in ..." campaigns struggle to sustain momentum, as consumers spend very little time making purchase decisions for many of the goods they buy, may simply assume certain goods are locally made, or understand that brands are sourced globally or the complexity of supply chains means even locally made products are rarely 100 percent locally produced.

Studies on authenticity have also shown how easy it is to appear to be local or connected in an iconic sense to a place. While brands such as BMW may not always be made in Germany, their design ethos ensures consumers can create a believable authentic connection between the brand and the country of origin. Likewise, clever use of local iconography by large brewers ensured consumers thought foreign beers were authentic local ones (and often more so than the truly local) (Beverland et al. 2008). Mythmaking has also been used to create a shared sense of nationhood, especially by Asian brands such as Singha beer (Cayla and Eckhardt 2008). Finally, brand morphing has been used to successfully suggest foreign brands have a long-established local tradition, even when they do not (Kates and Goh 2003).

In light of these differences, Kates and Goh (2003) encourage brand managers to **morph** aspects of their brand program when the need arises. Morphing is defined as: "Activities that bestow [a brand] with the strategic flexibility and dynamic capabilities that enable it to evolve into a very different type of [brand] in a relatively short period of time" (Kates and Goh, 2003, pp. 60–61).

Three types of morphing are identified in Table 9.2. These differences represent differences in degree, with customized uniformity representing the least change while creating new meanings represents the largest shift.

Table 9.2   Brand morphing practices

Brand Morphing Practice	Definition	Example
Customized uniformity	Adapting executional elements of global ads [and other brand elements such as product] to specific foreign-market meanings	Changing the execution of Kraft's Philadelphia Cream Cheese to reflect local cultural images of heaven
Changing brand positioning	The desired positioning itself is culturally objectionable or irrelevant, indicating that the brand should be positioned in different ways across countries.	It is difficult to position the Mars Bar as a convenience food in France because of cultural prohibitions against eating in public
Creating "new" meanings in a foreign country	A sense of local relevance is attained by transplanting images and meanings from one society to another	Whitman's chocolates created a positioning of a traditional Australian past using images commonly associated with the United States.

Source: Kates and Goh 2003, p. 63

Common adaptations in the case of foreign expansion relate to customized uniformity. Examples include:

1. Brand name and logo: The most common form of adaptation is to translate the brand names or brand-related endorsers and slogans into the local language in order to avoid confusion or ridicule. Logos may also be adapted to avoid offending locals—Nike for example found that its swoosh logo bore too much resemblance to the Arabic form of Allah in Islamic countries (Johansson and Carlson 2014, p. 168).

2. Product and service adaptations: Product and services can involve small adaptations to local tastes, such as Coke's recipe adjustments made to appeal to local preferences for sweetness/bitterness, or may require more substantial changes such as offering smaller vehicles in European markets (e.g., the Ford Ka and other smaller economy models were not sold in the US for many years) or adjusting footwear lasts (e.g., Jimmy Choo) to reflect South East Asian physiques (the failure of Nike and Adidas to adapt in this way initially provided an opportunity for local brand Li Ning to fill this demand). Service standards may also need to change as some countries have different norms regarding interaction between servers and customers and different beliefs about hierarchies—Australian servers for example tend to believe they are the equal of the customer, whereas in Japan servers are expected to treat the customer as their superior (and bow before them).

3. Communication and experiential adaptations: When William Grant decided to refresh their single malt whisky brand Glenfiddich around the tagline "Someday you will" the execution had to be adjusted for different market groupings. The idea was to contrast the brand with the overt success or achievement of Johnny Walker by emphasizing appreciation of the journey rather than the result. However, the content of the journey and what the end point was were different across different markets. For the UK and USA, the journey was usually placed in nature scenes, identifying how their target user largely saw personal success as an

escape from work. For Taiwan (one of the most important markets for single malt whisky) the journey was much more about financial achievement and building up wealth. In France (another key market for whisky), the campaign had to change altogether due to strict rules on advertising alcohol and limits on linking the category with success of any kind (resulting in advertising treatments focused on abstract links to key ingredients and associations such as water and purity).

The Brand Culture Perspective

The **brand culture approach** in the context of global versus local debates is less developed and much more fragmented. The key difference between this perspective and the managerial one focused on standardization vs. adaptation relates to who defines what is global, national, and local, and how users experience the effects of global brand culture. The managerial approach focuses on the brand and its geographic scope. The brand culture approach by way of contrast focuses on how the consumer views terms such as global, local, and national and how they see brands from different nations or those which transcend national borders (global brands).

The brand culture perspective also argues brands are part of culture and that therefore they are carriers of ideas (beyond the notion of country of origin imagery) and this can impact on how a brand is built and positioned. For example, American brands express a certain set of myths and lifestyles that have much to do with that nation's global reach and influence, whereas Japanese brands reject such lifestyle positioning in favor of technological performance, thereby limiting their equity and Japan's influence at a cultural level (although this has changed in recent times with the export of Japanese pop culture).

Although fragmented, the potential requirement to morph the brand across national borders is demonstrated in a number of studies suggesting brands can shape culture or experience a cultural backlash reflective of wider political ideals and tensions. For example:

1. In the lead-up to the 2002 FIFA World Cup in Korea and Japan, many advertisers focused on creating a shared culture around the idea of "New Asia" in order to generate brand equity and live the position of their brand around the world. This community was in so many ways imagined or invented since the history of the region is of vast cultural differences, mutual antagonism and distrust, and long periods of warfare. Cayla and Eckhardt (2008) found that advertisers studied historic Asian myths and used the shared codes across them to generate an idea of a "New Asia" (as urban, modern, and multicultural), and therefore a region of origin strategy that provided the basis for brands such as Singha beer to add to its prestige and take advantage of the world stage the 2002 FIFA World Cup provided. This strategy meant brands generated cultural content that then helped shift outsiders' image of the region, thereby benefiting Asian brands.

2. In New Zealand, the creation of community through brands is even more pronounced. As this country shrugged off its colonial links to the UK in the 1960s creatives found that the way in which to represent an indigenous (but Anglo-Saxon) New Zealand culture was to use everyday mundane brands because of their connective authenticity. Since every "Kiwi" (the nickname for New Zealanders, which was actually derived from an Australian brand of shoe polish) shared local brands of confectionery, toys, cheap fashion items, and national television icons, these provided the basis for a new form of identity in a way that high-brow art could not. Kiwis pass on the use of these brands in a variety of ways as a means of communicating cultural myths such as egalitarianism and innovation (Sands and Beverland 2011).

3. In Austria, local brands' adaptation to a multicultural environment (ostensibly local retailers offering products targeted at Turkish migrants) suffered a backlash from consumers because it clashed with what localism meant to native Austrians. Although tempting to suggest the locals were engaging in discrimination the picture was much more complex as native Austrians tried to maintain fealty to macro norms in favor of tolerance and micro traditions that were perceived as under attack by these adaptations (Luedicke 2015).

4. In India and Turkey the discourse of suppressed nationalist movements may be drawn upon as part of a backlash against globalization, opening up opportunities for local brands while also ensuring global brands come to be seen in a negative light or as "infidels" that spark a "consumer jihad" against them (Izberk-Bilgin 2012; Varman and Belk 2009).

5. Diasporas may provide the basis for a beachhead in local markets. The desire of many immigrants to retain connections with their homeland (while also adapting to local customs) means they will gravitate toward brands that are unchanged from their country of origin roots. For example, whisky brand Penderyn leveraged the Welsh diaspora to build a global audience (Schroeder et al. 2016). By being adopted by the diaspora, these brands are quickly perceived as real or authentic by cosmopolitan locals, thereby ensuring widespread adoption.

6. The complex history of some nations can give rise to opportunities for relatively neutral countries to generate the basis for populist worlds. The success of Korean pop culture throughout Asian (and through diasporas globally) fills a gap for populist worlds that neither Japan (with its World War II record) nor China (with its current regional hegemony) can provide. Brands can associate with Korean pop stars and cultural exports, thereby enhancing their authenticity throughout the region.

7. Consumers may use brands to assert competing visions of national identity. Studies in China and Vietnam identify that Western brands may be adopted or rejected by different consumer segments depending on their beliefs about desired national identities. Some Chinese consumers rejected Western brands as a means of righting past wrongs done by military domination in the nineteenth century, while others accepted them because China had now returned to its dominant place on the world stage and purchasing expensive foreign brands reinforced this (Dong and Tian 2009).

These findings, and more like them (see Brand Aside 9.6 on authenticity), suggest a richer more nuanced approach to global branding whereby adaptation may undermine brand equity, or enhance it, where what is local and global is defined dynamically in different ways by different groups of consumers, consumers may use brands to solve ideological schisms at the macro and local level, and brands can even provide the basis for national identity. The brand culture perspective steers clear of suggesting managerial principles, but much of what they find supports the case for morphing, standardization, and careful adaptation, and also the cultural positioning model.

BRAND ASIDE 9.6

Authentic and Fake: The Role of Context

Debates around authenticity are often framed in the dichotomy of real vs. fake. Real in this sense refers to the old trademark-driven notion of the "genuine article." These assumptions lead researchers and commentators to assume consumers are being duped when they are buying seemingly fake or counterfeit products. However, such a view ignores the role of the user in determining what is real and fake. An anthropological study of counterfeit consumption in Vietnam, for example, found that locals view fake and real as a continuum rather than absolutes (Vann 2006). For the Vietnamese, brands are discussed in terms of "model goods" (*hang lieu*), "mimic goods" (*hang nhai*), and true fakes. Model goods are what we would know as the original brand name, while true fakes are deceitful in that they deliver no functional performance. For example, a real Samsung Galaxy is a model good while a fake would be something that looked like a phone but was in fact just an empty shell. Mimic goods, however, are what we would know as counterfeits, in that they provide functional benefits but are nonetheless copies passing themselves off as brand-named goods (e.g., a working but fake Samsung Galaxy). Vann (2006, p. 290) describes the complex relationship between model and mimic goods as follows:

1. Mimic goods are normal and commonplace.
2. Their quality should be judged on how well they imitate the original.
3. They are not necessarily deceitful.
4. There is an interdependent and hierarchical relationship between model and mimic goods (i.e., one may buy the mimic but aspire towards the model).
5. Mimic goods are part of the competitive capitalist process.
6. Mimic goods enable the emerging middle class to balance two goals: to reflect the state's view that Vietnam is becoming a successful capitalist economy and

(Continued)

(2) to avoid the ire of their parents who having been brought up under the lean years of communism believe it is wrong to spend frivolously.

This framing also ignores the goals consumers may have when purchasing counterfeit products. For example, wealthy Chinese "tai-tais" (the wives of wealthy businessmen) often purchase counterfeit luxury products despite having the economic means to purchase the real thing. However, purchasing fake goods is often simply a backdrop to out-of-home socializing with friends, escaping the boredom that comes with having servants take care of everything at home, and having a workaholic husband. These consumers are not being duped, yet these goods serve a very real purpose in their lives, helping them achieve a sense of self-authentication with their friends, while the real items are retained for authoritative public performances where they wouldn't be seen dead with a counterfeit. Moreover, fears of theft or damage also mean these consumers often purchase the counterfeit item for daily use.

Outsourcing and Brand Equity

Scholars in operations management have been slow to realize the value of production or making to brand equity. Decisions on where to make things are framed in terms of "make or buy" or produce in-house or outsource. For manufacturing brands and even services, this had led to large-scale cost efficiencies, however such decisions have not always had a positive effect on brand equity. Why? As noted in Chapters 11 and 12, supply-chain-related issues often trigger an ethical backlash against brands. As the 2013 UK and Ireland horsemeat scandal demonstrated, traceability of problems is almost impossible in today's complex global networks of suppliers. Also, as Brand Asides 9.7 and 9.8 detail, such practices have also led to the rise of grey markets and counterfeits. As Oliver et al. (2007) identify in their comparison of low cost vs. upmarket automotive brands, lean production often results in a mean experience for users, resulting in lower prices and margins.

BRAND ASIDE 9.7

Grey Markets and the Global Brand Challenge

The pursuit of a global brand identity, guarding against counterfeits, and managing costs of expansion, is often driven by careful licensing strategies. In these cases, the licensee accepts influence and control from the global brand in return for the exclusive right to market and sell the brand in particular territories. This results in higher prices and slower release dates for new products in some markets (such as the UK, China, India, and Australia). However, web-based selling sites such as eBay and on-sellers enable consumers to subvert these arrangements, importing items at cheaper prices, before their official local release, or subverting licensee restrictions such as locked mobile-phone technology.

There are dangers to this for brand holders, however. In New Zealand, competition laws outlawed the ban on parallel importing (the ability to legally work around exclusive license agreements), resulting in low-cost retailers being able to sell globally branded goods without input from their owners. For example, Calvin Klein was aghast at their exclusive jeans being sold cut price (imported direct from Mexico) and dumped in large bins in discount retailer The Warehouse. However, there was little the brand could do to control this approach other than to focus on limited edition offers and faster-fashion cycles.

Consumer demand has also generated an entire industry dedicated to working around geographic restrictions. For example, sites such as Big Apple Buddy ship to consumers living outside of the USA (primarily Australia, Britain, Germany, Singapore, and the UAE), with the latest technological releases long before they are officially launched by licensees in their own markets (Courtenay, December 12, 2016). Consumers may also use virtual private networks (VPNs) to work around geographic restrictions on download content (which is common for high-rating shows such as *Game of Thrones* or *The Walking Dead*) and also use the dark web (Tor servers) to download content illegally.

BRAND ASIDE 9.8

The Challenge of Counterfeits

Brand counterfeiting is big business. Estimates suggest the global value of counterfeiting in 2015 was US$1.8 trillion or 5–7 percent of all global trade. Despite legal efforts, just over US$3 billion of counterfeit brands were captured by authorities. The luxury industry estimates that it loses at least 10 percent of its sales to counterfeit products. It is not only luxury fashion that is counterfeited. Counterfeiting effects a range of industries including consumer electronics, pharmaceuticals, wine, food and beverage (especially milk powder), fast fashion, toys, cigarettes, and even military hardware. Secondary markets such as eBay have implemented policies

(Continued)

designed to reduce counterfeit trade, however Chinese e-commerce giant Alibaba lists well over one billion fake products on its website.

Brands have fought back against this type of trade, with the Kering Group launching a suit against Alibaba in 2015, but despite winning the case, the luxury conglomerate has found it difficult to police such sales in China (the largest market for luxury products). The shift to online sales has made cracking down on counterfeits harder as buyers and sellers are often anonymous, goods traffic takes the form of millions of parcels, and many counterfeiters operate in legal jurisdictions with limited trademark protections or poor enforcement. Finally, the penalties for being caught are often relatively small, especially when considered against the volume of sales—many counterfeiters simply treat fines as a cost of doing business.

How dangerous are counterfeits to brand equity? Apart from lost sales, researchers and practitioners differ in their responses to this issue. Some argue that since only strong brands are copied, counterfeiting is a signal of brand health (i.e., brand managers should be more worried if their brands are not deemed worth copying). Consumer research also suggests a very nuanced picture, with most buyers being middle-class Western shoppers. Criminology research identifies no relationship between economic class and the purchase of fake goods (over 50 percent of UK consumers admit to purchasing counterfeit products; Price Waterhouse Coopers 2013). These buyers typically know their goods are fake, often buy the real thing along with counterfeit products, and counterfeit purchase may trigger interest in owning the genuine article (estimates suggest around 20 percent of counterfeit consumers buy the real item; Davenport and Lyons 2006). Furthermore, a 2013 Price Waterhouse report on British attitudes to counterfeits found that 75 percent of consumers view fakes as not only normal, but also the "new real." Are fakes potentially of higher status than the rather ubiquitous real thing? Could it be that the efforts to gain counterfeits, usually involving overseas travel or dealing with unofficial and often criminal sellers, represent an edgy type of cultural capital and point of status distinction? If this is the case then counterfeits pose a major threat to brand equity.

How have brand managers responded to the threat posed by counterfeits? Apart from working with legal authorities to clamp down on such sellers, technology including protein and DNA markers, invisible tracking devices, and complicated designs (similar to what currency producers use in banknotes), faster innovation cycles, and a shift to inconspicuous luxury is part of a coordinated strategy to try and stay ahead of entrepreneurial counterfeiters. Finally, some fashion labels have even co-opted counterfeiters, working directly with them to produce new lines. Versace Versus is one such line aimed at tapping into younger consumers' desire for edgy streetwear.

When organizations debate make or buy decisions, they often look at how value is created. If value creation and manufacturing can be separated then production is often sent offshore, potentially raising problems for brand identity (especially if brands draw on local associations) (Pisano 2009). Technology, fast fashion, and pharmaceuticals typically operate like this. For example, much of Apple's brand equity flows from its design and R&D teams, which are headquartered in Cupertino, California. However, once the prototype is decided upon and tested to satisfaction, production can shift to mass manufacture specialists in China. Apple, along with fast-fashion brands and pharmaceuticals, places no emphasis on the production process in their brand campaigns, instead playing up design, innovation capabilities, and newness.

If value creation and production cannot be separated, then production typically stays onshore, strengthening claims of place authenticity, albeit at a potentially higher economic cost (Beverland et al. 2015). Unsurprisingly craft brands find it difficult to outsource production as value is typically created in the production process itself. It would be difficult to imagine how a champagne brand such as Pol Roger could agree on a formula for its product and then outsource production offshore. In fact, many attempts to transfer skills and knowledge offshore through direct investment in vine-yards in Australia, New Zealand, and California have struggled in the marketplace, and many of the champagne houses have reduced their offshore holdings as a result (Beverland 2005b). These brands play heavily on the authenticity of place, and the cultural, mythological, and natural conditions that make their products or services special, as well as their time-honored traditions of craft expertise (Swiss watch brands for example) (Rokka and Canniford 2016).

What about brands that lie somewhere in between? Luxury fashion brands have struggled with this tension for some time. While many are tempted to attribute luxury brands' interest in offshore production to lower cost, this is often only a small part of the story (with the exception of products such as licensed glasses and accessories). Declines in apprenticeships and structural changes in the economy have led to skills shortages in the making arts (non-luxury manufacturers also struggle with this prob-lem), resulting in product shortages and concerns that the brands will be unable to replace their existing workforce.

However, luxury brands have often experienced a backlash when offshoring pro-duction, often for unpredictable reasons. For example, some fashion houses such as Louis Vuitton report that the output of Chinese artisans is "too good", leading consum-ers to believe the products could not possibly be handmade. Some have gone so far as to suggest the manufacturers should deliberately work in small flaws to give the illusion the product is handmade. Such responses flow from expectations about iconic authenticity—the notion of perfection directly contradicts consumers' shared beliefs about handmade production.

Furthermore, small challenger brands such as C.W. Dixey (see Chapter 8) have happily pointed out the lack of marketplace authenticity in terms of place of production. Finally, outsourcing production to countries with few copyright protections or little ability to enforce such claims has given rise to widespread counterfeiting, much of which is often better produced than the branded original.

Chapter Summary

Whether planned or unplanned, global exposure for brands is a fact of life. Brands in this sense are always "born global"—as soon as one consumer posts an image of the brand on Instagram or drops a pin on Pinterest, awareness of the brand diffuses through multiple consumer networks. Building a global brand is also a critical growth strategy, particularly as lifestyles become globalized, markets mature, and a middle class emerges in formerly developing economies.

This chapter has explored two approaches to global branding—**the managerial approach** and **the cultural approach**. Each approaches the global challenge from a different standpoint. The managerial approach focuses on the brand's geographic scope (as defined by financial measures of brand equity such as Interbrand's Top 100 Global Brands—see Chapter 3), and is primarily concerned with the challenges associated with entering new markets, and adapting to local conditions, while maintaining brand identity. The central problem for brand managers is balancing standardization of the brand program with adaptation to local conditions.

The cultural approach takes a different view, focusing on how consumers experience **globalization**. In this approach, the brand's geographic scope counts for little; rather it is how consumers define global, national, and local that determines the status of a brand. This approach focuses on the specific historical sociocultural conditions that frame consumers' experience of globalization and brands. This school is much more fragmented in its concerns than the managerial school, although one central concern is how consumers retain a sense of national identity or connection to place against a backdrop of blurring boundaries and hyperreality.

This is not the end of the book's focus on global brands. Chapter 11 presents a range of ethical challenges that have emerged as a result of globalization, including issues of sustainability, poverty, corruption, and supply-chain practices (particularly in relation to the treatment of employees). Chapter 12 identifies how polysemy, or multiple readings and interpretations of brand messages, can trigger brand crises.

Review Questions

1. Identify brands that have standardized their offer and some that have adapted. Pick one of each and identify three reasons why they chose to standardize or adapt.
2. Identify a brand that draws on country of origin imagery. Is the connection authentic or imagined?
3. Identify brands that have drawn on diasporas. How did they enter the market and why might a diaspora targeting strategy be effective?
4. Identify a brand that was born global. How was it launched?
5. Explore why a cultural tradition such as Christmas moves from a regional celebration to a global one. What does this offer for brands?

Case Example: HSBC: Becoming the World's Local Bank

HSBC Holdings plc. is a British-based multinational banking and financial services company headquartered in London, United Kingdom. It is the world's third largest bank by total assets, with total assets of US$2.63 trillion in 2015 (Cunningham 2015).

Few consumers know that HSBC did not exist as a brand in 1998. However, the Hong Kong and Shanghai Banking Corporation, founded in 1865 by a group of "canny" Scotsmen involved in the trade of Chinese goods from Hong Kong, had steadily grown from mercantile roots to become one of the top financial services organizations in the world. It bought banks, initially across Asia and the Middle East, and then Europe and the USA, evolving into a "hidden giant" by the mid to late 1990s. As a holding company it owned around 50 sizeable, independently powerful brands such as the British Bank of the Middle East, Midland Bank (UK), and Banko Bamerindus (Brazil), each of which had enjoyed decades of investment behind their own brand equities, and had loyal staff and customers, and typically strong brand metrics. Each brand was different—the only uniting factor being their ownership. From financing trade, the group now dealt in retail banking, credit

(Continued)

cards, investment, commercial, private, and online, with over 100 million customers in multiple countries.

The then chairman Sir John Bond recognized great changes on the horizon, including a globalization of trade and commerce, the rise of the Internet and the minimizing of borders, increasing international awareness and mobility, and a burgeoning middle class particularly in Asia. He saw these affecting the fabric of what his banks did. So he determined the need for an entirely new strategy, with the goal of doubling shareholder value in five years. In his words:

> HSBC is a worldwide organisation, operating in a global marketplace, offering world-class solutions ... we are placing increased emphasis on the development of banking and other financial services for personal customers. Our strategy calls for the development of a strong global consumer brand. (Sir John Bond, Group Chairman, December 1998)

This meant the creation of an entirely new brand—HSBC. Few people knew what these four letters meant or stood for (in the widest sense). With a new, clear focus on personal banking (vs. trade banking), building a strong consumer brand had to be a key component of the strategy—bringing together the multiple, disparate, brands they had been operating into one unified global brand. HSBC needed to reveal its global reach.

This decision to create a wholly new, global brand meant the disappearance of some very well-recognized names. Many commentators and marketers questioned the wisdom of such an initiative—throwing away the precious equity existing behind names that had been built up over years, indeed in many cases decades. HSBC calculated the risks—primarily of losing recognition and alienating customers. They were confident that if customers were satisfied with the service they were getting and were told what's happening, they wouldn't stop doing business with you simply because you had changed your name. The board's aim was to transfer positive equity elements of the subsidiary brands to the parent brand. And in doing so, create a world-beating global brand.

With (then) 170,000 staff in 6000 offices across 81 countries, the task was enormous. Very much a team effort, it involved getting people from all around the world to work together in ways they were not accustomed to. The authority came from the very top of the organization, empowering a strong central marketing team based in London.

From a branding perspective, this was a fundamental shift from the bank's previously federal structure to a centrally led and coordinated effort, leveraging traditional strengths of the organization—short lines of communication to key players, and quick, decisive, decision-making. The communications focus was initially toward staff—because if they didn't understand, they could not be expected to answer customer questions or project the new brand. Priorities were 1) staff, 2) customers, and 3) shareholders; and throughout, recognizing the different needs of staff and customers involved in retail, commercial, trade, investment, or private banking, and the other product and service divisions.

Costs of rebranding globally are enormous—developing a corporate identity, signage across 6,000+ offices, interior decors, uniforms, stationery, information cascades, training— so there was little budget remaining for global advertising. And the timing imperatives of making the switch "overnight" meant there was little time to develop a marketing campaign.

Although uncomfortable with relying on partners, the bank commissioned Lowe and Partners Worldwide, an advertising agency, to develop a campaign. The brief was to generate one approach, to be executed once all over the world, generating high visibility with low cost; and most important, it had to be neutral in image, culture, and linguistics so as to work effectively everywhere.

The agency decided on a phased approach, first to build awareness and recognition of the four-letter brand name and its red hexagon logo, reassuring and educating both customers and "followers" of HSBC. Then, as a second phase, broadening the application across products while adding softer elements of personality to aid understanding, add humanity, and build familiarity.

An exhaustive suite of formal and informal research followed, examining competitive positioning and context in major markets around the world. The in-depth analysis of the component parts of the new bank was interrogated, from directors to tellers, customers to critics, to gather a detailed understanding of values, differentiators, strengths and weaknesses. Finally, this was distilled into a global creative brief, primarily targeting the world's mass-affluent populations.

Phase 1: Awareness and Recognition: The creative genius here was to use symbols—icons understood by everyone everywhere (even before emoticons). Work was designed to be a-cultural (for economies of scale, simplicity of message); to cut through barriers of language, geography, history, sector, and eventually product; and to provide very simple recognition of the message: hexagon = bank. This approach aimed at communicating the spirit and substance of HSBC in the most concise way possible—to everyone, regardless of language or culture. Examples are presented in Figure 9.2.

(Continued)

Figure 9.2   'Your World of Financial Services'

Source: Lowe & Partners Worldwide

HSBC prided themselves on being straight talkers, with an aversion to jargon and unnecessary complexity. The real genius here was in devising a new language, a new advertising shorthand—so concise, it does not actually use words, but is based purely on symbols. And so clear, it is culturally agnostic, using universal symbols recognized around the world to stand for specific things: services, needs, emotions, and values.

The premise was that the HSBC logo would become another of those worldwide symbols—to make it a universally acknowledged sign of excellence and integrity in financial services.

Secondary benefits of this symbols approach included highly identifiable styling, low-cost production, low-cost media, and irrelevance of media quality. In addition to static advertisements in print and outdoor media, TV and cinema film versions were made to mirror the symbols approach, communicating the global nature of the bank and the universal appeal of its values.

The work ran successfully all over HSBC's world. Internally staff held a growing pride in the brand, overcoming concerns about the loss of previous brands. Importantly the brand was well received by customers–significantly in markets where HSBC replaced a long-standing, well-recognized brand. Brand awareness was climbing more rapidly than anticipated, building awareness and leading toward doubling shareholder value two years ahead of plan. Favorability ratings also improved; for example in the UK, HSBC became rated more favorably than the Midland Bank within the first year.

Phase 2: Personality and Familiarity: Consumer research at this time (2003) found that the advantages of a global bank's huge resources and stability were often outweighed by a perceived lack of personal engagement. Customers questioned the prevailing global brand model, the "McDonald's approach" that treats everyone/everything in the same way everywhere. There was an opportunity to use HSBC's multi-local approach to make "global" feel personally relevant, and so create what consumers perceive to be the ideal financial services brand, resolving the apparent paradox of providing all of the advantages of being both a global and local brand. In other words, people recognize the need for a global financial organization because they realize money markets are interconnected, and global scale suggests experience, knowledge, and security: but they still want to feel that their local banks know them, understand them and care about them as people, not just as numbers.

Using research and analysis findings, a "brand wheel" was used to distill the differentiating essence of the brand in the most compelling terms–"the world's local bank." Figure 9.3 provides further details.

The new slogan can be "exploded" to clarify its meaning as a communications idea:

Because our people are local people they have a genuine understanding of their peoples, countries and cultures that outsiders wouldn't know and could misunderstand.

Having used culturally agnostic work to date, the decision now was to highlight the bank's knowledge from one place that benefits people in another. Cultural differences, the and the celebration of them, were at the very core of the new creative idea. Examples of this are presented in Figure 9.4. Audio-visual work for television, cinema, and the emerging Internet featured cultural collisions, often depicting people in "foreign" situations. Ads were highly impactful, combining a light-hearted or

(Continued)

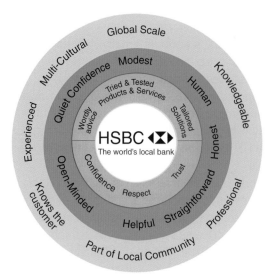

Attributes - The material facts of the company

Personality - Our distinctive values, beliefs and behaviour

Functional Benefits - What we offer our customers

Emotional Benefits - How our customers feel about us

Essence - The single defining thing we stand for

Figure 9.3   HSBC's Brand Wheel (2003)

Source: Lowe and Partners Worldwide

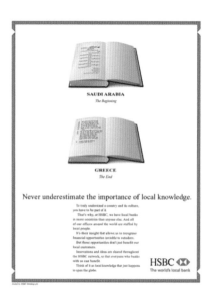

Figure 9.4   'Local Knowledge' Print Ads for HSBC

even humorous approach with a strong message—thereby cementing the conjoint of local approachability with global dependability. Increasingly the message was distributed through diverse, often highly localized media.

Results were impressive. Multiple awards were won in recognition of this advertising, but the single strongest appreciation came from customers and shareholders, who grew HSBC's audited brand value from virtually zero in 1999 to $10 billion in 2005 (Interbrand 2005). In 2005 HSBC changed their agency alignments, but retained this highly successful marketing strategy until 2011, when a new CEO in a difficult economic climate led to a revised commercial approach and retrenchment of many retail banking operations. This resulted in the demise of "the world's local bank" as the bank's positioning and—some would say—to the subsequent weakening of this once iconic brand.

(Case authored by Donald Lancaster, Teaching Fellow and PhD candidate, School of Management, University of Bath.)

Case Questions

1. Why did the HSBC seek standardization? Could they have used a local adaptation or glocalization strategy?
2. How did HSBC leverage local cultures to build brand awareness and identity?
3. Why did the brand shift its slogan and campaign? Was this a good idea?
4. What is HSBC currently doing? Examine their advertising and new campaigns. Have they remained on message or shifted? Evaluate their current campaign in terms of positioning strength.

Key Terms

Adaptation–standardization	Global brand/branding	International novice brands
Brand as culture	Global supply chains	Local–global tension
Brand morphing	Globalization	Long tail of markets
Country of origin	Glocalization	McDonaldization
Counterfeits	Imagined community	

Further Reading

Ahuvia, Aaron and Elif Izberk-Bilgin (2011), "Limits of the McDonaldization Thesis: eBayization and Ascendant Trends in Post-Industrial Consumer Culture," *Consumption Markets & Culture*, 14(4), 361–384.

Cayla, Julien and Giana M. Eckhardt (2008), "Asian Brands and the Shaping of a Transnational Imagined Community," *Journal of Consumer Research*, 35(2), 216–230.

Kates, Steven M. and Charlene Goh (2003), "Brand Morphing: Implications for Advertising Theory and Practice," *Journal of Advertising*, 32(1), 59–68.

Levitt, Theodore (1983), "Globalization of Markets," *Harvard Business Review*, 61(3), 92–102.

Schroeder, Jonathan, Janet Borgerson, and Zhiyan Wu (2016), "A Brand Culture Perspective on Global Brands," in F. Dall'Olmo Riley, J. Singh, and C. Blankson (eds.), *The Routledge Companion to Contemporary Brand Management*, Routledge, London, pp. 153–163.

10

CORPORATE BRANDING, SERVICES, AND BUSINESS-TO-BUSINESS BRANDING

Overall, because branding is about creating and sustaining trust it means delivering on promises. The best and most successful brands are completely coherent. Every aspect of what they do and what they are reinforces everything else. (Wally Olins)

Business-to-business work is about building a brand from the inside out. The brand message that we communicate to our clients' business constituents is often the same message that is carried through to the consumers in the marketplace. (Maureen Hall, *Advertising Age*, October 11, 2007)

Learning Objectives

When you finish reading this chapter, you will be able to:

1. Differentiate between corporate branding and other branding approaches
2. Explore the importance of a supportive corporate context for brand authenticity
3. Apply a range of strategies to build internal support for the brand
4. Differentiate between business-to-consumer and business-to-business branding approaches
5. Understand the unique aspects of services branding
6. Understand the different ways in which authenticity is achieved in the business-to-business context

7. Explore a range of strategies for building and maintaining brand equity in business-to-business markets
8. Identify the opportunities for branding for different positions within the supply chain
9. Identify the capabilities necessary for strong business-to-business to brands

Introduction

This chapter departs from the focus on growing brand equity and turns the lens back toward the firm. Chapters 5 and 6 examined the importance of launching the brand internally while Chapter 3 identified the potential for employment brand equity. Chapter 12 examines brand crises, many of which stem from failing to align the organization with the brand promise. Both models of brand positioning identify the need to make the firm "brand ready" in terms of aligning promises with systems, structures, procedures, practices, and employees. The mindshare model effectively does so through notions such as "living the brand" while the cultural model discusses organizational populism which ensures the firm aligns with the ethos at the heart of the populist world it draws power from.

Aligning the brand and organization with stakeholders (identified below) is the focus of **corporate brand** and/or **corporate reputation** researchers. The first half of the chapter will examine this area and build on what has been discussed thus far. The second half of the chapter will focus on branding in industrial or **business-to-business (B2B)** markets and services. Why B2B? First, although much of what has been covered so far is applicable to B2B, there are some contextual factors that make building brands in this sector different from building them with consumers. Second, given the nature of B2B practice, these organizations are more likely to engage in a branded house approach (see Chapter 7) or a single corporate brand (as are services, professional services, charities, think-tanks, and so on). The focus on corporate branding will flow into a discussion about services and B2B branding. Those aspects unique to services branding will also be covered.

Nonetheless, it is important to remember that the boundaries between B2B and B2C and products and services have blurred in recent times, corporate branding concerns such as stakeholder management and reputation affect all brands, product brands have service elements (and of course represent services to users in the broader sense), employee engagement is critical to brand delivery, and increasingly all sectors are considering a wider range of portfolio-management approaches (Brodie 2009).

What Is Corporate Branding?

Many writers on corporate reputation have a rather naïve view of branding as they tend to equate the brand with a product and view the origin of identity as generated by advertisers and therefore divorced from the organization per se. Of course, this is a mistake in light of what we know about branding, brand building, positioning, and reinforcement. They also fail to differentiate different types of brand architecture—a branded house for example is a corporate brand strategy. That said, corporate branding writers do focus on different, but important, areas.

1. They expand the scope of branding concerns to include the entire enterprise including its stakeholders. This includes employees (front-line and support service staff), managers (across all functions that impact on the delivery of the brand promise), investors (who provide resources and can trigger crises if unhappy), partners (including distributors, retailers, suppliers and co-branding alliances), customers (including all users), influencers (including the press and specialist industry insiders), NGOs (advocacy groups such as Greenpeace), and government (who can impact on the legitimacy of a brand's marketing operations).

2. They focus on the role of shared values or organizational culture in ensuring the firm can deliver on brand promises and of course keep the brand relevant. Chapter 6 identified the dangers that emerged from a lack of employee engagement with branded content. If employees see the brand in a different light from that intended, gaps will emerge between identity–image–culture and can ultimately lead to customer dissatisfaction. Consistency of delivery has been identified as central to services brands and failures relate more to training, poor HR–marketing relationships, reward structures, and systems that do not empower employees rather than a general lack of effort or skepticism toward branding per se (de Chernatony and Segal-Horn 2003). Likewise, gaps between culture and customer context are often why brands fail to build legitimacy with user communities (Cova 1997; Hietanen and Rokka 2015).

3. They highlight identity issues that occur beyond the brand such as employees' identity and tensions between different stakeholders and how they see the brand, as shown in the example of British Airways discussed below. Bang & Olufsen's successful turnaround had as much to with employees' co-creating and authenticating the firm's desire to shift its identity from design for design's sake to a more market-oriented approach (Ravasi and Schultz 2006).

4. In so doing, they also identify that in the case of a house brand, the holding company (e.g., Unilever) also has a reputation with stakeholders that requires careful management as it can affect the firm's ability to acquire resources from investors and governments and also the equity of individual brands (e.g., Dove, Axe) in the case of ethical challenges and crises. For example, Unilever has been subject to action from pressure groups because of their use of palm oil (the firm is one of the largest purchasers of this raw material) and has had to change its purchasing policies as a result.

(*Source*: adapted from Hatch and Schultz 2008, p. 9)

Who Are Stakeholders?

Corporate branding or reputation researchers identify the need to consider the impact of an organization's stakeholders on corporate identity and image, and in managing potential gaps arising between identity–image–culture (Hatch and Shultz 2008) and covered in Chapter 6. But who are a firm's stakeholders? Dowling's (2001) typology of stakeholders is widely used. He described four groups of stakeholders:

1. Customer groups: consumers and B2B customers.
2. Functional groups: employees, trade unions, suppliers, distributors, and service providers.
3. Normative groups: government, regulatory bodies, agencies, shareholders, and trade associations.
4. Diffuse groups: the media, special interest groups, and community members.

Figure 10.1 provides a tool for analyzing and managing different stakeholders. Be mindful that consumers can quickly mobilize (or be mobilized) online and through social media applications such as Twitter to challenge the practices of brands in unforeseen ways, as experienced by LEGO in Chapter 1.

Figure 10.1   Stakeholder Mapping

Source: Rosenbaum-Elliot et al. 2015, p.301

Aligning Multiple Identities

Research on corporate branding stresses the notion of identity or, more correctly, identities. Since an organization's reputation is a function of how it is viewed by a range of stakeholders, including senior management, employees, contractors, retailers, suppliers, distributors, alliance partners, media, shareholders, influencers, and customers, achieving a desired identity involves understanding how each stakeholder group views, or connects to, the firm and attempting to achieve a degree of congruence or **stakeholder alignment** between them over time.

For example, British Airways downplayed its Britishness in the 1990s, favoring instead an identity built around the multicultural nature of its customer base and aimed at reinforcing its position as the "world's favorite airline." Most notably, the tails of British Airways planes were repainted in styles reflecting many of the indigenous cultures of the Commonwealth (Pacific, Asian, African).

International users loved the redesigns. However, employees, key influencers (including former prime minister Margaret Thatcher), British flyers (who made up 40 percent of customers), hated the designs. Rival Virgin quickly grabbed the British flag-carrier mantle vacated by British Airways, in a publicity coup for Richard Branson's group. In failing to align its various identities, the brand suffered a backlash and eventually had to return to its original identity.

Lord Marshall, CEO of the airline at the time, reflected:

> As it turned out, the airline had gone too far, too fast for its key stakeholders—customers, shareholders, employees—and the British public. The change was too drastic and in the view of many weakened the strength of the brand. There was also the perception that the proud heritage of British Airways was being swept under a carpet of modernization. (In Balmer et al. 2009, p. 16)

John Balmer and Stephen Greyser are pioneers in the corporate branding arena. Balmer and colleagues have developed an **AC³ID model** to help us understand the different aspects of the corporate brand approach, as well as the means to manage various stakeholders. The AC³ID model is presented in Table 10.1. Balmer and colleagues make clear that a perfect alignment between all the identity types is difficult to achieve, and that managers instead should treat alignment over time as a goal. Their research, and that of others, demonstrate that identity is a powerful strategic tool, but as such needs to be understood from a range of stakeholder perspectives rather than preferring one (usually the desired identity). As the British Airways example above demonstrates, identity also needs to be evolved at a rate that all the stakeholders can handle, while radical, unplanned changes are unlikely to be viewed as legitimate by stakeholders and will therefore fail.

The different types of identity in Table 10.1 are described below:

Table 10.1   **AC³ID (Actual, Communicated, Conceived, Covenanted, Ideal, and Desired) Test of Corporate Brand Management**

Critical Concern	Identity Type	Concept	Time Frame
What we really are	Actual	Corporate Identity	Present
What we say we are	Communicated	Corporate Communications	Past/Present
What we are seen to be	Conceived	Corporate Image	Past/Present
What the brand stands for	Covenanted	Corporate Brand	Past/Present
What we ought to be	Ideal	Corporate Strategy	Future
What we wish to be	Desired	CEO Vision	Future

Source: Balmer et al. 2009, p. 7

1. Actual identity: distinctive attributes of the firm, often contained in the capability analysis.
2. Communicated identity: outward communications by the organization, usually in the form of desired brand identity.
3. Conceived identity: how other stakeholders view the firm, or the reputation or image of the brand among external authors such as users, influencers and society at large.
4. Covenanted identity: the underlying promise associated with the name or logo, or your communicated positioning.
5. Ideal identity: optimum future positioning of firm given the firm's legacy, competences, and the environment it exists within.
6. Desired identity: what the leaders of the firm would like the firm to be in the future.

(Source: Balmer et al. 2009, p. 20)

Figure 10.2 provides an example of how LEGO attempts to align different stakeholders in order to form a coherent image.

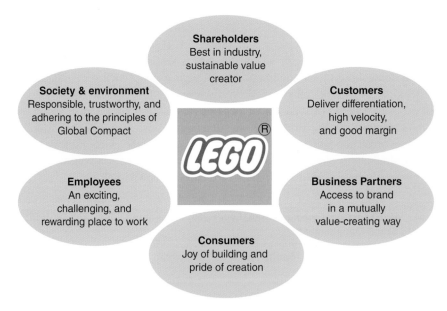

Figure 10.2   LEGO Stakeholder Alignment

Source: Hatch and Schultz 2008, p.152

The Vision–Culture–Image Alignment Model

Another tool for understanding corporate reputation management is Hatch and Schultz's (2008) **Vision–Culture–Image Alignment Model** (see Figure 10.3). This model has been highlighted previously in Chapter 6 as part of the internal brand launch section. Complementing Balmer and colleagues' AC³ID model that identifies the different types of identity and the means to align them, Hatch and Schultz provide tools for understanding how gaps between the various types of identities may emerge and therefore how to avoid the British Airways example identified above. Importantly this model is also useful for conducting brand audits and/or the internal branding approaches identified in the brand-building process (see Chapters 5 and 6).

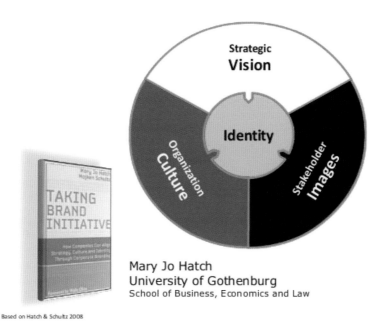

Based on Hatch & Schultz 2008

Figure 10.3   Hatch and Schultz V-C-I Model

Central to building a strong **corporate brand** and/or enhancing the reputation of the parent company is aligning the organization's vision, culture, and image. This approach is identified in the Vision–Culture–Image Alignment Model. What are these three things?

1. Vision: what the firm's leaders want the company to be.
2. Culture: what the company is perceived to be by its employees.
3. Image: how external stakeholders perceive the company.

Problems arise when gaps appear between the organization's vision, culture, and image. These gaps are:

1. Vision–culture: When employees' experience of the firm's practices do not match up with the firm's vision, this results in the company not delivering on its promises as employees focus on what is measured rather than on achieving the lofty ideals in the vision. For example, in the lead-up to the 2012 London Olympic Games Coca-Cola (UK) identified that many of its younger employees felt less than proud about working at the global drinks brand. Why? Employees were concerned about the firm's impact on the environment, both in terms of the lack of recyclability of their bottles and cans, the amount of packaging strewn throughout the countryside, and their heavy water use. They saw this as running counter to the long-term focus on sustainability promoted by the London Games. The brand leveraged the "legacy" theme of the London Games to build internal support for the brand, aligning their future vision of the firm with the Olympic focus on sustainability, and raising the internal status of "environmental strategies" to be equal with other core functions within the business (Farrelly et al. 2017).
2. Image–culture: When as employees we do not understand and support the strategic vision, a gap between who we are and how we are seen emerges. Chapter 6 identified the necessity of educating employees about the brand and aligning relevant systems with brand-related goals. Failure to do this is very common within large firms, especially among naïve first-time branders, with the result that promises are made to external users and then not delivered in those critical "moments of truth." For example, in 2009 my current university embarked on a secret brand program. While the external copy provided by experienced brand consultants was first class, staff were left wondering what the brand actually was, eventually viewing it as yet another change program and going back to their usual routines. Feedback from students at open days was that their expectations were significantly raised and often dashed when they subsequently received service that was far removed from that advertised. As a result a significant internal rollout program was developed.
3. Image–vision: When outsiders' images conflict with management's strategic vision, a credibility gap emerges between our desired identity and how others view us. Early corporate branding research was primarily focused on building an externally focused, corporate personality (Olins 1977). This was achieved via integrated marketing communications (IMC) that ensured the desired identity and

communicated identity was as one. One famous example was Wolff Olins' repositioning of British Petroleum as "Beyond Petroleum." This example is covered in depth in Chapter 12, but the brand's continued reliance on non-renewables, its lack of investment in renewable energy, and poor track record in environmental stewardship, have made it a constant source of ridicule. The "Beyond Petroleum" position backfired dramatically during the Gulf of Mexico Deepwater Horizon spill and subsequent clean-up fiasco in 2010.

(*Source of gap definitions*: Hatch and Schultz 2008, p. 75; examples as cited or collected by author)

Avoiding or reducing these three gaps involves aligning the organization's operations with stakeholder experiences. The vision–culture–image model provides the means by which firms attempt to do this, and the functions involved in aligning culture, identity (or vision), and image. Hatch and Schultz (2008, p. 79) identify several tools managers should use when attempting to achieve alignment across these three domains:

1. Stakeholder surveys: Compare reputational ratings across different stakeholder groups. Are there gaps, conflicts, tensions, or potential overlaps and points of agreement? What does each stakeholder seek from the corporate brand and how might you communicate with him or her?
2. Encourage dialogue between managers within different organizational functions: Interfunctional coordination is a key pillar of market or customer orientation and is beneficial because (a) teamwork is required to fulfill brand promises and (b) the different insights each function brings to address a problem or challenge are valuable.
3. Encourage dialogue between brand managers and stakeholders: This may seem obvious when it comes to your target user, but what about all the other stakeholders that impact on your reputation? Make sure you spend time listening to and engaging with your strongest supporters and also your biggest critics.
4. Hold events that connect stakeholders to each other via the brand: Drawing on the material covered under brand community (Chapter 6), events that bring different stakeholders together often help generate dialogue, understanding, and opportunity among different parties. This type of linking value is as valuable as that which you attempt to provide to end-users.

Internal Marketing

Corporate-branding strategists also stress the internal aspects of branding, including employment branding, brand-driven HR policies, and diffusing brand knowledge throughout the firm. All of these involve marketing the brand internally. To avoid gaps between vision, culture, and image, and also ensure alignment between the different stakeholders and identities identified by Balmer and colleagues (see Table 10.1), the following strategies are essential:

1. Brand-based recruitment: Southwest Airways in the US is a leader in the low-cost airline market. CEO Herb Kelleher is on record as saying "take care of your employees and everything else will follow" (Miles and Mangold 2005). However, the organization will also use its brand vision to hire staff. When recruiting pilots, the interviews were held inside a hot, humid hanger in the Arizona desert (at the firm's headquarters). Next to the seats where potential pilots were waiting was a large table with shorts on it. Those pilots that were prepared to strip off and put on the shorts to keep cool were most likely to get the job (they had all been vetted for flight proficiency obviously).

    Why? The airline requires everyone to pitch in to ensure the plane leaves on time. This means there can be no status barriers between pilots and cabin crew when it comes to loading bags, cleaning the cabin, and so on. The exercise with the shorts was designed to see who would be prepared to step out of their role (and formal suit) and be practical (Beverland 2009).

2. Brand-based performance assessment: Employees unsurprisingly tend to focus on doing what is measured. The Vegemite/iSnack 2.0 case, for example (see Chapter 2), involved not only engaging customers but also engaging employees. Prior to the change in approach, the firm was highly bureaucratic but, worse, employees were earning bonuses despite falling profitability and declining reputation. Simon and his team had to address performance-management issues before being able to engage in more customer-focused strategies, otherwise employees would naturally engage in off-brand actions, thereby leading to vision–culture gaps. Importantly, one of the reasons for dropping the iSnack 2.0 name was that employees felt betrayed by such a poor choice as it had not been generated by customers and also led to significant ridicule by the public (Keinan et al. 2011).

3. Brand-based training: Virtually all organizations have strong service elements. Although these can seem tangential to branding (such as call centers) it is these areas that often represent moments of truth for the brand (de Chernatony and Segal-Horn 2003). For example, Lloyds TSB had to turn around its reputation following the global financial crisis. Much of the problems facing the bank resulted from a lack of oversight and teamwork among their investment group (who were made up of strong, motivated individuals, who were driven to earn the most they possibly could). In repairing the bank's reputation with the public while also ensuring they had a successful investment arm, the bank hired specialist agency Lane 4 to use the logic of a high-performance team to enhance employee effectiveness. One exercise involved a Paralympian forcing the team to

play wheelchair rugby. This exercise forced traders to work together to achieve better results simply because they were all made equal through being placed in wheelchairs (Farrelly et al. 2017).

4. Brand-based volunteering: Gone are the days when outreach programs or sponsorships reflect the interest of the CEO or their partners. Brand-driven sponsorship and lobbying is critical for enhancing one's reputation with stakeholders while also reinforcing the brand. Volvo lobbies tirelessly for restrictions on in-car distractions such as television screens and mobile phones, as part of its commitment to safety and peace of mind. At the same time, it also stresses its innovations in hands-free technology. Likewise, large Australian home hardware retailer Bunnings is currently working with homeless charities to address the plight of rough sleepers in Australian cities. Being committed to the home, these volunteering efforts make sense and enhance the brand's reputation among multiple stakeholders.

5. Brand-based learning: Stories are powerful carriers of brand messages. Formalizing key stories and using them to reinforce brand understanding internally can help clarify how people should act in all situations. US retailer Nordstrom is renowned for its extraordinary customer focus and return policy. One story told involves an associate who refunded a customer who claimed his car tires were defective. Not only was it clear to the employee that the customer's claimed defect was due to wear and tear (the customer had mentioned he brought the tires a year ago), but the employee also knew that Nordstrom did not sell car tires! The message, however, is loud and clear—Nordstrom stands behind its guarantee of customer satisfaction or your money back.

Services Branding Challenges

Historically **services brands** trailed product brands in terms of financial valuation. However, the HSBC case in the previous chapter provides one example of an extremely valuable service brand. Much of what has been covered in the book can be transferred to services brands, especially given the focus on the internal audit and roll out in Chapter 6, and capability analysis in mindshare positioning, rendering the firm authentic in cultural branding, and the material covered above. Research reveals four important criteria for successful services brands. These are detailed below:

1. Focused position: A clear distinct positioning is important for all brands, but just as brands provide mental short-cuts for customers, so too does a focused brand enable employees to retain the essence of the service brand promise. Lloyds TSB's use of the idea of a journey in their advertising was used as much to remind

employees that customers' life changes required different products and services as it was targeted at external users.

2. Consistency: Consistency is a hallmark of all brands, regardless of their approach to positioning. However, service brands need to manage this carefully. All too often the scripting strategies deployed by services firms (which largely focus on ensuring employees interact with customers in a standardized way) are viewed as cold and robotic by customers, and can backfire when things go wrong and the user wants a more human encounter (Beverland et al. 2010). Consistency is also achieved via a whole organization roll out, in which the brand logic is diffused through all functions and relevant external stakeholders (see Chapter 6).

3. Values: All brands have values as part of their positioning; however, service brands in particular place an emphasis on "living the brand" (Ind 2014). This means that employees must be the living embodiment of the brand's values. For example, Singapore Airlines has built its brand image around its staff and a service culture where nothing is seen as too much hassle. Critically, management must all live these values as any gap between what is stated and what is actually done will undermine commitment to the brand. Importantly, systems, especially reward systems, must be aligned with the firm's culture to ensure consistency of delivery.

4. Systems: System alignment is critical for all brands, but particularly so for service brands as these can empower service staff to provide better outcomes.

Although they seem similar to the strategies underpinning successful brands, the differences are noted under each, and it is clear that services brands require a corporate branding approach and close working relationships between marketing, human resources, and operations. What is particularly apparent is the need to build **employee engagement** with the branding strategy (through **internal marketing**) as a means of ensuring consistency of delivery, authentic relating to end-users, and a focus on the customer. Figure 10.4 identifies the relationship between employee satisfaction and service brand performance.

Building on these four strategies and the material covered under corporate branding, Brodie (2009) developed an integrative approach to services branding, identifying links between external perceptions, external marketing, and internal perception and practice. Figure 10.5 provides detail. It identifies that the service brand is shaped by the input of staff, customers, and stakeholders, and the organization more generally. It also highlights three strategies that need alignment: the promises made about the service offer externally, internal marketing programs that ensure promises can be delivered, and the experience employees have in the service encounter (stressed or frustrated employees may be the outcome of poor service systems, organizational decisions, or poor resourcing).

Figure 10.4   Service Management Process

Source: de Chernatony and Segal-Horn 2003, p.1097

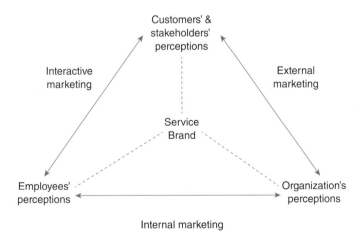

Figure 10.5   An Integrative Model of Services Brand Management

Source: Brodie 2009, p.109

Business-to-Business (B2B) Branding

For many years, **B2B brands** were seen as a contradiction in terms. Why? Business buyers were always thought to be rational, focused on getting the best deal or price, and therefore not susceptible to brand-driven claims. At best, a proven track record of delivery and performance was enough. As a result, many B2B organizations paradoxically traded on their reputation but rejected the need for branding per se.

This has changed in the last decade. Early studies on B2B branding demonstrated that the majority of buyers indicated that price competitiveness was the key driver (although this might be a function of surveying purchasing managers, all of whom are looking for cost and efficiency savings). However, as industrial markets have changed and become more competitive, supply chains have become more transparent, and business services have become more dominant in the sector (with the decline in manufacturing), branding as a means of creating value has become more popular within B2B (Graham and Mudambi 2016). And, unsurprisingly, those buyers were not always as rational as we were led to believe.

Furthermore, there are financial advantages to branding in business markets. Table 10.2 provides information on the financial impact of branding on B2B firms. Although the returns to branding are not as great as in B2C markets, nonetheless the outcomes are positive, particularly in light of the relative immaturity of B2B branding:

1. Brand power: Brand power is a function of customer loyalty to the brand. Brand power scores for the most powerful B2B brands are just ten points less than their equivalent B2C counterparts.
2. P/E ratio: A high price to earnings ratio generates expectations of greater earning growth in the future (it is often referred to as the multiple). The P/E ratio for B2B brands is intriguing. Studies like this are few and far between, so the numbers could be a function of the early development of B2B branding and booming commodity prices within some industrial sectors such as gold.

Table 10.2   Effects of brands on B2B financial rations

All Brands	Quintile	Brand power	P/E / ratio	Financial strength	Market cap/book value	Brand equity as % of market cap
Most powerful brands	1	48.8	15.8	5.4	2.5	13.3
	2	27.1	16.0	5.4	2.1	6.9
	3	16.3	14.9	5.4	1.2	3.3
	4	12.4	14.7	4.5	1.5	2.0
Least powerful brands	5	8.0	17.2	4.5	0.5	0.6

Source: Gregory and McNaughton 2004, p. 235

3. Market cap/book value: Market capitalization is the total value of the shares or the premium; i.e., the strongest brands are worth 2.5 times their book value, a substantial difference to the least powerful brands. By way of contrast, the strongest B2C branded firms are worth 4.7 times their book value.

4. Financial strength is simply an assessment of the health of the company's financial position: The financial strength of branded B2B firms is stronger than those with less investment, and although the differences do not appear great, they do involve substantial sums and give strongly branded firms more leverage with financial institutions and institutional investors.

5. Brand equity as percentage of market capitalization: The most powerful brands in the B2B sector have created substantial equity for their firms (by way of contrast the strongest B2C brands accounted for 15.6 percent of market capitalization). Other studies show that return on investment (ROI) is the strongest contributor to market capitalization, with brand equity a strong second. It is important to bear in mind that brand equity also contributes to ROI (Aaker 2014).

(*Source*: Beverland et al. 2015, p. 84)

In conclusion, branding in business markets matters in terms of financial performance, although the effects are likely to be industry specific—it is important to remember that the broadly defined B2B sector includes everything from highly branded professionals services (PriceWaterhouseCoopers) and technology firms (IBM) through to commodity sellers of highly desirable raw materials such as gold, diamonds, titanium, milk solids, and even water. Demand for these products may be such that branding offers little advantage to these producers (see Chapter 5 and the discussion of understanding the brand).

It is also worth keeping in mind that there are many other benefits to branding in business markets including:

1. B2B brands often represent ingredients in final products: For example, B2B brands such as Intel and Dolby offer important sources of trust for end-users and can add value to suppliers in highly competitive sectors. This is critical as demand is derived (see below) and concerns about traceability in supply chains are increasingly part of ethical brand crises (see Chapters 11 and 12).

2. B2B brands can add substantial value to other business firms and non-business users: Partnering with strong advertising agencies, architectural firms, financial institutions, travel providers, and so on can enhance the status of the buying firm and also send a strong signal to investors and other stakeholders.

3. As with B2C brands, B2B brands also have an employment function, with strong B2B brands as likely to attract and retain the best staff as their B2C counterparts.

4. Governments are likely to prefer known, trusted partners, especially in nations where trust-based relations dominate commercial contracts.

5. Co-branding possibilities exist for B2B brands, and may even add significant value to end-users: For example, lens producers Zeiss have long enjoyed strong brand partnerships that have increased the prices for cameras, mobile phones, spectacles and optical instruments, and generate marketing pull.

6. Salespeople are still a major part of B2B brand communication: Strong brands help prepare the way for salespeople, meaning they are more likely to gain appointments with key buyers, enjoy better terms and stronger relationships with senior buyers, and help with new innovations or extensions.

7. B2B innovation success rates are much higher than B2C rates, and much of this has to do with strong brands and the meaning they create with key users.

8. Brands reduce risk: There is an old saying, "no one got fired for buying IBM." This is a classic risk-reduction strategy, and despite the mythology about rational business buyers, B2B users are just as susceptible to so-called irrational impulses such as the fear of getting things wrong.

What Makes B2B Different?

Although there has been convergence between B2B and B2C over the past decade, there are some contextual differences that effect brand-building decisions and strategies. These are:

1. Multiple decision makers and influencers are involved in purchase: Although individual consumers are part of a network of influence, typically it is they or members of their household that decide on what to buy. In B2B situations, depending on the type of purchase (see below), many parties can be involved, including competitors, suppliers, government agencies, users, senior management, and purchasing managers (who may be the least important in the whole mix).

2. Different types of "buy" decisions affect the value of brands and the role of brands in choice: B2B purchases are usually classified in terms of their newness to the firm—new buy (purchasing goods or services for the first time), straight re-buy (repurchasing the same set of goods and services), modified re-buy (repurchasing the same goods and services with modifications), complex buy (purchasing complex projects such as new buildings, organizational transformation service, industrial networks, power plants, etc.). Purchases range from simple (such as bulk buying bed-sheets for hotels) to complex (such as appointing new brand agencies or buying complex IT service).

3. Derived demand: Most B2B purchases eventually flow through to end-users including consumers. Since B2B organizations often exist in complex supply chains or networks, demand for their brands is a function of the rest of the network, and ultimately the user of the final product or service. In practice this means two things: that your customer's customers matter and that one can experience wild swings in demand (called the "bullwhip effect") as sudden changes further

up the network (e.g., sudden changes in fashion) build momentum in the network, requiring sudden shifts in production or service provision. This also often means that a marketing budget must be allocated to stimulate marketing pull at the user end even though your direct relationships with immediate customers may require investment in push activities (Beverland and Lockshin 2003).

4. B2B has been subject to globalization and even pre-Internet technologies for much longer than B2C: Manufacturing in particular is characterized by complex supply chains, giving rise to challenges in relation to traceability and country of origin. Services however are also outsourcing many low-cost operations that can have an effect on the customer (e.g., call centers and service support). Brand position standardization may be more acceptable in this sector, while execution may require some local adaptation (usually in terms of training and materials).

5. Customer relationships are often much longer than in B2C: As Fournier (1998) demonstrated, consumers have a range of relationships with brands that can be fleeting or long term and highly involved. In contrast, B2B relationships are longer, with averages ranging between 7 and 11 years.

6. Relationships are longer but often less emotionally engaging: Much is made of the dark side of relationships in marketing, but in B2B relationship partners do not frame relationships in powerful emotional terms like consumers (although they may still have emotional content). They expect opportunism, things to go wrong, and even for partners to end relationships based on commercial decisions (Blocker et al. 2012).

7. Despite relationships being less emotional, personal connections still matter. Much has been made of the importance of after hours' social engagement between salespeople and their customers or suppliers and buyers. Studies have demonstrated, for example, that golfing days between buyers and suppliers help reinforce bonds and build trust, which ensure relationships last (Beverland 2001).

8. Your position within a network can affect your power, and therefore the ability to build a strong brand. For example, raw materials suppliers may struggle to build a brand because their direct contribution to the final product may be relatively small (although it can also be essential). In other cases, the critical nature of the raw material and the lack of choice may give the supplier immense power despite being far down the supply chain and therefore far removed from the end-user (e.g., suppliers of diamonds, so-called "super foods," and gene technologies). Toyota, for example, has a complex network of suppliers and sub-contracted suppliers. These suppliers have some power and therefore some ability to build a brand because they are the hub within the network. For sub-contractors, the picture is less positive, as they are separate network nodes that can be easily replaced and may experience the worst of the bullwhip effect (Ford et al. 2002).

9. Your customers may have more control over how the end-user experiences your offer. This necessitates working directly with customers and their staff to ensure the end-user gets the promised experience and your brand continues to be demanded (Beverland et al. 2007).

10. The complexity of many purchases and purchasing processes means buyers require more information than B2C consumers do (who are happy to draw on specific cultural codes or images). As a result, the marketing mix for B2B brands tends to favor salespeople, tradeshows, and professional presentations, with only a supporting role for advertising.

11. Although consumers often split their loyalty among several brands, business buyers do not always do this. Certainly, firms may have panels of service providers, such as market-research companies, largely to tap into specialist expertise, manage risk, and sometimes fit legal requirements, but for large-scale projects winning an account is often a zero-sum game, meaning that a lot is riding on meeting customer requirements and ensuring relationships are renewed. First-mover advantages in this context are particularly important, as one can quickly become the market leader or dominant player in the category and sustain that position for some time.

How Do Business Buyers Behave?

One characteristic of B2B markets is that long-term relationships between firms are normal. As Graham and Mudambi state: "Although B2B branding is anchored in an exchange relationship, the buyers and sellers often have close personal ties and common interests" (2016, p. 272). There are many reasons for this. B2B firms often exist within complex networks where each party is, to some degree, reliant on the other. Relationships are necessary because of the complexity of the product involved and the need for coordination. Relationships provide buyers with a sense of certainty that if something goes wrong, they can always call on someone they know and trust to help fix problems. Linking value in terms mentioned in Chapter 2 is as important in B2B as it is to B2C.

Figures 10.6 and 10.7 describe influences on B2B buyers and the **B2B buying process** respectively. As Figure 10.6 demonstrates, the buyers are influenced by a range of environmental, organizational, interpersonal, and individual factors, all of which make for complicated purchase decisions and often ones focused on balancing competing interests or tensions rather than focusing on the best offer in terms of price or functional performance. If you look at the diagram carefully, you can identify something very similar to the material covered in Chapter 2 which looked at users and self-authentication. Consider how a buyer's professional standing (to save money, contribute to the firm's success, reduce risk) represents authenticating acts while fealty to the organizational and environmental factors requires authoritative performances. Much like B2C brands that allow often-harried buyers to bridge both needs are likely to succeed.

As Figure 10.7 demonstrates, these unfold over the life of a relationship and each stage of the buying process can involve different stakeholders, different criteria, and different marketing actions, all of which will affect whether and how brands are considered.

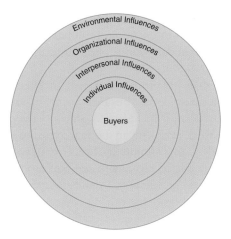

Figure 10.6   Influences on Business Buyers

Source: Based on Kotler et al. (2016), *Principles of Marketing European Edition*, 7th edition, p. 175.

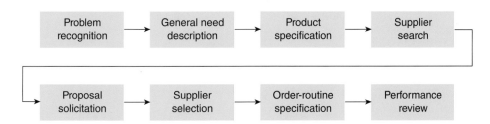

Figure 10.7   Business Buying Process

Since relationships are also the norm, many decisions are influenced by the potential future benefits that may flow as a result of close interpersonal interaction. For example:

1. Business buyers know that within complex projects characterized by uncertainty that things will go wrong: Therefore emphasizing service recovery, tracking ability, and building strong personal relationships ensure the buyer has confidence that when things go wrong, they can trust that those things will be righted and that they have a direct line to a real person who will take charge.
2. Since many purchases represent an input into the buying firm's competitive future, B2B brands are assessed not just on what functions they provide but also the capabilities of the firm behind them: B2B buyers often want firms with track records of process and product or service innovations as they'll require upgrades (computer software for example), efficiency savings (improved fuel efficiency for engines), and breakthrough ideas (new cultural marketing campaigns from advertising agencies) throughout the life of the relationship to ensure sustained leadership.

3. Business buyers also value the advice and adaptability of their partners: Freely given advice is often critical to ensuring the relationship is renewed while adaptability to unforeseen circumstances is often critical for minimizing relationship dissatisfaction (Beverland et al. 2007).

4. Business buyers often do not know their real problems: Much like consumers struggling to articulate their needs, business users' espoused problems are often symptomatic of deeper issues, including conflicts between the different levels of influence (see Figure 10.7), problems in the marketplace, problems with their products and services, and so on. Identifying firms' real problems and framing these solutions in ways acceptable to customers can add much value. Advertising agencies, for example, diagnose problems with sales figures as representative of deeper problems surrounding the brand, the quality of its associations relative to the competition, or performance on points of parity. In so doing, their advertising campaigns are often very different as a result of what the customer initially desired.

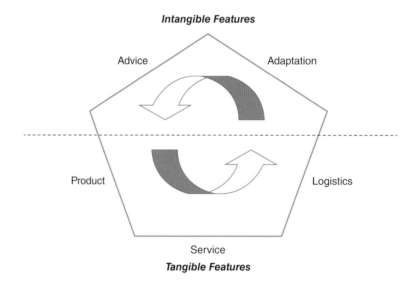

Figure 10.8   The Business Market Offer

The Business Marketing Offer and Brand

Together, the four factors above define the **business-marketing offer**, pictured in Figure 10.9. This offer forms the basis of a B2B brand position and strategy. The B2B branded-offer consists of those tangible features (much like a B2C brand) including products, services, and, critically, logistical support (or implementation). This last is essential as the success of the entire network is often driven by coordination between suppliers and ensuring that inputs arrive just in time for the next network member to use in the production process. However, these features, over time, are always points of parity for the B2B brand, given that product performance can quickly be matched, services replicated, and logistical systems purchased from off the shelf. Nonetheless, a poor performance on these features can trigger dissatisfaction, which, if left unaddressed, can trigger relationship dissolution.

The core part of strong B2B brands is what we do not see—the capabilities, investments, processes, and skills that ensure value is constantly delivered and renewed over the life of the relationship. Consistency in this sense takes on a different form, in that firms that are constantly able to renew their relevance are likely to build strong associations as an indispensable business partner (which is why so many technological brands such as Hewlett Packard and IBM or market-research firms such as TNS have shifted their overt identity toward one of a business partner, stressing the value they offer as solutions providers).

This part of the B2B brand consists of two interlocking parts: **adaptation** and **advice:**

1. Adaptation relates to the ability of the firm to be flexible within the relationship and critical to adapt to changes in customer desired value change (CDVC) (Beverland and Lockshin 2003; Flint et al. 2002, p. 107). Adaptation takes the following form:

   i. Hierarchy level: Customers demand for a move for performance on offer attributes, to attributes, consequences, and end-states. Australia-based commercial catamaran producer Incat had to adapt its offer to the changing customer environment resulting from rising fuel prices. Their ships were sold on the basis of speed, and were designed with this in mind, focusing on aerodynamic, light but strong frames that could carry large loads at high speed. As fuel prices skyrocketed, existing customers (boats cost upwards of GBP$300 million) asked Incat to help them reduce fuel costs while also meeting strict environmental controls that outlawed older and slower cargo boats. Incat's team redesigned the boats and their brand promise by refitting existing ships with smaller, fuel-efficient engines and stressing how their lightweight designs still traveled higher in the water (i.e., more efficiently) than traditional ships (Beverland and Farrelly 2007).

   ii. Newness: Customer demands for adaptations may take the form of not new, entirely new, or unexpected. For example, Interbrand's equity measure (The Top 100 Global Brands) was developed in response to customer's demands for "proof" that their brand advice worked. Typically, consulting companies such as Interbrand provide a standard framework to help firms develop brands or refresh existing ones, and then leave the business to get on with day-to-day management. The sheer cost of such advice raised concerns among brands' financial teams, resulting in marketers adding the new requirement of "proof" (brand equity) of Interbrand's effectiveness.

   iii. Bar raising: This represents a shift in performance standards to ensure the customer's firm is meeting market requirements, maintaining an edge, or addressing points of parity. Many B2C firms such as automotive firms use a process called reverse auctions to ensure continuous improvement among suppliers. What this does is essentially enable customers to put their requirements on an Internet exchange and let suppliers place the lowest bid or best quality bid. More often than not, this strategy is used in negotiations with existing suppliers to sharpen their game.

   iv. Priority changes: The example of Incat above also represents a shift in customer priorities that is part of a brand's adaptive ability. While speed was critical in a low energy cost environment, efficiency became more critical when fuel costs rose.

2. Advice is part of a proactivity strategy that is critical for renewing relationships or ensuring sustained brand loyalty within business markets. Whereas adaptation is essential for maintaining relational harmony, advice is critical for ensuring long-term loyalty, represented by the decision to renew relationships or increase the size of the account. **Relational proactivity** has four characteristics:

   i. Supplier initiative: Studies of relationship renewal identify that suppliers must play a proactive role in suggesting new opportunities and insights outside of the formal processes of account review (within the contract period and at the end). Failure to take the initiative often signals to customers that one is taking the relationship for granted, and that it might be time to put it out to tender.

   ii. Horizon expansion: This involves expanding customers' views of potential business opportunities. It is not crucial that customers adopt every insight or attempt to expand their horizons for potential markets or value opportunities; rather the act of doing so suggests one is interested in the future health of the customer's business and that one has invested further in ensuring combined success.

   iii. Strategic change: Research suggests such advice should be strategically focused and grounded in the interests of the customer (as opposed to self-interest on behalf of the supplier). This requires careful impression management and also an understanding of the customer's strategy and business environment. Investing in specific research projects that have the ability to expand customers' horizons in terms of strategic change can lend your offer significant credibility and enhance the intangible aspects of your positioning.

   iv. Signaling: Suppliers should take advantage of every mundane and formal opportunity (primarily the former) to signal their proactivity and therefore their interest in the customer's success. This is part of the reason B2B brands allocate marketing budget for social activities such as sporting events and invitations to seminars, as a means of getting time with relaxed customers. Even constant short elevator or water cooler conversations are critical to signaling one's intent.

(*Source*: Beverland et al. 2007, p. 52)

Leadership Capabilities for B2B Global Brand Leadership

In their book *Brand Leadership*, David Aaker and Erich Joachimsthaler identified that underpinning strong brands was a set of organization processes, practices, and capabilities. This aligns with the corporate branding approach's focus on the organizational aspects of brand reputation management. Recent studies identify the applicability of the Aaker and Joachimsthaler leadership model in the B2B context, albeit with subtle differences. These studies identify that global B2B brand leaders invest in the following capabilities that underpin **relational proactivity** and the aspects of the **business marketing branded-offer** presented in Figure 10.9:

1. Relational support: This is particularly important for the intangible aspects of the business marketing brand offer as it enhances a firm's reputation for adaptation and advice.
2. Network coordination: Coordinating multiple suppliers and other parties that affect how the brand is perceived or experienced is critical for ensuring product and service features are viewed positively, not to mention enhancing logistical support. Network coordination primarily helps with the tangible aspects of the business-marketing offer, although it also reinforces the intangible aspects especially through demands for value change (adaptation) and proactivity (advice).
3. Solutions focus: Either through coordinating other network partners or drawing on resources in-house, focusing on providing customer solutions, often to problems they themselves may not know (one common feature of many B2B customers is that, much like consumers, their espoused problems are not their real problems). Since relationships are long, being able to leverage resources and combine them in ways that deliver value over time is an essential capability of a B2B global brand leader.
4. Value-adding capabilities: In the context of branding this refers to the ability of the B2B brand to enhance the customer's brand, or the brands of network players. Since many business-to-business firms compete as networks, the stronger the reputational value of the entire network, the more competitive it is. Ingredient branding, investments in user-driven marketing to raise awareness (and generate pull), adding associations, playing to the cultural zeitgeist (ingredients, for example, are often the focus of doppelgänger attacks focused on sustainability, labor issues, and other sourcing concerns).

5. Measuring: B2B customers are often obsessed with measurement and precision. Since customers are usually purchasing or supply-chain managers, their training emphasizes quantification and efficiency. Being able to quantify quality claims, improve traceability, provide up-to-date tracking, and link consulting programs to measures of brand equity or performance, including enhanced perceptions of value, satisfaction, and authenticity among the customers' end-users, will help purchasing managers engage in authoritative performances with their finance team.

These specific capabilities are underpinned by a supportive organizational context that stresses customer focus, internal ownership of the brand, brand-driven marketing, innovation, entrepreneurship, and execution. Sustaining investments in the five areas is essential for maintaining **B2B brand leadership** (and often applies more generally to other brands). Their multi-disciplinary, cross-functional nature reinforces the need for a strong brand team, and a corporate branding approach in the B2B arena.

Chapter Summary

This chapter has shifted the focus away from individual brands and focused on the behind-the-scenes issues that enhance the brand's reputation. This focus is called corporate branding. Corporate branding considers how to balance competing interests or stakeholders, all of which will contribute to the organization's reputation. Three gaps are identified that have the potential to undermine the delivery of the intended brand strategy, and ultimately brand equity. Critically, an emphasis on reputation among stakeholders forces brand managers to attend to more than just customer-related issues in branding, putting effort into diffusing brand knowledge throughout the firm and working with powerful stakeholders such as influence groups, financial markets, and suppliers to ensure that crises are avoided.

The second half of the chapter focused on **services branding** and branding in industrial markets. B2B firms typically adopt a branded house or corporate branding approach because of the complexity of their value offer, the nature of these markets, and of course the more complicated purchase situations. This is not to suggest that **corporate branding** only applies in B2B; one can easily apply this model to B2C markets (especially in light of Chapter 12), professional service firms (law, finance, medicine, architecture), and new-to-branding contexts such as universities, charities, and government organizations, not to mention places.

B2B involves managing the interplay between tangible (points of parity) and intangible elements (points of difference) over time. Although it is unlikely that a cultural model will apply to B2B sectors, one should not automatically dismiss cultural considerations, especially when developing ingredient brands or branded programs such as Fair Trade for example. Beyond the qualifications in this part of the chapter, much of what is covered in the rest of this book applies to the B2B context, although B2B branding research and practice remain underdeveloped, potentially representing a larger opportunity for the aspiring brand manager.

Review Questions

1. What is the difference between corporate brand strategy and product or services branding as described in the rest of the text?
2. Why might gaps emerge between identity, image, and culture? Provide examples of each.
3. Why might service staff not deliver the brand as intended?
4. How does B2B branding differ from B2C? Are there similarities and crossovers?
5. Do business buyers reflect the purely rational stereotype? From your knowledge of influences on buying and the business-marketing offer, identify how brands may help buyers achieve self-authentication.

Case Example: Linatex—Branding Rubber Hoses

Linatex, founded in 1923, had long been associated with rubber protective solutions for heavy machinery in mining and minerals and general industrial uses. Their expertise was built around the quality of their rubber and their design team. Many of their processes had been patented and the firm built a global reputation for product quality and innovation. Despite this, they were latecomers to branding, only seeking to build a coherent, single corporate identity in the late 2000s after being acquired by Malaysian-based private equity firm Navis for US$31 million.

Like any private equity business, Navis had big plans for Linatex, aiming to double sales every three years. How? Linatex was tasked with leveraging their reputation and customer relationships into a formal branding program focused on (1) global coverage and (2) customer solutions that delivered efficiency savings. However, an internal review revealed that Linatex had anything but a clear brand identity.

Management decided to employ a respected brand agency, Futurebrand, to help reposition the company and focus the firm's marketing efforts. Branding was seen as critical because the firm was facing a number of strategic challenges including customers choosing lower-grade competitor products to save on purchasing costs (even though Linatex's products were more durable and therefore cheaper over the long run); the firm's expertise was based on different strengths in different regions (undermining the ability to leverage one identity), a confused communication offer, and fragmented branding approach (with many local operations developing their own brand materials).

(Continued)

Like many B2B organizations, the firm had a complex customer model including different industry contexts: mining, engineering, original equipment manufacturers, miners, and process focused business. Not including the people in these teams, there were many other stakeholders to consider including users, purchasing managers, site owners and managers, and maintenance staff. All of these stakeholders had different needs including managing costs, getting large projects up and running and keeping them on track and in budget, and risk management. Through careful research, markets were broken into three related audiences: corporate headquarters, mining sites, and operations.

After conducting research on the brand's reputation with key stakeholders and also an analysis of the firm's capabilities and associations, Futurebrand positioned Linatex as "superior flow enablers." Target users were clients engaged in extracting value from abrasive processes. The core promise of Linatex was to act as a partner to get the most out of flow rates through innovative product and service solutions. The brand's personality was presented as solid, understanding, adaptable, determined, and collaborative. The core brand challenge was to move customers' perceptions about the product and services from one of a cost to be minimized to a strategically important process that ensured positive outcomes at minimal risk. If the team could do this, a premium pricing strategy could be developed, although the total cost would involve substantial ongoing service support, and be amortized over a much longer period due to the durability of Linatex's products.

As a result, the brand was completely overhauled. Prior to change, the brand's architecture consisted of one global corporate brand coming from the firm's headquarters and lots of disjointed product brands largely flowing from local offices across the globe. The new approach would first focus on the customer and thereafter involve one consistent brand being spread across the group's entire product and service offerings. The new architecture would be built around customer solutions:

1. For corporate clients, solutions would be focused on enhanced project design and construction.
2. For site-based clients, solutions would be focused on improved project management.
3. For operations focused clients, solutions would be focused on maintenance.

This resulted in the firm's first corporate brand campaign with new imagery (see Linatex's "It's the Flow Here" ad posters) and the tagline "our strength, your endurance." Across the range of materials targeted at the three customer needs, brand-driven promises included:

1. Working with you, wherever your business is going
2. Local, wherever you are
3. Consistent delivery at every level
4. Continuous growth
5. Specifically built to meet your exacting requirements
6. "Flow"
7. "Made Tough"

The new corporate brand was rolled out in stages, first focused on unifying messages, then moving more aggressively, using the brand position and personality to drive through leadership, innovation, and an emphasis on expertise through added-on services such as design and process audits. The brand strategy paid off for Navis and the Malaysian-based group sold Linatex for US$200 million in 2010 to the Weir Group, a globally focused engineering firm based in Scotland.

Case Questions

1. Identify how the brand promises listed in the case appeal to each user group.
2. How did the rebrand of Linatex reflect the business-marketing branded-offer presented in Figure 10.9?
3. What were the strategic dangers of not branding? Could the benefits from the rebranding have been achieved in other ways?

Key terms

AC³ID model
Adaptation and advice
Corporate branding
Business-marketing offer
Business-to-business (B2B)

B2B brands
Business buying process
Corporate reputation
Employee engagement
Internal marketing
Relational proactivity

Services brand
Stakeholder alignment
Vision–Culture–Image Alignment Model

Further Reading

Balmer, John .M.T., Helen Stuart, and Stephen A. Greyser (2009), "Aligning Identity and Strategy: Corporate Branding at British Airways in the Late 20th Century," *California Management Review*, 51(3), 6–23.

Beverland, Michael B., Francis Farrelly, and Zeb Woodhatch (2007), "Exploring the Dimensions of Proactivity within Advertising Agency–Client Relationships," *Journal of Advertising*, 36(4), 49–60.

Brodie, Roderick J. (2009), "From Goods to Service Branding: An Integrative Perspective," *Journal of Service Research*, 9(1), 107–111.

Graham, Johnny L. and Susan Mudambi (2016), "Looking at the Future of B2B Branding," in F. Dall'Olmo Riley, J. Singh, and C. Blankson (eds.), *The Routledge Companion to Contemporary Brand Management*, Routledge, London, pp. 271–279.

Hatch, Mary Jo and Majken Schultz (2001), "Are the Strategic Stars Aligned for Your Corporate Brand?", *Harvard Business Review*, 79 (Feb.), 128–134.

11

ETHICS AND BRANDS

I earn a living fronting an organization that kills 1,200 human beings a day. 1,200 people! We're talking two jumbo jet planeloads of men, women and children. I mean, there's Attila, Genghis and me, Nick Naylor, the face of cigarettes, the Colonel Sanders of nicotine. (Aaron Eckhart playing tobacco industry lobbyist Nick Naylor, *Thank You for Smoking*, Fox Searchlight, 2006)

Ooh, you know what Bill's doing now? He's going for the righteous indignation dollar. That's a big dollar. A lot of people are feeling that indignation. We've done research—huge market. He's doing a good thing. (Late comedian Bill Hicks on advertising and marketing)

Learning Objectives

When you finish reading this chapter, you will be able to:

1. Examine the interplay between ethical worldviews and branding
2. Examine ethical issues from developmental and critical macro-marketing perspectives
3. Understand the deontological, teleological, and contextual approaches to ethics and branding
4. Understand the difference between normative and positive approaches to ethics
5. Explore contemporary issues in relation to branding and ethics

Introduction

In November 2016, Australian newspaper *The Age* broke a story regarding the systemic underpayment and exploitation of foreign laborers working in the horticulture industries (Mackenzie and Baker 2016). The essence of the story was that because these laborers had tenuous immigration statuses, had no awareness of local award rates, and were not unionized, they were paid substantially below the legal minimum and subject to abuse from unscrupulous brokers who often charged extortionate charges for renting the floor space where they slept. For many, after rent and money that was stolen by brokers, they were working for next to nothing (and in some cases were in debt). If they complained, they would be deported, often with nothing to show for months of backbreaking work.

The story seems simple enough, and for many posting on social media, it was easy to blame growers, brokers, lax enforcement of labor laws, a corrupt "system," or even the retailers who ultimately sold the fruit to consumers. One can treat this as a black and white story about workers being exploited by more powerful parties, or one can view it in terms of ethical shades of grey. If it is the former, then one can examine who is primarily at fault and who may have also indirectly contributed to the situation of workers via a failure to manage their supply chain, and the actions of their contractors, or enforce employment laws. If it is the latter, one may ask different types of questions, wondering if this type of exploitation is endemic within the market system at hand, or whether consumer demands for low prices may have indirectly contributed to growers turning a blind eye to exploitation. These two approaches frame the material in this chapter.

Why Brands and Ethics?

In many ways it's fair to ask "Why ethics?" when it comes to branding. Some consider brands to be commercial entities and hence their managers are motivated to maximize profits within the relevant legal frameworks they operate in. Others may go further, arguing that within the boundaries of the law, brand positioning and reinforcement sometimes requires breaches of social norms and values. For example, clothing retailer Abercrombie & Fitch is notorious for breaching social norms around acceptance and tolerance (what some might call "political correctness"). The brand was chastised for preferring a certain type of retail assistant (typically slim, muscular, and reinforcing stereotypes about attractiveness), going so far as to require disabled employees and those that don't fit the stereotype to work in back-office roles or roles that involve no front-stage engagement with the customer. Former CEO Mike Jeffries caused outrage when he responded by arguing that such companies are in danger of becoming "vanilla" by trying to appeal to everyone. (quoted in Lutz 2013).

However, are his actions unethical? From the viewpoint of brand positioning, he is correct. Abercrombie & Fitch survives because it is ruthless in reinforcing its position as being for cool rich kids aged 16–23 years old. The physical profile of the brand's retail assistants reinforces this, as does the in-store experience and the refusal to produce extra-large and above sizes. Technically, the brand is not breaching its legal obligations to hire the best qualified; rather it is reframing "best qualified" in brand-related terms.

Likewise, expectations regarding Exxon after the Exxon Valdez oil spill were low when compared to BP's Deepwater Horizon spill. Why? BP had rebranded itself as "Beyond Petroleum" whereas Exxon never deviated from its heritage of being a large oil producer. BP's mantra suggests it should act better, whereas our expectations of Exxon are low because they don't take an explicitly social stand. Brand Aside 11.1 explores this issue further, identifying why brands are held to a higher account than commodities.

BRAND ASIDE 11.1

Brands vs. Commodities: The Consumer Republic

Bruce Philp published an intriguing book in 2012 entitled *Consumer Republic: Using Brands to Get What You Want, Make Corporations Behave, and Maybe Even Save the World*. The book covers similar material to *No Logo*, and takes up where Klein left off, although is much more positive about brands as a tool for social good. Philp's view is that since brands are so visible, they are an easy target for critique and thus can become champions for positive change. Why? Similarly to Klein, with brands being so valuable, and their owners so concerned about protecting their image, they are much more sensitive to criticism and also to the potential that taking a leadership position (or at least being seen to) can have for brand equity.

Philp builds his case by comparing commodities and brands. He notes, for example, that Starbucks has faced criticism regarding the prices paid to farmers where coffee is grown, and for land clearing, biodiversity lost, and sustainability issues out of proportion to its actual impact on the global coffee trade. Most coffee is still sold as a commodity, and therein lies the rub. Commodity buyers engage in the same practices as Starbucks, but do so on a much larger scale, yet their very anonymity protects them. Thus Philp views brands as valuable, precisely because they can drive critical changes in developing economies and the supply chain.

So, as long as brand managers act legally, are their actions outside of ethical consideration? There are a number of reasons why it's important to consider the ethical implications raised by "branding" broadly. One is simple self-interest—as we cover in the final chapter (Chapter 12; see also Chapter 10 on reputation gaps), meaning creators are holding brands to account for their direct and indirect actions, and a failure to engage in ethical debates will result in falling brand equity and potentially the destruction of the brand.

Beyond that there are other issues (some would argue bigger more important issues) at stake, such as the impact of brand-driven consumption on the natural environment, on poverty and violence, on issues of body image and the representation of ethnic minorities, the exploitation of labor, corruption, encroachment into areas previously regarded as "sacred," the perceived sameness of local neighborhoods, exploitation of non-human animals, the appropriation of consumer-owned property, culture, spaces and even labor, and many other issues.

Chapter 2 identified that postmodernism had given greater power to brands as identity markers, focusing primarily on the benefits to brand owners of this shift. However, as Naomi Klein (2000) noted in her bestselling book *No Logo*, this success also makes brands a much bigger and more vulnerable target for activists and carries with it an obligation to ensure that the values at the heart of the brand's position are actually lived (rather than simply espoused) in all areas that the brand's operations touches. Thus "living the brand" may mean very different things to different stakeholders, giving greater importance to understanding how each views the brand's identity (see Chapter 10).

Brands have moved into many areas of the public realm, have benefited dramatically from their aspirational positioning and sub-cultural associations, from consumer support and moral sanction, and of course from globalization and the natural environment. Moreover, brands have also benefited from society, especially in terms of infrastructure and education, and indirectly through innovation policies (Mazzucato 2013). Since all marketers are now encouraged to be authentic storytellers and stewards in a more general sense (Holt 2002), and there is a need for moral legitimacy in order to operate successfully (Kates 2004), being aware of ethics is a necessity for any aspiring brand manager. Finally, brands can benefit substantially from taking ethical stances. The ban announced on travelers from seven Muslim countries by US President Trump (which was subsequently overturned in the courts) saw brands such as Airbnb, Audi, Bayern Munich, Google, Ikea, and Starbucks initiate programs supporting refugees and others hit by the restrictions.

Branding and Macro-concerns: Two Approaches

So far, this book has primarily approached branding from a micromarketing perspective. What does this mean? Micro approaches typically focus on the actions of individuals and organizations, including employees, activists, bloggers, brand managers, consumers, business customers, and of course brand-driven firms. By way of contrast, macro approaches focus on the marketing system ("the market"), whole sectors, the natural environment and society. In essence, macro-marketers attempt to understand how micromarketing can cause negative spillovers, what type of systems produce benefits for marketers, consumers and other users, how marketing and the natural environment can be aligned (assuming they can), and how marketing may be able to address its critics or help reduce harm (Hunt and Vitell 1986; Mittelstaedt et al. 2006).

Macro-marketing therefore becomes important for us to understand the ethical challenges facing brand marketers, and also the potential to address these concerns.

There are two general approaches to macro-marketing (Mittelstaedt et al. 2014):

1. **Developmental approaches**: This school views markets as critical systems for social development and human welfare (Mittelstaedt et al. 2014, p. 253). Any negative consequences of marketing action are treated much like they are in the dominant schools of economics—they are externalities or negative spillovers, resulting from information inefficiencies and asymmetries, poorly written regulation, or inadequate property rights.

   From this point of view, marketing can help correct some of these negative consequences, often through information campaigns, **corporate social responsibility (CSR)** programs, technological innovation, and behavioral change, usually drawing on the logic of "**nudging**" derived from behavioral science and extremely popular with many policymakers. Nudging is defined as follows:

   > Nudges are ways of influencing choice without limiting the choice set or making alternatives appreciably more costly in terms of time, trouble, social sanctions, and so forth. They are called for because of flaws in individual decision-making, and they work by making use of those flaws. (Hausman and Welch 2010, p. 126)

   This approach does not focus on regulating or banning actions that cause negative consequences; rather the focus is on understanding the limitations of decision-making in particular contexts and making small changes to nudge users to engage in "better" behavior (although who defines "better" is of course up for debate). For example, rather than banning sugary food, advocates of nudging might suggest better labeling systems, better placement of fruit in store, and so on.

   Nudging is not the only approach that these macro-marketers advocate as they often deploy frameworks other than behavioral science and its focus on experiments to solve problems (including ethnography, interviews, observations, and survey work). The developmental approach has also been instrumental in examining emerging ideas such as gross national happiness and quality of life (which draws heavily on the ideas of Abraham Maslow and seeks to improve markets to enhance human flourishing).

   Micro-marketing specialists have also framed much of their research in developmental terms, especially work on the behavioral tradition (see Brand Aside 11.2) and other work falling under the recent interest in transformational consumer research (TCR), which seeks to better the lives of consumers (Mick et al. 2012).

BRAND ASIDE 11.2

Predictably Irrational

Dan Ariely (2009) is one of the best-known proponents of behavioral science and nudge interventions in the consumer field. His book *Predictably Irrational* is a bestseller and, as the title suggests, is based on the idea that consumers deviate from the economist ideal of rationality, but in highly predictable ways. As a result, interventions or nudges can be designed to enable them to make the "right" decision. In one experiment, for example, Ariely examines the intention–behavior gap in relation to condom use. Why do consumers say they will use (or insist on using) a condom and yet don't do it? He demonstrates that when partners are aroused they are unable to make rational decisions, despite the best of intentions. Policy focused in this area therefore needs to equip consumers with the ability to make decisions in heightened emotional states, which contrast with the ways in which "safe sex" messages are framed.

Others use similar ideas in the area of overconsumption. Brian Wansink (2007), for example, is well known for his research into portion sizes and obesity. His work identifies how aspects of the environment in which one eats can lead people to over-eat, even when they desire to diet carefully. In one famous experience, he identifies how placing the same amount of food on a smaller plate actually leads to less consumption, while another experiment identifies how people pour more liquid into short squat glasses than tall ones, or eat more when presented with "low fat" labeled food. His results run counter to claims that the consumer is powerless to regulate their food intake in an environment saturated by food marketing and brands, and that consumers can make small changes to their behavior that ensure they eat less.

Although micro in its approach, this type of work aligns with a developmental approach to ethical issues and challenges conventional approaches to labeling, while reinforcing dominant discourses around consumer responsibility. Critical approaches in contrast suggest that placing responsibility back on to the consumer lets manufacturers and brands off the hook, a point reinforced by nutritional analyses that suggest sugar and high fructose corn syrup (used in many fast foods) make consumers more desirous of such foods while at the same time creating a feeling that one is hungry despite having consumed more than the recommended daily intake of calories.

2. **Critical approaches**: Unsurprisingly this school takes a more skeptical approach of the benefits of markets and marketing. Critical theorists view issues such as overconsumption, environmental degradation, speciesism, racism, gender discrimination, worker exploitation, tax avoidance, and so on as problems inherent in the capitalist system (Bradshaw and Zwick 2016; Tadajewski et al. 2014). In this

view, marketing is not so much the solution as the problem, or at least part of a system, which is based on unsustainable resource use, **overconsumption**, and so on. In this view, marketing and branding are part of many of the problems experienced by people within society.

Consider Stella McCartney's commitment to **sustainability** alongside her co-branding with fast-fashion brands such as Adidas and H&M. McCartney's brand expansion via partnerships is part of a strategy to challenge traditional stereotypes about sustainable fashion being for the wealthy or for those unconcerned with style. Developmental theorists would argue this is an example of market correction, of brands placing sustainability and animal rights on the agenda and shifting the practices of large fast fashion brands. In contrast, critical theorists would say that McCartney's belief in reconciling sustainability and fast fashion is hopelessly naïve (although motivated by good intentions).

McCartney after all is part of the Kering group, a large luxury conglomerate whose success is determined by meeting shareholder demands for increased quarterly profits. Although McCartney may take a position on sustainability, she in inevitably tied into a fashion system that is becoming evermore productive (gone are the days of seasonal releases; many luxury fashion houses such as Burberry now release as many as 14 collections a year and insiders suggest this is too slow). Should sustainability become "hot," demand for natural resources increases, more clothing is purchased, as eventually does waste (much fashion goes to landfill without ever being used), because unsustainability in inherent in the market for fast fashion.

Brand Aside 11.3 provides more details of slow vs. fast movements.

BRAND ASIDE 11.3

Slow vs. Fast Logics II

Metaphors of speed have been used to characterize different approaches to living. Slow living, for example, is offered as an alternative to the globalized, mass-branded, fast lifestyle. Emerging in the 1980s out of protests over McDonald's opening an outlet in the historic Italian town of Bra, Slow Food eventually extended its "brand" to include health, fashion, design, and even branding. The logic of slow makes some sense in relation to food as the focus is on tried and tested production techniques, enjoying meals over time, and celebrating variety. However, extending this logic into fashion-driven systems, such as design, technology, and fashion is more difficult. Furthermore, the notion of slow branding is challenging, as relevance remains central to brand equity.

(Continued)

Slow fashion, for example, advocates buying fewer but better clothing (i.e., classic pieces), vintage styles, and in some cases re-using, re-designing, re-purposing, or being able to re-sell clothing. However, even fashion practitioners identify how difficult it is to balance commitment to ethical fashion and sustainability with consumer desire for variety (itself an outcome of a system where everyone is always on a stage; Goffman 1957) and commercial viability (even for small labels not accountable to large shareholders) (Fletcher 2016).

Advocates of slow design, for example, identify that small changes in design can alleviate unsustainable actions. For example, small changes in bicycle design can make puncture repair much easier, thereby enabling the user to conduct the repair themself instead of feeling forced to use a specialist cycle shop who for cost-efficiency reasons will simply throw the damaged inner tube away and replace it with a new one (which adds to landfill and energy use) (Beverland 2011).

Although small changes like this can help, one must also be mindful of critical theorists' views that so-called sustainable design is part of a larger system of consumption and fashion. For example, design-for-sustainability advocate Stuart Walker (2006) details many ideas for re-using existing technologies in order to reduce the need for new goods. However, he tends to ignore the fact that such designs are likely to quickly become a new fashion (as few consumers in developed economies have the ability to repair things anymore), driving demand for slow style as the latest trend (Shove et al. 2007).

Nonetheless, the slow movement remains a powerful brand idea, and is one adopted by many in the revitalized "maker movement"; established brands focused on authenticity, services, cities, and regions, in response to consumer demand for at the very least a temporary escape from the fast market system.

The differences between the two approaches can be seen in discussions of environmental sustainability, a subject that will be covered in more detail below. The important thing to remember is both schools offer useful insights and tools to addressing challenges that arise in the marketplace (that go beyond sustainability and include the issues covered in this chapter), and help us understand why different stakeholders may frame problems and solutions in different ways. The critical school sensitizes us to the limitations of existing institutions (including brands) and their underlying assumptions, identifying why ethical challenges are inherent in existing arrangements. The developmental approach forces us to look at ways in which markets and brands can help address some of the ethical problems covered in this book.

Table 11.1   Developmental vs. critical approaches to sustainability

Dimension	Developmental School	Critical School
Technology	The focus here is on how markets and marketing systems can ensure technologies to deal with how environmental problems (including global warming) are created and adopted widely by market actors. Technological change (usually in terms of advancement) is the solution to environmental challenges.	Marketplace reliance on technological utopianism is misplaced and enables one to frame problems resulting from unsustainable economic systems as "manageable." This creates a false sense of hope amongst consumers, and represents a barrier to the changes necessary to avert global warming and other environmental disasters. Negative environmental impacts of technology are underestimated.
Political liberalism	Environmental problems are a result of the "tragedy of the commons" or the lack of property rights in relation to natural resources such as air, water, non-human species, and land. Strengthening property rights would enable current externalities to be internalized (for example, if people held rights in the atmosphere, pollution would become a cost that would need to be borne by the polluter).	The notion of voluntary exchange inherent in political liberalism is unrealistic. Nations, firms, and individuals are unlikely to change their behaviour and attempts to create voluntary exchanges to deal with carbon emissions for example have often failed.
Economic self-interest	How can we align the self-interest of actors with sustainability goals? Examples include identifying the price premium and market advantages of vegan products, organic produce, and CSR commitments.	The institutional systems in which we operate ensure the self-interests of some outweigh that of the environment, and that many of the Developmental School's initiatives (e.g., organic food) may be more harmful to the environment.
Anthropocentrism	Sustainability is defined in terms of our (i.e. humanity's) long-term survival.	Humanity's belief of dominion over nature and non-human species is part of the problem.
Competition	Competition necessitates innovation and change. Therefore markets should be harnessed to ensure sustainable outcomes, including emissions trading systems.	Competition consumes resources and more cooperative approaches are likely to render better results.

Source: adapted from Mittelstaedt et al. 2014, pp. 259–260

BRAND ASIDE 11.4

Consumer Responsibility

In response to many challenges, particularly claims of fueling obesity, gambling and other addictions, environmental destruction, debt, and overconsumption in general, many policymakers and corporate spokespeople place the onus back onto the consumer to take responsibility for their actions. In a recent study on the role of the Davos Forum, researchers Markus Giesler and Ella Veresiu (2014) noted how

(Continued)

criticisms of capitalism were reframed in terms of consumer responsibility. This shifts the moral obligation away from brands and onto consumers. Others have noted how this discourse is in fact a clever "governing mechanism" that allows brands to avoid ethical questions, and reinforces unsustainable practices among consumers. In many Western nations, the dominance of neoliberalism as a political-economic philosophy means consumers are hard wired to buy into the personal responsibility logic. While consumers undoubtedly have great market power (in terms of their ability to withdraw their patronage), others have noted that many actual improvements have been driven by legislated changes (Holt 2012) and supplier actions such as Fair Trade initiatives (Davies 2007), and that consumers often lack the ability to make the necessary changes (Longo et al. 2017).

Both approaches provide insight into how different stakeholders examine branding and ethical issues. Policymakers, brand managers, and industry representatives often focus on the developmental view, stressing market solutions, consumer responsibility (see Brand Aside 11.4), technological innovation, better labeling systems, corporate social responsibility (CSR), and partnerships between brands and not-for-profits among many other strategies aimed at reducing harm or flaws in the market mechanism. Elon Musk has built his entire Tesla brand around this idea, as have many of the proponents of access-based brands such as Airbnb, eBay, and Uber. The Etiko case at the end provides another such example. Activists, critics, consumer organizations (such as Community Supported Agriculture), and brands such as Vivienne Westwood typically take a more critical stance, arguing that many societal and environmental problems stem from the market system itself. Brand Aside 11.5 provides details on calls for anti-consumption.

BRAND ASIDE 11.5

Anti-consumption

Culture jamming collective Adbusters founded "Buy Nothing Day" (November 25 in the USA) as a reaction to a culture of consumption and materialism. There are many movements with similar motives, including downshifters, off-gridders, communes, freegans (who liberate perfectly edible food waste), and other waste liberators (such as those consumers who go through household trash for items of clothing that are still usable). Connecting all these groups is a commitment against overconsumption and the wastefulness of the present market system. Some brands have even built strong market positions around this. The most famous is environmentally positioned brand Patagonia with its 2011 "Do not buy this jacket" campaign. Others include Pret A Manger in the UK with its commitment to giving away unsold food to the homeless at the end of the day. Concerns over waste have forced many UK supermarkets to run "ugly fruit and vegetable campaigns," while in 2016 France became the first country to outlaw supermarket food waste (food waste is complex as covered in the section on sustainability).

This has given rise to an interest in anti-consumption research. However, is it possible to escape the market? One celebrated attempt is the Burning Man festival in the Nevada desert. Originally, this festival aimed to provide respite from the commercial world. The festival was formed around a large man sculpture, and ended when the sculpture was burned and no physical trace of the event remained. Studies of this festival identify that it is difficult to escape a market logic for long, and recently Burning Man has become seen as a playground for wealthy tourists, keen to add this event to their bucket list of must-see experiences. Eric Arnould (2007) argues that it is impossible and undesirable to escape the market, especially since those truly excluded from the market due to a lack of economic resources are most in need of the many goods and services provided by it. Anti-consumption also suffers from definitional challenges (by living we actually consume), and is best approached in terms of reduction, resistance, alternative markets and logics.

Marketing Ethics: The Classical Approach

Academics and practitioners have long given thought to the ethics of marketing, both in general and in relation to particular actions. The classical approach to marketing ethics is presented in Figure 11.1.

This approach combines the deontological and teleological approaches to ethical decision-making. What do these terms mean?

1. **Deontological**: ethical approaches using this view focus on behavior relative to a set of moral rules or principles. In this sense, ethics are judged in terms of right and wrong relative to universal principles. One obvious challenge arising in this approach is to decide which set of rules is universal as there has been (and still is) enormous debate as to the rights and wrongs of different religious views, moral philosophies, legal systems, and so on.

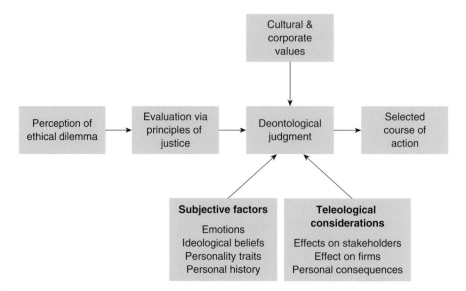

Figure 11.1   Standard Model of Marketing Ethics

Source: Thompson 1995, p.180

Normative approaches to ethics flow from deontological theories and focus on what "ought to be." Macro-marketing theorists Laczniak and Murphy (2006) outline seven basic perspectives that they propose ought to guide marketing activity:

i. Ethical marketing puts people first.
ii. Ethical marketers must achieve a behavioral standard in excess of the law.
iii. Marketers are responsible for whatever they intend as a means or ends as a marketing action.
iv. Marketing organizations should cultivate better (i.e., higher) moral imagination in their managers and employees.
v. Marketers should articulate and embrace a core set of ethical principles.
vi. Adoption of a stakeholder orientation is essential to ethical marketing decisions.
vii. Marketing organizations ought to delineate an ethical decision-making protocol.
(*Source*: Parsons 2009, pp. 125–26)

It is important to recognize that these seven principles work together and cannot be viewed in isolation from one another.

2. **Teleological**: teleology relates to goal-driven behavior and focuses more on the "likely consequences of an individual's actions" (Parsons, 2009, p. 124). Whereas deontological theories debate the nature of the set of rules to judge actions against, teleological theories differ over whose good to promote. Ethical egoism focuses on self-interest while utilitarianism focuses more on the greatest good for the greatest number.
(*Source*: Parsons 2009, pp. 123–24)

In contrast to normative approaches to ethics, teleological approaches are often called positive approaches. The approaches attempt to describe and explain what is (rather than what ought to be). However, in practice, such frameworks are often good in hindsight but not that useful for dealing with ethical issues as they arise (Thompson 1995).

In these cases, the focus is on understanding the influences on how actors perceive ethical problems and decide on what to do. The most influential model of marketing ethics per se is Hunt and Vitell's (1986) general theory of marketing ethics, and the classical approach to marketing ethics presented in Figure 11.1. As can be seen from Figure 11.1, how individuals think about ethical problems is a function of their context, their experience, their goals and assessment of consequences, and deontological values. In this model, brand managers do not act according to the seven ethical principles stated above but according to a mix of contextual influences, goals, and normative rules.

Each of these approaches frames brands' ethical obligations differently. **Deontological approaches** typically treat brands' ethical obligations from the standpoint of moral obligations, or a normative viewpoint. Many activists take this stance, suggesting it is simply wrong to pollute the natural environment, exploit humans and non-humans, misrepresent data, invade privacy, encourage overconsumption, reinforce existing gender, racial, and other stereotypes, avoid taxes, and so on. The **teleological approach** would examine these differently, possibly pointing out the benefits to workers in developing economies of increased employment opportunities, the benefits to society of economic growth, the trade-offs involved in privacy vs. information provision, and the supposed benefits from animal exploitation, and identify the commercial benefits of taking a strongly ethical stance.

Although advocates of the teleological approach critique the deontological focus on normative actions, many have noted that general theories of marketing ethics cannot entirely escape normative standards or values. Hunt and Vitell's general theory of marketing ethics, for example, includes a deontological element (see Figure 11.1).

These approaches are not without their limitations, however. Thompson (1995) notes that deontological approaches are not particularly helpful in addressing the many grey areas and paradoxes that confront marketers. For example, how does one balance home nation restrictions on paying bribes overseas with cultural norms in other nations where such actions are a necessary part of getting business done? And how does one balance personal values with the necessities of getting things done? Also, simple cautions not to invade consumer privacy, for example, fail to take into account the value consumers may gain from giving up some private information, or the benefits to society of allowing charities and research agencies to access consumer contact information (Yap et al. 2011). Abstract codes of ethical behavior often contained in corporate social responsibility (CSR) policies often lack usefulness in particular situations. Others note that ethical marketing and consumption discussions are characterized by problematic intention–behavior gaps as detailed in Brand Aside 11.6.

BRAND ASIDE 11.6

The Myth of the Ethical Consumer

It is common for marketers and the media to talk of ethical consumers as a type of market segment. This logic suggests there is a certain group of consumers who are intrinsically ethical, who use their values to guide their purchases. These consumers are believed to be both valuable and potentially quite influential in terms of setting trends and shaping the diffusion of so-called ethical products (such as Fair Trade, sustainable products, cruelty-free products, and so on). As economies develop, it is also believed that this segment will grow in size, as people become less concerned with economies and more concerned with morality. More importantly, these consumers will, through their actions, force companies into investing in corporate social responsibility policies and taking them seriously. How real is this ethical consumer? Research by Devinney et al. (2010) suggests "not very" (hence the title of their book *The Myth of the Ethical Consumer*).

These authors identify that apart from small groups of activists or groups such as ethical vegans, the number of consumers willing to pay more for ethical products resulting from corporate social responsibility strategies is limited. Ethical products that under-deliver on functionality are less likely to be chosen over their mainstream counterpart. This insight is why many early versions of "green" products failed; too often, they involved consumer sacrifice, something that the majority of users are not prepared to put up with, despite their stated commitment to ethical values. Insights like these led innovators such as Brigid Hardy of Beauty Engineered Forever to create environmental household cleaners that exceeded the performance and design value of their toxic counterparts.

Devinney and colleagues identified that context matters more than intent—when one asks consumers in private if they will buy Fair Trade, for example, few state they will; however, in public this number goes up to 70 percent. These types of intention–behavior gaps are common in ethical consumption research, green marketing, buy local, and so on, in that they fall prey to the rules governing an authoritative performance. No one after all wants to appear like they don't care about animals, the environment, overseas workers, and so on, but when it comes to the authenticating act of purchasing such products, investing their money in shares, functionality, price, and return win.

This leads consumer culture theory (CCT) scholar Craig Thompson (1995, p. 177) to conclude:

> Current models of marketing ethics do not sufficiently address the multitude of contextual influences that are intrinsic to ethical reasoning … and it is questionable whether research in marketing has led to significant improvements in the ethical climate of marketing practice.

A Contextual Approach to Marketing Ethics

Consumer culture researchers are reluctant to adopt either a deontological or norma-tive position, or teleological or positive approach to marketing ethics. Instead they focus on what helps or hinders self-authentication. However, it is possible to imagine a dark side of self-authentication, including how the desire for identity could lead to overconsumption and debt (Chung-Moya et al. 2017). There are also unintended spillovers from self-authentication. Consumers may engage in gambling as a means of affirming their connection to family or society, yet these actions can lead to real harm to themselves and others (Westberg et al. 2017). Identity factors such as associations between masculinity and meat eating have led to increases in consumption with spin-offs for the environment and national health systems (as lifestyle diseases increase) (Beverland 2014). These researchers argue that paying attention to the context, both current and historical, that led to such actions is essential for understanding the effec-tiveness of consumer and marketing action and social policy.

This approach, which lies at the heart of this text, emphasizes the important role of context, both individual and collective, in shaping expectations and actions. Although critics may argue that this results in relativism, this is not necessarily the case, as a **contextualist approach** is underpinned by an ethics of care and does not reject the possibility of actors following normative rules or codes of behavior. Attention to context is critical in dealing with the reality of ethical decisions, and would have helped avoid the tainted milk scandals in China (Fonterra, 2008, 2013), the UK horse-meat scandal (2013), and environmental disasters such as that which occurred in Bhopal, India (Union Carbide, 1984).

For example, scientists agree that bottled water is unsustainable and that con-sumers should be encouraged to drink tap water. However, bottled water was a solution to perceived dangers within existing water supplies, many of which had been polluted by industrial waste. As such, bottled water solved a genuine con-sumer need, but nonetheless resulted in air miles, energy use, plastic production, and waste (the solution would have been to clean up public water supplies). Despite the best intentions, consumers have over time become ideologically locked into the idea that bottled water is necessary for health and better than tap water (Holt 2012). How?

Over time, a combination of media scares about pollution, marketing claims about the need for constant hydration, and brand marketers' positioning of water using cul-tural codes expressive of purity, nature, and authenticity ensure that consumers take for granted the idea that bottled water is superior. This ethical approach aligns much more with the critical school and emphasizes government interventions (including bans) such as forced recycling (many European countries require bottlers to pay a small fee to people returning their used bottles) and forms of nudging (such as gov-ernment-subsidized in-home water filters) to overcome this ideology. Again, subsidization of solar panels in Australia has resulted in a significant uptake of renewal energy, with the result that consumers are now selling power back to the grid.

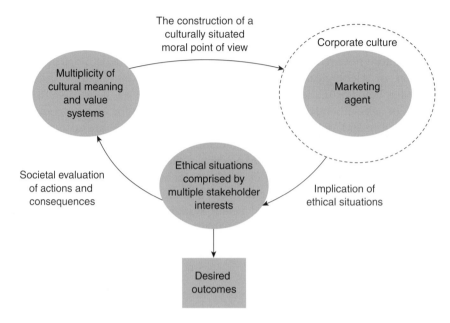

Figure 11.2   Contextual Model of an Ethical Dilemma

Source: Thompson 1995, p.182

Figure 11.2 presents an alternative model for marketing ethics, and one more in line with the framing of this text as laid out in Chapters 1 and 2.

As described in Figure 11.2, a contextualist approach argues that ethical dilemmas arise from the interplay of different contexts, ideologies, actors, interests, and evaluations. Each is described below:

1. The multiplicity of cultural meaning and value systems: Consistent with this discussion of authenticating acts and authoritative performances, contextualist approaches assume all chosen values are culturally situated. In practice this means that ethical dilemmas, such as those involving the clash of cultures, can at least be helped or addressed by attending to the subtleties of a target culture (including different nations and also consumer subcultures).

2. The culturally situated marketing agent: The context in which brand managers act is often defined by a set of values or beliefs, often called organizational culture. In reality, actors may draw on an organization-wide culture (shared across the firm), functional beliefs and values (e.g., the marketing philosophy or ideology), and personal values (Martin 1992). For example, ethical breaches in the UK banking system were often attributed to rogue individuals, yet investigations demonstrated that these traders were rewarded for risky actions, regardless of the ethical consequences. (Widespread knowledge of phone hacking was also demonstrated in the

News of the World case.) In this sense, firm culture, or subculture, may represent boundaries to authenticating acts, which is one reason why aspiring designers do not make fashionable clothes for plus-sized people.

3. Cultural meaning systems and the moral point of view: In contrast to many of the stylized ethical dilemmas presented in intention–behavior gap type studies (often "lifeboat" examples), real ethical decisions are often defined by their lack of certainty and clarity. Typically, everyday moral challenges occur in grey terms, which reflect the shifting and pluralistic nature of societies in general. It is rare, for example, for everyone in society to agree on a particular set of ethical standards—for example, open societies are characterized by ideological diversity, different viewpoints, and even seemingly contradictory approaches (atheists, for example, do not always reject religious values, while many religious institutions have suffered scandals at odds with their foundational teachings). What is subject to ethical consideration and the standards used also changes. Over the years, some societies have become more sensitive to environmental destruction, species loss, discrimination, privacy, and the rights of non-humans. These changes render many previous approaches to advertising, ingredient choice, information acquisition and use, and attitudes to globalization and profit maximization ethically suspect. Simple appeals to abstract principles or policies may not help in this regard because it may be difficult to know which competing stakeholders or interests one should preference and which principle to apply.

4. Interpretations of relevant stakeholders: Building on the previous point, defining stakeholders and their relative influence is difficult and the competing viewpoint of each renders normative principles impractical. Whose concerns should be taken into account? Why? How should one prioritize interests? How does one solve competing demands? CSR policies often struggle in this regard and, as identified in Chapter 12, societal expectations can change very quickly in this regard, generating doppelgänger images for brands and perpetuating crises of authenticity and negative brand equity.

5. Societal evaluations of marketing actions: Chapter 12 discusses the self-inflicted crisis experienced by the team at Tui Beer. The team suffered a backlash because its intended humor was seen as homophobic. However, it was not that long ago that depicting stereotypes of this nature was perfectly tolerable for the majority of consumers. Likewise, up until the mid-1980s, it was perfectly legal to advertise cigarettes in the mass media, and identify their use with images of coolness, sophistication, and romantic attractiveness. Now, however, these actions are legally forbidden (with widespread societal sanctions). Likewise, in Australia, the sale of semi-automatic firearms was accepted until the Port Arthur massacre in 1996 by a lone gunman led the government of the day to institute a gun buy-back scheme and subsequent ban. Now, lifting restrictions on the sale of guns is largely viewed as political suicide. Social mores change, and these affect the legitimacy of marketing actions. As mentioned earlier, what was once X-rated such as explicit sex on evening

television is now common in shows such as *Game of Thrones*, while reviews of an orgy scene in the remake of *Westworld* suggested televised sex was passé.

(*Source*: Thompson 1995, pp. 182–185, adapted by author)

Underpinning this approach is an **ethics of care**. An ethics of care orients us toward the interests of others. This approach is primarily empathetic, seeking to place ourselves in the shoes of others and look at issues from their standpoint. Empathy does not imply that we have to accept another's viewpoint as more valid than our own; rather it sensitizes us to alternative views and ways of seeing, opening up the possibility of dialogue and exchange.

Thompson (1995) proposes that an ethics of care aligns with much of the marketing philosophy or is an extension of it. For example, in framing customers in relational terms, we are obliged to look beyond their ability to provide us with resources to genuinely consider their wellbeing. If they truly are our partners, we should focus on their long-term interests. This may involve addressing issues of environmental sustainability, worker health, customer safety, and being sensitive to how stereotypes may affect their emotional states and those of their children. The same could be said for how marketing decisions affect the lives of employees, contractors, and the societies in which they operate overseas.

Corporate Social Responsibility

Corporate social responsibility (CSR) involves companies going beyond their legal obligations and their own interests to address and manage the impact of their activities on society and the natural environment (Lindgreen et al. 2016, p. 228). Some brands place CSR at the heart of their positioning (such as Patagonia and Stella McCartney), while others treat it is as a separate but related support program that is also focused on minimizing criticism and threats to corporate reputation. Lindgreen and colleagues identify that many approaches to CSR and branding fall short of an ideal, and as identified in the example of BP and "Beyond Petroleum" can backfire substantially (see Chapter 12). However, CSR investments can have a positive impact on reputation and therefore brand equity and firm value (Brammer and Millington 2008).

A detailed discussion of CSR strategies is beyond this text, but nonetheless it is worth considering how a contextualist approach to ethics would be embodied within the firm. Adopting a critical lens, many would be skeptical of such programs, suggesting they are simply ways of co-opting critics for financial gain or a form of loose coupling that ensures they deflect criticism and maintain legitimacy (Holt 2012; Meyer and Rowan 1977). However, advocates of a contextualist approach also suggest that ethics must be deeply embedded into marketing strategy instead of being seen as a separate group of programs or an extension of community engagement or public relations. Thompson (1995, p. 185) suggests that such an approach would involve the following questions:

1. What are the early warning signs of ethical dilemmas?
2. How are ethical concerns woven into strategic planning and everyday tactical activities?
3. Does the marketing organization tolerate expressions of conflict and dissonance over ethical matters? If so, how are these resolved?
4. What processes are used to negotiate conflicts among recognized differences in stakeholder interest?
5. What are the experiential consequences of engaging in unethical actions or being involved in a perceived ethical conflict?

(Source: Thompson 1995, p. 185)

Common Ethical Challenges Facing Brands

This section features a range of ethical charges typically leveled at brands. These are by no means exhaustive; rather they represent the most common or some emerging challenges that brand managers may confront. Answers to each are rarely easy, but nonetheless, as many of the examples testify, can have a dramatic impact on a brand's fortunes. Building on the contextualist approach above, it is important to remember how these may have emerged (to identify limitations to nudging or value-based calls for change), and to recognize that the importance and ways in which these are framed and expressed may shift over time and within different national and organizational contexts, while some may decline and unforeseen challenges emerge.

Consistent with previous chapters, examining anti-brand websites, activist materials, and cultural representations of the brand is essentially an early warning strategy to protect the brand's equity (where possible). Furthermore, being mindful of public and consumer sentiment, shifts in the wider political environment, and global changes is also critical for highlighting potential shifts and new sources of ethical dilemmas.

Sustainability and Resource Use

Marketing is part of a system geared toward cycles of consumption. Organizations accountable to shareholders are judged on their ability to improve on last quarter's results, often through stimulating more and more consumption of brands. To do so marketers have triggered status anxiety among consumers, resulting in ever quickening fashion cycles in clothing, technology, food, toys, entertainment goods, and so on. All of these have implications for resource use, global greenhouse emissions, climate change, carbon miles, and waste (among many other impacts on the natural environment). Even goods marketed as "green" or "environmentally friendly" can have larger carbon footprints than we would care to admit (organic food production is not necessarily more environmentally friendly, for example), and such actions can be little more than greenwashing that enables consumers to convince themselves they are consuming sustainably, while continuing to consume well beyond their needs.

Status Anxiety

Post-World War II, marketers realized that playing to people's fears over status and being left behind (e.g., "keeping up with the Joneses") was a way to encourage more consumption and ensure shorter product lifecycles and greater returns (initially this occurred in the automotive context with the shift from technological improvements to stylistic changes every season to encourage people to upgrade their vehicles). **Status anxiety**—the concern about one's position relative to that of others— has not only fueled increases in consumption, it has also generated increased consumer debt, seen the emergence of a negative relationship between material wealth and happiness, and in some cases resulted in deaths—for example, over 1,200 people are killed in the USA each year for their sneakers alone according to the documentary *Sneakerheadz*.

Unpaid Consumer Work

Many brands with the highest equity valuation by Interbrand and Brandz and those viewed as future stars rely on consumer work. The emergence of Web 2.0, where internet sites became truly interactive, enabling collaboration between consumers and other consumers and consumers and marketers, resulted in a blurring of boundaries between consumption and production. Today we know this as "**prosumption**" involving "prosumers" engaged in a range of activities including ratings, reviews, likes, shares, direct collaboration such as with LEGO (Chapter 1), and crowdsourcing (Ritzer and Jurgenson 2010). This has benefited firms in many ways, especially social media brands that rely on the size of their web-based community for their value proposition (e.g., eBay is valuable because of the number of sellers it has).

Review websites such as TripAdvisor are based on unpaid work by consumers, whose reviews generate traffic to the website, which provide the basis for the brand's advertising platform. Studies on eBay sellers have identified just how effortful maintaining one's reputation is, and how much of this is unpaid work. Even behemoths such as Amazon rely substantially on the value of quality reviews to sell more of their products. Web-based social media platforms are based on consumer-generated content, without which they would not have a large enough audience to use as an asset for advertising and direct selling. Often referred to as the "sharing economy," access-based consumption models or cooperative consumption models such as Uber, Zipcar, and Airbnb place user ratings at the heart of their business models.

Yet how much of this value is returned to the consumer? Many of these brands use notions of community, consumer sovereignty and savviness, and co-creation in their positioning and messaging (Bardhi and Eckhardt 2012). Despite claims of co-creation and consumer ownership, many of these businesses claim all consumer-generated content as their own, have user agreements that allow them to on-sell consumer details to marketers, and have the right to change these terms and conditions at will. Although users benefit from these services, the financial returns to the brand holders are also substantial, and not captured directly by the very users that generate content.

Brand Aside 11.7 raises another ethical challenge in relation to benefiting from consumer work, this time in relation to the co-optation of images and consumer-generated materials (Arvidsson and Petersen 2016).

BRAND ASIDE 11.7

The Conquest of Cool

Fashion brands such as Urban Outfitters regularly draw on images of rebellion, ethnicity, and counterculture in their designs. Think of all those people walking around wearing t-shirts with "The Ramones" on them. It is unlikely that they're all fans of the seminal 1970s New York punk band (in fact it's unlikely they've even heard of them!). Likewise, all those Che Guevara images printed on jackets, t-shirts, and coffee cups are hardly precursors to the revolution or a celebration of communism. As discussed elsewhere in this chapter and book, leveraging consumer-driven associations has long been common practice amongst brand marketers. A presentation in the 1970s at JWT entitled "X becomes G" captured this approach. What is today X-rated will tomorrow be for general consumption. Marketers are thus encouraged to use the ideas and images of fringe groups to add significant cool and authenticity to their brands.

Thomas Frank's (1998) book *The Conquest of Cool* identifies how firms eventually commercialized the 1960s counterculture in the United States. Naomi Klein updated this argument in her crossover bestseller *No Logo* (see Chapter 12), suggesting that brands have encroached into areas previously resistant to commercialization such as university campuses. Such encroachment enables brands to soften their commercial edges, thereby being seen as relatively benign. In a twist on this argument, Heath and Potter (2006) in *The Rebel Sell* argue that counterculture is no longer threatening because, through co-optation, it has become consumer culture. These authors suggest far from conformity being at the

(Continued)

heart of consumer culture, markets are driven by their ability to package rebellion. While in this past "cool" was a political statement of rebellion, now consumer rebellion or subversion is simply a status claim, one that will quickly be copied by others, requiring more co-optation of new forms of distinction.

These critics raise some interesting ethical challenges for brands, however. Although consumers do not "own" cultural content such as those associated with musical movements (rap, reggae, punk, indie, etc.), identity subcultures (e.g. gamers, slackers, etc.), and so on, they nevertheless psychologically own this material. Psychological ownership represents a felt ownership over material, or a moral claim to its use. Because such material is often collectively created, it is rarely subject to copyright control or licensing requirements, enabling brands to use it freely, and even trademark such expressions and forbid the originators to use it. Studies have identified that consumers will seek to de-authenticate myths that brands use to co-opt such material (Arsel and Thompson 2011), while others have called such a model "cultural parasitism" and suggested that successful cultural brand positioning requires a much more authentic approach, involving respectful use, acknowledgment, shared benefits, and a contribution back to the subculture (Holt 2002; see also Beverland and Ewing 2005).

However, if both the mindshare and cultural models build equity via cultural associations that they do little to create, is it ethical to simply co-opt this material without compensation?

Representation and Stereotyping

Brands have long struggled with where to draw the line between offensive stereotypes, manipulating vulnerable consumers (e.g., body image), and creative advertising. Unilever's Dove brand has championed this issue, through its Real Beauty and "You're more beautiful than you think" campaigns, although these have also been criticized on grounds of insincerity (the models featured on many billboards were subject to careful Photoshopping), questionable authenticity (see Chapter 7 and the problem of combined brand architectures for Dove vs. Axe/Lynx), and emotional manipulation. Brands such as Calvin Klein and the now defunct American Apparel have also been accused of sexualizing young women, through their creation of the "tween" segment (Cook and Kaiser 2004) and drawing on associations with the pornography industry.

Furthermore, the representation or lack of representation of certain groups had also triggered calls for change and even boycotts. Mattel's Barbie has long been criticized not just for its idealized body image but also for its lack of ethnic diversity and its reinforcement of traditional gender stereotypes. Victoria's Secret has long been accused of promoting body-image anxiety among women. The brand's high-profile Secret Angels emerged from the supermodel era in the 1990s, which placed an emphasis on a singular definition of beauty involving slim, large-breasted, white females. The brand's "perfect body" campaign raised the ire of activists, resulting in an online petition. The subsequent backlash saw the brand change its campaign to "A body for every body" which featured the same models in the video, resulting in further criticism.

Tax Avoidance

Emerging out of the global financial crisis in 2007–2008, which led to greater pressure being placed on national tax revenues and declines in social spending, the most high-profile brands (with the highest equity) have faced significant scrutiny over their global taxation arrangements. Apple was recently ordered to pay the Republic of Ireland billions of euros in back taxes by the European Court of Justice, while Amazon, Facebook, Starbucks, Google, Uber, and many others have been outed by activists for effectively paying little or no tax in the nations they trade in, or within the nations where they are headquartered.

Although these firms commonly argue that what they are doing is perfectly legal (and often it is) and that they provide employment to thousands of people who do pay taxes, this is countered with the argument that many of the jobs are insecure (especially within the "gig economy"), relatively low paid, and subject to offshoring. Furthermore, some of these brands' practices shift costs onto the state (whose revenues are stretched), such as Walmart's reliance on welfare topping up staff wages, and the requirement for police to monitor supermarket customers after automated check-out technology saw a spike in theft (prior to this, theft had been monitored by employees at cash registers).

Others critics have also pointed out that the basis of many innovations at the base of global corporations revenue streams is in fact funded by the state through investments in research and innovation within universities. Large pharmaceutical firms have been shown to conduct little breakthrough research, preferring instead to invest in low-risk "me too" products, while claiming copyright protection for drugs and processes funded by the state. Mariana Mazzucato's *Entrepreneurial State* (2013) identified how virtually all of Apple's technological breakthroughs were funded through government investments in space and weapons technology. Others have noted that a failure to pay taxes may undermine the very basis of the ecosystem underpinning business innovations, particularly as firms send production offshore (often investment in research and skills shifts as a result), further undermining the ability of governments to engage in the blue-sky research that underpins much economic development and productivity improvements (Pisano 2009).

Supply Chain Transparency

For many manufacturers and increasingly services, cost advantages have led to complex global supply chains involving numerous contractors, many of whom have been accused of unscrupulous labor practices, and health and safety violations. For example, the regular fires and building collapses in Bangladesh's garment district have triggered widespread criticism of many high-profile fashion brands as well as retailers such as Sainsbury's who use these manufacturers for their own-label ranges (Press 2016). Naomi Klein's bestseller *No Logo* (see Chapter 12) further exposed the poor pay and conditions, long hours, physical and mental abuse, use of child labor, and other violations that occurred in supply chains for aspirational lifestyle brands such as Nike.

The 2013 horsemeat scandal involving many readymade meals in the UK and Ireland provides another example, where supermarkets literally have little idea what goes into their products simply because supply chains are now so complex. Other supply-chain challenges include the use of unsustainable materials, testing on animals to get around EU bans, bribery and corruption, environmental pollution, and tax avoidance. *Riverblue* (2014), a documentary on the impact of our desire for cheap denim, details the damage done to river systems in Bangladesh, China, and India, and the human costs in terms of access to clean drinking water. Outsourcing of production to these countries occurred after the signing of the NAFTA free-trade agreement, where brands such as Levi's sought cost efficiencies.

Animal exploitation

Although animal rights activists have always held organizations to account for their use of non-humans, for the most part these issues remained on the fringes of society. Recently, however, this issue has become more prominent, as the case study on *Blackfish* and SeaWorld in Chapter 12 demonstrates. Scientists have highlighted the impact of animal agriculture on the planet, identifying the sector as the leading driver of climate change emissions (primarily through methane, which is more toxic than carbon dioxide). Activist groups such as People for the Ethical Treatment of Animals (PETA) have exposed many brands (such as Hermés) for their cruel practices in relation to the keeping and killing of animals. Other groups have highlighted the miserable conditions of many farm animals, forcing supermarkets to change who they purchase meat, eggs, and milk from (Beverland 2014). The recent 2012 Cambridge Declaration on Animal Consciousness has also triggered difficult ethical debates about how we treat non-human beings and whether we have the right to harm them.

Brands have also benefited from this concern, with disrupters such as Beyond Meat, Tofurkey, Vegg, and other vegan alternatives (such as Etiko below) garnering support from wealthy high-profile investors such as Microsoft founder Bill Gates. Rates of veganism are increasing exponentially within Western economies, as is the value share for food and other products that are vegan and/or have animal welfare commitments. Beyond food, concern with the treatment of non-human animals has been felt in entertainment, fashion, pharmaceuticals, household cleaners, and many other categories.

Chapter Summary

In this chapter, the ethical implications of branding and marketing have been explored. A shift to co-creation means that brands can no longer act without regard for ethics. This is particularly so for brands that take a strong aspirational or even moral stand, or whose positioning and supportive strategies stakeholders can frame ethically. Ethical debates within marketing are framed in ways that view the market system and marketing as a positive force for good, or in more skeptical, critical ways, whereby marketing is often viewed as part of the problem.

Three approaches to ethics were examined. In line with the previous chapters and the emphasis on co-creation that frames this book, this chapter has presented a contextualist approach to ethics, underpinned by an ethics of care. This approach suggests ethical dilemmas emerge between various cultural, societal, institutional, organizational, temporal, and personal beliefs and rules, and require ethical reasoning to be engineered into marketing planning and brand strategy. The chapter concluded with some common ethical concerns involving brands that can form the basis of class discussion, and also set the stage for the final chapter on brand crisis.

Review Questions

1. Reflecting on the example of Abercrombie & Fitch's treatment of disabled employees, how would their actions be judged from a normative, positive, and contextual approach?
2. What other ethical concerns can you identify (beyond those listed here) that have the potential to impact on brands?
3. Drawing on the different macromarketing perspectives, examine one of the ethical concerns raised in the book and identify how brands might be able to (or not) address it.

Case Example: Etiko—Wear No Evil

Etiko founder Nick Savaidis had long been passionate about ethical issues in manufacturing, and fashion in particular. Growing up in Brunswick, Melbourne's historic garment production area, he had seen the disparity between the piece rates his hard-working mother had received for her garments versus the retail prices for those clothes in Melbourne's designer stores. Moving through university, he lived in second-hand clothes as a protest against worker exploitation in offshore garment factories and also became involved with Oxfam's Community Aid Board. Graduating as a teacher, he had worked in many outback communities, helping Aboriginal communities earn money through social enterprise. Nick had been instrumental in setting up local supply chains that were able to make clothing featuring prints by Aboriginal artists. This ensured consumers received an authentically Aboriginal item, and that the funds spent went to communities of creators rather than to large firms who often used stylized versions of those designs without paying the creators anything.

These formative years paved the way for Nick's own ethical brand, Etiko, which has become a recognized leader in Fair Trade sourcing, sustainable fiber use, and transparency. Etiko originally emerged from Nick's desire to make footballs from sustainable materials, and then evolved into a range of footwear and now clothing. The main product lines are casual footwear, ostensibly copying the design of Converse's famous Chuck Taylor high-top and low-rise sneaker, and a range of rubber thongs (an everyday facet of Australian life) using sustainable rubber and co-branded with a number of charity groups including Animals Australia, Free the Bears, and Sea Shepherd. Recently the brand has expanded into underwear made from sustainable Fair Trade cotton. Figure 11.3 contains examples. The brand's vegan-friendly status (Nick himself is not vegan but sees no reason to harm animals) has ensured it has a strong following within this community, featuring strongly on social media and in specialist stores such as local chain Vegan Wares.

However, the brand is also at a turning point. Nick aims to grow the business and desires to sell 30 percent of it to raise funds for expansion. To do this, he knows he must expand beyond his current loyal, vegan/ethical fanbase and appeal more widely to a lifestyle of health and sustainability segment. This group spans ages and incomes although is primarily female, located on Australia's Eastern seaboard, and consists of those who strongly believe in consuming, representing around 5–10 percent of a population of 25 million people. Nick also suspects that if he can appeal to this group, he may open up the other 40 percent of the population who are leaning toward sustainable consumption (the remaining 50 percent largely do

Figure 11.3   Etiko Products

not care). Etiko products are competitively priced, and available through specialist channels and the brand's own web store.

Nick was aware of the size of this challenge. Attending a talk by Tim Devinney years earlier, he understood that there was no so-called "ethical consumer." Confronting Professor Devinney afterwards, he asked whether a brand such as his should simply give up. Devinney countered by arguing that the success of Nick's business lay in building strong points of difference that would appeal to consumers, with the ethical aspect representing a positive spillover effect. Nick also believed the brand represented a solution to consumers' frustration with intention–behavior gaps. He recalls giving a talk at a school where upon describing the conditions under which clothes were produced offshore, students were visibly upset and outraged and wondered what they could do about it. At the same time, those students were dressed head to toe in the very same brands that were engaged in the exploitation. Nick's takeaway from this encounter was that the market was frustrating consumers' desires for more ethical products.

Nick wondered whether he could expand the brand without compromising his ethics. Although veganism was becoming more popular in Australia, the community remains small, and for some consumers divisive (although this was fast changing). His brand's tagline "Wear No Evil" was uncompromising, but was this a

(Continued)

turn-off? Consumers' historical experience of sustainable fashion brands was also potentially a problem, with many brands being low on fashionability, comfort, and style, in favor of using material such as hemp and bamboo. The brand has strong moral credentials, being recognized in an industry fashion report as the only A+ awarded ethical producer in Australia. Much of its communications stressed this, but Nick wondered whether this would have crossover appeal (see http://good onyou.eco/etiko-leading-the-way/ for examples).

Source: author's notes.

Case Questions

1. Using Thompson's model, identify how Nick's brand helps consumers address their ethical needs.
2. What is the essence of the Etiko brand?
3. Nick desires to expand his brand to later adopters. These potential users are ethically minded but less adventurous than his loyal users. Build a persona of this consumer and identify the types of messages they will respond to.
4. What are the dangers and benefits of expanding the Etiko brand to new users?

Key Terms

Consumer responsibility
Contextualist ethics
Corporate social responsibility (CSR)
Deontological ethics
Ethics of care

Fast vs slow
Macro-marketing: critical view
Macro-marketing: developmental view
Normative approaches

Nudging
Overconsumption
Prosumption
Status anxiety
Sustainability
Teleological approaches

Further reading

Arnould, Eric J. (2007), "Should Consumer Citizens Escape the Market?," *Annals of the American Academy of Political and Social Science*, 611 (May), 96–111.

Holt, Douglas B. (2012), "Constructing Sustainable Consumption: From Ethical Values to Cultural Transformation of Unsustainable Markets," *Annals of the American Academy*, 644(Nov.), 236–255.

Longo, Cristina, Peter Nuttal, and Avi Shankar (2017), "'It's not easy living a sustainable lifestyle': How Greater Knowledge Leads to Dilemmas, Tensions and Paralysis," *Journal of Business Ethics*, DOI 10.1007/s10551-016-3422-1.

Mittelstaedt, John D., Clifford J. Schultz II, William E. Kilbourne, and Mark Peterson (2014), "Sustainability as Megatrend: Two Schools of Macromarketing Thought," *Journal of Macromarketing*, 34(3), 253–264.

Thompson, Craig J. (1995), "A Contextualist Proposal for the Conceptualization and Study of Marketing Ethics," *Journal of Public Policy & Marketing*, 14(2), 177–191.

YouTube, "Ethics of Consumption—Cultural Capitalism" https://www.youtube.com/watch?v=GRvRm19UKdA.

12

MANAGING BRAND CRISIS

In the business world, the rear view mirror is always clearer than the windscreen. (Warren Buffett, Berkshire Hathaway)

Events, dear boy, events. (Response by UK Prime Minister Harold Macmillan to a journalist's question about what could cause the government to go off course)

Learning Objectives

When you finish reading this chapter, you will be able to:

1. Understand the importance of managing brand crises to brand equity
2. Understand the different types of crises and the nature of each
3. Develop strategies for managing crises of authenticity
4. Understand the financial impact of crises
5. Examine impression management techniques used in crises

Introduction

Imagine you are the brand manager of Greggs (a large bakery chain in the UK) waking up (on August 19, 2014) and being greeted with phone calls from your frantic social media team (and a few messages from the press) after your banner that appeared in Google was hacked and was going viral. Replacing the slogan "Always Fresh. Always Tasty." is a particularly vicious parody. The message, reflecting class divisions in the UK, quickly went viral and necessitated a response.

Not for nothing is Greggs a high-street institution. The brand team quickly swung into damage control, issuing press releases thanking their customers for 70 years of patronage, and using social media to turn the tide in their favor. The Greggs team were quick to link to Google UK offering them some tasty treats to quickly fix the problem (which was done with good humor). Figure 12.1 identifies the various messages used to not only avoid the crisis getting out of hand and hurting the brand image, but also turning it to the brand's advantage, and quickly reminding customers that it was on their side, while also generating widespread awareness resulting in many new recruits.

Barely a day goes by when a brand is not suffering some crisis—be it an exposé on the treatment of foreign workers, the impact of the brand on the environment, our health, our politics, plant closures, a store opening ruining the character of the neighborhood, product and service failures, mis-tweets, David vs. Goliath legal cases (usually involving perceived infringements against copyright), or outright disasters involving death, environmental contamination, and disease. And those are just a few examples. Brands today are under such scrutiny that every social media post can be dissected, parodied, and twisted in unplanned ways. And since what is on social media stays on social media, such misdeeds or slights (true or not) can be endlessly recycled, forcing another wave of denials and responses.

Crisis lies at the heart of modern brand management. This affects not just brands on social media but also the social media platforms themselves. Twitter has to balance its commitment to free expression with its overwhelmingly liberal user base. For example, Twitter permanently banned high-profile "alt-right" provocateur Milo Yiannpoulos for

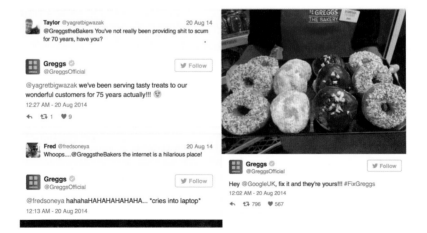

Figure 12.1

inciting hatred and encouraging his many followers to troll various speakers. Even venerable business-to-business brands are affected, as official Oscar's partner PwC found following the 2017 Oscar night Best Picture debacle.

With co-creation, globalization, hyperreality, and increasingly branded worlds, brands face attacks from multiple unforeseen angles, that can have very real impacts on financial valuation, customer-based brand equity, cultural brand authenticity, and share price or other forms of legitimacy necessary to access resources. One definition of a crisis suggests it represents a critical turning point in development. For some brands, crises proved too much (Valujet) and they suffered negative equity or a slow decline. For others, such as Coca-Cola, Johnson & Johnson, and to a lesser extent Vegemite and iSnack2.0 (see Chapter 2), crises represent forced refocusing on core brand truths and often become part of the brand's myth or folklore.

Some suggest that such crises may have been planned all along, just to generate interest in the brand. Either way, with institutional shareholders so concerned about reputation, planning for a crisis is a necessity for the brand team. And with the potential for doppelgänger images, parodies, or other authenticity attacks to go viral on global social media, even seemingly small missteps, if left to fester, can become full-blown crises relatively quickly. This chapter concludes the examination of co-creating brand meaning by looking at what happens when things go wrong (even when you're not necessarily at fault).

What Is a Crisis?

In the context of brand management, let's start by excluding the type of equity decline that was discussed in Chapter 8. Crises, unless left to fester for a long time, do not necessitate revitalization, refreshing, or re-launch. Typically, crises effect brands regardless of their "health" and, if managed well, can hopefully avert sustained declines in equity (it is likely there will be some short-term downturn, however).

So what is a **brand crisis**? Let's start by examining the dictionary definition of "crisis." Crisis is defined in the following ways:

1. A crucial or decisive point or situation; a turning point (general)
2. An unstable condition, as in political, social, or economic affairs, involving an impending abrupt or decisive change (general)
3. A sudden change in the course of a disease or fever, toward either improvement or deterioration (medicine)
4. An emotionally stressful event or traumatic change in a person's life (psychology)
5. A point in a story or drama when a conflict reaches its highest tension and must be resolved (literature)

(*Source*: http://www.dictionary.com/browse/crisis,
accessed November 15, 2016)

As we shall see further on this chapter, there are many different types of brand crisis, some minor, some major, and, in rare cases, some fatal. The above definitions identify that a crisis represents an episode characterized by uncertainty, tension, and conflict, with potential for harm or decline. Intriguingly, however, a crisis can be a turning point for good, whereby the solution to the conflict results in a transformation. Following the literary definition in point 5 above, in hindsight a crisis may represent a key turning point in the brand's myth, often coming to represent important moral lessons for employees, users, and other meaning makers.

For example, the New Coke episode helped the organization understand the nature of the consumer–brand relationship in ways that arguably their dominant way of operating could not. The subsequent result was Classic Coke, a return to the brand's roots, while also providing the impetus to dethrone Pepsi and win the "cola wars" in the US. This is perhaps why New Coke is seen as one of marketing's greatest blunders and greatest triumphs (Klaassen, 2010). Vegemite's iSnack2.0 troubles also helped clarify the belief that Australians owned the brand. In fact, the team had little choice but to change the name, not so much due to external pressure (unlike New Coke, iSnack2.0 was successful in terms of sales, and targeted different users to Vegemite), but because brand manager Simon Talbot had stressed the importance of customer orientation to Kraft's revival in Australia.

However, the downside is that left untreated, a crisis can represent a turning point for the worse. In hindsight, this crisis might become part of branding folklore for all the wrong reasons! However, there are some critical reasons why **brand crisis management** is essential.

Why Manage Crises?

Barclays' CEO Bob Diamond seemed untouchable, until an ongoing series of crises involving unethical and at times illegal behavior saw the bank's reputation decline and its share price plummet. Institutional shareholders had little choice but to remove the outspoken CEO as part of a damage limitation strategy. The backlash from the phone-hacking scandal was so damaging to *News of the World* that owner Rupert Murdoch was forced to close the 169-year-old paper. The self-acceleration crisis that forced Toyota to recall some of its cars turned into a much larger and costlier crisis because of initial mismanagement. What was a simple product failure has cost the company US$3.1 billion in recall and class action settlement costs. The cost in brand equity is substantial, and the misstep also breathed life into struggling Ford and General Motors who benefited as a result.

Apart from the possibility of losing one's job and brand death, why it is important to have a proactive approach to crisis management?

1. The share market understands the value of reputation: This chapter began with a quote from famed institutional investor Warren Buffett. Buffett encapsulates a common view that damage to a firm's reputation is harmful to shareholder value

and therefore requires quick management. He has made clear to his own staff that all of them must act ethically to protect the reputation of his firm Berkshire Hathaway. As he stated (at the peak of the banking and investment scandals) in his internal memo to Berkshire Hathaway senior managers: "If you lose dollars for the firm by bad decisions, I will be understanding. If you lose reputation for the firm, I will be ruthless" (Hill 2011).

In the same memo, Buffett made clear that culture rather than formal rulebooks governed how firms should behave and expected to see significant changes in firms he invested in that had fallen foul of the law and societal expectations.

Given the success of the brand-as-asset model, share-market analysts (those who advise shareholders to "buy," "sell," or "hold" a stock) are particularly susceptible to crises that have the potential to damage the brand's reputation, thereby undermining its equity and its ability to generate returns over time. Should customer-based brand equity decline (i.e., the brand becomes less meaningful to users) then loyalty declines and markets adjust the value of a stock down to bring it into line with changed expectations regarding lifetime value and discounted cash flow.

Even small errors, if amplified by social media, can have enormous financial implications. "United Breaks Guitars" is a well-known example. When country and western singer Dave Carroll uploaded his song "United Breaks Guitars" onto YouTube the stock market took notice, wiping US$180 million off the value of the airline's stock (which for many undercapitalized US airlines is a huge amount). The song is available on YouTube and is a corny but cutting tale of poor service quality and the lack of customer focus at United Airlines (an airline with historically strong negative net promoter scores).

2. Changes in media mean that crises can quickly get out of hand: Before social media, information about crises could often be contained or localized, and diffused slowly, often taking days or weeks to be picked up by the mainstream media such as television news channels, newspapers and so on. With the advent of social media, information is often difficult to contain and diffuses rapidly. By the time the traditional media pick up the story, it is likely that the crisis is already spiraling out of control. This is demonstrated in Figure 12.2 that identifies the speed at which stories diffuse through social media, and Figure 12.3 showing how the "United Breaks Guitars" story broke.

Activist groups (including those critical of specific brands or brands in general) were early adopters of social media, and have become extremely effective at generating content and diffusing it quickly and widely. Many of these groups have their homepages hosted in countries with strong laws protecting free speech and their activities sit just outside of legal jurisdictions. Activist groups have a diffused structure, often switching between multiple homepages and

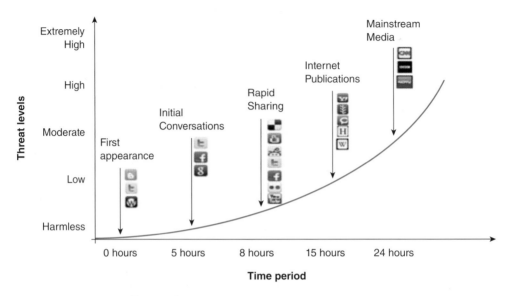

Figure 12.2   Media Diffusion of Crisis

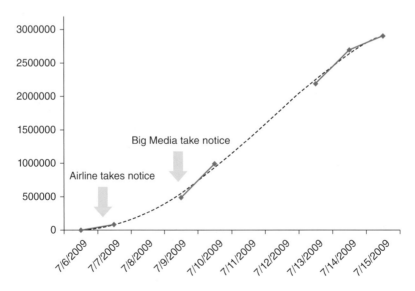

Figure 12.3   United Breaks Guitars Diffusion

accounts to avoid legal action (in terms of libel, defamation, and trademark infringement). Also, as the "McLibel" case demonstrated in the 1990s, while brands can often win on legal technicalities against activists (particularly in the UK where libel laws favor the plaintiffs), they can easily lose the **public relations** battle (Klein 2000).

3. Lying is increasingly harder to get away from: Crisis-management professionals focus on managing public perceptions about the disaster. Their main focus is first to contain the crisis, and minimize damage. Prior to social media, fact checking became difficult, particularly in the case of major crises where local governments may have wanted to reduce the chance of widespread panic or had more nefarious motivations such as covering up corruption, poor enforcement, or avoiding liability. Today this is increasingly difficult to achieve as fact checkers can easily challenge official press releases, insider leaks can spread widely, and we have seen the advent of hacker brands such as Wikileaks and Anonymous dedicated to challenging corporate and government interests.

   A graph showing the variances in reported spill flow rate shows how easy it is for the official version of events to be challenged or "fact checked." This identifies differences between BP's official version of how much oil was flowing into the Gulf of Mexico after the Deepwater Horizon spill and the actual rate as measured by scientists and other groups. BP is one of many companies criticized regularly for "green washing" (the attempt to project an image of being sustainable despite the reality of your operations). Repositioned in the 1990s, British Petroleum became "Beyond Petroleum" in order to position themselves away from non-renewable energy sources. However, activists have regularly challenged this, and point out that in 2008, for example, the company still had 93 percent of their income flowing from oil and gas.

   The classic approach of deny and contain is now much harder. Not only are claims subject to fact checking and insider leaks diffusing widely across social media, but also false claims can diffuse just as quickly and create a brand crisis.

4. The double-edged sword of "truthiness": Tommy Hilfiger has long been dogged by rumors that he has made racist comments about African Americans. There is no truth to this rumor, but nonetheless it has stuck and, with the advent of social media, re-emerges every now and again, necessitating another round of denials and press releases. Chapter 2 discussed the phenomenon of "truthiness" in relation to authenticity claims by brands. As long as the claims by the brand help consumers achieve self-authentication, which of course involves matching preconceived notions of real and fake, the brand's claim is judged positively.

   Truthiness, however, cuts both ways. Truthiness reflects a process of motivated reasoning, whereby we select information based on what we want to achieve, and screen out contradictory input. In the context of social media, writers talk about the "echo chamber" whereby like-minded people network together and create their own reality. In the aftermath of the 2015 UK election, for example, Twitter users expressed shock at David Cameron's Conservative (Tory) Party victory. Tweets and posts on other social media forums state, "No one I know voted Tory!" This of course could be true—after all we screen out information that does not fit with our desired identity (usually by "unfollowing" posters of such material) and avoid people and their networks that hold alternate views to our own (by "unfriending" them).

How does this affect brands? In the aftermath of Apple CEO Steve Jobs's death, some non-fans were quick to criticize him, arguing that his company had invented little and that, unlike Microsoft's Bill and Melinda Gates, he had given little to charity. Many fans were outraged, and quick to condemn such posters, closing off debate about the founder, despite that fact that such claims have some validity. In a story involving the wife of the leader of the Chinese Red Cross, it was alleged that she was siphoning money from the charity and using it to buy luxury goods. The claims turned out to be false, but nonetheless seemed true (truthy) in the context of widespread allegations and anger against corporate and government corruption in China. This allegation still affects the Red Cross and has damaged the charity's reputation and fundraising ability in that country.

5. Polysemy: This refers to the coexistence of many possible meanings for a word or phrase (Puntoni et al. 2010). In the context of branding, this can also include multiple meanings for codes, situations, and narratives. In previous chapters, we identified that this has a positive benefit when communicating across multiple audiences—for example, in the way that certain images are used to communicate with straights and gays, thereby reinforcing cultural legitimacy with the latter. However, polysemy also has a negative side, especially in the context of globally connected consumers and influencers.

In 2010, KFC faced a backlash against its advertising campaign. African American consumers saw the advertisements as reinforcing racist stereotypes, and quickly picketed outside the company's headquarters in Louisville, Kentucky. KFC was quick to pull the advertisements and apologize for any offence. The campaign, however, involved KFC's Australian operation, who had ran a sponsorship campaign involving the West Indian cricket team who were touring during the annual Summer of Cricket series. So what went wrong?

The advertisement played on the friendly fan rivalry between the two teams. West Indian fans have long brought a party-like atmosphere to cricket matches in Australia and are seen as boisterous, fun-loving, and passionate about the game. The advertisement in question featured a lone Australian fan in the middle of the West Indian fans, looking rather nervous and uncomfortable as he prepared for the inevitable jokes at his expense. His solution was to offer the fans a bucket of KFC. The advertisement ends with everyone partying and having a good time, something that reinforced the tradition of "play hard, party hard" of West Indies tours.

Australian fans read this ad as intended. The brand had a long history of sponsoring the West Indian team, and supportive campaigns showed the team relaxing after a day's play with KFC products. African American activists saw it in another light—as an openly racist advertisement where a lone white man, clearly uncomfortable, placates African Americans with fried chicken. The situation was read as reinforcing stereotypes that African Americans are dangerous, and that one can pay them off with fried food. Australian fans expressed surprise at this, reinforcing the feeling that Americans were ignorant of local traditions and simply "didn't get it." However, the relative market size of Australia versus America meant head office quickly pulled an advertising campaign they had authorized.

Polysemy is tricky to manage, as advertisements can be read in many different ways. Careful testing and segmentation can help, as the discussion of 42 Below's seemingly homophobic advertisements demonstrates (see Chapter 6). Nonetheless, the coexistence of multiple meanings can easily generate a backlash, especially when one is communicating as a subcultural insider under the cultural positioning model.

6.   A quick response, with the right tone of voice, can represent a win for the brand: Johnson & Johnson's decision to quickly pull all of their Tylenol from store shelves after they received a tip-off that someone had poisoned some with cyanide is seen as the industry standard for dealing with such crises. The corporate brand's reputation was reinforced because they were seen as placing the health of the public above commercial concerns. This approach to recall is defined by risk-management techniques that stress that the harm from not doing anything and being wrong is greater than the chance that the fault does not exist or no one will be harmed.

As the Greggs example shows, a fast response and the appropriate tone (in this context playfulness complemented by messages about the quality of their products and their customer focus) can quickly turn a crisis into a positive. One needs to be careful, however—although the idea of the "service recovery paradox" is still popular (see Brand Aside 12.1), it has largely been disproven in numerous studies and is no longer taken seriously by service marketing academics. As the very least, good recovery helps minimize harm rather than provide a positive lift for the relationship (the brand relationship typically declines somewhat after a significant failure). For minor crises, including customer parodies such as that of Greggs, a quick, self-deprecating response can turn a negative into a positive.

BRAND ASIDE 12.1

The Service-recovery Paradox – Real or Fake?

In 1992, scholars at the annual American Marketing Association Summer Educators Conference presented some intriguing results from a study of service recovery and satisfaction. Service recovery is an important idea in service management and stresses the importance of having strategies in place to ensure that failures (which are likely) are managed and that the inconvenienced customer is "recovered" so they do not switch. The 1992 paper drew on an old idea that strong service recovery could in fact make customers more loyal. The authors went one step further suggesting service recovery could be used to ensure retention and encouraged the belief that getting things wrong and then righting them might, paradoxically, be a great strategy.

The authors' follow-up paper where they were unable to replicate their results quickly recanted the idea of a paradox. However, the idea of a service-recovery paradox caught on and led many to believe that transgressions represented opportunities to make loyal customers even more committed to the brand. Subsequent studies, including a meta-analysis, have demonstrated that the service-recovery paradox rarely occurs, and only really operates in fairly mediocre service systems. Things will always go wrong in human systems, and service recovery strategies are important to avoiding a full-blown crisis, but greater value can be gained by investing in service quality beforehand.

Are All Crises the Same?

This chapter covers a number of examples of crisis. They can seem relatively innocuous, such as Apple's iPhone 4 signaling problems, self-inflicted (such as those of New Zealand brewer Tui), position-defining events such as New Coke, fatal disasters such as those involving *News of the World*, or shifts in public perception that challenge the legitimacy of entire industries or related practices (see the SeaWorld and *Blackfish* case at the end of the chapter).

It is common to treat all brand-related crises in the same way; however, different types of crisis require different responses. Much depends on the brand's position and how consumers frame their relationship.

For example, while oil spills and environmental damage are unfortunately a fact of life for many resource extraction industries, the disasters triggered by failures at Exxon and BP had very different outcomes for each brand. Why? Positioning. BP after all was "Beyond Petroleum" whereas Exxon does not have a strong brand-driven approach and certainly not a sincerity-based position focused on environmental sustainability. Brands positioned in terms of emotions, aspiration, culture, and identity, or social missions often suffer a different "authenticity crisis" from brands positioned on functional performance advantages. Although it is commonly believed that stronger brand relationships provide the brand with a buffer against mistakes, research suggests transgressions may heighten consumer anger resulting in a **"love becomes hate" effect** (Grégoire et al. 2009). Brand Aside 12.2 provides more details.

BRAND ASIDE 12.2

The "Love Becomes Hate" Effect

With the emergence of relationship marketing in the 1990s much has been made of the ability of strong relationships to act as a protective buffer when things go wrong. One of the reasons firms are encouraged to increase loyalty to their brands is that customers are believed to be more forgiving in the case of failures, transgressions, or crises. Much of this idea is drawn from personal relationships, where the harmed partner may forgive the transgressor because of how much they have invested in the relationship, perceptions of future gain from remaining together, and social norms stressing the importance of forgiveness. However, studies have questioned these assumptions, identifying that customers do not treat brand relationships in exactly the same way as interpersonal ones (Blocker et al. 2012), that the ways in which customers frame the relationship can impact on how they respond to transgressions (Beverland et al. 2010), and that love can quickly turn to hate (Grégoire et al. 2009).

In regard to the latter effect, Grégoire et al. (2009) identified that those customers with the strongest relationships may hold a grudge after a failure much longer than those with weaker ones. Not only do your best customers hold a grudge for longer, over time they are more likely to ruminate over the transgressions, engaging in a process called "counter-factual" thinking (whereby they compare what happened to their beliefs about what should have happened and reposition the relationship accordingly), and are more likely to seek revenge and/or switch to another provider. That is, love, quickly turns to lasting hate. The authors identify that any form of service recovery, financial or a mere apology, can help lessen the likelihood that your best customers will hold a lasting grudge.

Table 12.1   Understanding different types of brand crisis

Crisis type	Nature of	Cause	Solution	Danger
Reputational	Crisis affects firm behind brand.	Major disaster or breach of social norms that lies outside of brand management team.	Whole of firm response; CEO critical.	Negative brand equity
Authenticity	The basis of the brand's identity is challenged.	For functional brands, performance failures are the key driver. For emotionally positioned brands, failures relate to value-gaps.	Functional: fix the problem and recompense for any losses. Emotional: apologize, acknowledge fault, restore customer trust, and rebuild authenticity.	Functional: left too long, costs can escalate, scrutiny can remove focus from organization; competitors can take advantage; equity can decline. Emotional: equity can decline, grudge holding can occur.
Legitimacy	The activities at the heart of the brand lose moral legitimacy.	Society or a sub-set of society withdraws moral support for all or some part of the brand's operations; often triggered by activist groups or media investigations.	Whole of firm response; work with stakeholders; recognize that legitimacy may never be regained.	Possibility of brand death unless a major reposition occurs.
Self-inflicted Wounds	Unplanned but easily avoided ("known knowns"), minor mistakes that affect brand image.	Firm employees make mistakes that breach expected brand norms or more likely societal expectations.	Marketing team and guilty organizational parties need to quickly respond, and take ownership of fault; training and brand policing critical.	If untreated, can become major crisis; ongoing mis-steps can effect reputation.
Deliberate	Firm triggers faux crisis in order to generate a buzz and clarify positioning.	Brand team engages in guerrilla style tactics to breach societal norms, or leverage institutions to generate a buzz about brand that implicitly reinforces its position in a positive way.	Brand manager sign off. Know the brand's position and know the target audience in depth. Seed key networks.	It could backfire and spiral into a full-blown crisis; viral campaigns quickly move beyond marketer control; consumers may feel cheated.

So what types of commonly occurring crises are there? Five are listed below. Table 12.1 provides further details of each. It's important to remember these crises may overlap, may occur to different degrees, may be perceived differently by different meaning creators, and require different strategies. And failing to manage each appropriately can ensure a small transgression or mistake can turn into a much larger, equity threatening disaster that quickly gets out of hand. The five are:

1. **Reputational crises**: Reputation is something that applies more to the organization than to the brand per se. This can get blurred in the case of corporate brands (see Chapter 10), but nonetheless reputational crises are often things that

are largely out of the control of the brand team, may not be directly caused by brand or marketing issues, and require a wider organizational response. However, it is critical that they be addressed as the future of the brand may be at stake, and it's almost certain that negative associations may drive down the brand's equity.

So what is a reputational crisis? Examples include the BP Deepwater Horizon disaster, Johnson & Johnson's Tylenol experience, the *News of the World* and the phone-hacking scandal, the recent Malaysia Airlines experience involving one airliner that was lost at sea (and has still to be found) and one shot down over disputed territory in the Ukraine. Other examples would include the ValuJet Flight 592, Iceland's horsemeat scandal, the Costa Concordia sinking off the coast of Italy, and Dior designer John Galliano's drug-fueled anti-Semitic rant. Reputational crises are those that affect the brand indirectly, and require an all of firm response.

How should one respond to reputational crises? The answer very much depends on how bad the crisis is. In the case of ValuJet, subsequent investigations revealed major shortcomings in maintenance and safety checks, largely out of a desire to save money. These revelations dealt a killer blow to the discount airline, and broke a core point of parity (safety) in the airline sector. Like the *News of the World*, the ValuJet brand's equity was negative. Despite being cleared for operation by civil aviation authorities, the brand's name turned away wary customers, and eventually it had to be rebranded as AirTran. Similar examples affected American Insurance Group (AIG) (and other financial institutions) after the global financial crisis. The brand's problems were primarily located in the United States, but the entire global group suffered as a result, necessitating a de-merger and dropping of the AIG name in offshore markets.

As identified in Table 12.1 reputational crises require a whole of firm response. The Deepwater Horizon spill, for example, presented the BP brand team with problems, but ending the crisis involved the CEO, teams of engineers, public relations experts, lawyers, and operational experts. In these instances, the brand team probably needs to consider whether further advertising campaigns or other forms of brand reinforcement or innovation are best delayed, lest they fail due to widespread anger and negative publicity about the brand.

Critical to solving these crises is taking responsibility for the problem, ensuring it gets fixed as soon as possible, openness and honesty, and compensating those who have suffered. Subsequent change in organizational practices is also advised. The correct tone of voice is crucial, as can be seen by the anger surrounding BP's then CEO Tony Hayward's claim that he wanted his life back during the peak of the crisis.

BRAND ASIDE 12.3

No Logo: Holding Brands to Account

Released in 1999 at a time defined by waves of protests against free trade and globalization, Canadian Naomi Klein's bestselling *No Logo: Taking Aim at the Brand Bullies* quickly became a rallying point for those concerned about the increasing power of brands in the social sphere. Klein's book covers a lot of ground, focusing on the increased power of brands, and how people have begun to push back against this power. From a branding point of view, *No Logo* holds a mirror up to those brands with highly emotional or aspirational positions. Thus Nike's off-shore manufacturing partners' labor practices were not just criticized because they breached duties of care or ethical beliefs; they were attacked because they ran counter to the brand's aspirational lifestyle.

In effect this is an authenticity attack, and a particularly damaging one. Klein identified that such critiques were powerful because they could quickly reframe brand image in the minds of customers in wealthy markets and other influencers, thereby leading to further activism, protests, picketing, and boycotts, and, of course, declining equity. The aftermath of the labor scandals saw Nike's profit performance drop sharply (while that of Adidas improved), much to the chagrin of shareholders. Although written about events where the Internet was only in its infancy, Klein identified that social media would be a powerful tool in the fight against global brands, and also identified the basis for doppelgänger brand image in her chapter entitled, "Brand Boomerang."

2. **Authenticity crises**: Naomi Klein's influential *No Logo* (see Brand Aside 12.3) book represented an authenticity attack on brands. In essence, she argued that brands said one thing, but did another. Any aspirational claims they made were, when subject to scrutiny, fake. In many ways these types of critiques blur the lines between different types of crises, but the logic of brands not living up to their stated identity represents an authenticity crisis. There are two common types of authenticity crises: functional and emotional.

For functionally positioned brands, **authenticity crises** stem from some failure, typically in product performance or service that undermines key brand claims. Toyota's recent experience with its automatic acceleration problems is a classic example. The venerable Japanese brand is known for reliability and quality, so the failure of such an important feature of any vehicle creates a crisis of authenticity. Nonetheless, these crises (despite Toyota's initial mismanagement) are relatively easy to solve because customers simply want the problem to be fixed and, critically, want to feel the company is working on that problem.

Responding to these crises involves the brand team working with the relative parties to ensure the problem is solved. Critical to addressing many of these crises in products is a recall and replacement or compensation strategy. Toyota, for example, recalled its faulty vehicles, did a thorough check on all its fleet, and recalled several other vehicle types as a result. The cost was significant, but over time trust in the brand returned and the effect of the crisis was short-lived (and could be used again to reinforce the brand's commitment to quality, especially internally).

For service brands, such authenticity failures typically involve revisions to hiring, training and procedures, and compensation. Again, the effect of these is often short-lived.

BRAND ASIDE 12.4

When Good Brands Go Bad?

Does brand image affect how consumers respond to crises? Aaker et al. (2004) demonstrate that it does, and in surprising ways. Conducting experiments with hypothetical brands with "exciting" and "sincere" (i.e., authentic) personalities, the authors found that sincere brands suffered more from failures, while exciting ones seemed to benefit from transgressions. As a result, brand relationships for sincere brands weakened after transgressions while the opposite happened with exciting brands. Why? Both brands encouraged different types of relationship—sincere brands encouraged much closer, more intimate relationships, whereas exciting brands resulted in looser relationships, more akin to a short-term "fling" or "affair." Thus, when the exciting brand did go wrong, it was expected and in many ways reinforced the brand's exciting status (rebels after all are supposed to be dangerous), while the sincere brand was the equivalent of a spouse finding out about a marital affair—the hurt was much deeper and longer lasting (relationships with sincere brands never returned to their pre-transgression status).

This article is one of several that began to question the tendency to oversell relationship strategies or ignore the negative implications of strong brand relationships or emotional framing of brands.

Emotional brands present a different authenticity crisis. Beverland et al. (2010) examined how consumers dealt with relationship transgressions in brand-related behavior. Much to their surprise, they found that consumers could engage in extended grudge-holding that in some cases was seemingly out of all proportion to the harm done, while they could also appear quite relaxed in cases where it was reasonable to be angry. Others have found similar effects (see Brand Aside 12.4). Depending on how the consumer framed their brand relationship, they could engage in negative or positive conflict-management styles, with very different outcomes for brand equity.

This research identifies the downsides of emotional or identity positioning. When brand managers frame their brand position in highly personal terms, consumers reframe not only the relationship, but also their expectations of behavior, including what is right, appropriate, and fair. Unsurprisingly, they react much more negatively when an emotional or sincere brand breaches key norms and, critically, offering them economic compensation only makes matters worse.

How should one deal with this type of **authenticity crisis**? This very much depends on the cause. If it is a lack of authenticity relative to the populist world one is attempting to relate to, then any reaction must be framed in terms that will be acceptable to members within those communities (economic compensation may not cut it). Tommy Hilfiger, for example, eventually asked premier civil rights organization the Anti-Defamation League (ADL) to investigate whether he made a series of racist comments about ethnic groups central to his brand's image and cool. After an exhaustive investigation the ADL concluded there was no case to answer (nonetheless Hilfiger is still dealing with such rumors, thanks to regular re-tweets of old allegations).

In all cases, **empathetic communication** is the key. This type of communication demonstrates that you understand the breach from the point of view of the aggrieved party and are communicating in a respectful way and that reasserts the user's previous relationship status. It is critical to do this quickly, as hurt consumers can ruminate over the episode, reconfigure brand relationships, and engage in extensive grudge-holding including deliberate damage to the firm and negative word of mouth.

3. **Crises of legitimacy**: There are many activities that were once acceptable but are no longer (and vice versa of course). **Moral legitimacy** relates to whether society or a critical (to the brand) subset of society believes you have the right to operate as you do. The *Blackfish* vs. SeaWorld case at the end of this chapter provides one such example. In this case, increasing questions about the rights of non-human animals (including the Cambridge 2012 Declaration of Animal Consciousness) mean that society re-evaluating certain activities including using them for entertainment, causing them pain and harm, keeping them in conditions at odds with their

emotional flourishing, and even killing them for food (Beverland 2014). Historically, other industries, including human slavery, tobacco and alcohol production, and weapons, have faced or periodically faced societal censure.

Many of these issues have been covered already in Chapter 11 on brand ethics, but suffice to say when such a crisis emerges, it can quickly get out of hand as SeaWorld has found, and may represent an existential challenge to the brand per se. How after all can a brand focused on animal entertainment reposition when the core activity that has generated value is increasingly being seen as illegitimate, and turning away customers (resulting in a plummeting share price)?

Dealing with these threats is tricky, and often by the time they have emerged into the mainstream, the crisis is already beyond the control of management. In the case of tobacco and alcohol, greater regulation may lend the industry some legitimacy in the eyes of users, while reframing concerns about gun-related deaths in the US as an issue of personal freedom has been very successful (although arguably this relies on a very particular historical and legal context).

Working with critics may also help, but again, typically brands start to engage when the crisis is spiraling out of control. One critical approach would therefore be to monitor anti-brand websites and be aware of those opposed to your operation and proactively work with them, or develop strategies to deflect criticism.

For example, in their operation there is often little difference between entertainment organizations like SeaWorld and zoos, but many zoos have been more proactive in managing perceptions of legitimacy—they have stopped taking animals from the wild, developed critical breeding programs to conserve species, often used animals that have been hurt and cannot be returned to the wild, and rebuilt many enclosures so the captive animals have a more natural existence. On a recent (February 2017) visit to one popular zoo, Healesville Animal Sanctuary in Melbourne, staff noticeably stressed the role zoos play in staving off extinction, by emphasizing breeding programs and re-release into the wild. This was done to counter criticism from animal rights groups arguing they are little more than exploitative entertainment empires.

4. **Self-inflicted wounds**: We can all recall silly "what were they thinking" errors made by brands. Usually these involve what seem to be known knowns or things we could easily predict should be avoided—the iSnack2.0 name being an obvious example. These can easily occur in very large, diffuse organizations and/or those that rely on contractors and outsource much of their operations. Things can and do go wrong, and a lack of clear policing and internal brand guidelines can result in self-inflicted wounds.

New Zealand brewer Tui experienced this with the 2013 vote to legalize gay marriage. The vote passed relatively easily and was seen as an example of democracy at its best. Members were allowed to vote their according to their consciences, ensuring a respectful tone and general feeling that everyone's voice was being heard. New Zealand society is relatively liberal and there was little doubt the move was extremely popular as it reinforced the leadership position on social issues that the country had become famous for. So how did Tui miss this?

Tui is an old regional beer brand that was refreshed and launched on a national scale in the 1990s. Since 1994, quirky billboard campaigns have lain at the heart of its success and growth (to be one of the biggest brands locally). Figure 12.4 provides three examples, including the offending one. The billboards typically play on local colloquial expressions and everyday humor. Critically, every message is ended with the ironic saying "yeah right." For example: "It actually makes your bum look small," "I'm actually going to study really hard this year" (placed outside universities), "England is the best" (used during cricket test matches), and so on. These are so popular that they have been published in a bestselling book.

The brand has become known for quickly launching new billboards to respond to local memes, celebrity errors, and key events. The day after the gay marriage vote the brand once again launched a billboard, but this one did not have the intended effect: "Dad's new husband seems nice. Yeah right." The brand made things worse by defending their choice amidst widespread anger and consumer backlash, potentially placing its cool factor in jeopardy.

Tui's response was not particularly clever, and despite defending the billboard as one that "might not always hit the mark" it was quickly removed. However, it's

Figure 12.4 Tui Roadside Billboards

Source: author's file

hard to understand how a brand team known for understanding local sentiment made such an error in the first place. A better response might have been to pull the campaign quickly and, being a beer brand, sponsor the local Hero party, and run a series of self-deprecating billboards (poking fun at the marketing team) instead. These types of crisis can quickly get out of hand, but it's critical to re-examine internal sign-off processes and training to ensure employees do not make these errors regularly.

5. Deliberate: A search on the Internet will quickly identify web pages (http://www.obscure.org/~bob/stuff/coke.html) sites dedicated to identifying large crises as conspiracies—New Coke is a favorite, but Vegemite has also generated its own conspiracy theories. The idea is simple; brands struggling for relevance deliberately create a crisis to re-engage the public. Since it works in politics, the logic of creating a distraction and then managing it to an effective, but planned, outcome is brilliant impression management. For Vegemite, iSnack 2.0 was a foolish mistake handled well, whereas for New Coke, the sheer expense and ethos of the company mean any conspiracy is highly unlikely (albeit such claims are not unfavorable to the brand's mythology). However, the question remains, can, and should, brands manufacture a crisis?

In many ways, shocking customers and breaching societal conventions have always paid off. Everyone in the music industry knows the value of a record being banned (just ask The Sex Pistols), while French Connection's FCUK campaign and Benetton's confronting billboards all paid off handsomely. Ryanair is also known to regularly entertain the idea of customers having to pay to use the toilet on flights, or of offering stand-up "second-class" fares. Such campaigns regularly generate outrage, usually on the front page of big-selling tabloids such as the *Daily Mail*, all of which reinforces to their target customer that the airline will stop at nothing to get fares down.

UK-based brewery BrewDog has built much of its brand equity around a punk ethos (its flagship IPA is called "Punk"), often refusing to withdraw advertisements judged to breach accepted standards, only for journalists to discover much later that the complaints against the advertisement came from the brand's CEO, James Watt (Henley 2016). New Zealand's 42 Below similarly stimulated a crisis, criticizing industry behemoth Absolut and falling foul of the industry regulator. The response can be found in 42 Below's public retraction, where the firm apologizes for stating Absolut was the vodka judges "least favourite" rather than the more correct "no kind words to say about Absolut".

One needs to be careful in engaging in this tactic. Firms that do this do run the risk of a backlash if customers feel cheated—it is a fine line between appreciating being punk'd and feeling like one has been taken for a ride. Nevertheless, these campaigns are usually thought through carefully. Clearly, brand managers behind the Ryanair announcements know their audience and also know that the tabloid press is infinitely gullible. Likewise, 42 Below, run by former Saatchi & Saatchi creatives, know that in printing their letter they are sending a powerful message about priorities—that unlike Absolut, 42 Below are focused on producing great vodka. Much the same can be said for BrewDog, who are deliberately trying to shake up conventions in the traditional world of craft brewing.

The benefits to this approach are obvious—one can generate a buzz and publicity, remind people about the brand's benefits, and increase social media awareness, sentiment, and mentions, all at little cost.

Tone of Voice

Tone of voice has been covered in Chapter 5 in terms of bringing the brand position to life. However, public relations specialists and reputation managers also use the phrase when discussing how to communicate information within a crisis (and in general, how to communicate to preempt them). So what do they recommend? The following information comes from studies on how key stakeholders including financial markets judge communication from brands (Spratt 2011):

1. In descending order, brand reputation leaders are typically those that inform (in their area of expertise), listen, educate, engage, and solve problems.
2. In descending order, tactically, those brands with the strongest reputations speak plainly, speak only when they have something useful to say, engage in a two-way conversation, have a global outlook, and are first to comment on news relevant to their sphere of activity.
3. In descending order, the tone of voice used by senior spokespeople should be positive, human, friendly, concise, and humorous (where appropriate).
4. In descending order, brand leadership comes from expertise, driving change within an industry, fronting the media in good times and bad, being big enough to admit fault, and sharing information where relevant.

US airline Delta was roundly criticized for its failure to apologize to Dr Tamika Cross after she alleged flight attendants refused to believe she was a medical doctor during an emergency because she was an African American (see Chapter 11). The story is one of many that reflects the prejudice minorities experience every day, and came at a time (October 2016) of increased attention on issues of discrimination including micro-aggressions, alleged police brutality, and increased support for far-right groups in the USA. It also triggered reports of many other instances of large brands discriminating against minorities in the USA. Delta's official Facebook statement regarding the incident reaffirmed its formal commitment to diversity, but failed to address a single allegation made by Cross, and was widely condemned as being insincere.

Reframing

Macworld events involving the launch of new products by former CEO Steve Jobs usually went without a hitch. Carefully planned and scripted, these events became part of the brand's folklore, were heavily over-subscribed, reported as news around the world, and provided the launch pad for the next generation of innovations from one of the world's premier technology brands. The launch of the iPhone 4 did not, however, go to plan. Unable to get a Wi-Fi connection during Jobs's presentation, the crowd quickly started to jeer and boo—this was the type of failure competitors were known for. The problem was that the product had been shipped to thousands of customers and it was too late to do anything about it.

So how did Apple respond? Taking a technique straight out of a public relations manager's handbook, they **reframed** the problem. The problem arose because the firm wanted to push the capabilities of the phone further while at the same time making the handset sleeker and lighter. Their failure to identify the problem prior to launch seemed to be a classic amateurish error. Clearly, it was a firm-level fault and one of the few missteps by Apple at the time. However, Jobs reframed this problem as an "industry problem" and immediately took the heat out of the failure. This reframing deflects blame for the fault, and is an attempt to change the nature of the conversation and, of course, control it. Customers were provided with a sleeve design that enabled perfect Wi-Fi connection and subsequent releases fixed the problem.

Contingency Planning

Why did Simon Talbot and his team at Vegemite change tack so quickly when consumer sentiment quickly went against iSnack2.0 as a name choice? Simple—they had prepared. Talbot had the benefit of learning about New Coke in his MBA course and as part of the brand extension program had compiled an impressive dossier on previous attempts to change iconic brands. The one key lesson—when public perception goes against you, don't swim against the tide (in contrast the team at Coke spent months defending their New Coke decision, arguing that "a little push back was to be expected").

The brands as asset approach has historically been framed in terms of a growth logic—that is, how do we grow the value of the brand? However, financial markets complement this with **risk management** logic (higher risks are associated with higher returns). Risk management is not cautious about growth; rather, the focus shifts to identifying, minimizing and preparing for any reasonable threats to growth. With so much firm value tied up in intangibles, for brands in particular, preparing for crisis is a sensible strategy for protecting the brand asset and also for ensuring more nuanced approaches to brand growth that take into account the potential for backlash among meaning creators, and place reputation at the heart of scenario planning and risk assessment.

In closing, apart from tone of voice, brand crisis planning and management can be enhanced in four ways (these are particularly critical if you intend to engage in deliberate crises):

1. Understand your position: Many crises stem from disconnects between the espoused brand position and your actions. The Tui example is a classic example—the brand's image is one of an everyday expression of Kiwi (New Zealand) life. Had the brand team realized this, they would have thought twice about running the offending billboard. Likewise, Vegemite's belief that the brand was owned by the consumer would have told them that the strategy of choosing a brand name behind closed doors, rather than further engagement through a public vote, had the potential to fail.

2. Understand co-creation: Be aware that your brand's meaning is shaped by the four meaning makers identified in Chapter 1 and in Figure 1.1. In so doing, you are more likely to draw on more sources of information and pick up on emerging concerns, critiques, and parodies that will enable you to craft responses to preempt crisis and potentially reinforce or clarify your brand position and claims of authenticity.

3. Understand how information flows: Influencer networks are so critical in determining the impact of information and speed of diffusion. Figure 12.5 identifies how information flows in the UK and US stock market. Equity analysts are those that publish advice on stocks to buy, sell, or hold. If you understand how information

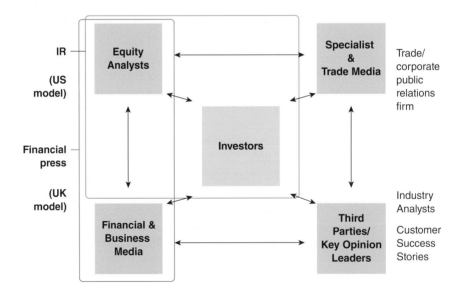

Figure 12.5   Information channels in US/UK share markets

Source: Spratt 2011

flows, not only can you track those sources, you can also be mindful of when things are likely to start impacting on analysts, who may decide to write down your stock, which might ensure you avoid a uncomfortable meeting with an irate CEO.

4. Understand stakeholder concerns: Building on the above example from the share market, it is critical to understand the information that concerns stakeholders. For example, Figure 12.6 identifies how shareholders judge different types of crises. By examining this we can understand why "United Breaks Guitars" had such a big effect—the poor service articulated in a corny country and western song identified United Airlines' famed service improvement program had failed to have any effect on the brand's long-term negative rating.

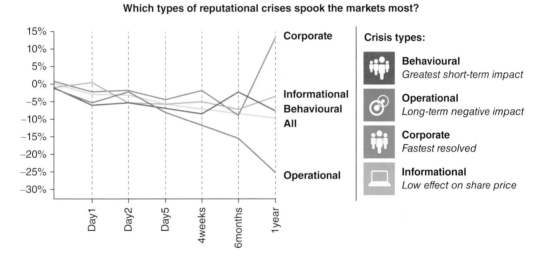

Figure 12.6   Reputation Crises and Impacts

Source: Freshfields Crisis Management Study, 2012

Chapter Summary

The concern with defining and measuring brand equity arose from branding existential crisis (represented by "Marlborough Friday"), so it is perhaps apt to end with a focus on managing brand crises (albeit of a different order). The emergence of social media has increased the likelihood of brand crisis. The nature of much social media discussion also means that the truth or falsehood of such claims do not matter, so much as how one responds. Brands are also victims of their own success. The very ubiquity of brands means they attract criticism, sometimes unfair (often not), or are viewed as resources by activists seeking to drive social change (you can easily adjust Figure 3.3 to include activists as meaning makers and what they seek from brands).

Crisis is therefore something that is likely to happen, is hard to predict, and potentially damaging, although possibly represents an opportunity.

This chapter has identified the nature of a brand crisis, and discussed why the brand as asset approach has led to increased concerns over reputation and necessitated the need to manage brand crises strategically and quickly. It has identified five types of brand crises, suggesting different types of responses, and discussed the importance of tone of voice. Finally, the chapter has emphasized the need for contingency and scenario planning, as part of the shift towards greater risk-management logic in branding.

Review Questions

1. Identify five common criticisms directed toward brands that could affect their value.
2. Identify five potential areas where brands could face criticism. These issues are unlikely to yet concern the brand's target audience, but nonetheless could represent a threat to any brand.

Case Example: SeaWorld and *Blackfish*

SeaWorld is a US-based chain that features cetaceans and sea lions in a range of entertainment shows. Long a target of animal rights groups, the brand has been rocked by a 2013 documentary called *Blackfish* that was produced after a trainer was killed by an orca or killer whale. The critically lauded documentary focused around one male orca, Tilikum, who was taken from the wild when he was very young, and who had been involved in three deaths in the park. The heart-rending scenes of the young orca being removed from his family pod (where the mother was heard screaming), and allegations of abuse and mental damage resulting from being confined in a tiny pool without company, generated a crisis for SeaWorld, leading to plummeting stock prices, reduced visits, and widespread criticism from former employees and animal welfare advocates.

The documentary focused on the deaths of experienced trainers due to what the company maintained were accidents or even trainer error during shows involving close interaction with Orcas. In telling Tilikum's backstory, the documentary team drew on whale experts identifying that cetaceans are extremely intelligent beings, and that it is entirely possible, due to isolation and abuse, that Tilikum was in fact killing trainers due to frustration and anger. The fault for this was laid squarely at the feet of the corporate brand, SeaWorld Parks & Entertainment (who had experienced similar deaths in their operations around the world). SeaWorld did not take part in the documentary, but much of the film focused on the lengths the brand would go to co-opt other trainers to lay the blame for accidents and deaths on staff error to avoid legal reparations from families and manage the impression that keeping orcas in confinement did not have a detrimental effect on their welfare or mental wellbeing.

SeaWorld invested heavily in public relations, refuting the claims made in *Blackfish*, threatening the documentary crew legally, and even going so far as to doctor a poll in the *Orlando Business Journal* where they asked readers' opinions of whether the film had changed their view of SeaWorld—most said "no," but the brand team were caught out when it was found 55 percent of the votes came from a SeaWorld ISP address. The reaction of a range of stakeholders was swift with major music artists such as Heart and The Beach Boys (among many others) withdrawing from planned concerts at the Orlando theme park, attendance dropped 5 percent, Southwest Airlines ended its partnership with SeaWorld in 2014 after public pressure to do so, and numerous states and countries adopted legislation to the ban keeping cetaceans in captivity. After further criticism, SeaWorld announced a shift in its shows to focus on education. However, the Orca Encounter shift was quickly condemned by animal rights activists and did little to stem the brand's slide.

Animal rights issues have advanced substantially in the past 20 years and have crossed over from the fringe into the mainstream. Recently courts in India and Argentina have attributed non-human rights to certain species, including cetaceans, while the non-human rights project in the US has been slowly building a case for habeas corpus (an ancient law banning unlawful detention or imprisonment) to be applied to highly intelligent animals such as bears, apes, and whales. In July 7, 2012 scientists gathered at Cambridge to make the Cambridge Declaration of Animal Consciousness, identifying that the scientific consensus was that vast numbers of non-human species were conscious, and therefore deserving of rights. Around the globe, industries using animals for entertainment have been banned or heavily criticized, including the Ringling Brothers Circus (which closed down in May 2017), animal testing for pharmaceuticals and cosmetics, and horse and carriage rides, while movie and television shows are subject to sustained criticism for using live animals given CGI capabilities.

The impact on share price was substantial, falling 50 percent in 2014, triggering a lawsuit by shareholder representatives who alleged that a refusal to

(Continued)

acknowledge and address the *Blackfish* claims may have amounted to management negligence. By 2015, SeaWorld had announced it would end its captive orca shows (by 2019) and its breeding programs, although activists quickly pointed out that the firm had plans to expand in countries such as China where animal rights laws are less developed (although public opinion is fast catching up with that elsewhere and many of the emerging national economies are seen as the new battle-line for animal rights groups impressed at the speed of change and shift in opinions).

On January 8, orca Tilikum died at the young age of 36 from poor health. The park had kept him in solitary confinement in a small pool and withdrawn him from shows since his fatal attack on trainer Dawn Brancheau in 2010. SeaWorld announced it was ending its orca shows, laying off a number of staff, while opening their first non-orca show in Abu Dhabi.

Case Questions

1. Do you think the SeaWorld brand can continue to operate in the same way as it has in the past? Identify reasons why and why not.
2. What type of authenticity crisis is SeaWorld suffering? Was this a result of failing to deal with an earlier type of authenticity crisis?
3. How could SeaWorld have avoided its current fate?
4. How should SeaWorld deal with the current brand crisis?

Key Terms

Authenticity crisis
Brand crisis
Brand crisis
management
Contingency
planning

Crises of legitimacy
Empathetic
communication
Love becomes hate
effect
Moral legitimacy

Public relations
Reframing
Reputational crises
Risk management
Self-inflicted wounds

Further Reading

Aaker, Jennifer, Susan Fournier, and S. Adam Brasel (2004), "When Good Brands do Bad," *Journal of Consumer Research*, 31(June), 1–16.

Beverland, Michael B., Steven M. Kates, Adam Lindgreen and Emily Chung (2010), "Exploring Consumer Conflict in Service Encounters," *Journal of the Academy of Marketing Science*, 83, 617–633.

Blackfish: Never Capture What You Can't Control. http://www.blackfishmovie.com.

Earl, Steve and Stephen Waddington (2012), *Brand Anarchy: Managing Corporate Reputation*, Bloomsbury: London.

Grégoire, Yany, Thomas M. Tripp, and Renaud Legoux (2009), "When Customer Love Turns into Lasting Hate: The Effects of Relationship Strength and Time on Customer Revenge and Avoidance," *Journal of Marketing*, 73(Nov.), 18–32.

References

Aaker, David (2014), *Aaker on Branding: 20 Principles that Drive Success*, Morgan James Publishing, Virginia.

Aaker, David A. (2012), "Win the Brand Relevance Battle and Then Build Competitor Barriers," *California Management Review*, 54(2), 43–57.

Aaker, David (1996), *Building Strong Brands*, Simon & Schuster, New York.

Aaker, David (1991), *Managing Brand Equity*, The Free Press, New York.

Aaker, David and Erich Joachimsthaler (2009), *Brand Leadership*, Simon & Schuster, London.

Aaker, David and Erich Joachimsthaler (2000), "The Brand Relationship Spectrum: The Key to the Brand Architecture Challenge," *California Management Review*, 42(4), 8–23.

Aaker, Jennifer, Susan Fournier, and S. Adam Brasel (2004), "When Good Bands Do Bad," *Journal of Consumer Research*, 31(June), 1–16.

Ahuvia, Aaron and Elif Izberk-Bilgin (2011), "Limits of the McDonaldization Thesis: eBayization and Ascendant Trends in Post-Industrial Consumer Culture," *Consumption Markets & Culture*, 14(4), 361–384.

Albrow, Martin and Elizabeth King (1990). *Globalization, Knowledge and Society*, Sage, London.

Anderson, Benedict (1983). *Imagined Communities*, Verso, London.

Anderson, Chris (2006), *The Long Tail: Why the Future of Business is Selling Less is More*, Hyperion, New York.

Ariely, Dan (2009), *Predictably Irrational: The Hidden Forces that Shape Our Decisions*, HarperCollins, New York.

Arnould, Eric J. (2007), "Should Consumer Citizens Escape the Market?", *The Annals of the American Academy of Political and Social Science,* 611(May), 96–111.

Arnould, Eric J. and Linda L. Price (2000), "Authenticating Acts and Authoritative Performances: Questing for Self and Community," in S. Ratneshwar, David G. Mick, and Cynthia Huffman (eds.), *The Why of Consumption: Contemporary Perspectives on Consumer Motives, Goals, and Desires*, Routledge, London, pp. 140–163.

Arnould, Eric J. and Craig J. Thompson (2005), "Consumer Culture Theory (CCT): Twenty Years of Research," *Journal of Consumer Research*, 31(4), 868–882.

Arsel, Zeynep and Craig J. Thompson (2011), "Demythologizing Consumption Practices: How Consumers Protect Their Field-Dependent Identity Investments from Devaluing Marketplace Myths," *Journal of Consumer Research*, 37(5), 791–806.

Arvidsson, Adam and Alessandro Caliandro (2016), "Brand Public," *Journal of Consumer Research*, 42(5), 727–748.

Arvidsson, Adam and Nicolai Petersen (2016), *The Ethical Economy: Rebuilding Value After the Crisi*s, Columbia University Press, New York.

Avery, Jill, Tonia Junker, and Daniela Beyersdorfer (2016), *Longchamp*, Harvard Business School Teaching Case # 9-316-086.

Balmer, John M.T., Helen Stuart, and Stephen A. Greyser (2009), "Aligning Identity and Strategy: Corporate Branding at British Airways in the Late 20th Century," *California Management Review*, 51(3), 6–23.

Bardhi, Fleura and Giana M. Eckhardt (2012), "Access-Based Consumption: The Case of Car Sharing," *Journal of Consumer Research*, 39(4), 881–898.

Bastos, Wilson and Sidney J. Levy (2012), "A History of the Concept of Branding: Practice and Theory," *Journal of Historical Research in Marketing*, 4(3), 347–368.

Baudrillard, Jean (1994), *Simulacra and Simulation*, University of Michigan Press, Ann Arbor, MI.

BBC (2016, January 29), "Lego Reveals New Disabled Figures after an Online Campaign," http://www.bbc.co.uk/newsbeat/article/35429774/lego-reveals-new-disabled-figures-after-an-online-campaign (accessed January 3, 2017).

Belk, Russell W. (2013), "Extended Self in a Digital World," *Journal of Consumer Research*, 40(3), 477–500.

Belk, Russell W. (1988), "Possessions and Self," *Journal of Consumer Research*, 15(2), 139–168.

Belk, Russell W., Melanie Wallendorf, and John F. Sherry, Jr. (1989), "The Sacred and the Profane in Consumer Behavior: Theodicy on the Odyssey," *Journal of Consumer Research*, 16(1), 1–38.

Berger, Arthur Asa (2010), *The Objects of Affection: Semiotics and Consumer Culture*, Palgrave Macmillan, London.

Beverland, Michael B. (2014), "Sustainable Eating: Mainstreaming Plant-Based Diets in Developed Economies," *Journal of Macromarketing*, 34(3), 369–382.

Beverland, Michael B. (2011), "Slow Design," *Design Management Review*, 22(1), 34–43.

Beverland, Michael B. (2010), "Right-Wing Customers—The Enemy of Innovation," *Design Management Review*, September, 64–71.

Beverland, Michael B. (2009), *Building Brand Authenticity: 7 Habits of Iconic Brands*, Palgrave Macmillan, London.

Beverland, Michael B. (2007), "Can Cooperatives Brand? Exploring the Interplay between Cooperative Structure and Sustained Brand Marketing Success," *Food Policy*, 32(4), 480–495.

Beverland, Michael B. (2005a) "Managing the Design-Innovation Marketing Interface: Resolving the Tension between Artistic Creation and Commercial Imperatives," *Journal of Product Innovation Management*, 22, 193–207.

Beverland, Michael B. (2005b), "Crafting Brand Authenticity: The Case of Luxury Wine," *Journal of Management Studies* 42(5), 1003–1029.

Beverland, Michael B. (2004), "Wither Haute Couture: Emergent Change and Future Value Creation in Luxury Fashion Markets," *Business Horizons*, 47(2), 63–70.

Beverland, Michael B. (2001), "Contextual Influences and the Adoption and Practice of Relationship Selling in a Business-to-Business Setting: An Exploratory Study," *Journal of Personal Selling and Sales Management*, XX1(3), 207–215.

Beverland, Michael B. and Michael T. Ewing (2005), "Slowing the Adoption and Diffusion Process to Enhance Brand Repositioning: The Consumer Driven Repositioning of Dunlop Volley," *Business Horizons,* 48 (Sept.–Oct.), 385–391.

Beverland, Michael B. and Francis J. Farrelly (2011),"Renewing Subcultural Ideology: Reclaiming Surf's Soul", *Advances in Consumer Research* Volume 39, eds. Rohini Ahluwalia, Tanya L. Chartrand, and Rebecca K. Ratner, Duluth, MN: Association for Consumer Research, pp. 273-274.

Beverland, Michael B., and Francis J. Farrelly (2010), "The Quest for Authenticity in Consumption: Consumers' Purposive Choice of Authentic Cues to Shape Experienced Outcomes," *Journal of Consumer Research,* 36(5), 838–856.

Beverland, Michael B. and Francis J. Farrelly (2007), "What Does It Mean to Be Design-Led?" *Design Management Review*, 18(4), 10–17.

Beverland, Michael B., Francis J. Farrelly, and Pascale G. Quester (2010), "Authentic Subcultural Membership: Antecedents and Consequences of Authenticating Acts and Authoritative Performances," *Psychology & Marketing*, 27(7), 698–716.

Beverland, Michael B., Francis Farrelly, and Zeb Woodhatch (2007), "Exploring the Dimensions of Proactivity within Advertising Agency–Client Relationships," *Journal of Advertising*, 36(4), 49–60.

Beverland, Michael B. and Karen Fernandez (2016), "The Future Is Analog: Managerial Implications of Consumers' Experiences of Legacy Technology," *23rd Innovation and Product Development Conference*, Glasgow, June 12–14.

Beverland, Michael B., Steven M. Kates, Adam Lindgreen, and Emily Chung (2010), "Exploring Consumer Conflict in Service Encounters," *Journal of the Academy of Marketing Science*, 83, 617–633.

Beverland, Michael B. and Adam Lindgreen (2002), "Using Country of Origin in Strategy: The Importance of Context and Strategic Action," *Journal of Brand Management*, 10(2), 147–167.

Beverland, M.B. and Lindgreen, A. (2004), "Relationship Use and Market Dynamism: A Model of Relationship Evolution," *Journal of Marketing Management*, 20(7–8), 825–858.

Beverland, M.B., Lindgreen, A., and Vink M. (2008), "Projecting Authenticity through Advertising: Consumer Judgments of Advertisers' Claims," *Journal of Advertising*, 37(1), 5–15.

Beverland, M.B. and Lockshin, L.S. (2003), "A Longitudinal Study of Customers' Desired Value Change in Business-to-Business Markets," *Industrial Marketing Management*, 31(8), 653–666.

Beverland, Michael B., Pietro Micheli, and Francis J. Farrelly (2016), "Resourceful Sensemaking: Overcoming Barriers between Designers and Marketers in NPD," *Journal of Product Innovation Management*, 33(5), 628–648.

Beverland, Michael B., Julie Napoli, and Francis J. Farrelly (2010), "Towards a Typology of Brand Position and Innovation Effort," *Journal of Product Innovation Management*, 27(1), 33–48.

Beverland, Michael B., Julie Napoli, and Adam Lindgreen (2007), "Global Industrial Brands: A Framework and Exploratory Examination," *Industrial Marketing Management*, 36, 1082–1097.

Beverland, Michael B., Beverley Nielsen, and Vicky Pryce (2015a), *Redesigning Manufacturing: Rebalancing the UK Economy*, Palgrave Macmillan, London.

Beverland, Michael B. and Sarah Reynolds (2010), "Sociocultural Brand Management: Exploring Branding Practices in the Postmodern Age," 2010 Thought Leaders International Conference in Brand Management, Lugano, April 18–20.

Beverland, Michael B., Maria Sääksjärvi, and Avi Shankar (2015b), "Reconsidering Innovation Adoption: Insights from Consumer Culture Theory," 22nd Innovation & Product Development Management Conference, Copenhagen, June 13–17.

Beverland, Michael B., Sarah J.S. Wilner, and Pietro Micheli (2015c), "Reconciling the Tension Between Consistency and Relevance: Design Thinking as a Mechanism for Achieving Brand Ambidexterity," *Journal of the Academy of Marketing Science*, 43(5), 589–609.

Blocker, Christopher P., Mark B. Houston, and Daniel J. Flint (2012), "Unpacking What a "Relationship" Means to Commercial Buyers: How the Relationship Metaphor Creates Tension and Obscures Experience," *Journal of Consumer Research*, 38(5), 886–899.

Borel, Laurence-Helene and George Christodoulides (2016), "Branding and Digital Analytics," in F. Dall'Olmo Riley, J. Singh, and C. Blankson (eds.), *The Routledge Companion to Contemporary Brand Management*, Routledge, London, pp. 255–268.

Bourdieu, Pierre (1984), *Distinction: A Social Critique of the Judgement of Taste*, Harvard University Press, Cambridge, MA.

Bradshaw, Alan and Detlev Zwick (2016), "The Field of Business Sustainability and the Death Drive: A Radical Intervention," *Journal of Business Ethics*, 136(2), 267–279.

Brakus, J. Joško, Bernd H. Schmitt, and Lia Zarantonello (2009), "Brand Experience: What Is It? How Is It Measured? Does It Affect Loyalty?", *Journal of Marketing*, 73(3), 52–68.

Brammer, Stephen and Andrew I. Millington (2008), "Does It Pay to Be Different? An Analysis of the Relationship between Corporate Social and Financial Performance," *Strategic Management Journal*, 29(12), 1325–1343.

Brodie, Roderick J. (2009), "From Goods to Service Branding: An Integrative Perspective," *Journal of Service Research*, 9(1), 107–111.

Brown, Andrew D., Patrick Stacey, and Joe Nandhakumar (2008), "Making Sense Of Sensemaking Narratives," *Human Relations*, 61(8), 1035–1062.

Brown, Stephen (2016), *Brands and Branding*, Sage, London.

Brown, Stephen (2003), *Time, Space and the Market: Retroscapes Rising*, M.E. Sharpe, London.

Brown, Stephen, Robert V. Kozinets, and John F. Sherry Jr. (2003), "Teaching Old Brands New Tricks: Retro Branding and the Revival of Brand Meaning," *Journal of Marketing*, 67(3), 19–33.

Calderwood, Imogen (2015, August 4), "Lego Criticised by Disability Group…," http://www. dailymail.co.uk/news/article-3184721/Lego-criticised-disability-group-stereotypical-figure-elderly-man-wheelchair-claiming-sends-message-disabled-children-old-people-use-them. html (accessed January 14, 2017).

Canniford, Robin (2011), "How to Manage Consumer Tribes," *Journal of Strategic Marketing*, 19(7), 591–606.

Canniford, Robin and Avi Shankar (2013), "Purifying Practices: How Consumers Assemble Romantic Experiences of Nature," *Journal of Consumer Research*, 39(5), 1051–1069.

Cayla, Julien, Robin Beers, and Eric Arnould (2014), "Stories that Deliver Business Insights," *MIT Sloan Management Review*, 55 (2), 55–62.

Cayla, Julien and Giana M. Eckhardt (2008), "Asian Brands and the Shaping of a Transnational Imagined Community," *Journal of Consumer Research*, 35 (2), 216–230.

Christensen, Clayton M. (1997), *The Innovator's Dilemma: When New Technologies Cause Great Firms to Fail*, Harvard Business School Press, Boston, MA.

Chung-Moya, Emily, Francis J. Farrelly, Michael B. Beverland, and Ingo O. Karpen (2017), "Loyalty or Liability: Resolving the Consumer Fanaticism Paradox," *Marketing Theory*, DOI: 10.1177/1470593117705696

Churchman, C. West (1967), "Wicked Problems," *Management Science*, 14(4), B-141-146.

Cohen, Heidi (2011, August 8), "30 Branding definitions," http://heidicohen.com/30-branding-definitions/ (accessed June 8, 2016).

Cohen, Lindsey (2016, May 12), "Abercrombie & Fitch: Marketing in the Grey Area," https://medium.com/@lindzcoh/abercrombie-fitch-marketing-in-the-grey-area-5194894b3a73 (accessed January 3, 2017).

Conejo, Francisco and Ben Wooliscroft (2015), "Brands Defined as Semiotic Marketing Systems," *Journal of Macromarketing*, 35(3), 287–301.

Conklin, Jeff (2003), "Dialog Mapping: Reflections on an Industrial Strength Case Study," in P. Kirschner, S.J.B Shum, and C.S. Carr (eds), *Visualizing Argumentation—Tools for Collaborative and Educational Sense-Making*, Springer-Verlag, London.

Cook, Daniel Thomas and Susan B. Kaiser (2004), "Betwixt and Be Tween," *Journal of Consumer Culture*, 4(2), 203–227.

Coupland, Jennifer C. (2005), "Invisible Brands: An Ethnography of Households and the Brands in Their Kitchen Pantries," *Journal of Consumer Research*, 32(1), 106–118.

Courtenay, Adam (2016, December 12), "Australian Couple Make $2.5 Million Delivering Hard-to-get American Products," *The Age*, http://www.theage.com.au/small-business/entrepreneur/australian-couple-make-25-million-delivering-hardtoget-american-products-20161208-gt6jug (accessed December 12, 2016).

Cova, Bernard (1997), "Community and Consumption: Towards a Definition of the 'Linking Value' of Product or Services," *European Journal of Marketing*, 31(3/4), 297–316.

Cova, Bernard and Véronique Cova (2002), "Tribal Marketing: The Tribalisation of Society and Its Impact on the Conduct of Marketing," *European Journal of Marketing*, 36(5/6), 595–620.

Cova, Bernard, Robert V. Kozinets, and Avi Shankar (2007), *Consumer Tribes*, Routledge, London.

Criado, Elisa (2014, August 5), "Lego Launches First Ever Female …," http://www.independent.co.uk/life-style/health-and-families/lego-launches-female-scientist-set-months-after-7-year-old-requested-they-make-more-lego-girl-people-9650341.html (accessed January 14, 2017).

Cromie, John G. and Michael T. Ewing (2009), "The Rejection of Brand Hegemony," *Journal of Business Research*, 62(2), 218–230.

Cunningham, Andrew (2015), "Best Global Brands," *Global Finance Magazine*, November, https://www.gfmag.com/magazine/november-2015/biggest-global-banks-2015 (accessed March 3, 2017).

Dall'Olmo Riley, Francesca (2016), "Brand Definitions and Conceptualizations," in F. Dall'Olmo Riley, J. Singh, and C. Blankson (eds), *The Routledge Companion to Contemporary Brand Management* (pp. 3–12), Routledge, London.

Dameron, Kenneth (1939), "The Consumer Movement," *Harvard Business Review*, 17(3), 271–289.

Darley, William K. (2016), "Brand Building via Integrated Marketing Communications," in F. Dall'Olmo Riley, J. Singh, and C. Blankson (eds), *The Routledge Companion to Contemporary Brand Management* (pp. 201–217), Routledge, London.

Davenport and Lyons (2006), Counterfeiting Luxury Report, http://www.intangiblebusiness.com/news/legal/2007/08/counterfeit-copycat-keeping-it-real (accessed February 2, 2016).

Davies, Iain A. (2007), "The Eras and Participants of Fair Trade: An Industry Structure/Stakeholder Perspective on the Growth of the Fair Trade Industry," *Corporate Governance: The International Journal of Business in Society*, 7(4), 455–470

de Chernatony, Leslie and Susan Segal-Horn, (2003) "The Criteria for Successful Services Brands," *European Journal of Marketing*, 37(7/8), 1095–1118.

Deephouse, David and Suzanne M. Carter (2005), "An Examination of the Differences between Organizational Legitimacy and Organizational Reputation," *Journal of Management Studies*, 42(2), 329–360.

Deighton, John (2003), *Snapple*, Harvard Business School Teaching Case 599126.

Deshpande, Rohit and Anat Keinan (2015), "Brands and Brand Equity," *Harvard Business School Teaching Note* 8140-HTM-ENG.

Devinney, Timothy M., Pat Auger, and Giana M. Eckhardt (2010), *The Myth of the Ethical Consumer*, Cambridge University Press, Cambridge.

Dickinson-Delaporte, Sonia, Michael B. Beverland, and Adam Lindgreen (2010), "Building Corporate Reputation with Stakeholders: Exploring the Role of Message Ambiguity for Social Marketers," *European Journal of Marketing*, 44(11/12), 1856–1874.

Dobele, Angela, Adam Lindgreen, Michael B. Beverland, Joëlle VanHamme, and Robert Wijk (2007), "Why Pass On Viral Messages? Because They Connect Emotionally," *Business Horizons*, 50, 291–304.

Dong, Lily and Kelly Tian (2009), "The Use of Western Brands in Asserting Chinese National Identity," *Journal of Consumer Research*, 36(3), 504–523.

Dougherty, Deborah (2008), "Bridging Social Constraint and Social Action to Design Organizations for Innovation," *Organization Studies*, 29(3), 415–434.

Dowling, Grahame (2001), *Creating Corporate Reputations: Identity, Image and Performance*, Oxford University Press, Oxford.

Earl, Steve and Stephen Waddington (2012), *Brand Anarchy: Managing Corporate Reputation*, Bloomsbury, London.

Eckhardt, Giana, Russell W. Belk, and Jonathan Wilson (2015), "The Rise of Inconspicuous Consumption," *Journal of Marketing Management*, 31(7/8), 807–826.

Edwards, Helen and Derek Day (2014), "Passionbrands: The Extraordinary Power of Belief," in Kartikeya Kompella (ed.), *The Definitive Book on Branding*, Sage, London.

Edwards, Helen and Derek Day (2005), *Creating Passionbrands: How to Build Emotional Connections with Customers*, Kogan Page, London.

Epp, Amber M. and Linda L. Price (2010), "The Storied Life of Singularized Objects: Forces of Agency and Network Transformation," *Journal of Consumer Research*, 36(5), 820–837.

Epp, Amber M., Hope Jensen Schau, and Linda L. Price (2014), "The Role of Brands and Mediating Technologies in Assembling Long-Distance Family Practices," *Journal of Marketing*, 78(3), 81–101.

Farrelly, Francis J., Michael B. Beverland, and Ingo O. Karpen (2017), "Creating Internal Legitimacy for Cultural Market Orientation," working paper, School of Economics, Finance and Marketing, RMIT University.

Firat, A. Fuat and Alladi Venkatesh (1995), "Liberatory Postmodernism and the Reenchantment of Consumption," *Journal of Consumer Research*, 22(3), 239–267.

Fletcher, Kate (2016), *Craft of Use: Post-Growth Fashion*, Routledge, London.

Flint, Daniel J., Robert B. Woodruff, and Sarah Fisher Gardial (2002), "Exploring the Phenomenon of Customers' Desired Value Change in a Business-to-Business Context," *Journal of Marketing*, 66(4), 102–117.

Florida, Richard (2002), *The Rise of the Creative Class*, Basic Books, New York.

Forbes, Thayne (2006), "Valuing Customers," http://www.intangiblebusiness.com/news/financial/2006/08/valuing-customers (accessed June 6, 2016).

Ford, David, Pierre Berthon, Stephen Brown, Lars-Erik Gadde, Peter Naudé, Thomas Ritter, Ivan Snehota, and Håkan Håkansson (2002), *The Business Marketing Course: Managing in Complex Networks*, Wiley, London.

Forden, Sara G. (2000), *The House of Gucci*, William Morrow, London.

Fottrell, Quentin (2012), "What Starbucks' $7 Coffee Is Really Worth," http://www.marketwatch.com/story/what-starbucks-7-coffee-is-really-worth-2012-11-29 (accessed December 12, 2016).

Fournier, Susan (2016), "When the Brand Is a Person: Understanding and Managing Corporeal Brands," IVEY Business School Marketing Seminar Series, IVEY Business School, London, Ontario, November 1.

Fournier, Susan (1998), "Consumers and Their Brands: Developing Relationship Theory in Consumer Research," *Journal of Consumer Research*, 24(4), 343–373.

Fournier, Susan and Jill Avery (2011), "The Uninvited Brand," *Business Horizons*, 54(3), 193–207.

Fournier, Susan and Lara Lee (2009), "Getting Brand Communities Right," *Harvard Business Review*, 87(4), 105–111.

Frank, Thomas (1998), *The Conquest of Cool: Business Culture, Counterculture and the Rise of Hip-Consumerism*, University of Chicago Press, Chicago.

Gardner, Burleigh B. and Sidney J. Levy (1955), "The Product and the Brand," *Harvard Business Review*, March–April, 33–39.

Gebhardt, Gary F., Gregory S. Carpenter, and John F. Sherry Jr. (2006), "Creating a Market Orientation: A Longitudinal, Multifirm, Grounded Analysis of Cultural Transformation," *Journal of Marketing*, 70(4), 37–55.

Gerzema, John and Ed Lebar (2008), *The Brand Bubble: The Looming Crisis in Brand Value and How to Avoid It*, Jossey-Bass, New York.

Giddens, Anthony (1991), *Modernity and Self-identity: Self and Society in the Late Modern Age*, Polity Press, Cambridge.

Giesler, Markus (2012), "How Doppelgänger Brand Images Influence the Market Creation Process: Longitudinal Insights from the Rise of Botox Cosmetic," *Journal of Marketing*, 76(Nov.), 55–68.

Giesler, Markus and Ela Veresiu (2014), "Creating the Responsible Consumer: Moralistic Governance Regimes and Consumer Subjectivity," *Journal of Consumer Research*, 41(3), 840–857.

Gilmore, James H. and B. Joseph Pine (2007), *Authenticity: What Consumers Really Want*, Harvard Business School Press, Cambridge, MA.

Gladwell, Malcolm (2002), *The Tipping Point: How Little Things Can Make a Big Difference*, Abacus, London.

Gobé, Marc (2007), *Brand Jam: Humanizing Brands through Emotional Design*, Allworth Press, New York.

Goffman, Erving (1957), *The Presentation of Self in Everyday Life*, Penguin, New York.

Graham, Johnny L. and Susan Mudambi (2016), "Looking at the Future of B2B Branding," in F. Dall'Olmo Riley, J. Singh, and C. Blankson (eds.), *The Routledge Companion to Contemporary Brand Management*, Routledge, London, pp. 271–279.

Grayson, Kent and Radan Martinec (2004), "Consumer Perceptions of Iconicity and Indexicality and Their Influence on Assessments of Authentic Market Offerings," *Journal of Consumer Research*, 31(2), 296–312.

Grégoire, Yany, Thomas M. Tripp, and Renaud Legoux (2009), "When Customer Love Turns into Lasting Hate: The Effects of Relationship Strength and Time on Customer Revenge and Avoidance," *Journal of Marketing*, 73(Nov.), 18–32.

Gregory, James R. and Lawrence McNaughton (2004), "Brand Logic: A Business Case for Communications," *Journal of Advertising Research*, 44(3), 232–236.

Hall, Maureen, (2007), "In Praise of B2B Work," *Ad Age*, http://adage.com/article/small-agency-diary/praise-b2b-work/121056/ (accessed April 5, 2017).

Hatch, Mary Jo and Majken Schultz (2008), *Taking Brand Initiative: How Companies Can Align Strategy, Culture, and Identity through Corporate Branding*, John Wiley & Sons, London.

Hatch, Mary Jo and Majken Schultz (2001), "Are the Strategic Stars Aligned for Your Corporate Brand?", *Harvard Business Review*, 79 (Feb.), 128–134.

Hausman, Daniel M. and Brynn Welch (2010), "Debate: To Nudge or Not to Nudge," *Journal of Political Philosophy*, 18(1), 123–136.

Hayashi, Alden M. (2014), "Thriving in a Big Data World," *MIT Sloan Management Review*, 55(2), 35–39.

Heath, Joseph and Andrew Potter (2006), *The Rebel Sell: How the Counter Culture Became Consumer Culture*, Capstone, Mankato, MN.

Heath, Robert (2012), *Seducing the Subconscious: The Psychology of Emotional Influence in Advertising*, Wiley-Blackwell, London.

Heding, Tilde, Charlotte F. Knudtzen, and Mogens Bjerre (2016), *Brand Management: Research, Theory and Practice*, Routledge, London.

Heller, Stephen (2008), *Iron Fists: Branding the 20th Century Totalitarian State*, Phaidon Press, London.

Henley, Jon (2016, March 24), "The Aggressive, Outrageous, Infuriating (and Ingenious) Rise of BrewDog," *Guardian*, https://www.theguardian.com/lifeandstyle/2016/mar/24/the-aggressive-outrageous-infuriating-and-ingenious-rise-of-brewdog (accessed March 24).

Hietanen, Joel and Joonas Rokka (2015), "Market Practices in Countercultural Market Emergence," *European Journal of Marketing*, 49(9/10), 1563–1588

Hill, Andrew (2011, February 28), "Buffett's Exceptional Style of Leadership," https://www.ft.com/content/73e667a8-436b-11e0-8f0d-00144feabdc0 (accessed June 15, 2013).

Holbrook, Morris B. (1999), *Consumer Value: A Framework for Analysis and Research*, Psychology Press, Abingdon.

Holbrook, Morris B. and Elizabeth C. Hirschman (1982), "The Experiential Aspects of Consumption: Consumer Fantasies, Feelings, and Fun," *Journal of Consumer Research* 9(2), 132–140.

Holt, Douglas (2016), "Branding in the Age of Social Media," *Harvard Business Review* 94(3), 40–50.

Holt, Douglas B. (2012), "Constructing Sustainable Consumption: From Ethical Values to Cultural Transformation of Unsustainable Markets," *The Annals of the American Academy*, 644 (Nov.), 236–255.

Holt, Douglas B. (2006), "Jack Daniel's America Iconic Brands as Ideological Parasites and Proselytizers," *Journal of Consumer Culture*, 6(3), 355–377.

Holt, Douglas B. (2004a), *How Brands Become Icons: The Principles of Cultural Branding*, Harvard Business School Press, Cambridge, MA.

Holt, Douglas (2004b), "What Becomes an Icon Most?" *Harvard Business Review*, 81(3), 43–49.

Holt, Douglas B. (2003), "Brands and Branding," *Harvard Business School Teaching Note* 9-503-045.

Holt, Douglas B. (2002), "Why Do Brands Cause Trouble? A Dialectical Theory of Consumer Culture and Branding," *Journal of Consumer Research*, 29(1), 70–90.

Holt, Douglas B. (1998), "Does Cultural Capital Structure American Consumption?", *Journal of Consumer Research*, 25(1), 1–25.

Holt, Douglas B. and Douglas Cameron (2010), *Cultural Strategy: Using Innovative Ideologies to Build Breakthrough Brands*, Oxford University Press, Oxford.

Holt, Douglas B. and Craig J. Thompson (2004), "Man-of-action heroes: The Pursuit of Heroic Masculinity in Everyday Consumption," *Journal of Consumer Research*, 31 (2), 425–440.

Homburg, C., A. Vomburg, M. Enke, and P. H. Grimm (2015), "The Loss of the Marketing Department's Influence: Is It Really Happening? And Why Worry?", *Journal of the Academy of Marketing Science*, 43 (1): 1–13.

Horst, Peter and Robert Duboff (2015), "Don't Let Big Data Bury Your Brand," *Harvard Business Review*, November, 2–9.

Hultink, Erik-Jan, Abbie Griffin, Susan Hart, and Henry S.J. Robben (1997), "Industrial New Product Launch Strategies and Product Development Performance," *Journal of Product Innovation Management*, 14(4), 243–257.

Hunt, Shelby D. and Scott M. Vitell (1986), "A General Theory of Marketing Ethics," *Journal of Macromarketing*, 6(Spring), 5–15.

Hsu, Liwu, Susan Fournier, Shuba Srinivasan (2016), "Brand Architecture Strategy and Firm Value: How Leveraging, Separating, and Distancing the Corporate Brand Affects Risk and Returns," *Journal of the Academy of Marketing Science*, 44(2), 261–280.

Ind, Nicholas (2014), "Living the Brand," in Kartikeya Kompella (ed.), *The Definitive Book on Branding*, Sage, London, pp. 199–218.

Interbrand (2016), Best Global Brands Ranking 2016, http://interbrand.com/best-brands/best-global-brands/2016/ranking/ (accessed March 2, 2017).

Interbrand (2014), Best Global Brands 2014, www.bestglobalbrands.com/2014/ranking/ (accessed April 4, 2015).

International Monetary Fund (2000, April 12), *Globalization: Threats or Opportunity*, IMF Publications, http://www.imf.org/external/np/exr/ib/2000/041200to.htm (accessed November 22, 2016).

Izberk-Bilgin, Elif (2012), "Infidel Brands: Unveiling Alternative Meanings of Global Brands at the Nexus of Globalization, Consumer Culture, and Islamism," *Journal of Consumer Research*, 39(4), 663–687.

Jayasinghe, Laknath and Mark Ritson (2013), "Everyday Advertising Context: An Ethnography of Advertising Response in the Family Living Room," *Journal of Consumer Research*, 40(1), 104–121.

Johansson, Johny K and Kurt A. Carlson (2014), *Contemporary Brand Management*, Sage, Newbury Park, CA.

Johansson, Johny K., Claudiu V. Dimofte, and Sanal K. Mazvancheryl (2016), "The Performance of Global Brands in the 2008 Financial Crisis: A Test of Two Brand Value Measures," *International Journal of Research in Marketing*, 29(3), 235–245.

Johnson, Steven (2006), *Everything Bad Is Good for You: How Popular Culture is Making Us Smarter*, Penguin, New York.

Kapferer, Jean-Noel (2014a), "Brands and Innovation," in Kartikeya Kompella (ed.), *The Definitive Book on Branding*, Sage, London, pp. 149–170.

Kapferer, Jean-Noel (2014b), "The Artification of Luxury: From Artisans to Artists," *Business Horizons*, 57, 371–380.

Kapferer, Jean-Noel (2012), "Abundant Rarity: The Key to Luxury Growth," *Business Horizons*, 55, 453–462.

Kates, Steven M. (2004), "The Dynamics of Brand Legitimacy: An Interpretive Study in the Gay Men's Community," *Journal of Consumer Research*, 31(2), 455–464.

Kates, Steven M. and Charlene Goh (2003), "Brand Morphing: Implications for Advertising Theory and Practice," *Journal of Advertising*, 32(1), 59–68.

Keinan, Anat and Michael B. Beverland (2016) *C.W. Dixey & Son*, Harvard Business School Teaching Case 9-517-019.

Keinan, Anat and Sandrine Crener (2015), *Stella McCartney*, Harvard Business School Case 9-515-075.

Keinan, Anat, Francis J. Farrelly, and Michael B. Beverland (2012), *Introducing iSnack2.0: The New Vegemite*. Harvard Business School Case 9-512-020.

Keller, Kevin Lane (2003), "Brand Synthesis: The Multidimensionality of Brand Knowledge," *Journal of Consumer Research*, 29(4), 595–600.

Keller, Kevin Lane (2000), "The Brand Report Card," *Harvard Business Review*, Jan.–Feb., 147–157.

Keller, Kevin Lane (1999), "Managing Brands for the Long Run: Brand Reinforcement and Revitalization Strategies," *California Management Review*, 41(3), 102–124.

Keller, Kevin Lane (1993), "Conceptualizing, Measuring, and Managing Customer-Based Brand Equity," *Journal of Marketing*, 57(January), 1–22.

Keller, Kevin Lane, Brian Sternthal, and Alice Tybout (2002), "Three Questions You Need to Ask about Your Brand," *Harvard Business Review* 80(9), 80–89.

Kim, Suyong Joh (2016), *Pantone*, Joh & Compnay, Seoul.

Kim, W. Chan and Renee Mauborgne (2015), *Blue Ocean Strategy: How to Create Uncontested Market Space and Make the Competition Irrelevant*, Harvard Business School Press, Cambridge, MA.

Klaassen, Abbey (2010, April 23), "New Coke: One of Marketing's Biggest Blunders Turns 25," *Advertising Age*, http://adage.com/article/adages/coke-marketing-s-biggest-blunders-turns-25/143470/ (accessed November 15, 2016).

Klein, Naomi (2000), *No Logo*, Fourth Estate, New York.

Kotler, Philip, Gary Armstrong, Lloyd C. Harris, and Nigel Piercy (2016), *Principles of Marketing European Edition*, 7th Edition, Pearson Education, Harlow.

Kozinets, Robert V. (2009), *Netnography: Doing Ethnographic Research Online*, Sage, London.

Kozinets, Robert V. Kristine de Valck, Andrea C. Wojnicki, and Sarah J.S. Wilner (2010), "Networked Narratives: Understanding Word-of-Mouth Marketing in Online Communities," *Journal of Marketing*, 74(2), 71–89.

Laczniak, Gene R. and Patrick E. Murphy (2006), "Normative Perspectives for Ethical and Socially Responsible Marketing," *Journal of Macromarketing*, 26(2), 154–177.

Lee, Z., Hang, H., and Beverland, M.B. (2017), "Evolution of Brand Equity: Knowledge Co-Creation between Manufacturer Brands, Advertising Agencies and Academics, 1950–2000," *Association of Business History Conference*, June 30, Glasgow.

Levitt, Theodore (1983), "The Globalization of Markets," *Harvard Business Review*, 61(May–June), 92–102.

Levitt, Theodore (1960), "Marketing Myopia," *Harvard Business Review*, July–August, 45–56.

Levy, Sidney J. (1959), "Symbols for Sale," *Harvard Business Review*, July–August, 117–124.

Lindgreen, Adam, François Maon, and Christine Vallaster (2016), "Building Brands via Corporate Social Responsibility," in F. Dall'Olmo Riley, J. Singh, and C. Blankson (eds), *The Routledge Companion to Contemporary Brand Management*, Routledge, London, pp. 228–254.

Longo, Cristina, Avi Shankar, and Peter Nuttall (2017), "It's Not Easy Living a Sustainable Lifestyle": How Greater Knowledge Leads to Dilemmas, Tensions and Paralysis," *Journal of Business Ethics* DOI 10.1007/s10551-016-3422-1

Low, George S. and Ronald A. Fullerton (1994), "Brands, Brand Management, and the Brand Manager System: A Critical-historical Evaluation," *Journal of Marketing Research*, XXI(May), 173–190.

Luedicke, Marius K. (2015), "Indigenes' Responses to Immigrants' Consumer Acculturation: A Relational Configuration Analysis," *Journal of Consumer Research*, 42(1), 109–129.

Lutz, Ashley (2013, May 4) "Abercrombie & Fitch Refuses to Make Clothes for Fat People," https://www.businessinsider.com.au/abercrombie-wants-thin-customers-2013-5 (accessed March 10, 2017).

Macintosh, Gerrard and Lawrence S. Lockshin (1997), "Retail Relationships and Store Loyalty: A Multi-Level Perspective," *International Journal of Research in Marketing*, 14(5), 487–497.

Mackenzie, Nick and Richard Baker (2016, November 15), "Special Investigation: The Fruits of Their Labour", *The Age*, http://www.theage.com.au/interactive/2016/fruit-picking-investigation/ (accessed November 15, 2016).

Madden, Thomas J, Frank Fehle, and Susan Fournier (2006), "Brands Matters: An Empirical Demonstration of the Creation of Shareholder Value through Branding," *Journal of the Academy of Marketing Science*, 34(2), 224–235.

Martin, Dianne M., John W. Schouten, and James H. McAlexander (2006), "Claiming the Throttle: Multiple Femininities in a Hyper-Masculine Subculture," *Consumption, Markets and Culture*, 9(3), 171–205.

Martin, Joanne (1992), *Cultures in Organizations: Three Perspectives*, Sage, Newbury Park, CA.

Mazzucato, Mariana (2013), *The Entrepreneurial State: Debunking Myths Public vs. Private Sector Myths*, Anthem Press, London.

McAfee, Andrew and Erik Brynjolfsson (2012), "Big Data: The Management Revolution," *Harvard Business Review*, October, 2–9.

McCracken, Grant (2010), *Chief Culture Officer: How to Create a Living Breathing Corporation*, Basic Books, New York.

McCracken, Grant (1990), *Culture and Consumption: New Approaches to the Symbolic Character of Consumer Goods and Activities*, Indiana University Press, Bloomington, IN.

McCracken, Grant (1989), "Who Is the Celebrity Endorser? Cultural Foundations of the Endorsement Process," *Journal of Consumer Research*, 16(Dec.), 310–321.

McCracken, Grant (1986), "Culture and Consumption: A Theoretical Account of the Structure and Movement of the Cultural Meaning of Consumer Goods", *Journal of Consumer Research*, 13(1): 71–84.

Merz, Michael A., Yi He, and Stephen L. Vargo (2009), "The Evolving Brand Logic: A Service-Dominant Logic Perspective," *Journal of the Academy of Marketing Science*, 37(3), 328–344.

Meyer, John W. and Brian Rowan (1977), "Institutionalized Organizations: Formal Structure as Myth and Ceremony," *American Journal of Sociology*, 83(2), 340–363

Micheli, Pietro, Sabeen Bhatti, Sarah J.S. Wilner, and Michael B. Beverland (2017), "Towards a Definition of Design Thinking," *International Product Development Management Conference*, June 11-13 Reykjavik University.

Mick, David Glen, Simone Pettigrew, Cornelia Pechmann, and Julie L. Ozanne (2012), "Origins, Qualities, and Envisionments of Transformative Consumer Research," in D.G. Mick et al. (eds.), *Transformative Consumer Research for Personal and Collective Well-Being*, Routledge, London, pp. 3–24.

Miles, Sandra J. and W. Glynn Mangold (2005), "Positioning Southwest Airlines through Employee Branding," *Business Horizons*, 48(6), 535–545.

Mintzberg, Henry (1987), "Crafting Strategy," *Harvard Business Review*, July–August, 66–74.

Mittelstaedt, John D., William E. Kilbourne, Robert A. Mittelstaedt (2006), "Macromarketing as Agorology: Macromarketing Theory and the Study of the Agora," *Journal of Macromarketing,* 26 (2), 131 - 142

Mittelstaedt, John D., Clifford J. Schultz II, William E. Kilbourne, and Mark Peterson (2014), "Sustainability as Megatrend: Two Schools of Macromarketing Thought," *Journal of Macromarketing*, 34(3), 253–264.

Moazzez, Navid (2016, November 30) "50 Amazing Personal Branding Quotes You Need to Know," http://www.navidmoazzez.com/best-personal-branding-quotes/ (accessed February 2, 2017).

Moon, Youngme (2004), *Burberry*, Harvard Business School Teaching Case 504048.

Moore, Karl and Susan Reid (2008), "The Birth of the Brand: 4000 Years of Branding," *Business History*, 50(4), 419–432.

Morhart, Felicitas, Malär, Lucia, Guèvremont, Amélie, Girardin, Florent and Grohmann, Bianca (2015), "Brand Authenticity: An Integrative Framework and Measurement Scale," *Journal of Consumer Psychology*, 25(2), 200–218.

Muñiz, Albert M. Jr. and Thomas O'Guinn (2001), "Brand Community," *Journal of Consumer Research*, 27(4), 412–432.

Naidoo, Rajani, Avi Shankar, and Ekant Veer (2011), "The Consumerist Turn in Higher Education: Policy Aspirations and Outcomes," *Journal of Marketing Management*, 27(11/12), 1142–1162.

Napoli, Julie, Sonia Dickinson-Delaporte, Michael B. Beverland and Francis J. Farrelly (2014), "Measuring Consumer-based Brand Authenticity," *Journal of Business Research*, 67, 1090–1098.

Neumeier, Marty (2005), *The Brand Gap: How to Bridge the Distance Between Business Strategy and Design*, New Riders, San Francisco, CA.

Olins, Wally (1978), *The Corporate Personality: An Inquiry into the Nature of Corporate Identity*, Mayflower Books, New York.

Oliver, Nick, Lee Schab, and Matthias Holweg (2007), "Lean Principles and Premium Brands: Conflict or Complement?" *International Journal of Production Research*, 45(16), 3723–3739.

Park, C. Whan, Sung Youl Jun, Allan D. Shocker. (1996), "Composite Branding Alliances: An Investigation of Extension and Feedback Effects," *Journal of Marketing Research*, 33 (4) 453–466.

Park, C. Whan, Deborah J. MacInnis, Joseph Priester, Andreas B. Eisingerich, and Dawn Iacobucci (2010), "Brand Attachment and Brand Attitude Strength: Conceptual and Empirical Differentiation of Two Critical Brand Equity Drivers," *Journal of Marketing*, 74(6), 1–17.

Parmentier, Marie-Agnès (2011), "When David Met Victoria: Forging a Strong Family Brand," *Family Firm Review*, 24(3), 217–232.

Parsons, Elizabeth (2009), "Ethical Debates in Marketing," in E. Parsons and P. Maclaran (eds.), *Contemporary Issues in Marketing and Consumer Behaviour*, Routledge, London, pp. 121–140.

Parsons, Elizabeth and Pauline Maclaran (2009), *Contemporary Issues in Marketing and Consumer Behaviour*, Routledge, London.

Patnaik, Dev (2009), *Wired to Care: How Companies Prosper When They Create Widespread Empathy*, Financial Times/Prentice Hall, London.

Peters, Tom (1997, August 31), "The Brand Called You," *Fast Company*, https://www.fast company.com/28905/brand-called-you (accessed March 17, 2017).

Petty, Ross D. (2011), "The Codevelopment of Trademark Law and the Concept of Brand Marketing in the United States before 1946," *Journal of Macromarketing*, 31(1), 85–99.

Philip-Jones, John (1998), *How Advertising Works: The Role of Research*, Sage, London.

Philp, Bruce (2012), *Consumer Republic: Using Brands to Get What You Want, Make Corporations Behave, and Maybe Even Save the World*, Emblem, London.

Pine, B. Joseph and James H. Gilmore (1998), "Welcome to the Experience Economy," *Harvard Business Review*, July–August, 97–105.

Pisano, Gary P. (2009), *Producing Prosperity: Why America Needs a Manufacturing Renaissance*, Harvard Business School Press, Cambridge, MA.

Potter, Andrew (2011), *The Authenticity Hoax: Why the "Real" Things We Seek Don't Make Us Happy*, HarperPerennial, New York.

Prahalad, C.K. and Venkat Ramaswamy (2004), "Co-Creation Experiences: The Next Practice in Value Creation," *Journal of Interactive Marketing*, 18(3), 5–14.

Press, Clare (2016), *Wardrobe Crisis: How We Went from Sunday Best to Fast Fashion*, Penguin, Melbourne.

Price, Linda L. and Eric J. Arnould (1999), "Commercial Friendships: Service Provider–Client Relationships in Context," *Journal of Marketing*, 63(4), 38–56.

PriceWaterhouseCoopers (2013, October), "Counterfeit Goods in the UK: Who Is Buying What and Why," https://www.pwc.co.uk/assets/pdf/anti-counterfeiting-consumer-survey-october-2013.pdf (accessed February 2, 2016).

Puntoni, Stefano, Jonathan Schroeder, and Mark Ritson (2010), "Meaning Matters: Polysemy in Advertising," *Journal of Advertising*, 39(2), 51–64.

Quester, Pascale G. (1996), "Consumers' Perceptions of Sponsorship Sources," *Asia Pacific Advances in Consumer Research*, 2, 13–18.

Ravasi, Davide and Majken Schultz (2006), "Responding to Organizational Identity Threats: Exploring the Role of Organizational Culture," *Academy of Management Journal*, 49(3), 433–458.

Reichheld, Frederick F. (2003), "The One Number You Need to Grow," *Harvard Business Review*, 81(12), 46–54.

Reynolds, Simon (2012), *Retromania: Pop Culture's Addiction to Its Own Past*, Faber & Faber, London.

Ries, Al and Jack Trout (1981), *Positioning: The Battle for Your Mind*, McGraw-Hill, New York.

Ritson, Mark (2012, July 11), "Mark Ritson's Seven Rules of Brand Management," *Marketing Week* (Online Edition), p. 6. https://www.marketingweek.com/2012/07/11/mark-ritsons-seven-rules-of-brand-management/

Ritson, Mark (2010), "Should You Launch a Fighter Brand?" *Harvard Business Review*, 87(10), 86–94.

Ritson, Mark (2004, July 14), "Focus Group Fiasco Gives Research a Bad Name," http://www.campaignlive.co.uk/article/mark-ritson-branding-focus-group-fiasco-gives-research-bad-name/216518 (accessed August 3, 2017).

Ritzer, George (1983), *The McDonaldization of Society*, Sage, Newbury Park, CA.

Ritzer, George and Jurgenson, N. (2010), "Production, Consumption, Prosumption," *Journal of Consumer Culture*, 10(1), 13 –36.

Roberts, Kevin (2004), *Lovemarks: The Future Beyond Brands*, Powerhouse Books, New York.

Rokka, Joonas and Robin Canniford (2016), "Heterotopian Selfies: How Social Media Destabilizes Brand Assemblages," *European Journal of Marketing*, 50(9/10), 1789–1813.

Rose, Randall L. and Stacy L. Wood (2005), "Paradox and the Consumption of Authenticity through Reality Television," *Journal of Consumer Research*, 32(2), 284–296.

Rosenbaum, Mark, S. Mauricio Losada Otalora, and Germán Contreras Ramírez (2017), "How to Create a Realistic Customer Journey Map," *Business Horizons*, 60(1), 143–150.

Rosenbaum-Elliott, Richard H, Larry Percy, and Simon Pervan (2015), *Strategic Brand Management,* 3rd Edition, Oxford University Press, Oxford.

Salinas, Gabriella (2016), "Brand Valuation: Principles, Applications, and Latest Developments," in Francesca Dall'Olmo Riley, Jaywant Singh, and Charles Blankson (eds), *The Routledge Companion to Contemporary Brand Management*, Routledge, Abingdon.

Sean Sands and Michael B. Beverland (2011), "Kiwiana: National Identity and Consumption," *European Advances in Consumer Research* Volume 9, eds. Alan Bradshaw, Chris Hackley, and Pauline Maclaran, Duluth, MN, Association for Consumer Research, pp. 491.

Saw, M. Astella (2015), "The Context," *Viewpoint*, 35, 28–29.

Schau, Hope J., Albert M. Muñiz, Jr., and Eric J. Arnould (2009), "How Brand Community Practices Create Value," *Journal of Marketing*, 73(5), 30–51.

Schutte, Shané (2014, June 16), "6 Worst Brand Extensions from Famous Companies," http://realbusiness.co.uk/business-growth/2014/06/16/6-worst-brand-extensions-from-famous-companies/ (accessed April 3, 2017).

Schouten, John W. and James H. McAlexander (1995), "Subcultures of Consumption: An Ethnography of the New Bikers," *Journal of Consumer Res*earch, 22(1), 43–61.

Schroeder, Jonathan, Janet Borgerson, and Zhiyan Wu (2016), "A Brand Culture Perspective on Global Brands," in F. Dall'Olmo Riley, J. Singh, and C. Blankson (eds), *The Routledge Companion to Contemporary Brand Management*, Routledge, London, pp. 153–163.

Seo, Jaewoo and Yeongmin Kim (2016), *Netflix*, Joh & Company, Seoul.

Shankar, Avi and Fitchett, James (2002), "Having, Being & Consumption," *Journal of Marketing Management*, 18(5/6), 501–516.

Shove, Elizabeth, Matthew Watson, Martin Hand, and Jack Ingram (2007), *The Design of Everyday Life*, Berg, Oxford.

Silk, Alvin J. (2006), *What is Marketing?* Harvard Business School Press, Cambridge, MA.

Singer, Melissa (2016, November 26), "Discount Universe Farewell Australia with an Exhibition of Star-spangled Glamour," *Sydney Morning Herald*, http://www.smh.com.au/lifestyle/fashion/discount-universe-farewell-australia-with-an-exhibition-of-starspangled-glamour-20161125-gsxdgj.html (accessed November 26, 2016).

Singh, Jaywant and Uncles, Mark (2016), "Measuring the Market Performance of Brands: Applications in Brand Management," in F. Dall'Olmo Riley, J. Singh, and C. Blankson (eds), *The Routledge Companion to Contemporary Brand Management*, Routledge, London, pp. 13–31.

Spiggle, Susan, Hang T. Nguyen, and Mary Caravella (2012), "More than Fit: Brand Extension Authenticity," *Journal of Marketing Research*, 49(6), 967–983.

Spratt, Tim (2011), "Corporate Reputation Management," MBA Guest Lecture, School of Management, University of Bath, April 3.

Suárez, Fernando F. and James M. Utterback (1995), "Dominant Designs and the Survival of Firms," *Strategic Management Journal*, 16(6), 415–430.

Tadajewski, Mark., Jessica Chelekis, Benet Deberry-Spence, Bernardo Figueiredo, Olga Kravets, Krittenee Nuttavuthisit, K., Lisa Peñaloza and Johanna Moisander (2014), "The Discourses of Marketing and Development: 'Towards Critical Transformative Marketing Research,'" *Journal of Marketing Management*, 30(17–18), 1728–1771.

Teece, David, Gary Pisano, and Amy Shuen (1997), "Dynamic Capabilities and Strategic Management," *Strategic Management Journal*, 18(7), 509–533.

Thomson, Matthew Deborah J. MacInniss, and C. Whan Park (2005) "The Ties that Bind: Measuring the Strength of Consumers' Emotional Attachment to Brands," *Journal of Consumer Psychology*, 15(1), 77–91.

Thompson, Craig J. (1995), "A Contextualist Proposal for the Conceptualization and Study of Marketing Ethics," *Journal of Public Policy & Marketing*, 14(2), 177–191.

Thompson, Craig J. Aric Rindfleisch, and Zeynep Arsel (2006), "Emotional Branding and the Strategic Value of the Doppelgänger Brand Image," *Journal of Marketing*, 70(1), 50–64.

Trout, Jack and Steve Rivkin (2009), *Repositioning: Marketing in an Era of Competition*, Change and Crisis, McGraw-Hill, New York.

Twitchell, James (2004), *Branded Nation: The Marketing of Megachurch, College Inc., and Museumworld*, Simon & Schuster, New York.

Tybout, Alice and Brian Sternthal (2005), "Brand Positioning," in Alice M. Tybout and Tim Calkins (eds), *Kellogg on Branding* , John Wiley & Sons, Hoboken, NJ, pp. 11–26.

Underhill, Paco (2000), *Why We Buy: The Science of Shopping*, Texere Publishing, Knutsford.

Vann, Elizabeth F. (2006), "The Limits of Authenticity in Vietnamese Consumer Markets," *American Anthropologist*, 108(2), 286–296.

Vargo, Stephen and Robert V. Lusch (2004), "The Service-Dominant Logic of Marketing," *Journal of Marketing*, 68(1), 1–17.

Varman, Rohit and Russell W. Belk (2009), "Nationalism and Ideology in an Anticonsumption Movement," *Journal of Consumer Research*, 36(4), 686–700.

Verganti, Roberto (2011), "Designing Breakthrough Products," *Harvard Business Review*, 89(10), 114–120.

Verganti, Roberto (2009), *Design Driven Innovation: Changing the Rules of Competition by Radically Innovating What Things Mean*, Harvard Business Press, Cambridge, MA.

Völckner, Franziska and Henrik Sattler (2006), "Drivers of Brand Extension Success," *Journal of Marketing*, 70(2), 18–34.

Walker, Rob (2010), *Buying In: The Secret Dialogue between What We Buy and Who We Are*, Random House, New York.

Walker, Rob (2008), "Can a Dead Brand Live Again?", *The New York Times Magazine*, May 18, 49–53.

Walker, Stuart (2006), *Sustainable by Design: Explorations in Theory and Practice*, Routledge, London.

Wansink, Brian (2007), *Mindless Eating: Why We Eat More than We Think*, Bantam, London.

Weinberger, Michelle F. and Melanie Wallendorf (2012), "Intracommunity Gifting at the Intersection of Contemporary Moral and Market Economies," *Journal of Consumer Research*, 39(1), 74–92.

Wells, James (2017, February 24), "Students Vote Google Most Desirable Employer Again," https://www.campusreview.com.au/2017/02/students-vote-google-most-desirable-employer-again/ (accessed March 3, 2017).

Westberg, Kate, Michael B. Beverland, and Samantha Thomas (2017) "The Unintended Normalization of Gambling: Family Identity Influences on the Adoption of Harmful Consumption Practices," *Journal of Macromarketing* DOI: 10.1177/0276146717720979

Wheeler, Alina (2003), *Designing Brand Identity: A Complete Guide to Creating, Building, and Maintaining String Brands*, John Wiley & Sons, Hoboken, NJ.

Willett, Megan (2015, February 28), "Louis Vuitton Is Now a "Brand for Secretaries" in China," http://www.businessinsider.com.au/louis-vuitton-losing-sales-in-china-2015-2 (accessed August 14, 2016).

Yap, Jo En, Michael B. Beverland, and Liliana L. Bove (2011) ,"Doing Privacy: Exploring the Nature of Consumer Privacy and Privacy Management Strategies", *Advances in Consumer Research* Volume 39, eds. Rohini Ahluwalia, Tanya L. Chartrand, and Rebecca K. Ratner, Duluth, M: Association for Consumer Research, Pages: 515-516.

Zaltman, Gerald (2003), *How Customers Think: Essential Insights into the Mind of the Market*, Harvard Business School Press, Cambridge, MA.

Zaltman, Gerald and Robin H. Coulter (1995), "Seeing the Voice of the Customer: Metaphor-based Advertising Research," *Journal of Advertising Research*, 35(4), 35–51.

Wikipedia Cites

https://en.wikipedia.org/wiki/Blackfish (film) (accessed March 10, 2017).

https://en.wikipedia.org/wiki/History_of_Lego#Decline.2C_1992.E2.80.932004 (accessed March 10, 2017).

https://en.wikipedia.org/wiki/Hofstede's_cultural_dimensions_theory (accessed March 10, 2017).

https://en.wikipedia.org/wiki/McDonald's_legal_cases (accessed March 10, 2017).

Index